MARTIN SCORSESE

THE ICONIC FILMMAKER AND HIS WORK

IAN NATHAN

Quarto

First published in 2025 by White Lion Publishing,
an imprint of The Quarto Group.
One Triptych Place, London, SE1 9SH,
United Kingdom
T (0)20 7700 9000
www.Quarto.com

EEA Representation, WTS Tax d.o.o., Žanova ulica 3, 4000 Kranj, Slovenia
www.wts-tax.si

A catalogue record for this book is available from the British Library.

ISBN 978-1-83600-643-5
Ebook ISBN 978-1-83600-644-2

10 9 8 7 6 5 4 3 2 1

Designed by Sue Pressley and Paul Turner, Stonecastle Graphics
Edited by Nick Freeth
Publisher Jessica Axe
Editorial Director Jennifer Barr
Editor Róisín Duffy
Art Director Paileen Currie
Senior Production Controller Rohana Yusof

Printed in Pontian, Johor, Malaysia PC072025

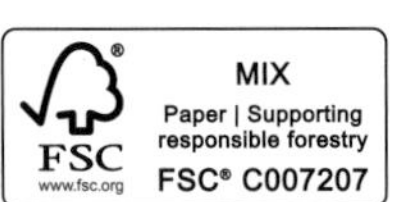

MARTIN SCORSESE

THE ICONIC FILMMAKER AND HIS WORK

IAN NATHAN

UNOFFICIAL AND UNAUTHORISED

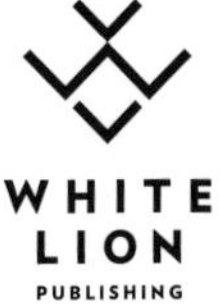

WHITE
LION
PUBLISHING

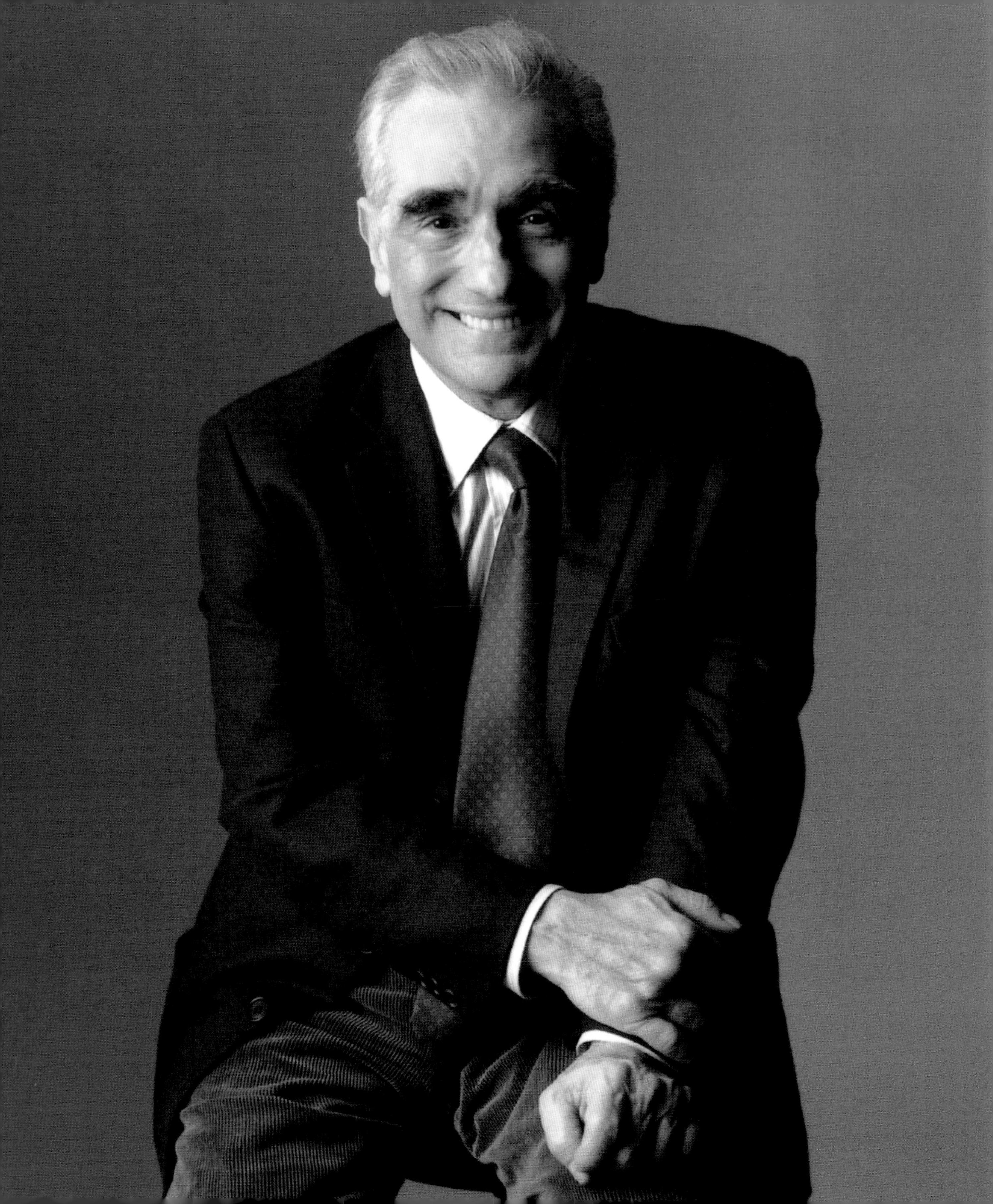

CONTENTS

Opposite: *The maestro at ease – Martin Scorsese photographed in 2010, for the release of* Shutter Island.

INTRODUCTION

'Of course it's not life – it's the invocation of life, it's an ongoing dialogue with life.'[1]
Martin Scorsese

Martin Charles Scorsese is surely the most revered director alive. By peers, critics, fans, by pretty much anyone who has an interest in film. For decades, he has simply been considered the best – if such distinctions must be drawn. It's not about box office, or awards, it's about film itself. Such is his distinction that there is an official Martin Scorsese Professor of Cinema Studies at the Tisch School of the Arts in New York. Not bad for the asthmatic little Catholic kid from Lower Manhattan, who considered the priesthood, daydreamed of becoming a gangster (like the toughs he saw coming out of shadowy bars, shielded in suits, seemingly untouchable), but yearned to make movies.

But what does it even mean to be the 'the best'?

Certainly, Scorsese's storeyed career is one of the defining statements on the possibility of film: *Mean Streets, Taxi Driver, Raging Bull, Goodfellas, The Age of Innocence, The Wolf of Wall Street, The Irishman*. His entire filmography is so varied, yet fully the work of one man.

Has any director been more devoted to the idea of filmmaking as an art form? Whatever the size of canvas, or subject matter, for Scorsese film is always personal. That is the only way to make it *authentic*. And even while defying the rigid strictures of commercial thinking or genre imperatives, he has found audiences. Somehow, he has found a way of combining the naturalism born of a childhood watching the life outside his windows and the glorious dream-like potential of film to augment reality. Between those two views, he has created a new genre: 'A Martin Scorsese Picture.'

Stretching from the late sixties to right now, this is a story of filmmaking daring set against an industry and a country in upheaval. Scorsese is America's greatest living artist, in all that term implies. More than Francis Ford Coppola, he has chronicled a nation of immigrants (his family line stretches back to Sicily) and the treacherous pursuit of the American Dream. The suite of gangster films, from *Mean Streets* to *The Irishman*, for which

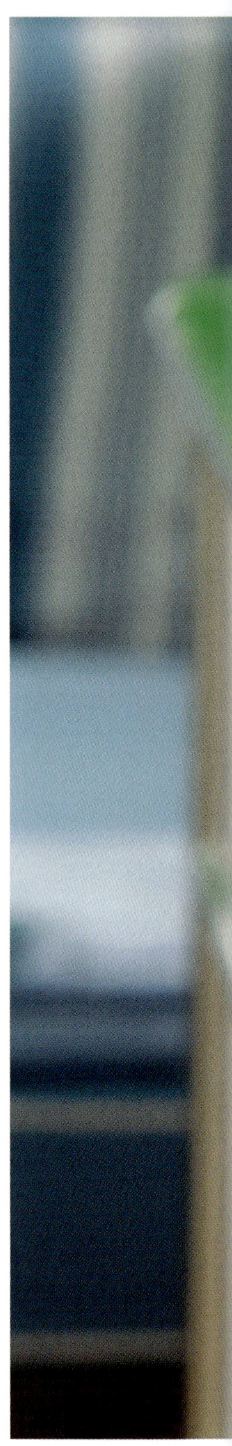

Right: *The man in his element, Martin Scorsese is never more alive than on a movie set. In this case, during the making of* The Wolf of Wall Street *in 2012.*

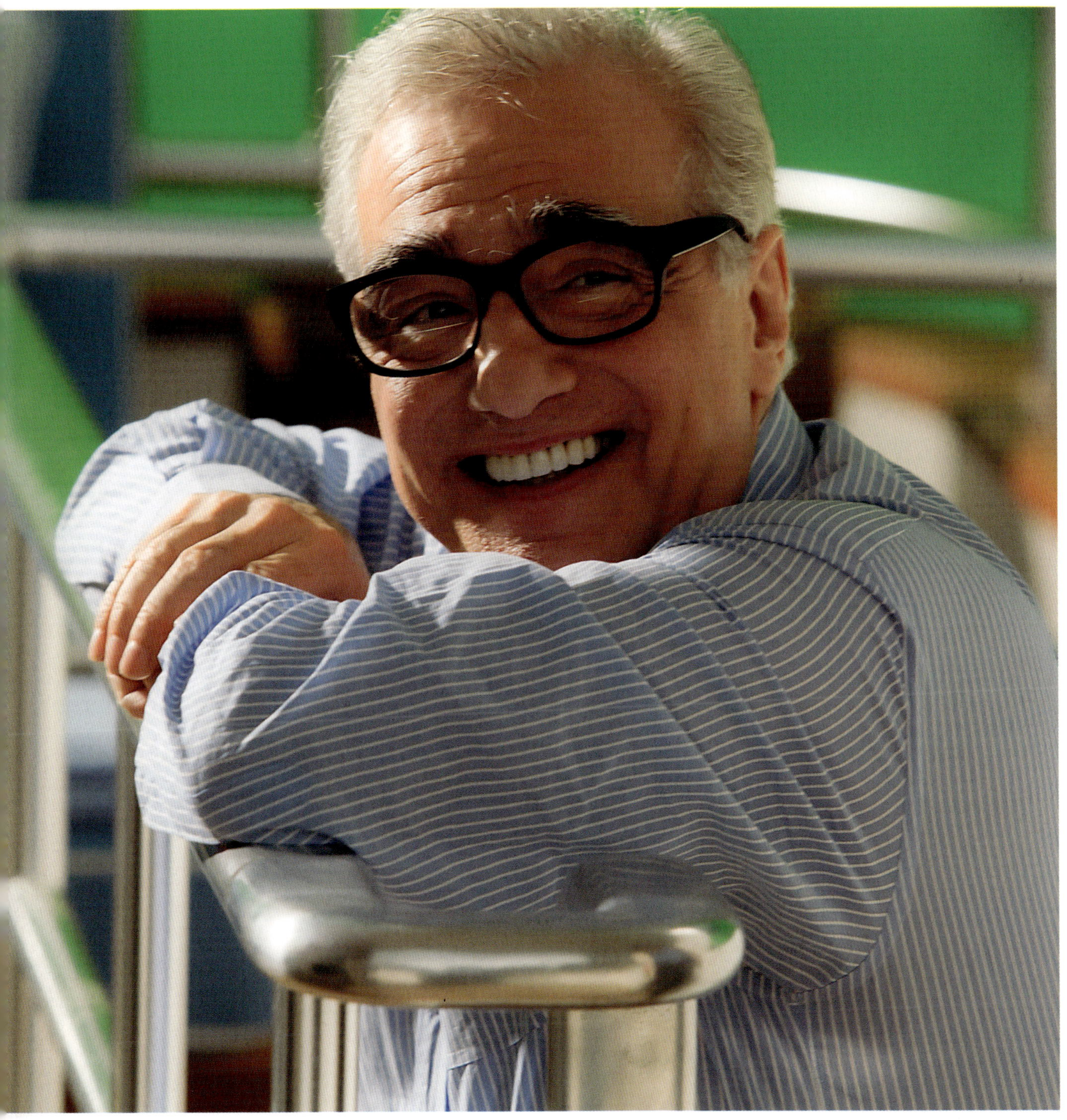

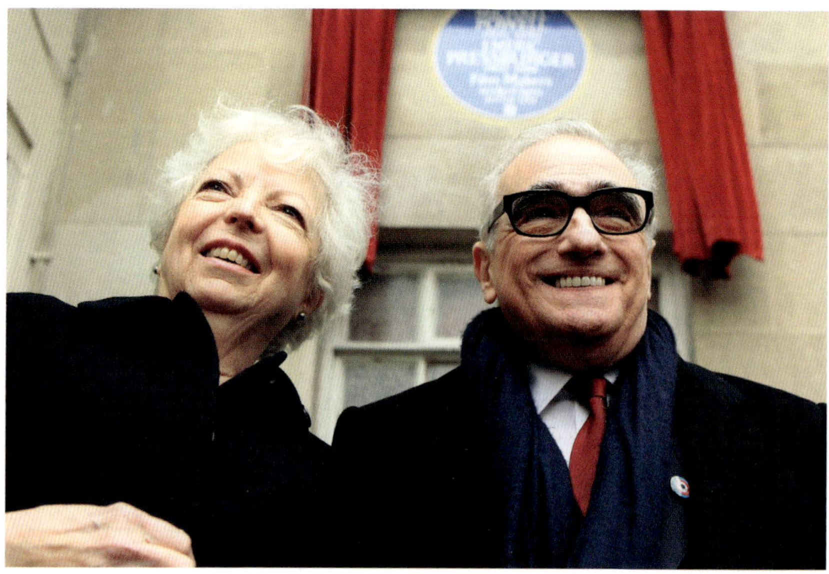

Right: *Hero worship – editor Thelma Schoonmaker and Martin Scorsese unveil a blue plaque, in London, to her late husband and his filmmaking idol Michael Powell in 2014.*

he is best known, form a captivating journal of American history. The Italian-American psyche is one of his abiding themes. All his gangsters, peacocks and killers, are so very human.

This book considers the making of all twenty-six of his films, but equally seeks out the thinking within them. All those Scorsesean themes, expressed with such style. We see so many currents that pass from one film to the next. Scorsese is fascinated by the codes that tie society together, from the knife-edge ethics of *Goodfellas* to the porcelain constraints among New York's nineteenth-century upper classes in *The Age of Innocence*. There is that absorption with men thrust, willingly or not, to the margins of society: Robert De Niro's deluded stand-up in *The King of Comedy*; Nicolas Cage's paramedic fragmenting on the nightshift in *Bringing Out the Dead*; and, of course, De Niro's Travis Bickle in *Taxi Driver*, a man who suspects he may be in a movie instead of a life. And there are those wrestling with God, just as the director has: the covert missionaries of *Silence*, the boy born to be Dalai Lama in *Kundun*, and the human Jesus of *The Last Temptation of Christ*. *Raging Bull* alone is a broiling ocean of sin and symbolism.

News flash: film can be so much more than entertainment.

Notions of good and bad are not found in the dream-tinged, life-scorched cityscapes of Scorsese. As confidant and critic Richard Schickel once said of the canon, 'there has never been and never will be a "triumph of the human spirit" in a Scorsese film. He's too intelligent for that.'[2] Is this what elevates him away from his peers? The doubt that remains in the existential altar boy. The idea that human darkness is a fascinating as the light.

Scorsese is also the purest of the Movie Brats, that great clan of filmmakers of the 1970s to which he belonged, certain that all film must be nourished by the past. He has seen as many films as one man can see. He is a fanatic, a collector, a preservationist, and a documentarian. He holds wild and vivid opinions, professorial in his understanding of the medium's power. Yet he is far from an old-fashioned director. Bending tradition to his will, he turns genre into new forms: be it the neo-noir of *Taxi Driver*, a musical with *New York, New York*, a crime caper in *The Departed*, or the Western elements of *Killers of the Flower Moon*.

He is the auteur who loves company. There are a series of extraordinary, career-defining partnerships. With Robert De Niro, his great muse and alter ego, the canvas on which Scorsese has painted so many of his visions. With Leonardo DiCaprio, a wellspring of youth turned trusted star. With Thelma Schoonmaker, his editor of choice who influences the shape of a Scorsese picture like no other. All the significant names: Paul Schrader, Nicholas Pileggi, Jay Cocks, Robbie Robertson, Harvey Keitel, Joe Pesci, Daniel Day-Lewis.

'I am an American director, which means I am a Hollywood director,'[3] he once claimed, fascinated, even stimulated, though as often tormented by the artistic dilemma presented by the studio system.

While being critical of Hollywood conformity, he has managed (just about) to chart a course between the shoals of the establishment, even when shipwreck looked certain.

Over a long career, patterns emerge, cycles of commercial failure and rebirth, despair and triumph. He is a great survivor. Quite literally, when it came to a near-fatal drug addiction. Addiction is another theme sewn into the films: not only to drugs or money, but life itself and its opposite: self-destruction.

He has never compromised, even when accused of selling out. The so-called dalliances in populism, *Cape Fear, The Aviator, The Departed* (with its four Oscars), or *Shutter Island*, offer as much experimentation as his artier numbers.

Meeting Scorsese is like meeting someone you already now. His mannerisms are so familiar: the gusts of laughter, the impish liveliness, the tumbling thoughts. Researching this book has meant standing beneath a waterfall of knowledge and reflection that threatens to overwhelm any writer. All the life he packs into his films is written into that small frame and lined face, with those wizardly eyebrows, and the compelling turns of phrase as busy as a New York city block.

As the avuncular Marty enters his ninth decade, his ambitions call for eye-watering budgets, but mortality has entered the frame. Each new film seems to contain a calculus of the old, as if he is making his own reckoning, writing his own book in film form. But his mind is still so full that it is impossible to think of him retiring. Where will we be without the new Scorsese?

Is this what it means to be the best? He has made addicts out of us all.

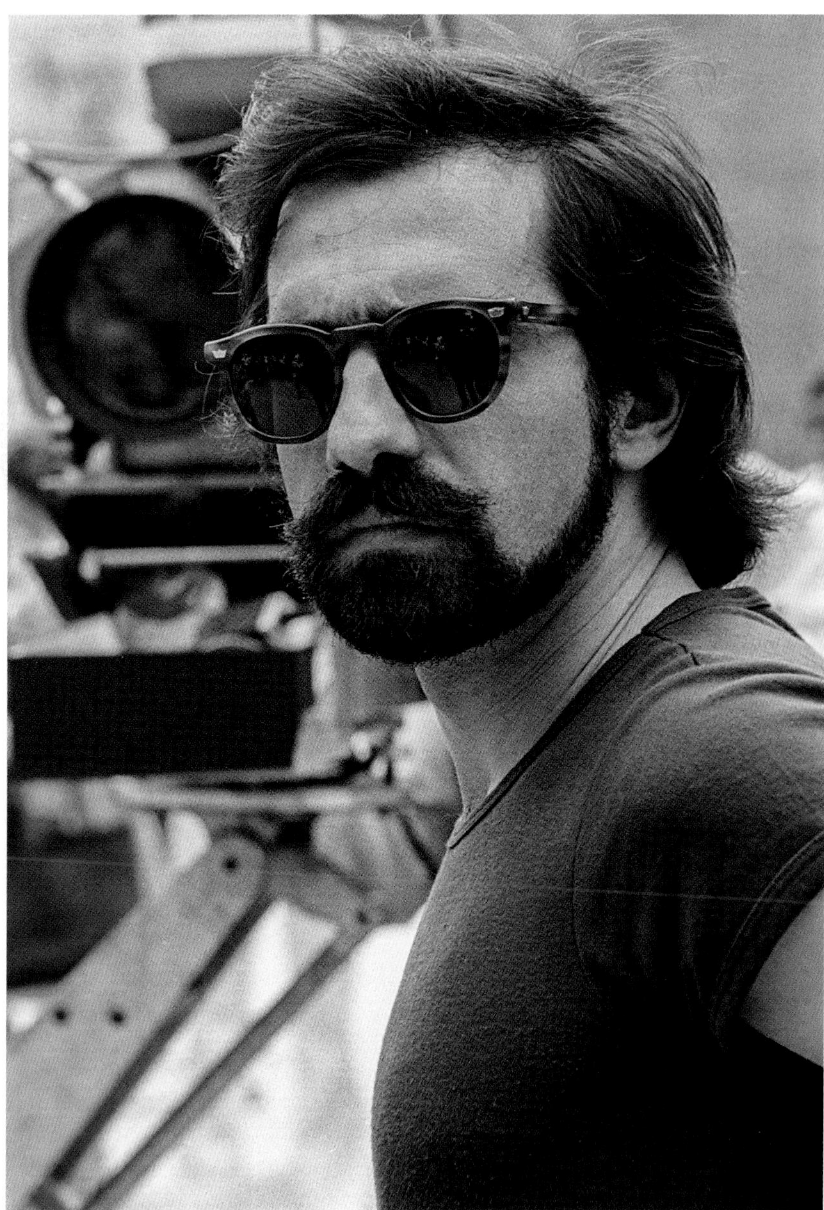

Above: *Marty the Movie Brat – the 1970s-style Scorsese at loose on the streets of New York shooting his early masterpiece* Taxi Driver.

Sometime in his teens, Martin Scorsese went to confession. Not in itself an unusual occurrence, he had been an observant Catholic since boyhood; God and His rituals played a significant part in his youth, and He would have plenty to say in the movies to come. As biographers tend to point out, the young Scorsese had seriously considered entering the priesthood, but didn't have the grades for Jesuit university, so went instead to New York University, the auspicious NYU, to study film. His other religion.

Scorsese admitted to the hidden priest that he had recently been to see Ingmar Bergman's spider's web of infidelity and passion *Smiles of a Summer Night*. What was troubling him was that he really couldn't understand what was so problematic about the film, which had been condemned by the church – Bergman's output was covered with a blanket condemnation by the Catholic Legion of Decency. The priest went kindly on the young man. While the watching of Bergman films should not be encouraged 'for the masses,'[1] an exception might be made for those hoping to make film their work.

Scorsese smiled at the recollection. 'I mean, how many guys from the Lower East Side were going to see *Smiles of a Summer Night*?'[2]

All the same, the open-minded priest can't have imagined he was oiling the wheels on a career that would one day lead to *The Last Temptation of Christ*.

Despite the many words that have been spent on the subject, in the end this greatness we have bestowed upon Scorsese boils down to three things. God, film, and crime. Put them together in a large New York-shaped pot and cook them to the richness of his mother's meatballs and you have the greatest living American filmmaker.

Martin Charles Scorsese was born in 1942 in Corona, Queens, though the telling years of his childhood years belonged to Little Italy, the warren of streets at the foot of Manhattan, the island at the heart of New York, his great muse. As far as his memory was concerned, Corona had

Opposite: *A cinema-obsessed Martin Scorsese pictured in 1969, about the time of his transition from NYU film student to professional director with* Who's That Knocking at My Door.

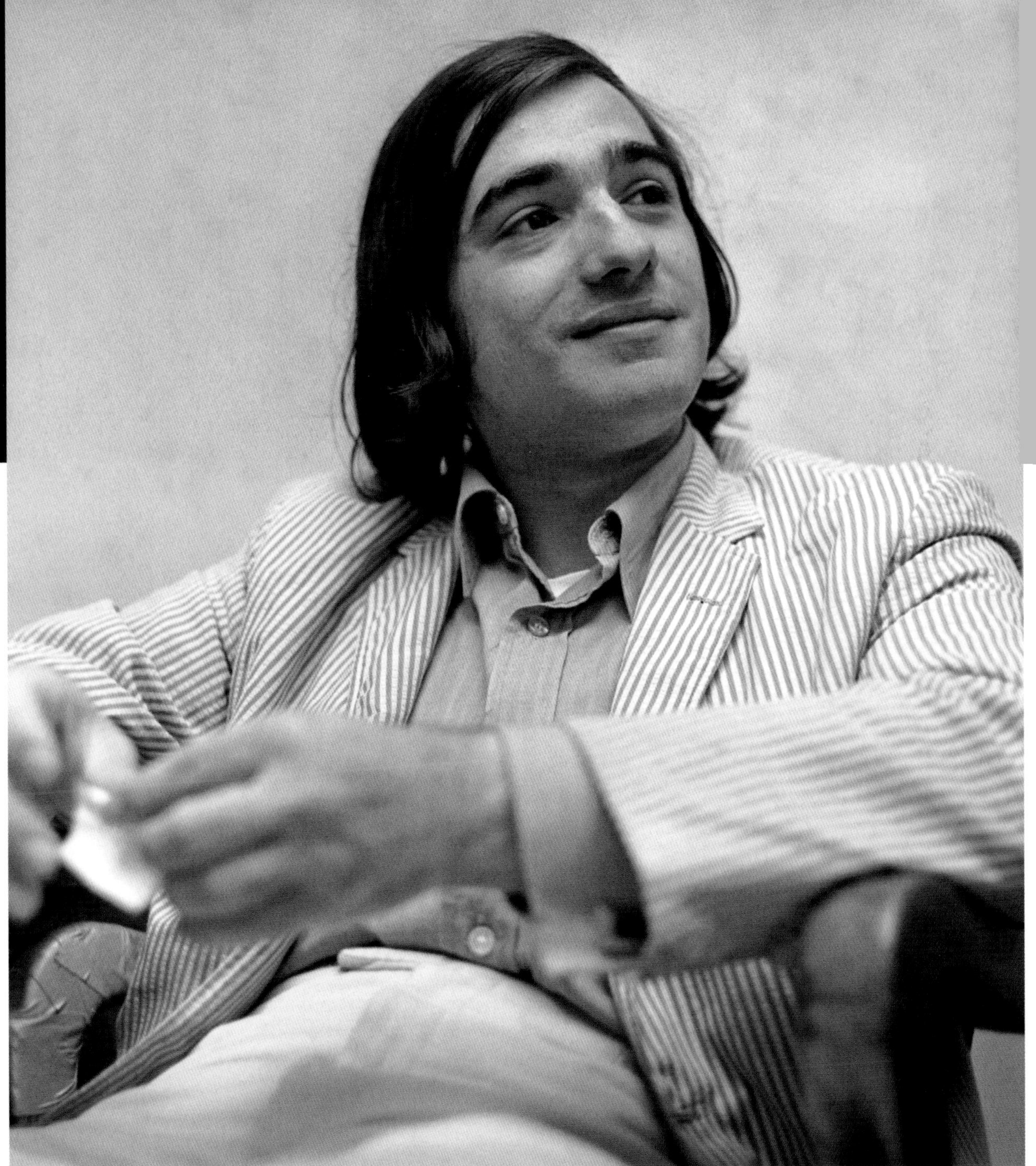

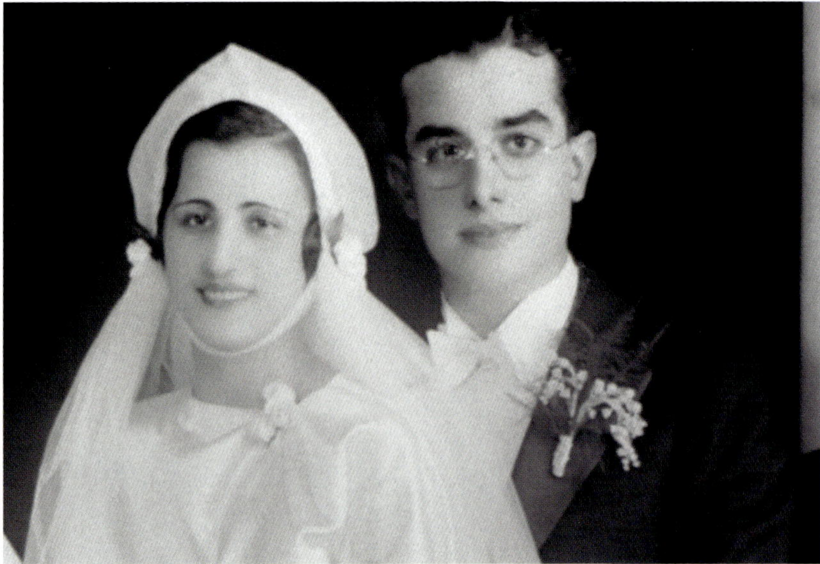

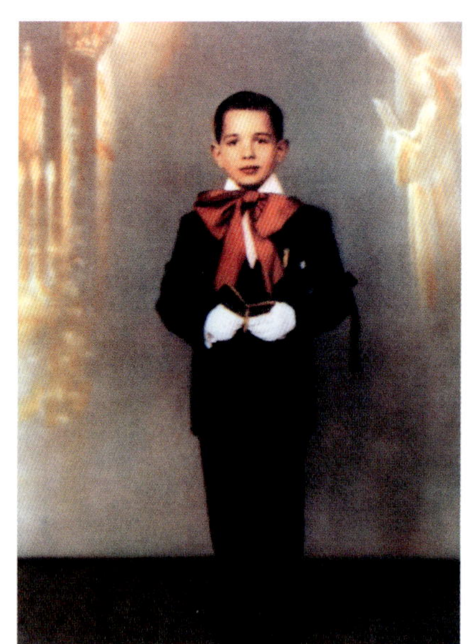

been an idyll: the family had a yard, he could walk in the park, at least until he was overtaken by an asthma attack. At the age of two Scorsese had almost died from Whooping Cough (there was an epidemic sweeping through Queens), which he thinks may have wrecked his lungs. At the age of three he was diagnosed with acute asthma. Almost eighty years later, he can still find himself gasping for air.

All four of his grandparents had emigrated from Sicily, their blood thick with a history of loyalty and betrayal. Landing by ship, the family name had been misspelled to Scorsese from Scozzese. In life, it is properly pronounced *Scorsezze*, but he accepts most know him as Scorsese. His parents, Charles and Catherine, worked in the garment district. Both have made engaging cameos in the family business introduced by their youngest son; his father was also put to work on the costumes of *Raging Bull*. In Scorsese's first and most personal documentary, *Italianamerican*, an exploration of his heritage made in 1974, after he won backing from the National Endowment for the Humanities, and broadcast as part of the series *A Storm of Strangers*, he joins his parents in their apartment for wine and pasta, slowly drawing them into vivid stories of their youth and the struggles of immigrant life in Little Italy.

The candid footage is a delight: his middle-aged parents, unsure when the camera is rolling or not, treat Marty as if he's still twelve years old. 'When are you going to leave?'[3] his mother demands at the end, done with the questions, but beaming still in the limelight that has entered her home. A counterpoint to the darkness of *Mean Streets*, life spills into the lens, with Scorsese keeping the sparse crew, equipment, and his own nervy presence in the frame. It's beautifully messy. We come to understand that this is what his upbringing was like, all the bustle and bickering that would stir a style. Here is a lodestar for the Scorsesean gift. His parents are such captivating performers and storytellers, with his mother's recipe

Above left: *The wedding photo of Martin Scorsese's beloved parents and frequent collaborators Catherine and Charles Scorsese – an image used in his 1974 documentary* Italianamerican.

Above right: *The age of innocence – an angelic nine-year-old Scorsese posing for the camera in 1951.*

Opposite: *Scorsese interviewed his parents for* Italianamerican, *a fascinating portrait of a marriage, emblematic of how he would mine his own family stories for his art.*

for meatballs written out in full in the credits like the masterplan for a career (cooking will take on an almost mystical aura in the films – the stuff of life).

While still a student, Scorsese had overheard his parents discussing his hopes of becoming a filmmaker as 'madness.'[4] But they backed him, and when the awards and endowments began to accumulate their belief in him grew solid. This 40-minute film stands as a confirmation of his devotion to this complex but loving couple, the first of Scorsese's many portraits of marriage.

Notably absent from the lens is his elder brother Frank, who shrinks from his brother's story, a ghostly presence who died in 2021.

The move to Elizabeth Street in Little Italy came with the startling immediacy of a jump cut, and was triggered by trouble with the landlord. There is an unfinished script Scorsese was writing with Nicholas Pileggi (his *Goodfellas* companion) called *The Neighborhood* that tells the story (among many). About how his errant Uncle Joe Bug fell out with the local mob and the lengths his father went to keep him out of trouble. In truth, to keep him from getting shot. 'I don't know if I can bring myself to do it,' remarked Scorsese, this was 2010. 'It's complicated... My father was assisted by a crime family.'[5]

Mean Streets is always taken to be imprinted with an autobiographical map of Scorsese's youth, but Harvey Keitel's burdened Charlie is as much his father in disguise and Robert De Niro's mooncalf Johnny Boy, the gurning troublemaker, is Uncle Joe. 'The whole picture of *Mean Streets*, it's really him, my father, not me,'[6] said Scorsese.

Back in his memories, their landlord got wind of things. He didn't like Uncle Joe, he knew he was trouble. He started to suspect that Scorsese's father was getting involved with underworld figures in order to fix Joe's debts. There came a confrontation, their language turned sour, it came to blows, and the landlord pulled an axe. If Charlie Scorsese's sister-in-law hadn't intervened who knows what might have happened. Scorsese likened it to a scene in John Ford's *The Quiet Man*. There was another tussle later, in a bar. 'And the next I knew we had to leave,'[7] he recalled.

So the family came to live in a third floor walk-up from the same street where his father was born. Uncle Joe moved into the floor below, unable to stay out of trouble, feeding his nephew's imagination. It was more cramped than Corona, leaving no escape from the family dramas, the heated discussions among aunts and uncles, news of storm-tossed tributaries of familial disaster. Marty was the youngest,

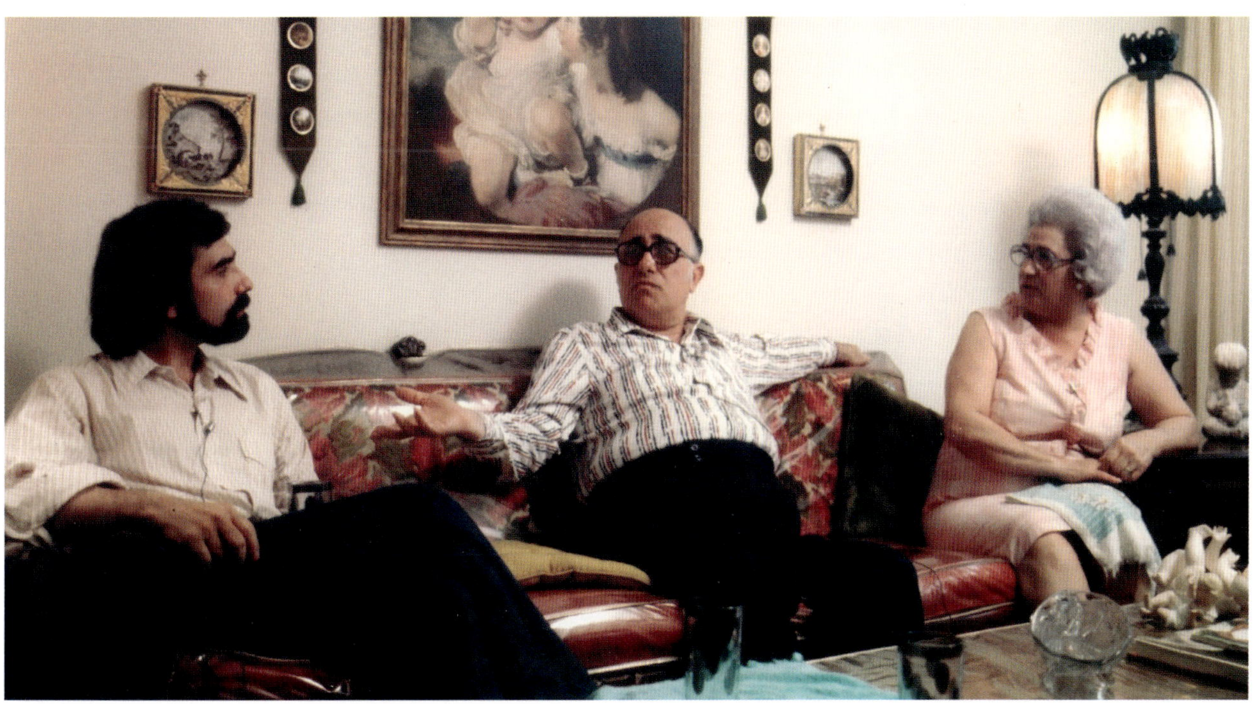

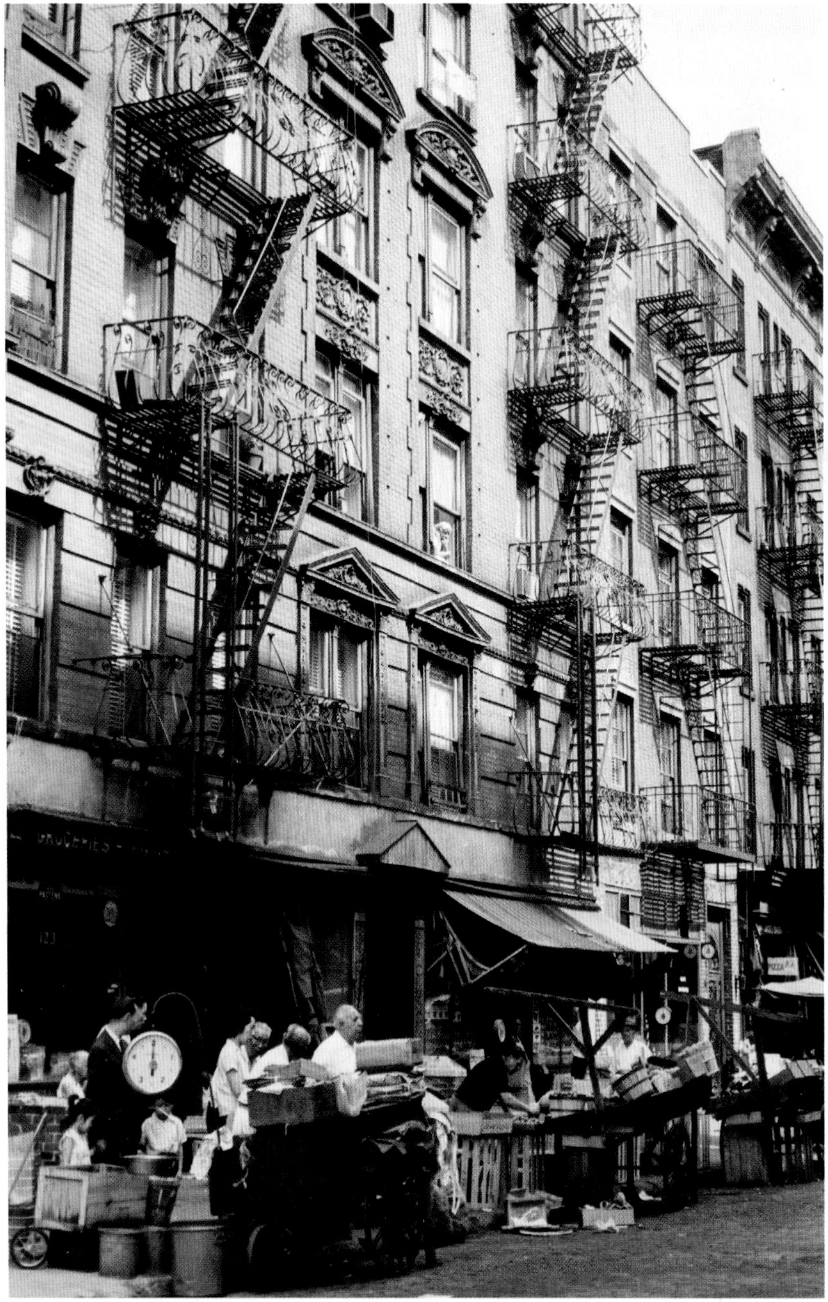

Above: *Little Italy in Lower Manhattan, New York circa 1960, the bustling streets that served as Martin Scorsese's great muse.*

always present but told to keep quiet, only making his voice heard in his imagination. We can feel it awakening within: the need to speak, to tell the stories from the kitchen table and the streets below, life and art as tight as the boy's stricken lungs.

'I grew up on the Bowery,' said Scorsese, his mind ranging to the rough-edged Skid Row of drop-outs, many of whom he came to know, a street or two over. 'And that was like being in a Bosch painting.'[8] All his films teem with the life he observed on the ten blocks from Houston Street to Chinatown: the bustle, the energy, the sparks that fly in a family, the preening mobsters in their suits, a family of a different kind, talking their way around the American Dream. Even the sparse, far-flung meditations on faith, a *Kundun* or a *Silence*, still carry that nervous undercurrent. Violence is always close to hand in the world of Scorsese, as it was outside his childhood door. 'There were even fights in the movie theatres,'[9] he admitted.

He observed it all.

Trapped floors above Little Italy, forbidden from joining the kids in their scuffles and hijinks, even their laughter would cause him to reach for oxygen, he would gaze from his window (his first frame) or the fire escape at the melting pot below. The roof at Elizabeth Street, which gave a view of the entire city, was 'as close to heaven as you could get.'[10]

Religion was an external influence; his parents were hardly pious. It came through Catholic school, run by the Sisters of Mercy, a body of apocalyptic Irish nuns in an Italian neighbourhood, which didn't sit well. And through the solace of St. Patrick's Cathedral (being built among the clashes of *Gangs of New York*), where he escaped from the turmoil of home, lulled by the rituals of Mass. Think of his films: from Travis

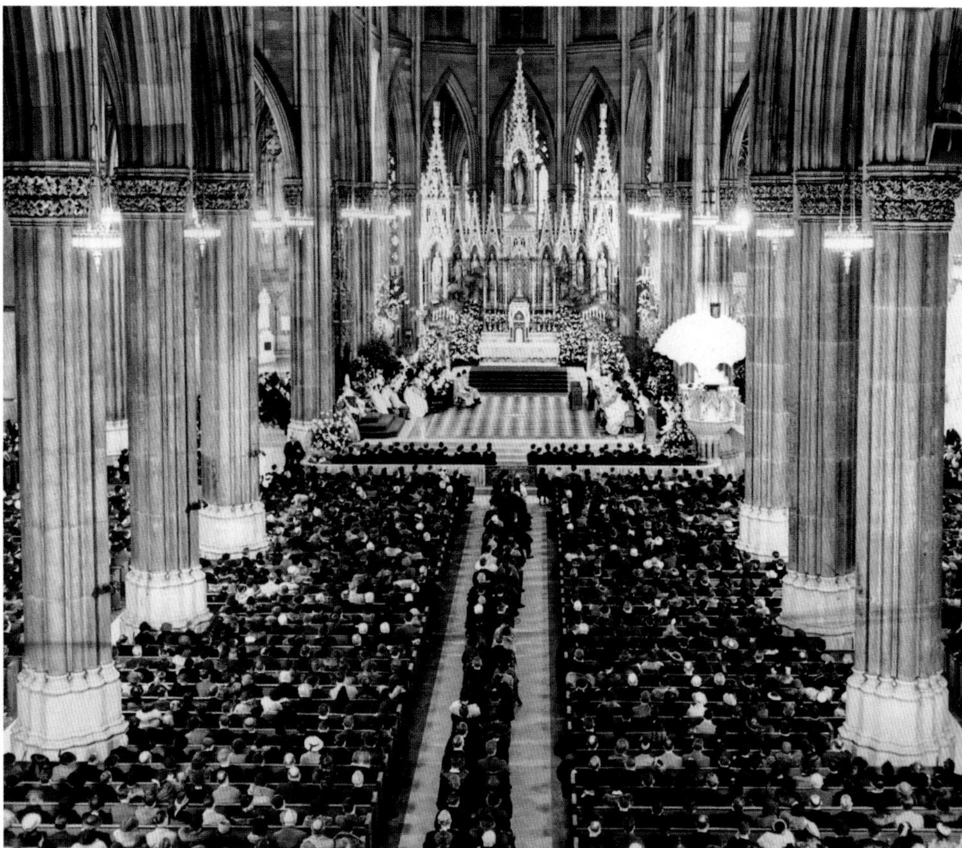

Left: *Easter Service at St Patrick's Cathedral in New York – this great Gothic building was central to Scorsese's early devotion to Catholicism, and his recurrent use of rituals as a theme.*

Bickle's purifying rigours in *Taxi Driver* to the montage of money passing through the gaudy cathedrals of *Casino*, they are filled with the mesmerising power of ritual. All those voice-overs carry the sermonizing cant of priests.

At the age of eight, he became an altar boy, struggling to rise for 7 a.m. Mass, but imbibing the catechism of Catholic doctrine, good and evil, moral certainties that will be picked apart by his art. Yet church gave him a clear view of American corruption and its allure.

God, crime, and film. He could have been pulled in any one of these directions, but film spoke to him as might a heavenly messenger, a Damascene vision of projected light. Film answered his imagination in ways that even God couldn't match. And film saved him from the underworld temptations he would turn into fabulous fiction: the good life offered by the glamorous men, which was as encoded as the conventions of Mass.

'And it came out of a loneliness, which I still have,' he confessed, 'which had to do with my father and my mother. And they couldn't do anything with me. So they took me to the movies.'[11] It was all they could think to do with this pale boy. His father had loved the films of the thirties and forties, and it was mainly his father who was forced to take him uptown to 42nd Street or the Academy of Music on 14th Street. Scorsese saw more of his father in Manhattan than in Queens or Little Italy, sitting beside him in the dark. It became another ritual, asking for another kind of belief – a suspension of disbelief. To look up and see heaven on a giant screen. When it came to film, Scorsese was devout.

This is the gospel of Martin Scorsese: the director built from an obsession with cinema from the day he was taken to watch the heated melodrama of *Duel in the Sun* (the first title he can recall seeing), in which Jennifer Jones and a cold-hearted Gregory Peck, enemies and lovers, will destroy one another. 'That led me to King Vidor... There you're dealing with the whole idea of personal expression within the

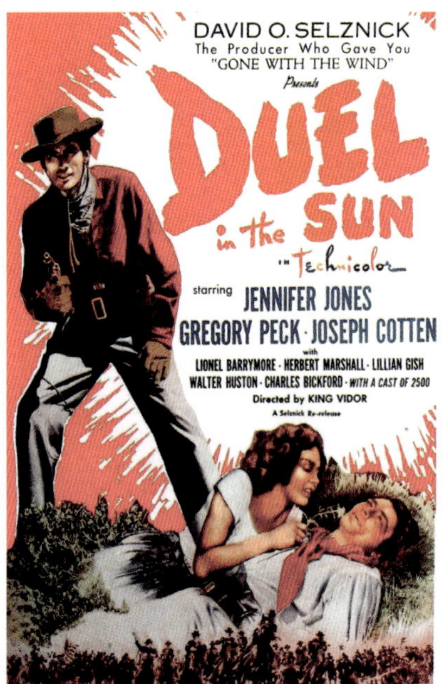

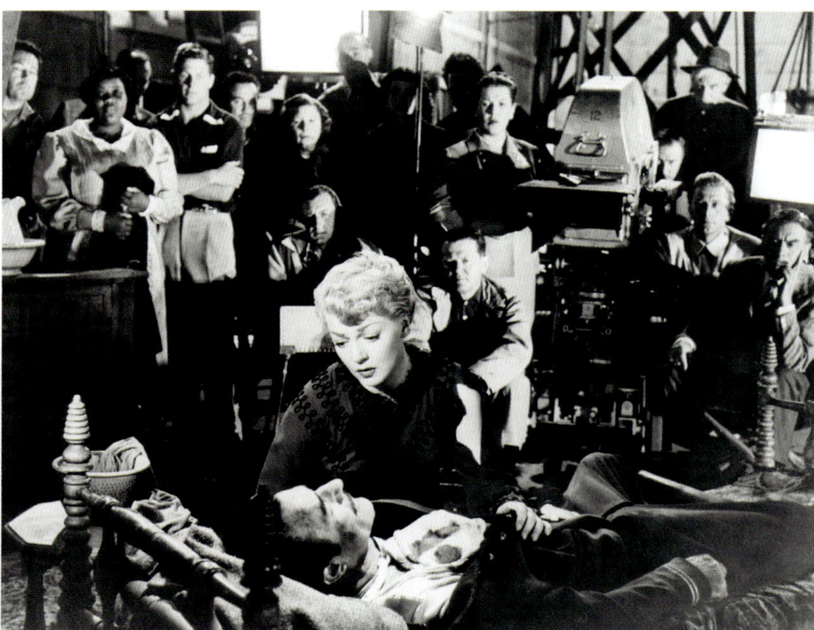

studio system. Vidor made a very personal film.'[12] There were hardly thoughts he could articulate at the time, swept up in passions he didn't understand, but felt nonetheless.

An entire book could be filled with the films that have left their indelible mark on the great director (indeed he has made beautiful documentaries that list and poeticize his lifelong affair with film history). The influences on each of his own films form a path through the dense forest of genre and mood. For now, we should mark *The Bad and the Beautiful*, the first film to show him behind-the-scenes of filmmaking. And *Sunset Boulevard*, which he recalled seeing at the age of ten, certain it was a form of glamorous horror movie. At first, he loved genre, all the musicals, Biblical epics and Westerns, which swept him up into the great outdoors he could never reach. John Ford was the first director he could name, and with him came the concept of a presence behind the story, an author of these images. Elia Kazan revealed things he hadn't thought possible: he recognized the world of Marlon Brando in *On the Waterfront* as his own. 'I must have seen it twenty times,' he recalled, 'then came *East of Eden*, which also reflected some of my own emotions and experience.'[13]

The excitement of cinema, all of it, had a 'seduction to it,'[14] he said. He yearned to find himself there, within the dream, far from the streets he called home. Yet those streets were the source of stories. Embracing that contradiction, the escape and the reality, was another defining factor of his miraculous style.

When his father arrived home with a sixteen-inch RCA Victor television set (the first on the block), Italian Neorealism entered his life. Every Friday night (in the fifties, with Hollywood still resisting television, the schedules turned to Italian, French, and British cinema) he would see his family reflected in *The Bicycle Thieves, Rome: Open City,* and *Paisan*. He sensed how

Above left: *The poster for David O. Selznick's fraught Western* Duel in the Sun *(1946) – the first film that truly made an impression on the young Martin Scorsese.*

Above right: *Vincente Minnelli's behind-the-scenes drama* The Bad and the Beautiful *(1952) was one of the movies to reveal how filmmaking worked to an awe-struck Scorsese.*

powerful these films were, how truthful, as equally drawn to the emotional European sensibility and the glories of Golden Era Hollywood. He knew himself to be American, but the personal expression of Visconti, Pasolini, and Rossellini was deep in his DNA. What made humanity tick.

That same priest, Father Francis Principe, who had salved his mind when it came to Bergman, was the first to warn him about the Oscars. Principe had watched the telecast and saw the giant stage Oscar – 'like three storeys high,'[15] recalled Scorsese – as a 'Golden Idol.'[16] Success can be a dark god.

This passion for cinema pours out of Scorsese like a river. He readily quotes his masters within his films, yet is never derivative. He understands what it is to pay homage. But is also aware that he can seem absurd. Given the chance, he will launch into streams of filmic consciousness, details of obscure pictures, lost directors, still pin-sharp in his impeccable memory. Indeed, you can match his exuberant style to the way he speaks: the energy, the restlessness, the excitement, the depth, the unstoppable flow, how his thoughts spin wildly into tangents, and then tangents within tangents, before reassembling to make perfect sense.

Nevertheless, it was not a simple thing to become a filmmaker, no matter how many classics you had logged in your psyche. And for a working-class boy, short and short of breath, whose world was hemmed in by New York's glowering tenements, the odds looked tall indeed. But the need to express himself was too strong to resist.

Below left: *The release poster for the legendary* On the Waterfront *– New Yorker Elia Kazan's 1964 film was a revelation for Scorsese, showing him that a bold, naturalistic approach could be applied to the big screen.*

Below right: *Vittorio De Sica's* Bicycle Thieves *(1948), one of the leading examples of Italian Neorealism, films that felt more like life than fiction to Scorsese.*

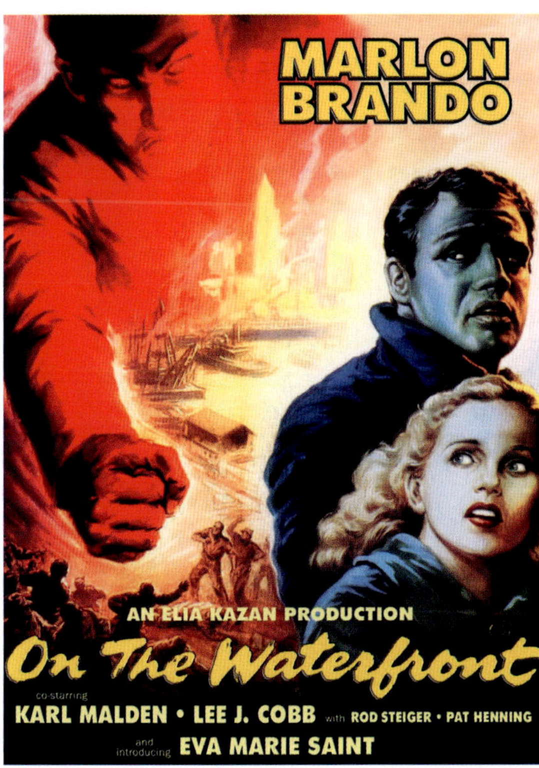

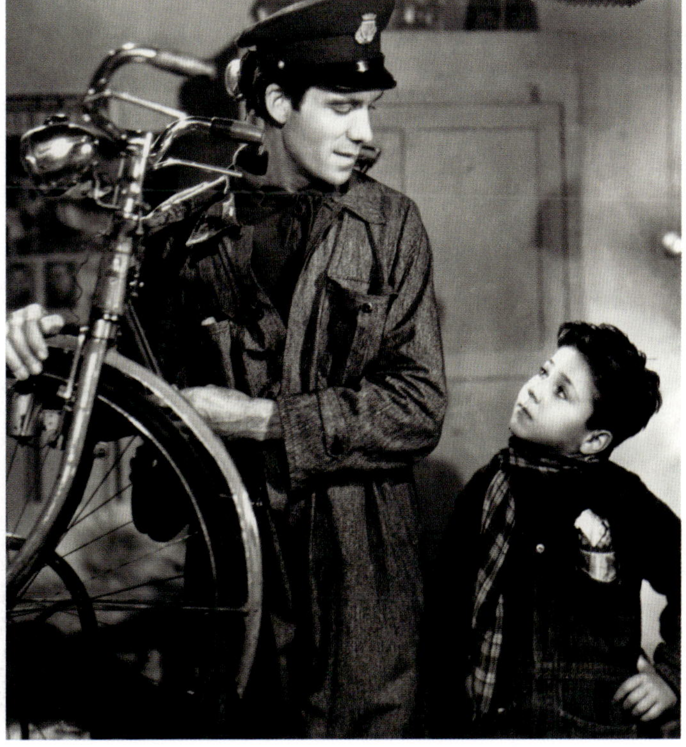

In fact the exalted career began at the age of five or six, with the first in a series of elaborate drawings (at one stage, he had considered becoming a painter), in which he began to translate the stories he saw in his head into sequential images like a comic-book. He didn't know it yet, but these were storyboards for improbable films. They came complete with credits: the flourish of MarSco Productions, with a winged logo, directed and produced by Martin Scorsese. With the images that followed in aspect ratio or Cinemascope, he began to perceive that the lines dividing the pictures denoted a camera move or a cut. Only one has survived, an epic entitled *The Eternal City*. The first Scorsese film on record is *Vesuvius VI*, made in 1959, a Roman epic inspired by the television series 77 *Sunset Strip* and shot on a Super8 camera lent to him by his friend Joey (unlike Spielberg he never owned a camera as a child), produced under the MarSco banner.

Then came the liberation of NYU in 1960. Walking the blocks uptown to Greenwich 'was like going to Mars,'[17] he said. This is where he encountered Haig Manoogian, the Armenian-American who became his first mentor and taught a three-hour film class, instilling in his students - those that lasted - a fearsome seriousness about the subject. Not that Scorsese necessarily agreed with his tutor. When he handed in a treatise on *The Third Man*, it was returned with a B+ and note scribbled on the front: 'Forget this, it's just a thriller.'[18]

Below: *Starring the great Joseph Cotten and Orson Welles, Carol Reed's glorious film noir* The Third Man *(1949) was the subject of a treatise from the student Martin Scorsese, and would be homaged throughout his career.*

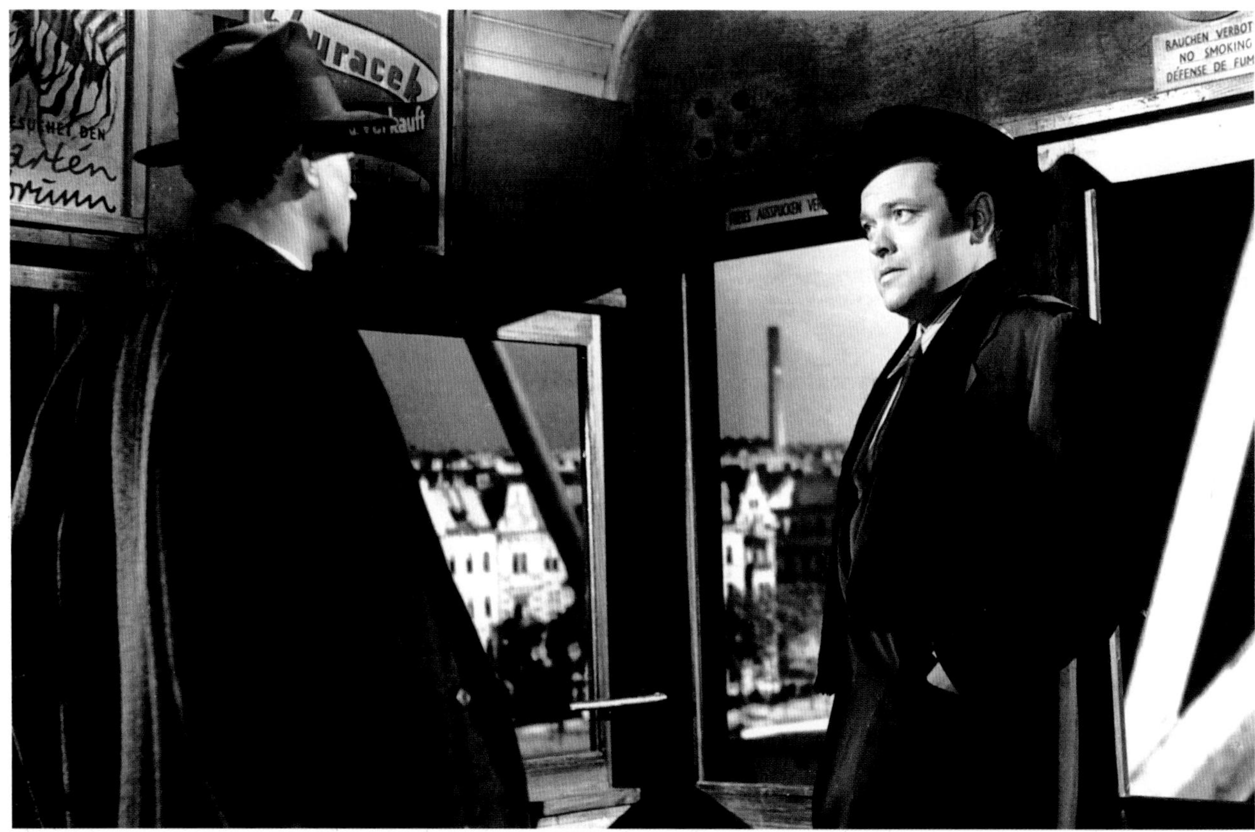

1959
VESUVIUS VI (Short) Director / Producer / Writer / Cinematographer

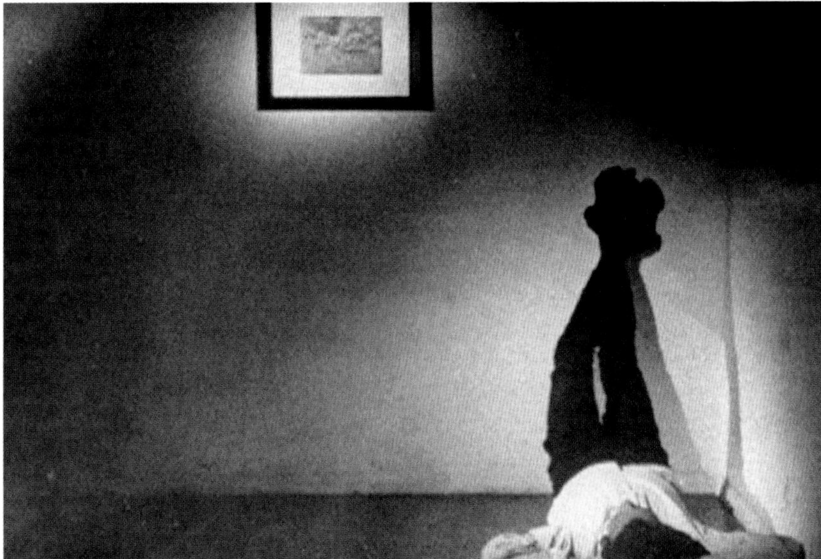

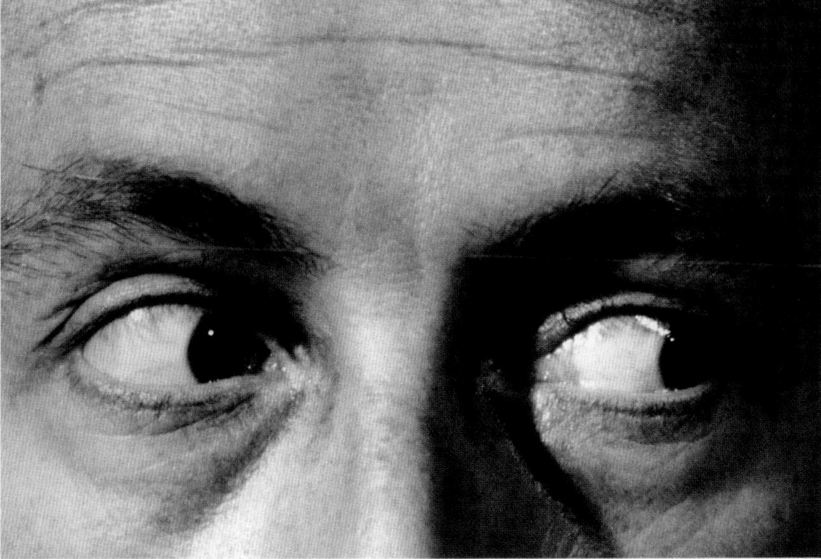

Top: *Scorsese's first short film,* What's a Nice Girl Like You Doing in a Place Like This?, *stars Zeph Michaelis as a young man who becomes obsessed with a painting, code for the director's all-consuming love of movies.*

Above: *Even in his first film, Scorsese was revealing the stylistic flourishes that would define his style, including the extreme.*

Scorsese was a film student from 1960 to 1965. What a time to be a cinéaste: every week brought a new masterpiece to the arthouses he and his peers (among them Brian De Palma, the first Movie Brat he became acquainted with) stalked, smoking, drinking, and mulling over their experiences in nearby cafés. It was almost overwhelming. The French New Wave crashed on American shores. All these directors, not much older than them, ripping up the Hollywood rulebook, while celebrating the likes of Ford and Hitchcock as auteurs. Godard and Truffaut taught him that linear storytelling need no longer apply. There were the Eastern Europeans and the later Italians, Fellini and Antonioni, asking questions but never answering them. Every Bergman was a challenge. And from within America, indeed within New York, came John Cassavetes, fomenting an independent scene with films raw with human experience. *Shadows* had been shot on a 16mm camera. 'If he could do it, so could we,'[19] decided Scorsese.

As much a practical course as theoretical, it was at NYU that Scorsese's first ventures into filmmaking truly took shape with a set of short films, made with the assistance of his fellow students and produced and championed by Manoogian. There is a danger of over-reading such early forays, yet each of these experiments unmistakably bears the signature of Little Italy's favourite son.

Shot in black and white, *What's a Nice Girl Like You Doing in a Place Like This?* was completed in a summer workshop in 1963, and introduced us to the writer Harry (Zeph Michaelis), so obsessed with a picture in his apartment featuring a man in a boat that he is overcome with writer's block. He can't even sleep, the presence of the painting too vivid in his head. To break its hold, he throws a party and meets a

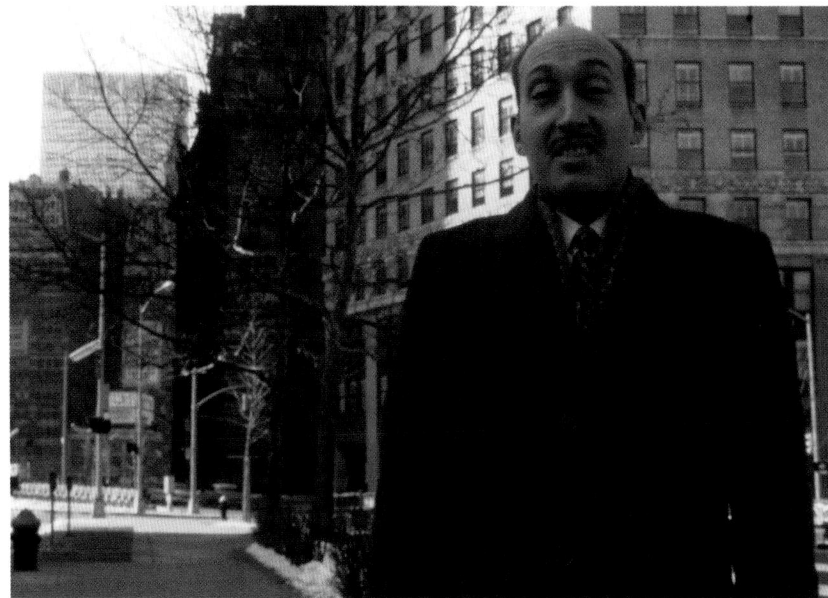

Right: *Ira Rubin in* It's Not Just You, Murray! *– recalled from middle age by Murray, Martin Scorsese's whimsical second short from 1964 introduces his biographical mode of storytelling.*

beautiful girl (Mimi Stark), who turns out to be a painter, into whose boat-themed work he will eventually disappear.

Immediately evident is the sheer zeal Scorsese has for the medium's possibilities, something he has never lost: montage, voice-over, freeze frames, still photos, shades of autobiography, even animation. He described it as a tale of 'pure paranoia.'[20] It is tempting to take it as a metaphor for the director's own obsessions with cinema. The tone is unsettlingly larkish, hinting at the edgy formulations of *The King of Comedy* and *After Hours*. Funny, but funny how?

'What makes it so watchable,' wrote the critic Bilge Ebiri, when the early shorts were collected on DVD in Scorsese's honour, '... isn't its underlying meaning, but rather the frantic, fractured, contrapuntal fashion in which it unfolds.'[21] It feels like life.

The excellent *It's Not Just You, Murray!*, made in 1964, brings us closer still to the imprimatur of Scorsese. Shot on location on the Lower East Side, this could be said to be his first gangster movie; it's certainly a prelude to *Mean Streets* and inspired by the cornucopia of Little Italy gossip. 'It's basically *Goodfellas*,'[22] admitted Scorsese. Motored by voice-over, the story traces the rise of two small-time wiseguys, while building toward the betrayal that lies beneath their jocular brotherhood. Murray is our guide (Ira Rubin, whose slick, fourth-wall-breaking appraisal of his own success hints at Leonardo DiCaprio's effervescent guide to *The Wolf of Wall Street*), while his enigmatic partner Joe (Sam DeFazio) hovers suspiciously in the background. Of note, Catherine Scorsese makes her first appearance in one of her son's enterprises as Murray's overbearing mother, forever trying to spoon-feed him meatballs.

When Murray goes into show business, Scorsese takes the chance to mount a dime-store musical number, an urge that would wend its way to *New York, New York*. Not really knowing how to bring his tale to a satisfying close, he opts for an extended homage to Fellini's *8½*.

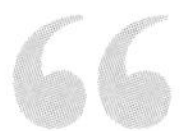

What makes it so watchable ... isn't its underlying meaning, but rather the frantic, fractured, contrapuntal fashion in which it unfolds.

BILGE EBIRI

Right: *Following the lives of two small-time New York hustlers masquerading as businessmen,* It's Not Just You, Murray! *is essentially Scorsese's first gangster movie.*

Below: *Love triangulated – marking the first appearance of another recurrent Scorsese theme, Rubin's Murray (left) remains blind to the infidelity of his wife (Andrea Martin) with partner and best friend Joe (Sam DeFazio).*

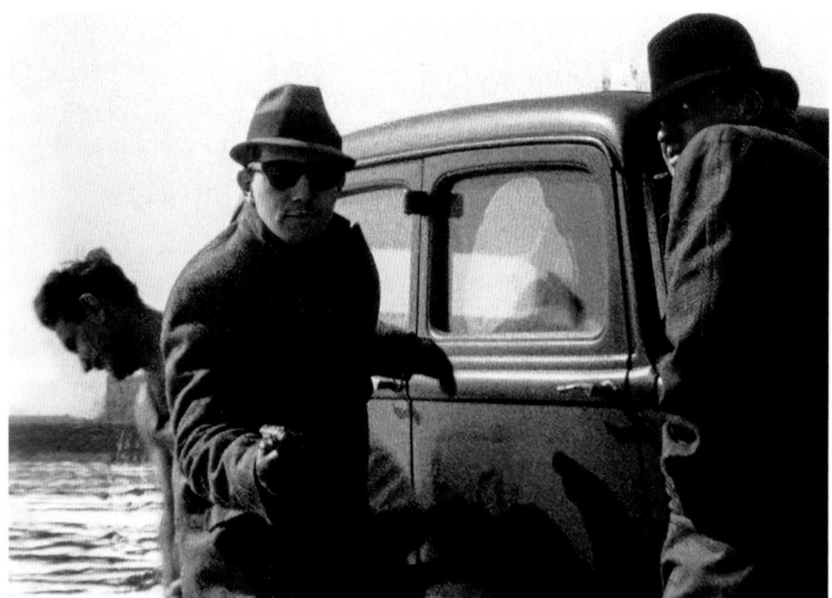

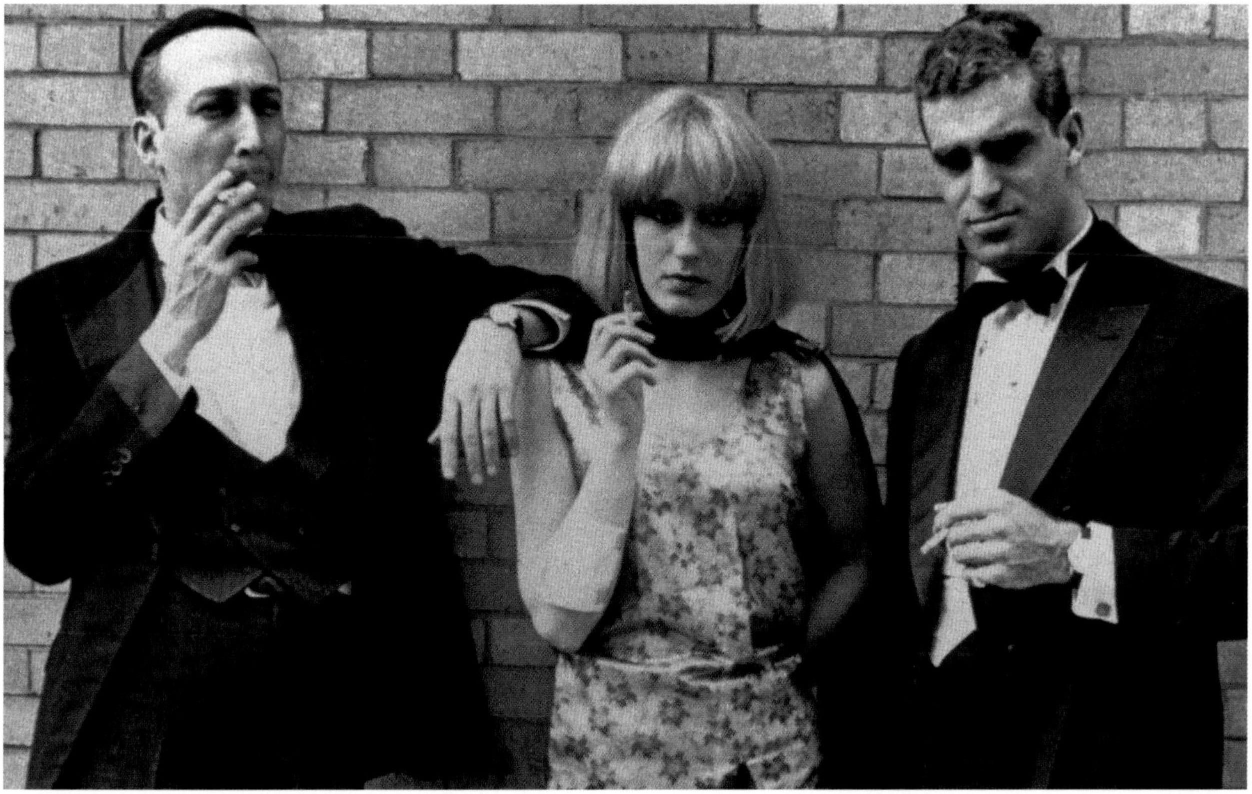

1966
NEW YORK CITY... MELTING POINT (Short) Director / Editor / Writer

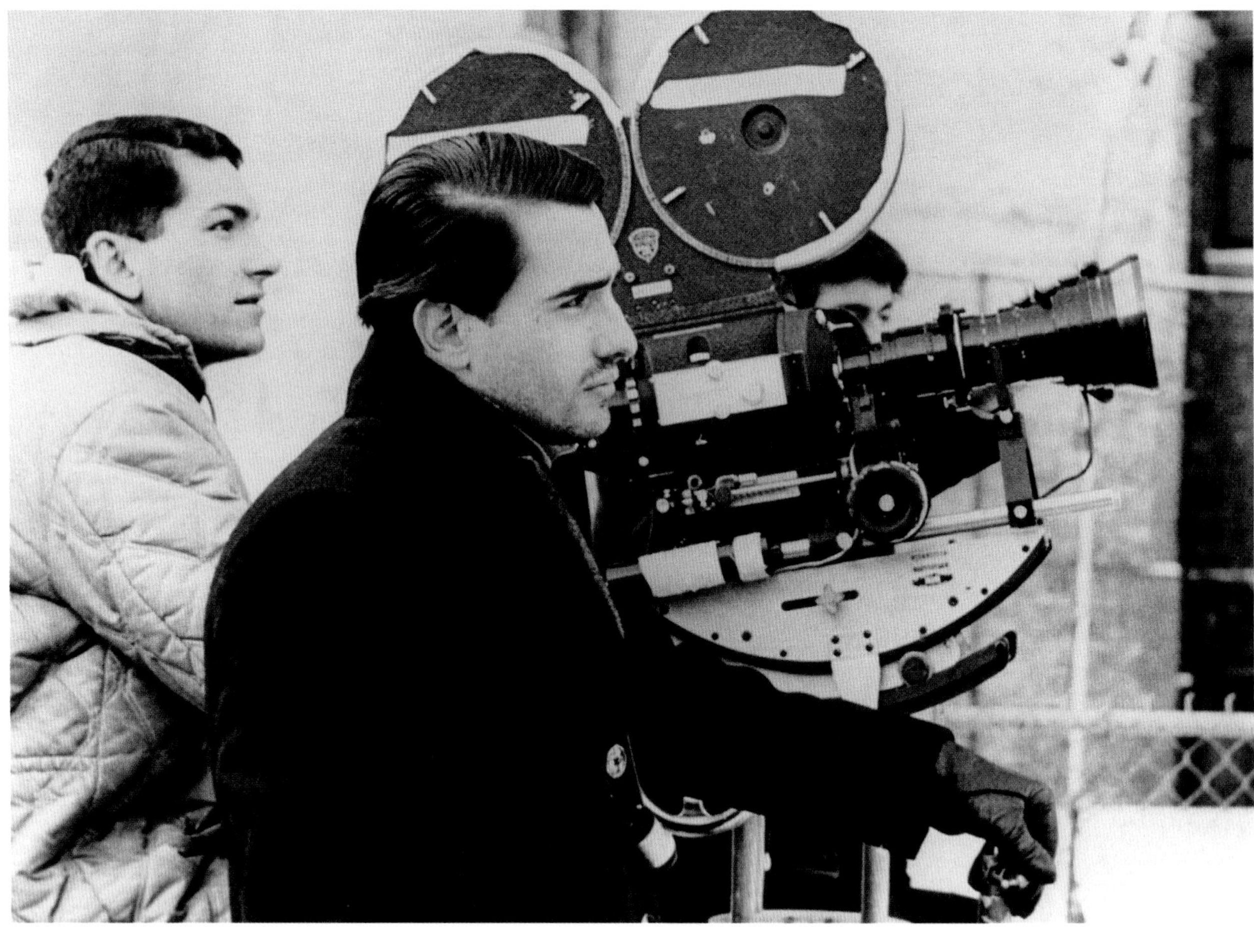

Above: *A portrait of the director as a young man – Martin Scorsese takes up his career-long station beside the camera on the chilly New York set of* It's Not Just You, Murray!

Made in 1967, after Scorsese won a batch of colour film, *The Big Shave* presents the startling sight of the young director embracing Buñuelian surrealism. Eager to keep filming, Scorsese devised a five-minute short of a young man (Peter Bernuth) going through the ritual of his morning shave in an impeccably polished bathroom. In intense close-up, he begins to cut his skin deeper and deeper, building to a savage torrent of jam-like blood, covering his face, throat, and chest (a shot reminiscent of the sweat pouring down Jake La Motta's chest in *Raging Bull*) and onto the faucets. It is the first sighting of Scorsese's unblinking yet aloof treatment of violence. Screened at European festivals, it was met with storms of outrage and laughter – an augury of things to come.

It is also a rare sighting of Scorsese making a direct political statement (his politics tend to well up from within story), when he claimed that it was designed to be a comment on America's involvement in Vietnam, as represented by the concept of self-harm. With time, he recognized that it also embodies a growing sense of disillusionment and anger with the false starts of his career. He was struggling to find a distributor for his first feature,

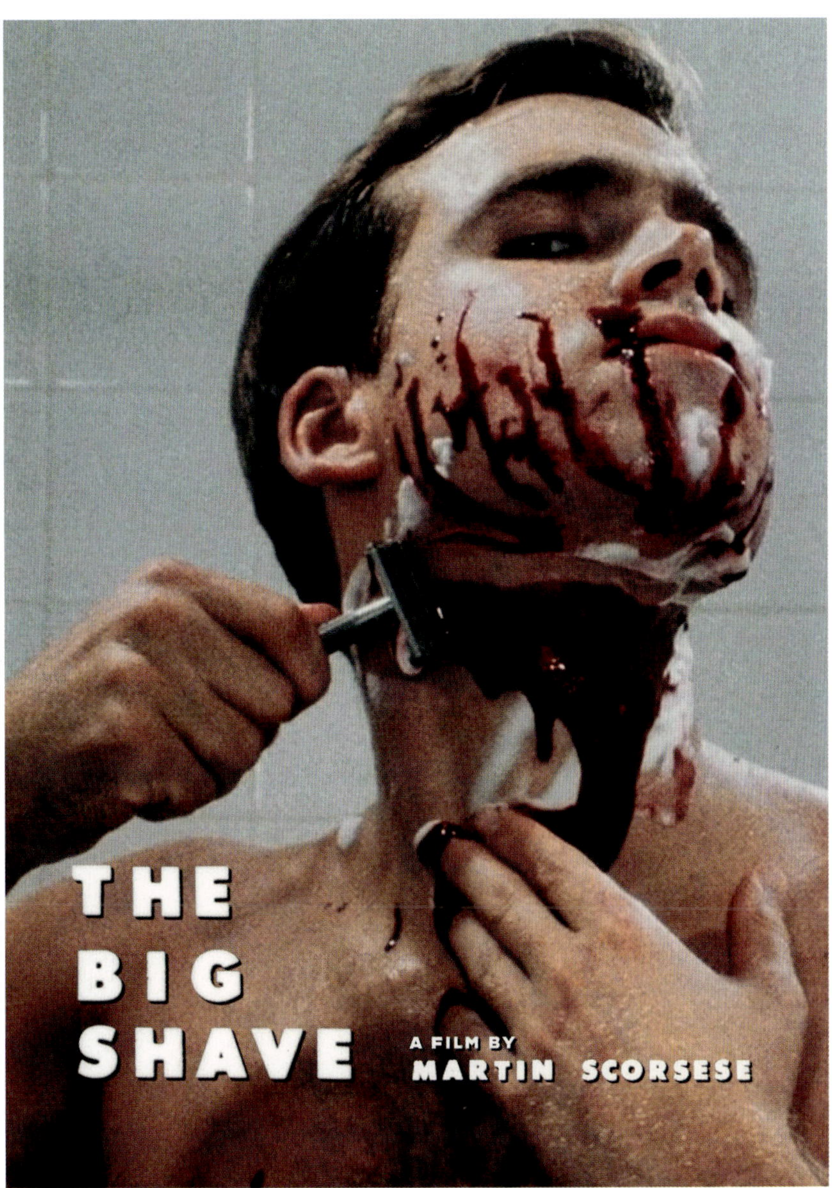

Who's That Knocking at My Door, and having won an internship at Paramount (all these prizes are a clear signal of his promise), was dismayed when it was withdrawn due to a régime change at the studio. There are hints here at the bloody storm that will conclude *Taxi Driver.*

Scorsese emerged from the cocoon of university ready to fly. But as the next chapter attests, it will be a fitful beginning to his professional career. From the very start, almost by instinct, the style that emerged was electrified by personal expression, not something Hollywood yet had an appetite for (though times were about to change).

The films that emerge over the decades of his career will be marked by their doubleness: the need to fulfil the potential of cinema (let's call it that, he needs the temple in which to worship) and also uproot the tangles of life. The inner and outer worlds of his films are infinitely entwined. Then these films are all influenced by the streets on which he grew up. In every one, even those cited as career-rescuing commercial ventures (there will be a few) it is possible to see within the outline of the characters the presence of the filmmaker. This is the stamp of auteurship, the inescapable thumbprint, as slowly, surely, Scorsese, or *Scorsezze*, the little man from Little Italy, transformed the medium.

'I'm too close to the pictures,' he once said, pained to consider even his masterworks. 'A lot of them are too damn personal.'[23] Amen to that.

Above: *Scorsese's first colour film,* The Big Shave *from 1967, is still his most alarmingly surreal. Concealing an anti-Vietnam message, it calmly observes a young man (Peter Bernuth) shaving his jaw to a bloody pulp.*

REEL LIFE

Who's That Knocking at My Door (1969), *Boxcar Bertha* (1972), *Mean Streets* (1973), *Alice Doesn't Live Here Anymore* (1974)

New York in the mid-sixties: a Bosch painting, a melting pot, America in ebullient microcosm. The bohemian possibilities of the Village are blocks away from a career in crime, Madison Avenue only streets from the rich scents of immigrant life. Still a student, based out of the Tisch School of the Arts (the media arts faculty of the NYU) on Broadway, grabbing what time he can with the limited amount of equipment on offer, Martin Scorsese itches to make a movie, the city itself is energizing him. Getting his first feature film even finished will take four years. 'I was trying to make a reputation,'[1] he admitted. Even now, he is still trying.

Alongside his immersion in cinema, Scorsese had become well read. There had been few books at home, they weren't part of what he termed his parents' cultural makeup. Late in high school, a literature course had introduced him to the introspection of Thomas Hardy, Graham Greene, James Baldwin, and Dostoevsky. James Joyce's *A Portrait of the Artist as a Young Man* reinforced what he called his 'growing atheism.'[2] A battle was underway with a faith he has never brought himself to fully reject. He also discovered in Joyce the allure of 'fatalism'[3] within the Irish flavour of Catholicism, an Italian-Irish divide which will draw him to *Gangs of New York* and *The Departed*. He had enrolled in university as an English student, convinced the only path forward was becoming a teacher. As a filmmaker he will display a novelistic vein – a psychological inquest into character.

University had made him more American, even worldly, but the stories that filled his head sprang from the font of Elizabeth Street. Write what you know; film what you know. It is 1965 and his life unfurls like a movie directed by Martin Scorsese, cascading with montages, a patchwork of memory. As far back as he could remember, he always wanted to be a director…

Yet the momentous debut, eventually called *Who's That Knocking at My Door* (from The Genies' hit over the closing credits), wasn't the thunderclap over

Opposite: *The auteur theorising – a young Martin Scorsese contemplates a scene on his first full studio film* Alice Doesn't Live Here Anymore *(1974).*

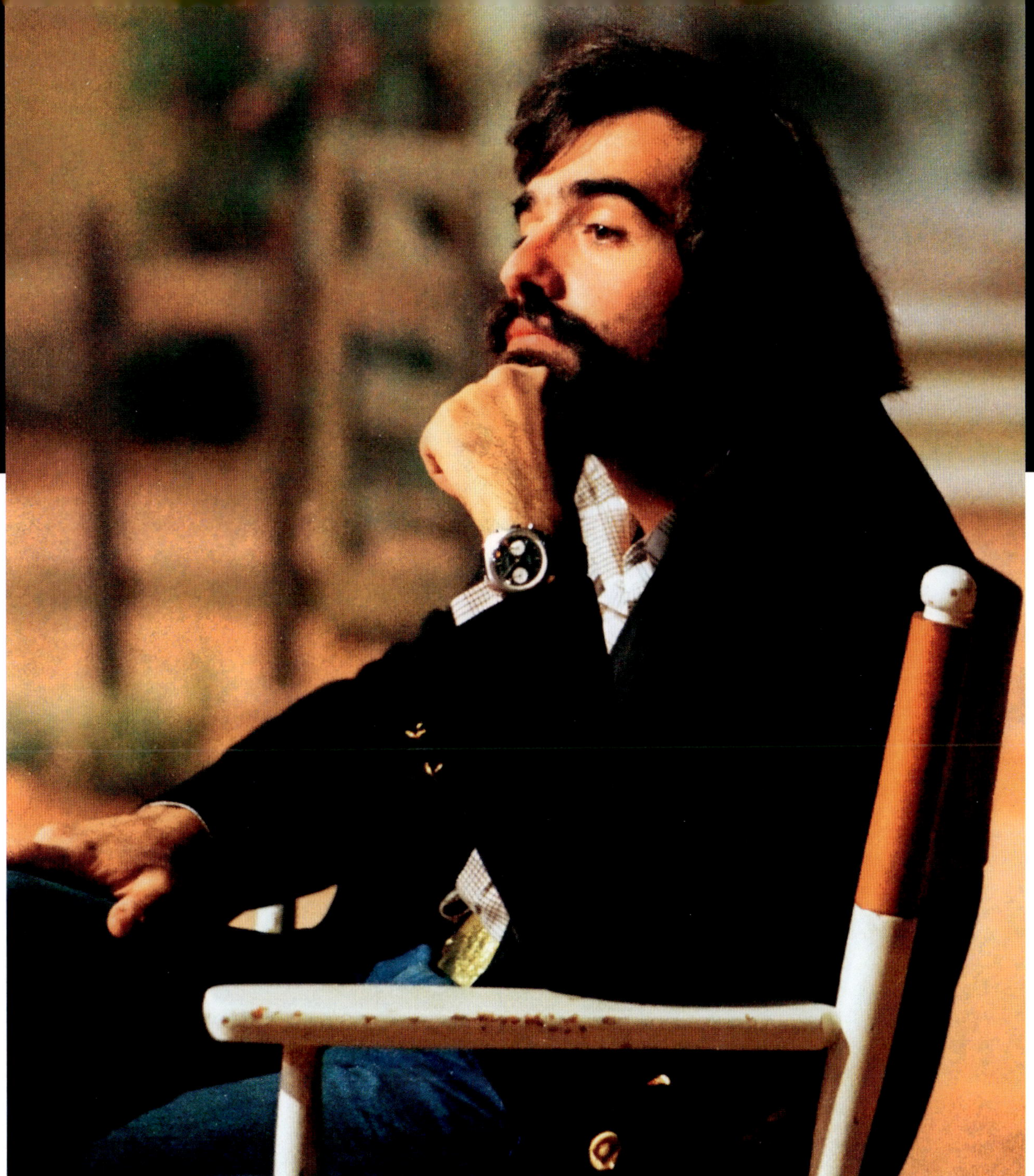

the mountainside we might expect. Not that there weren't prophets who proclaimed the artist in utero. Catching the film at the Chicago Film Festival in 1967 (under the title *I Call First*), Roger Ebert, legendary critic of the *Chicago Sun-Times*, cited scenes that are 'among the most evocative descriptions of American life I have ever seen.'[4]

As with the shorts, there is a tendency to inventory the earliest films for the Scorsese to come rather than watch them for their own sake. Pondering the director's debut on one of its numerous, rose-tinted re-releases, the *New Yorker's* Michael Sragow claimed the film is best viewed as 'a fascinating portfolio piece: a black-and-white blueprint for *Mean Streets*.'[5] And beyond that the mighty career.

It began as part of Scorsese's masters program at NYU, under the title *Bring on the Dancing Girls*. It was still a short, the work of a group of friends, fellow students, and those looking for a start. Lifelong collaborations were underway.

In 1961 he met Mardik Martin, who had arrived in New York from Baghdad at the age of eighteen, switching from business to the miracle of film studies. Martin recalled Scorsese as the only fellow student who ever talked to him. Both made up for their short stature with a prolix nature. Both were outsiders. Both storytellers. A friendship was born, as well as a working relationship, with Martin as co-writer, assistant, fixer, producer, and devotee of the Scorsese cause.

They were equally desperate to get a film off the ground. At one point pitching a sexploitation movie called *This Movie Will Save Your Marriage*. 'In the Swedish style,'[6] laughed Martin. Anything that might work. For a while, Scorsese temped as an assistant cameraman for John G. Avildsen, who would later direct *Rocky*.

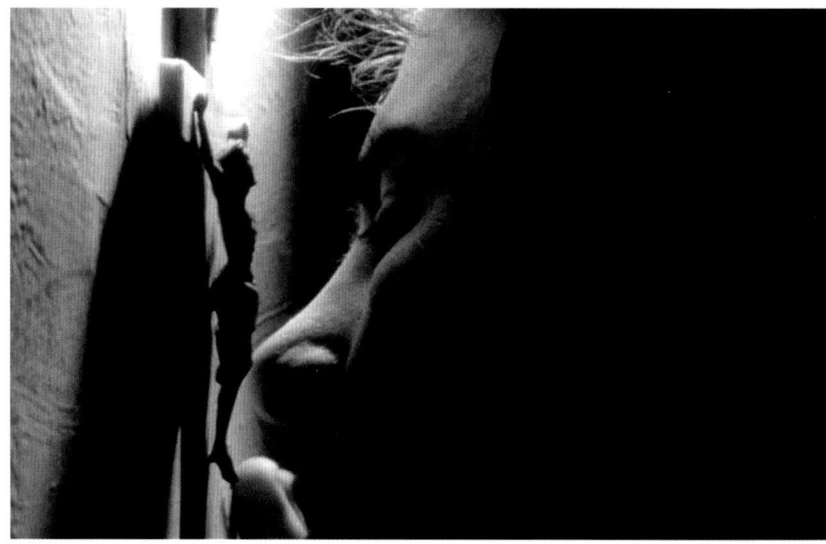

Above: *Altar ego – Martin Scorsese would later admit he had overdone the Catholic symbolism of his debut feature film* Who's That Knocking at My Door *(1969).*

Opposite: *Part-time court stenographer Harvey Keitel was the first of Scorsese's great leading men, bringing the troubled J.R. to life, while adopting many of the mannerisms of the director.*

The young Scorsese had a trilogy of films mapped out, which flowed directly from the Little Italy of the fifties and sixties, all the life he had observed from his window. Three stories forming a Joycean rite of passage for a cadre of young men at the fringes of crime (guns are casually glimpsed and they strut the streets in territorial mood), with the Catholic Church and boorish cultural traditions looming large in their lives. The first part, *Jerusalem, Jerusalem*, got no further than a treatment, which followed the group as boys heading out from the city to a Jesuit retreat. It introduced J.R., evidently an alter ego for Scorsese – he is remarkably film-literate for a street kid. What follows are the events of *Who's That Knocking at My Door* and finally *Mean Streets*, though the narrative threads holding the trilogy together would come loose.

Scorsese and Martin found their leading man by putting an ad in the industry rag *Show Business*, and a handsome young court stenographer and former marine from Brighton Beach arrived for an audition. With the dominance of Robert De Niro and

Leonardo DiCaprio in the canon, it is easy to forget that Harvey Keitel was Scorsese's first muse (despite being Polish-Jewish, the actor does a fair approximation of the director's Italianate mannerisms as J.R.). They had instant rapport, and the same sense of humour, recalled Keitel, 'and we seemed to possess a similar common denominator, a need for something – a certain truth, a need to express what we saw.'[7]

Bring on the Dancing Girls, as it began, was shot in Little Italy, indeed on Elizabeth Street. Crewed by a handful of eager students, they filmed at weekends, subsisting during the week. There was no talk of permits, Scorsese grabbed his shots on the fly, documentary-style, despite the cumbersome weight of the 35mm Mitchell BNC under loan from the university. They used their own homes, their own narrow hallways, their own mothers (the ever-willing Catherine Scorsese takes a symbolic cameo in the opening scene serving up Italian pie).

This was a stylish glance at the prototypical young men of the Lower East Side, their nights out pitched at a carefully calibrated clamour (we can hardly pick up what they are saying), riffing on a boisterous mix of the Italian Neorealists, the French New Wave, and the edgy, in-a-room verisimilitude of John Cassavetes, New York's crown prince of indie. Scorsese storyboarded every shot. Experimental in vein, narrative was almost non-existent in its tonal snapshots of parties, bar talk, scuffles, and the sudden breathing space of an excursion upstate where J.R. drinks in the epiphany of the great American landscape – a mythical life beckoning from beyond the city limits.

In 1967, with the encouragement of tutor-turned-producer Haig Manoogian (who also found him financial backing) and a student loan secured by his father, Scorsese set about expanding what he had into a feature film. Utilizing a lighter 16mm camera (with the footage blown up to 35mm), he went back onto the streets of New York intent on a romantic plot. Keitel's overwrought J.R. will meet an unnamed

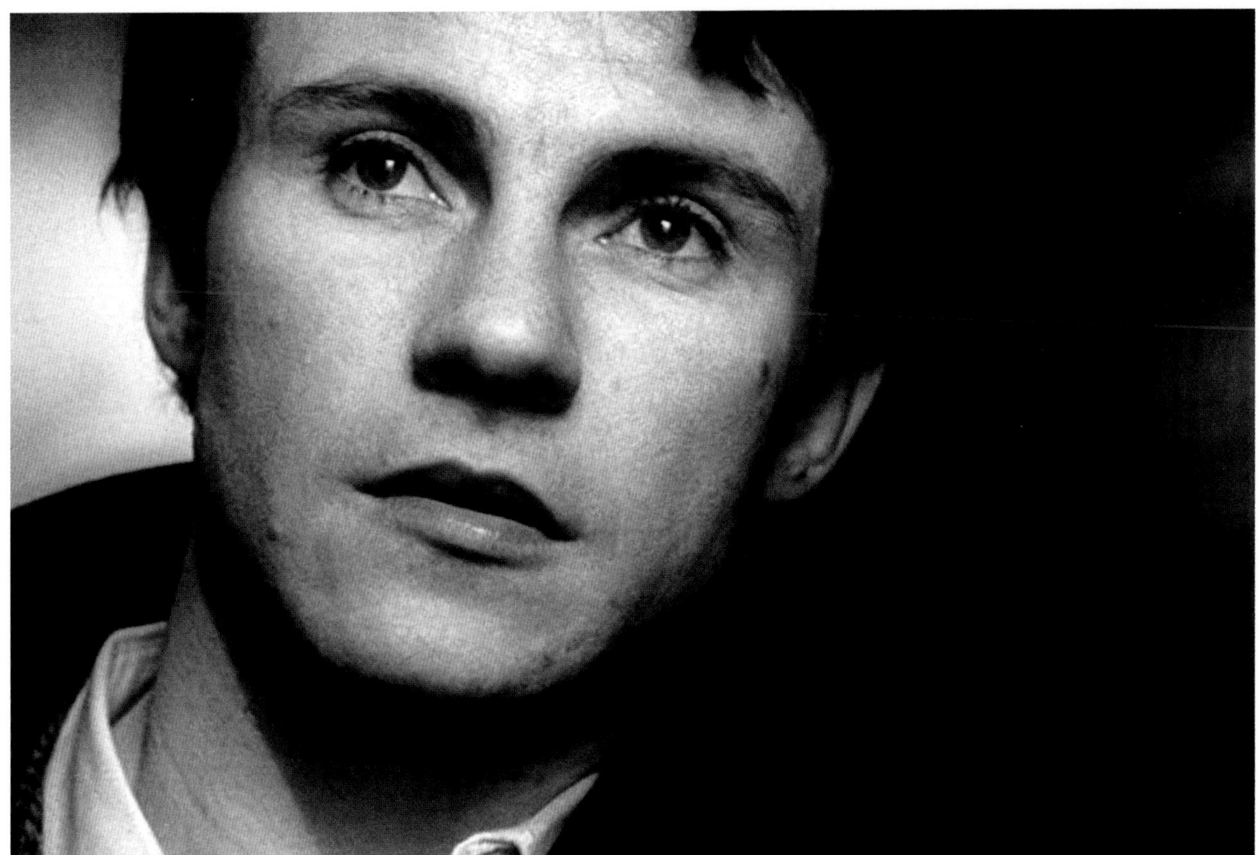

blonde (the striking Zina Bethune, a former ballet dancer who had appeared in soap operas) in the waiting room for the Staten Island Ferry, the camera dollying past like an eavesdropper. A connection is made via talk of John Wayne, rooftop montages, and visits to the movies: inverting the self-sabotage of Travis Bickle taking Betsy to a porno in *Taxi Driver,* the couple exit *Rio Bravo* deep in happy discussion (Scorsese's perfect date).

To unite his twinned stories, he needed a good editor. He had a great one. Born in Algeria, where her father worked in the oil industry, Thelma Schoonmaker had ended up at Cornell learning Russian, with Nabokov as a tutor, and then studying primitive art at Columbia. 'America was like a foreign country to me at first,'[8] she said, another outsider. She got into editing by chance, answering a newspaper ad for an assistant editor, and ended up butchering art films by Antonioni, Godard, or Truffaut to fit late night television slots. Versions Scorsese was watching. She knew as well as he did what had gone missing. That led her to a six-week summer film course and NYU, Marty, and the rest of her life.

'Marty had edited [*What's a Nice Girl Like You Doing in a Place Like This?*] but someone had miscut the negative. Since I knew about negative cutting from the terrible job that I'd had, the professor for the course asked me to help Marty fix his film.'[9]

Still his closest collaborator, the indomitable Schoonmaker has been 'fixing' his films ever since. All those energies, all that sublime timing, that ineffable *Scorsese-ness* is evoked in the ethereal dark of the edit suite with Thelma.

Intercut with the highlights of the existing footage of the roistering gang – a counterpoint of immaturity and adulthood

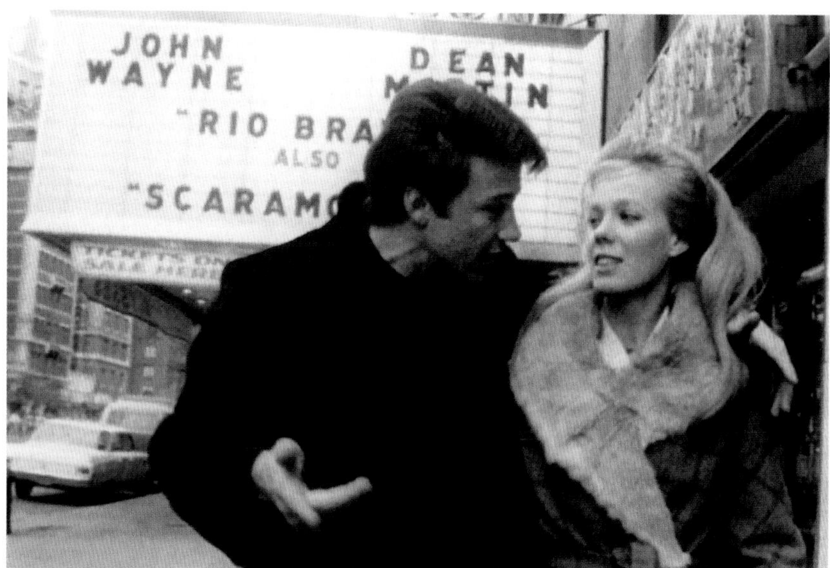

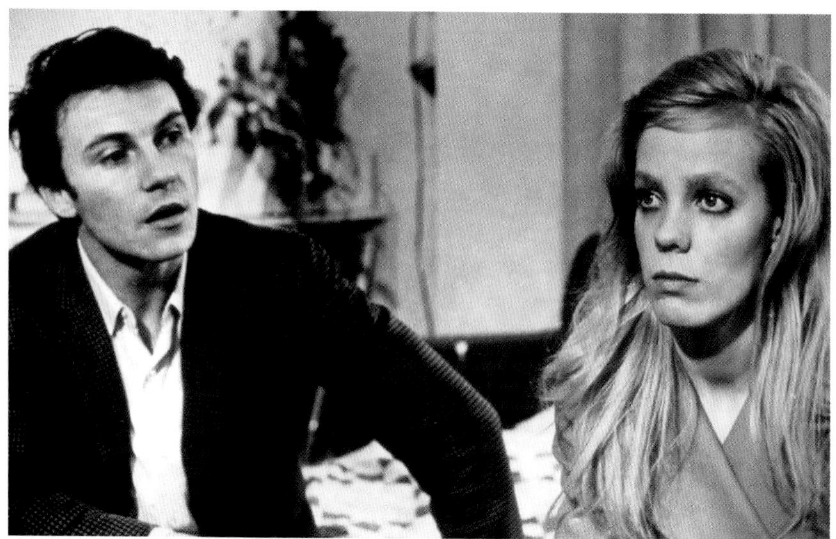

Top: *Martin Scorsese's biographical signature is all over* Who's That Knocking at My Door *(1969), including a scene of J.R. (Harvey Keitel) and his date (Zina Bethune) exiting a* Rio Bravo *matinée, discussing the merits of Howard Hawks' Western.*

Above: *Scorsese's first feature would take four years to finish, with the actors visibly maturing between scenes, but Scorsese's great frankness of style was fully formed. Mentor John Cassavetes loved it.*

– J.R.'s relationship founders when he can't handle the revelation that his upper-crust girl was the victim of a rape (expressed in an unnerving staccato flashback). By his antiquated dictum, there are the 'nice girls' you marry, and the 'broads'[10] you sleep with. She has in his confusion become a broad. He flees, but is left racked by guilt. What biographer Mary Pat Kelly called Scorsese's 'spirit-flesh dichotomy.'[11] The old Madonna and the whore syndrome. His wrong-headedness verges on social commentary. 'He's bred not to mature, not to move ahead,'[12] insisted Scorsese.

They sought a distributor for the film, now entitled *I Call First*, and got nowhere. That was until Manoogian brought it to the attention of an old army buddy, Joseph Brenner, who had gone into the softcore market. Brenner offered to distribute the film on the condition they add a sex scene. Scorsese was away in a turbulent Europe of 1968 shooting commercials, so Keitel was flown to Amsterdam, where the director set about sheepishly creating an extended fantasy of J.R. having sex with various beautiful sex workers in a dreamy loft. All artfully composed, but a patent non sequitur within a film essentially about sexual repression. Scorsese literally had to smuggle the celluloid back through customs in his raincoat pocket.

Finally released as *Who's That Knocking at My Door*, it's a disjointed, often heavy-handed piece; the Catholic symbolism is laid on thick (including close-ups of J.R. kissing a crucifix). Yet moment by moment here are the stirrings of the great style: the editing rhythms, the combination of music and image (the jukebox of Scorsese's imagination), the wild surges of natural energy, that sense of a director making his film from *within* the world of the story.

With next to no promotion, it made no money at all. Scorsese and Martin even took to the streets to hand out fliers in front of their one Manhattan cinema. It opened in Chicago on the very same street as the Biograph, outside which John Dillinger was shot. 'That makes two things that died on that block,'[13] smirked one of Scorsese's uncles.

His directing career might have been stuck in first gear, but Scorsese began to accumulate meaningful experience. He edited news footage for CBS; the snapshots of the Vietnam war, roughhewn but redolent of danger, stuck with him. Manoogian landed him a job teaching at the university, where Vietnam vet Oliver Stone attended his class. He was also hired by Michael Wadleigh (cameraman for portions of *Who's That Knocking at My Door*) to be an assistant director on *Woodstock*, the epochal record of the music festival that ignited a generation. It was

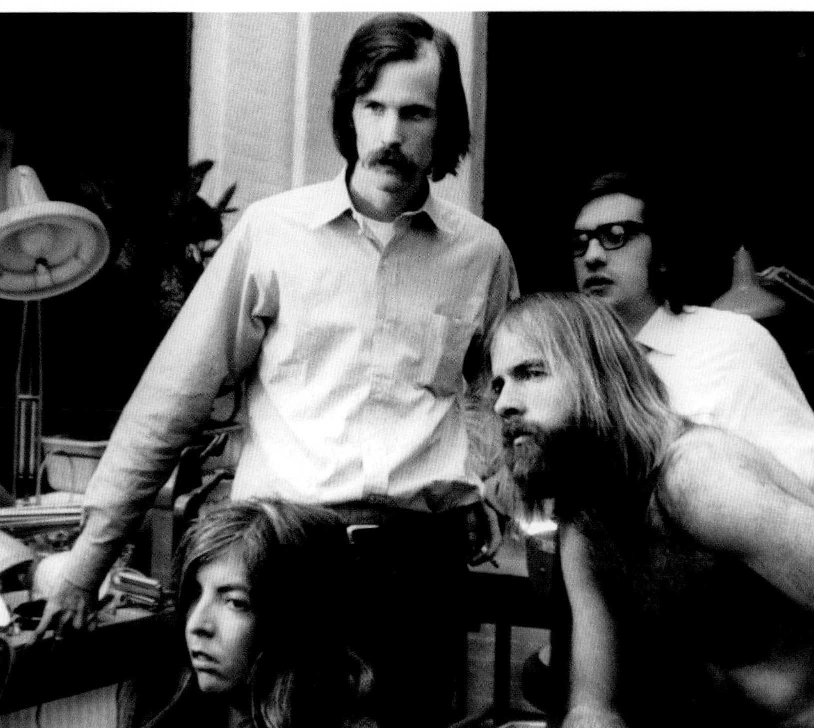

Above: *Scorsese (far right) worked as editor and assistant director on concert documentary* Woodstock *in 1969, with fellow former NYU students Thelma Schoonmaker (bottom left) and director Mike Wadleigh (shirtless), who eventually fired him for intruding on his turf.*

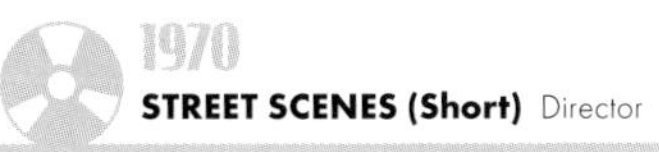

1970
STREET SCENES (Short) Director

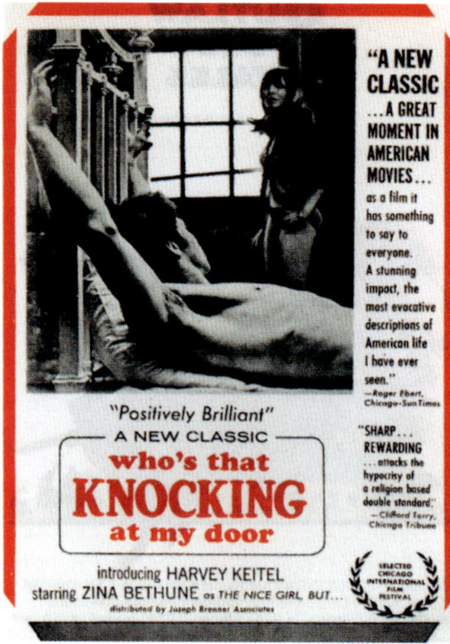

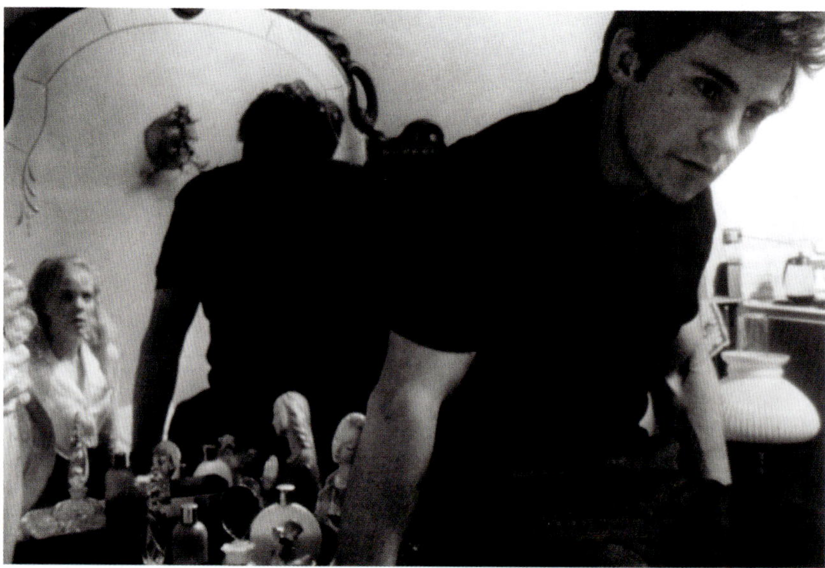

Above left: *Although* Who's That Knocking at My Door *received good reviews, it barely made a murmur at the box office, leaving Martin Scorsese to head to Los Angeles in search of a career.*

Above right: *The film is filled with a growing sense of the director to come, intent on bringing the personality of the characters into his shots.*

thrilling chaos, nothing went to plan, but the counterculture began to flow through his bloodstream.

And in 1969, Scorsese was fired from his first, bona fide professional directing gig after a week. *The Honeymoon Killers* came his way via his agent Harry Ufland, and the forties-set biopic of serial-killing couple Martha Beck and Ray Fernandez suggests a ready Scorsesean enterprise. Finding no connection to the long-winded script, he went overboard in an attempt to affect a *style* for a simple noir, concentrating on long, dawdling master shots like a Carl Dreyer picture. 'I was trying to impose myself as a master of camera,'[14] he rued, unable to handle the rigour of playing a genre straight. Eventually directed by Leonard Kastle, it became a cult classic, even Scorsese thinks so.

In 1971, this son of New York did the unthinkable and headed West to the land of the setting sun: California, Los Angeles, and Hollywood, the locus of the film industry. Scorsese had been working as an assistant for Cassavetes on *Minnie and Moskowitz* in 1971 – basically trailing him around, absorbing his wisdom – when he took up the offer of editing flower-power documentary *Medicine Ball Caravan*, imagining directing opportunities had to follow. It is startling to be reminded that Scorsese resided in California for thirteen years, during which time he made many of his great New York movies.

As is well documented, he fell in with a legendary faction of talented hopefuls, the colloquial movie brats, readying themselves to storm the gates of the studios. He knew Brian De Palma from New York, but at the beach parties and nocturnal gatherings, he could talk film and the film business with likeminded souls such as Francis Ford Coppola, Steven Spielberg, George Lucas, John Milius, and a writer named Paul Schrader.

And yet, Scorsese had at first imagined slipping into the studio system. He thought he could be more Californian, he laughed, 'a movie director in the old Hollywood style, making genre films at a rapid pace. But the old Hollywood was dying.'[15]

One of the fascinating contradictions of the New Hollywood era was that these young directors were trying to keep something of the old Hollywood alive. But they brought the counterculture with them; doing conventional things unconventionally. Scorsese recalled deliberately going against the established filmmakers he admired.

As a city, Los Angeles didn't suit him, it brought out his asthma. He was hospitalized for the first time (but far from the last), growing ever more dependent on cortisone. Living in an old Hollywood Hills house, the warm air stoked his anxieties, all his Catholic-fuelled superstitions, giving him a sense of poetic doom. The old guilt. Addictions were entering his life: prescribed drugs soothed his breathing, recreational drugs stoked his muse, therapy inspired more obsessions. He was constantly hustling to direct. 'People had no idea. You pushed here and it gave there, you slipped in,'[16] he recalled. The question was whether he was losing himself at the feast or finding himself.

Made in 1971 for Roger Corman's New World Pictures, *Boxcar Bertha* is generally viewed as an outlier at best, a quick exploitation flick to keep Scorsese solvent and sane. But he was gaining a crucial understanding of how he might forge a career in the industry. What he classified as a crash course in 'the realities of the marketplace.'[17] And equally a lesson in what could be achieved, even if your film was destined for drive-ins.

Z-grade-movie mogul Corman was the industry's great catalyst. Working with the producer was a matter of mutual exploitation: Corman exploited nascent talent for cheap labour, they exploited him for the chance to direct something, anything, that might awaken the major studios to their gifts. Coppola had made his debut on a dirt-cheap Corman affair, the horror-with-pretentions *Dementia 13*, and hadn't he just dazzled America with *The Godfather*? In different ways, Peter Bogdanovich, Ron Howard, Jonathan Demme, John Sayles, Joe Dante, and James Cameron all gained a start at Corman's makeshift studio in Santa Monica.

Boxcar Bertha was a classic Corman cash-in on the notoriety of *Bonnie and Clyde* (so stands as a Hollywood B-movie). Shot on location in Arkansas at a twenty-four-day dash, this Depression-era road movie centres on boxcar-jumping itinerant Bertha (Barbara Hershey) who falls in with (and into bed with) union organizer Big Bill Shelly (David Carradine). Alongside fellow fugitives, card-sharp Rake Brown (Barry Primus) and erstwhile musician Von Morton (Bernie Casey), they clatter through a procession of holdups and getaways, with the railway authorities in hot pursuit.

Corman left strict instructions for ample portions of nudity and violence. Scorsese stuck to the script, delivering a rough-edged (and bare-bodied) thriller, made with the devotion of a man who knew his way around the proposed genre. Even exploitation flicks deserved due care and attention.

'Marty went to Arkansas ahead of everybody to scout locations,' recalled Corman. 'And when we arrived, we found that he had sketched all of the shots and tacked them to the walls of his motel room.

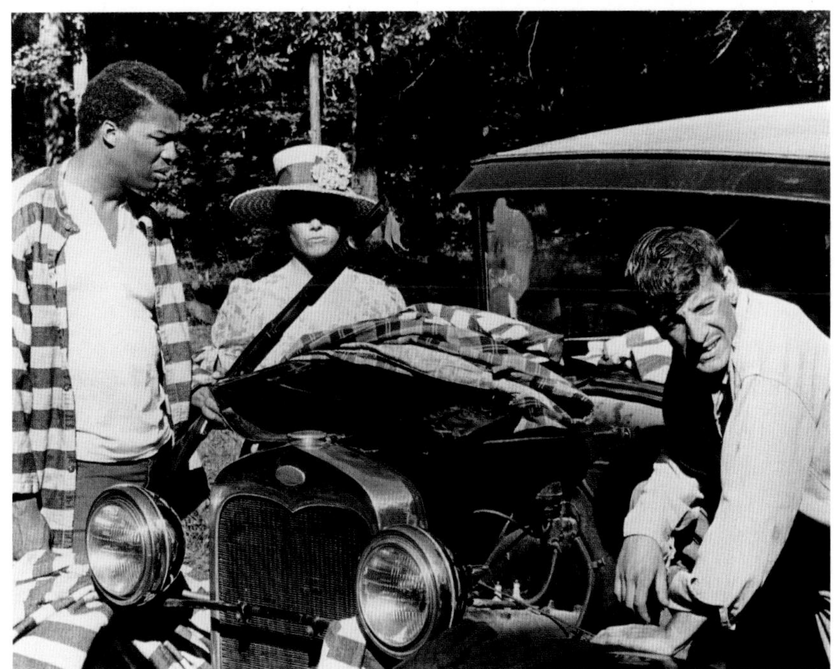

Above: *Bernie Casey, Barbara Hershey, and Barry Primus in Scorsese's unexpected second feature,* Boxcar Bertha *(1972), a Depression-era thriller backed by exploitation king Roger Corman.*

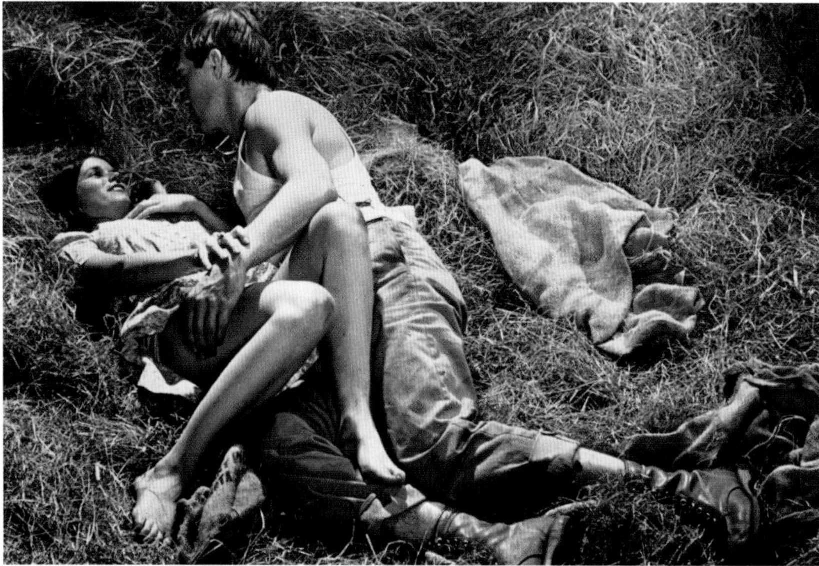

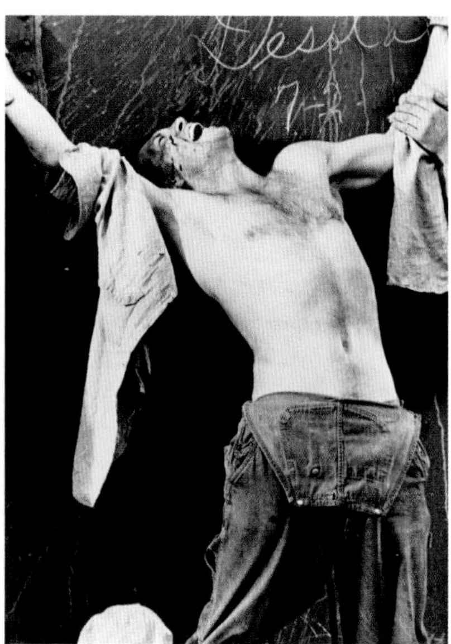

It was the most complete preparation of a picture I had ever seen.'[18]

'Every shot was very, very specifically designed, every one of them,'[19] insisted Scorsese.

'Yet the film keeps fighting Scorsese,' sighed *The Ringer*, looking back on this oddball second with a common complaint. 'The director's touches often feel like ornamentation on a story that doesn't have a lot of nuance...'[20]

While formulaic, piquant historical detail, vigorous camerawork, those outbursts of violence, and the spirited, edgy performance from Hershey (Bertha is swept up in a life of crime) prove that Scorsese's invention is irrepressible, even with blunt tools. What the *LA Free Press* highlighted as 'a crudely compelling lifeforce.'[21] The image of Carradine crucified to a railway carriage leaves no doubt as to who is behind the camera. There are whimsical allusions: the four main characters are modelled on the heroes of *The Wizard of Oz*. And traditional ones: to John Ford and John Steinbeck. Though a world and a career away in terms of budget and credibility, this is historical terrain he would revisit in *Killers of the Flower Moon*.

Corman returned with tempting offers: Blaxploitation flick *I Escaped From Devil's Island* due to be shot in Costa Rica, and gladiator picture *The Arena*, to be made in Spain. A Hollywood career started to look possible. But Cassavetes had been clear on the matter. He was better than this. Scorsese had shown his idol the two-hour rough cut of *Boxcar Bertha*, and Cassavetes didn't hold back. 'Marty, you've just spent a whole year of your life making a piece of shit. It's a good picture, but you're better than the people who make this kind of movie.'[22]

That stuck with him, Sermon on the Mount style, to be requoted in interviews as the primal philosophy: don't get hooked into the exploitation market for the sake of getting something made. He knew that everything in his life added up to *Mean Streets*. It was like an image coming into focus, a calling realized, a lungful of oxygen.

Above left: *Barbara Hershey and David Carradine share a quiet character moment amid the mayhem of* Boxcar Bertha *– Scorsese finding extra dimensions within the proposed genre...*

Above right: *...and he has never been shy of overt religious symbolism, here with Carradine's final crucifixion pose – a herald, perchance, for* The Last Temptation of Christ, *the novel of which was given to him by Hershey?*

Opposite above: *Hershey's untamed Bertha is a rare female lead in a Scorsese film, the only other being the title character of* Alice Doesn't Live Here Anymore *(1974).*

Opposite below: *The gang make a getaway – even though* Boxcar Bertha *was a desperately needed job, it is a part of Scorsese's career-long American crime saga.*

> Marty, you've just spent a whole year of your life making a piece of shit. It's a good picture, but you're better than the people who make this kind of movie.
>
> JOHN CASSAVETES

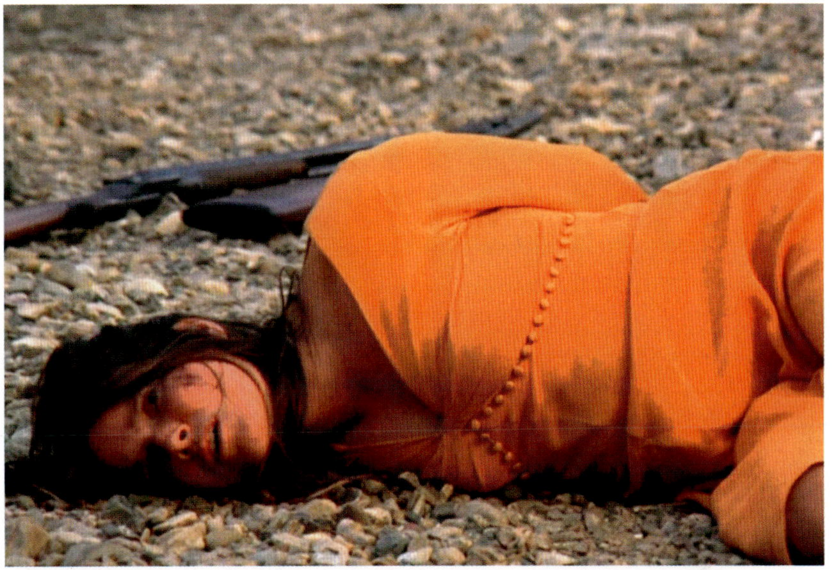

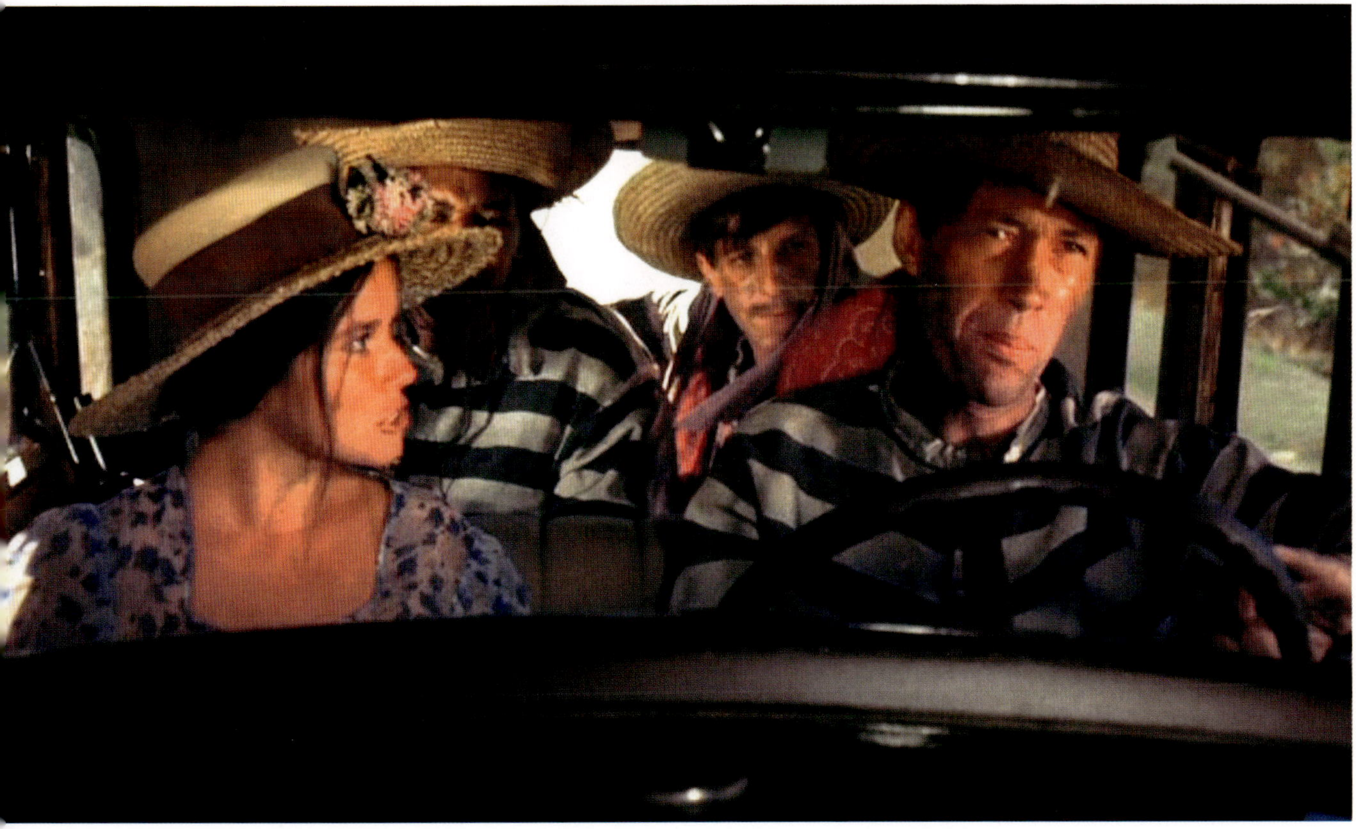

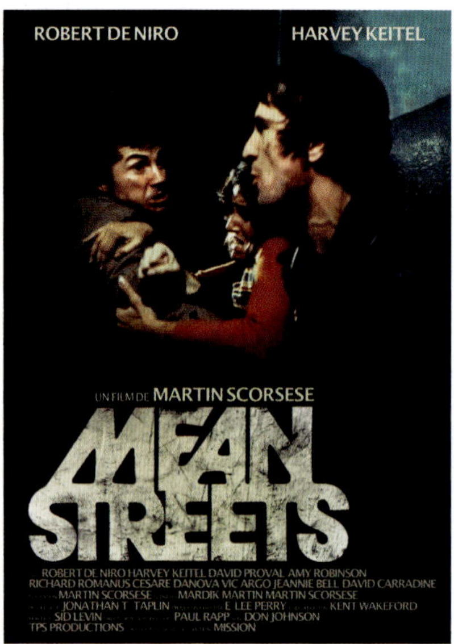

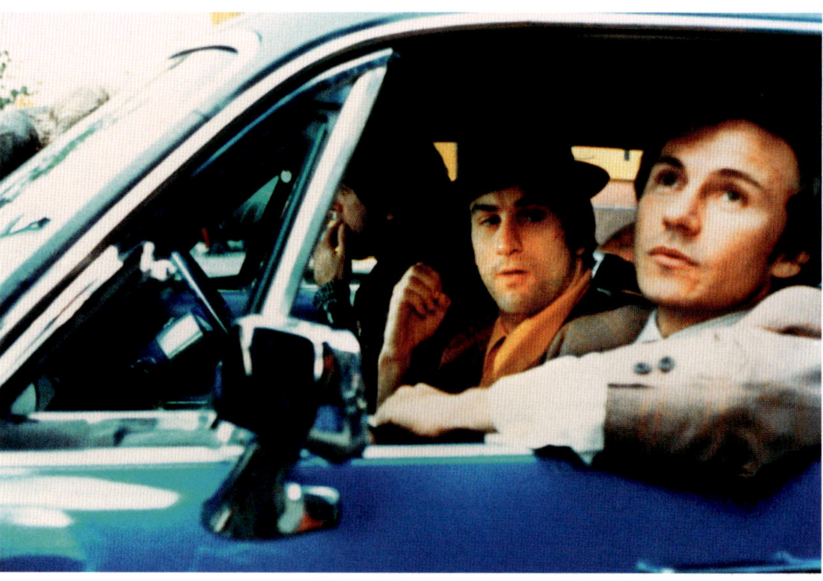

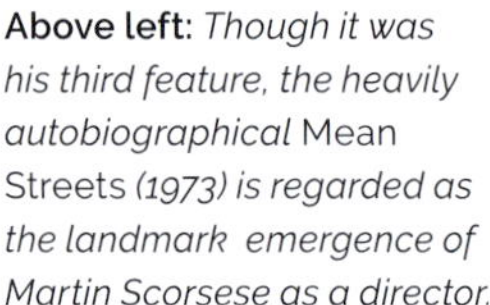

Above left: *Though it was his third feature, the heavily autobiographical* Mean Streets *(1973) is regarded as the landmark emergence of Martin Scorsese as a director.*

Above right: *Life on the streets – Robert De Niro makes his Scorsese debut as the erratic Johnny Boy alongside Harvey Keitel's Charlie. Both are based on various real figures the director knew from Little Italy.*

Mean Streets is the film that reveals Scorsese.

Though at the time it was still called *Season of the Witch*, the third part of his semi-autobiographical New York trilogy, and it was in need of a rewrite. It lacked the chatterbox vibrancy of his dinner-table stories, the way he recalled his youth. That was a moviemaking challenge – to translate the buoyancy of table talk, even street talk, onto the movie screen. He took out much of the religion that had weighed down *Who's That Knocking at My Door*, put in the pool-hall fight (to The Marvelettes' *Please Mr. Postman*), emphasizing the lure of the mob lifestyle. Almost without thinking, the rewrite 'paid homage'[23] to the Warner Brothers gangster movies of decades earlier, another fixture of Scorsese's imprisoned youth. Like *Little Caesar*, Columbia's *The Big Heat*, or his favourite, *The Public Enemy*, which were a little overdone and heavily acted. If he was venturing into genre, it was to be the same realistic milieu as *Who's That Knocking at My Door*. A chronicle of the Italian-American social order that would run through his career. The criminal heartbeat of his city, his country, that fabled 'disruption'[24] of the American Dream. 'If you can't get rich by legal means,' he laughed, recalling the neighbourhood ethos, 'then illegal means will do.'[25]

Scorsese loved how William Wellman, director of *The Public Enemy*, blended in popular tunes of the era with a standard score. Songs provided another layer of narrative, all these tunes he heard pouring out of the neon-fringed bars at three in the morning. These streets were his stage, a living set, a world that ran on blood and twisted ethical codes, the binds of loyalty. 'I never thought of it as one place,' he said. 'To me, Manhattan is the universe.'[26]

On the film's 50th anniversary, *The Guardian* classified his third feature an 'ultraviolent urban pastoral.'[27] Thrillingly sensual and effortlessly fluent, they added, it was his 'early masterpiece.'[28]

The title was changed. *Season of the Witch* was lifted from the Donovan hit from 1966, about a man gazing out of his window

1973
MEAN STREETS Director / Writer (screenplay) / Actor (uncredited)

(insert the young, breathless Scorsese) and pondering the strangeness of life. Jay Cocks, film critic for *Time* (it was an era when the good critics befriended directors), suggested *Mean Streets*, after the Raymond Chandler quote from *The Simple Art of Murder:* 'Down these mean streets a man must go who is not himself mean…'[29]

'I thought it a little pretentious,' admitted Scorsese, 'but it turned out to be a pretty good title.'[30]

Shooting on location, six days squeezed out of the limited $650,000 budget (raised by Bob Dylan's former road manager Jonathan Taplin, before Warner picked up the project) among the granite canyons of the Lower East Side - Bowery and Bleecker, Hester and Baxter, Cleveland Place, and by the cathedral on Mulberry Street - the locals spotted the title on a slate and took against the production. 'There's nothing wrong with these streets!'[31] they remonstrated, exasperated hands reaching for the heavens. He wanted to change the name, but never did.

Apart from those days in his old haunt, the film was made in Los Angeles in the autumn of 1972, but the joins never show. Against the clock, Scorsese grabbed more and more footage to cover his tracks, moving guerrilla-style, street to street, a student. He framed his actors against the urban world, 'and let the buildings do the talking.'[32] He shot the ends of scenes weeks before their beginnings. When David Carradine's drunk is riddled with bullets in the john, spilling out onto the street in pursuit of his assailant before being halted by the sudden onset of death, those are doubles in New York, old friends from the hood blocked so as not to show their faces. Carradine's stand-in, slumping to the sidewalk, was Larry the Box - a local safecracker.

Below: *Home sweet home - Scorsese poses on a New York sidewalk, during only six days of location shooting for* Mean Streets.

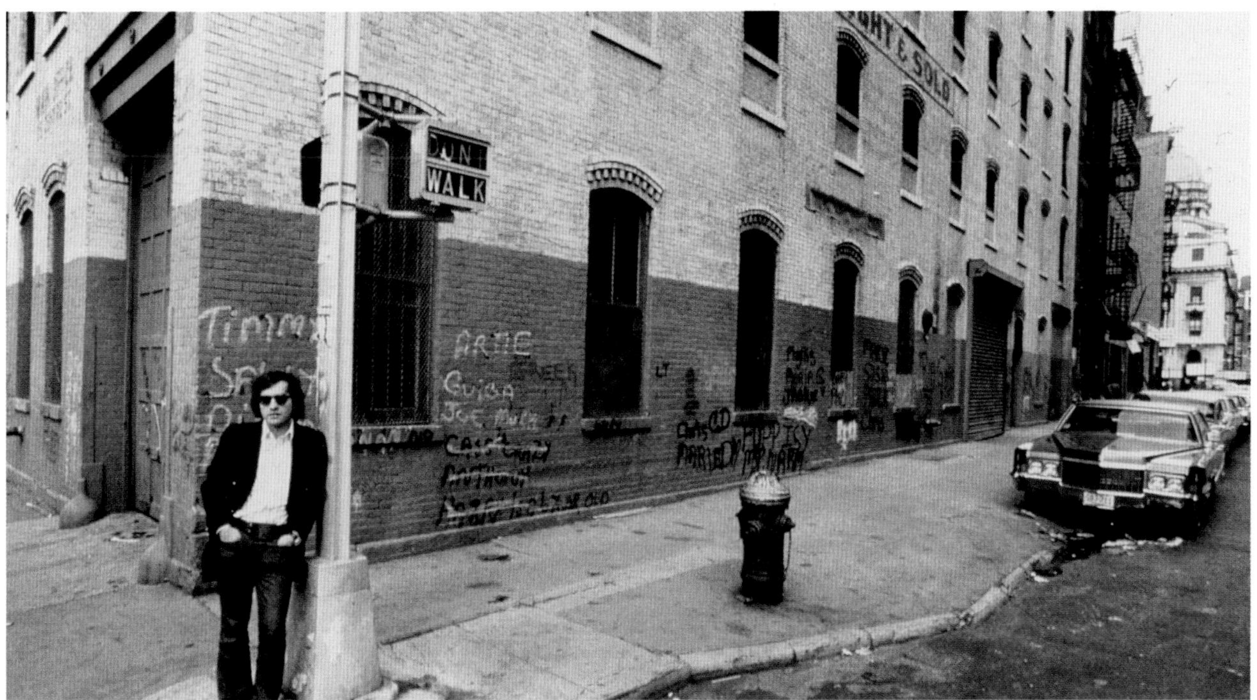

Chandler's poetics make perfect sense. *Mean Streets* is a study of a man finding or losing himself on these neon-streaked New York sidewalks. This is a crime picture nestled inside a character piece. Then character was plot, as far as Scorsese could tell, with Harvey Keitel as Charlie, his alter ego (the name changed from J.R.), who is smart enough to glimpse a future elsewhere, but the neighbourhood won't let go. He still wants to please his uncle, a local mob boss (Richard Romanus), and is drawn to the flame of power (threads that would form a tapestry in *Goodfellas*). A tortured Catholic, guilt presses in on him over his affair with his cousin Teresa (Amy Robinson), who suffers from epilepsy. And for better and much worse he is devoted to his best friend Johnny Boy, the hot-tempered hustler, sinking into debt, as doomed as the setting sun, and played by a newcomer named Robert De Niro.

At a Christmas dinner held by Cocks and his wife, the actress Verna Bloom, Scorsese and De Niro had got talking. Naturally, they had heard of each other. They were from the same blocks, knew the same people, had seen each other at dances regularly enough to say hello. De Niro had liked *Who's That Knocking at My Door.* It was 'accurate,'[33] he told Scorsese.

The director wanted to cast people who understood the world as he did. The worst thing was getting to set and having an actor ask 'What does this scene mean?'[34] They needed to know for themselves.

Below: *Directed with a powerful, unpredictable urgency,* Mean Streets *defies convention, including the relief of a happy ending – Charlie's attempts to escape the neighbourhood are doomed.*

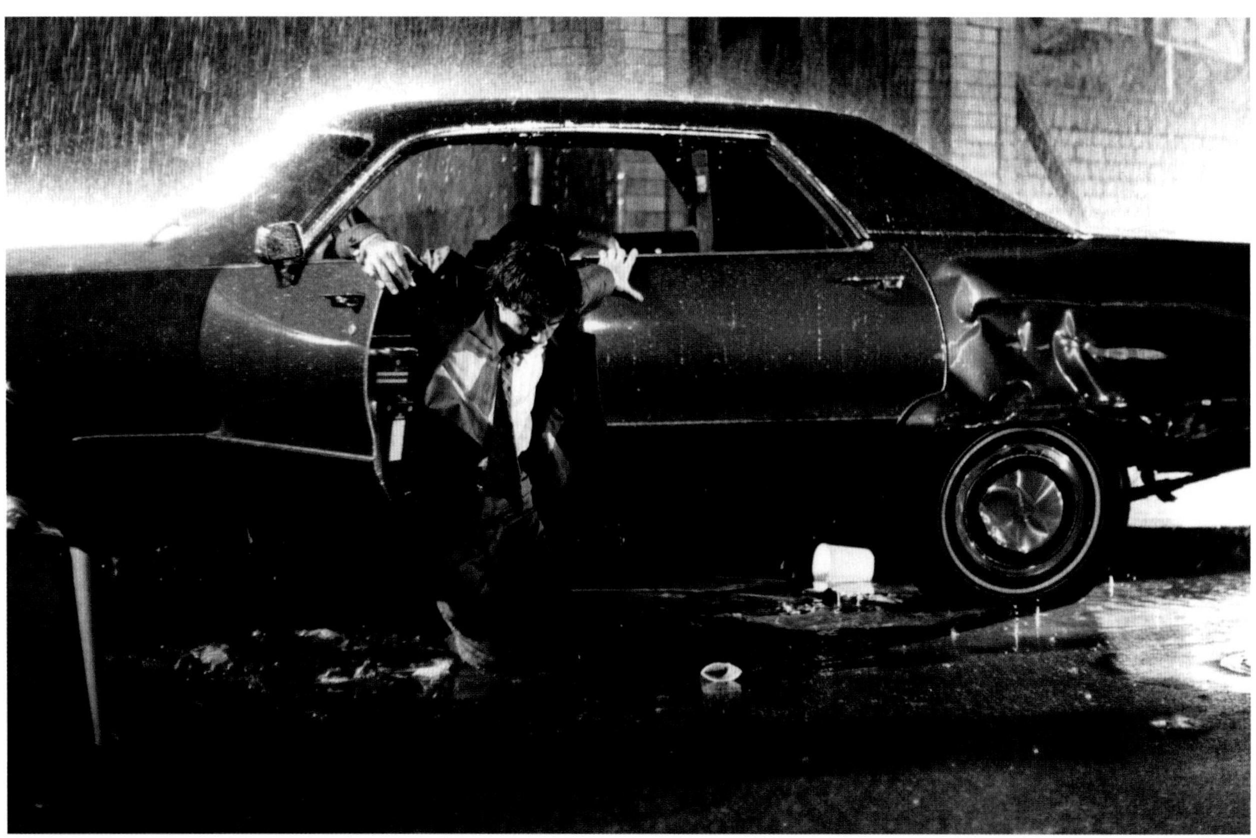

Right: *Simpatico – Robert De Niro (left) and Harvey Keitel (right) listen to their director's instructions. From the very beginning, Scorsese cast actors who understood the world as he did.*

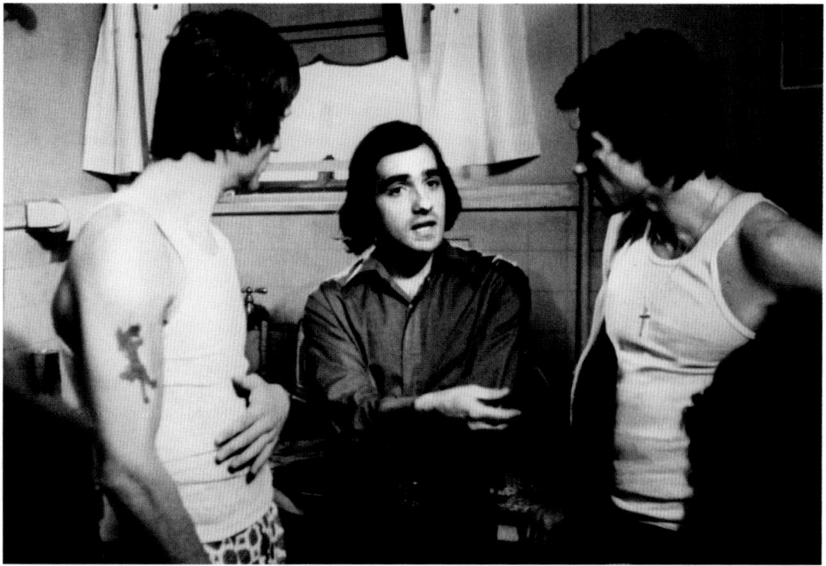

Keitel, De Niro, all of the cast, were liberated from the concerns of reaching a dramatic goal. They could explore the moment as if events were unfolding before them. *Mean Streets* has the jagged, off-the-hip agitation of improvised scenes – gags whipped up on the spot under the needling pressure of the lurking camera. In fact it was a spontaneity captured during rehearsal then written in: the shots were tightly controlled, Scorsese certain now of what he wanted to express.

The film gets bounced around like a pinball by circumstance. Changes of scene or tone come without the standard building of suspense. Nothing is telegraphed. 'In watching Martin Scorsese's film for the sixth or seventh time,' reflected Hunter Lanier in *Film Threat*, 'there's still the feeling that it could go anywhere, that anything could happen.'[35]

Yet there is a sense of ritual – repeated events, actions, familiar hustles, a cycle of damnation. Pauline Kael, aloft in the *New Yorker*, celebrated a 'riper sense of evil'[36] than is conventional to the genre.

Scorsese makes a cameo appearance – a habit – as the hired gunman whose bullet pierces Johnny Boy in the tragic finale. He laughed at the significance. 'I was raised with them, the gangster and the priests. And now, as an artist, in a way I am both...'[37]

When Cassavetes saw the rough cut, he turned to Scorsese and gave him another piece of advice: 'Don't cut it whatever you do.'[38]

Mean Streets took Scorsese to Cannes, and it was the first work the New York Film Festival deigned to show. The reviews were glowing, but the box office remained muted (documented figures for his first three films are sketchy). It played well in New York, but made little impact elsewhere, smothered by the oncoming release of *The Exorcist*. But there is no doubt that this was the film that made Scorsese's reputation. *Mean Streets* is now considered the foundation stone to the Scorsese era. *Mean Streets* led to *Taxi Driver.*

But first a sign that the times were indeed changing. Scorsese was offered a studio movie in the truest sense with *Alice Doesn't Live Here Anymore*, backed by Warner. But one that asked for him to remain Scorsese. Ellen Burstyn, having missed out on an Oscar for *The Exorcist*, decided her next would be Robert Getchell's script about a recent widow and wannabe singer named Alice Hyatt and her precocious son Tommy (Alfred Lutter) destined for California in a station wagon via the arid stretches of Arizona – only to be waylaid in Tucson, where Alice works tables at a diner. Burstyn wanted someone young and exciting behind the camera, who wasn't institutionalized by the system. De Palma had introduced her to Coppola who mentioned Scorsese, suggesting she watch *Mean Streets*. 'What this script needs is the opposite of a polish,' she insisted. 'It needs roughing up.'[39] Scorsese was just the man for a bit of roughing up.

Ironically, one of the reasons Scorsese took the picture was a growing concern that he would become known as a director of gangster films in a realistic Italian idiom. In other words, he was worried he would be typecast as Scorsese. 'At that

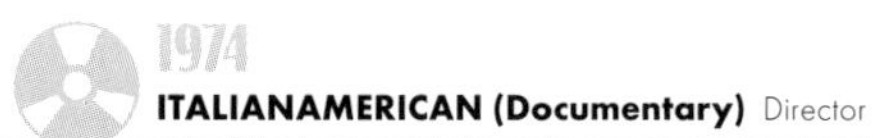

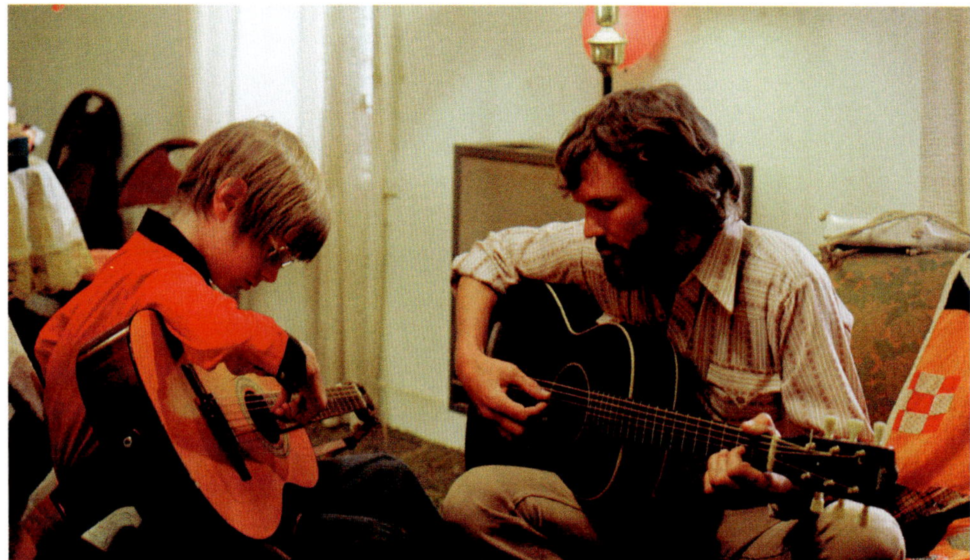

Left: *Alfred Lutter and Kris Kristofferson get in tune in* Alice Doesn't Live Here Anymore *(1974), a studio film that came Martin Scorsese's way because he didn't make studio-style films.*

Below: *Midwestern streets – with his fourth picture, Scorsese again found himself miles from New York, drawn to the chance to shoot the kind of American movie he adored as a kid. Yet he could never escape his own naturalistic sensibility.*

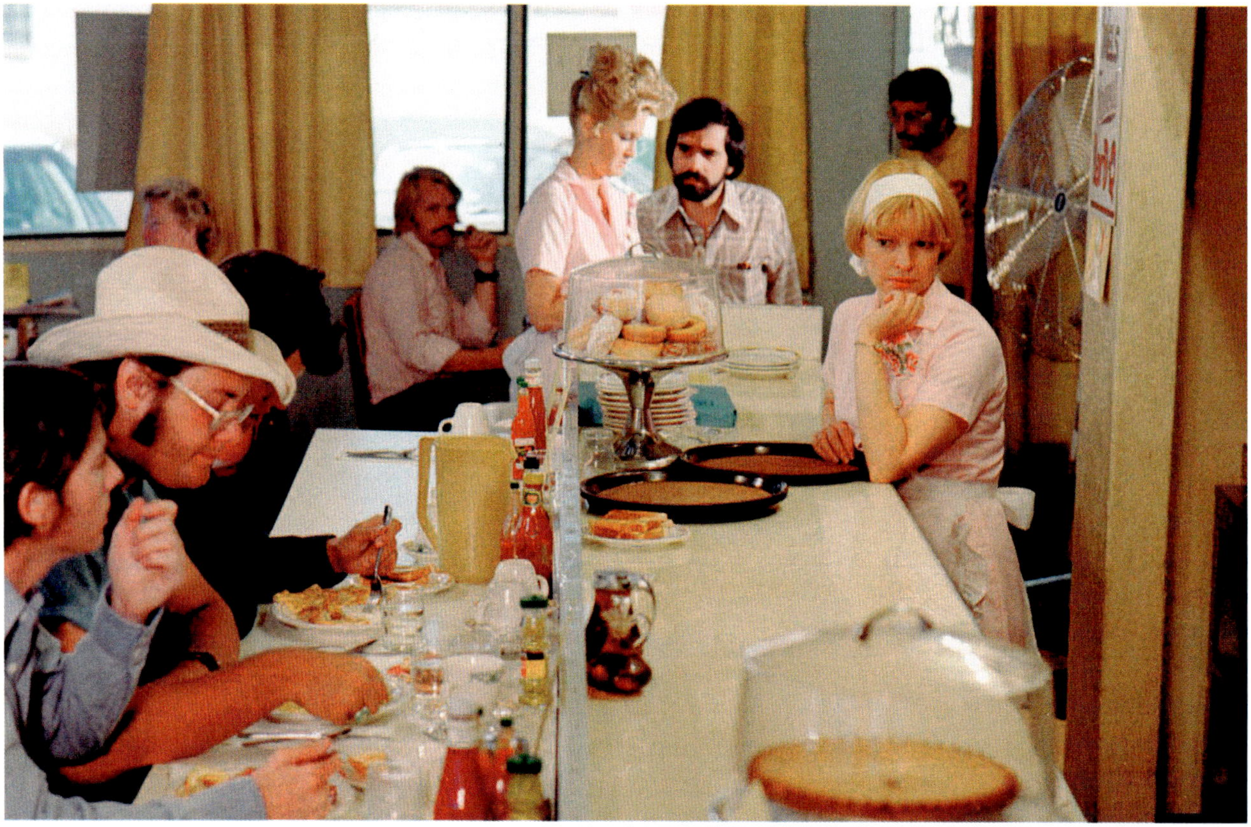

1974

ALICE DOESN'T LIVE HERE ANYMORE Director / Actor (uncredited)

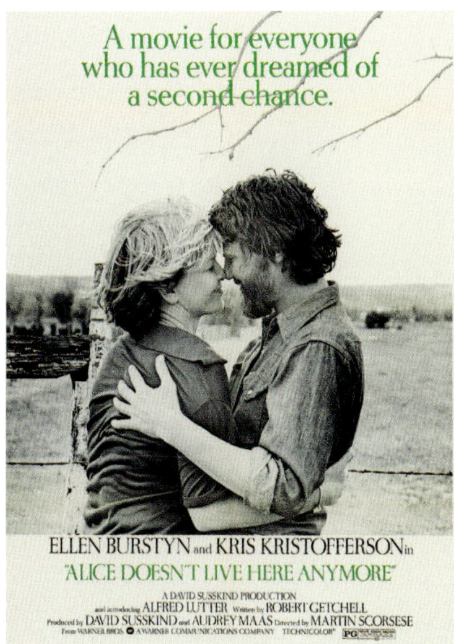

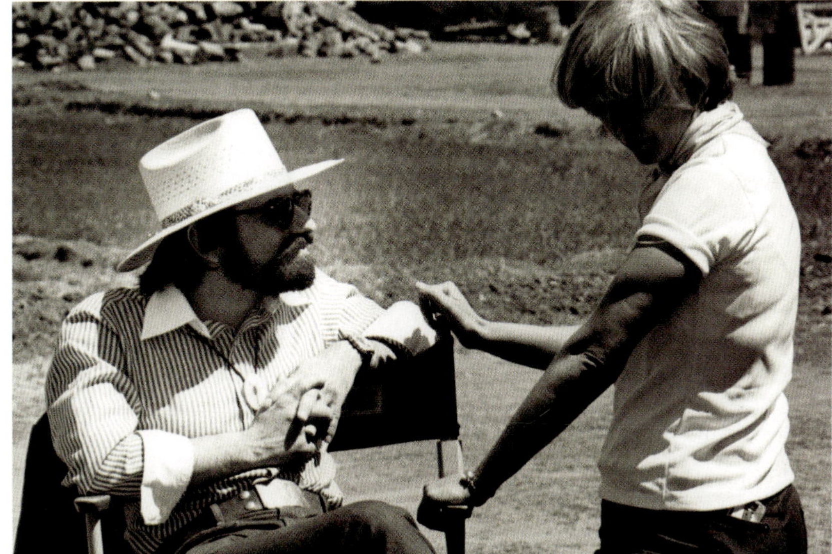

point, there was a part of me that wanted to erase everything of where I came from,'[40] he said. *Mean Streets* had felt like laying his past to rest.

Another irony: although hired for his realism, he took the chance to pay homage to the landscaped beauty of *East of Eden*, *Gone with the Wind*, and *Duel in the Sun*, what he called a 'New Yorker's view of the West.'[41] For the opening flashback to Alice's childhood, he tried out the ravishing colour schemes of Douglas Sirk melodramas and *The Wizard of Oz* – the first sighting of conscious artifice in a Scorsese film. There are hints of musical, though Alice's songs are purely diegetic.

It was its own revolution. At $1.8 million, the budget was three times that of *Mean Streets*. For the first time in his career, Scorsese could build sets; he had a West Coast crew, including Marcia Lucas (George's then-wife) as editor. He shot on location in Arizona, and on the old Columbia lot in Los Angeles. This erstwhile romcom was his first hit, making $18 million. It was a fine balancing act. As the *Times* reported, 'The film is an odd mixture of the commercial-predictable and real insights. The places have a painful reality.'[42]

After *Boxcar Bertha, Alice Doesn't Live Here Anymore* is his only other female-led feature, which would win Burstyn her Oscar. 'That time with Marty was probably the most creative experience I have ever had with a director,'[43] she said. He was reminded of his own relationship with a spirited mother. It was Scorsese who pushed for a more ambiguous ending, where despite the chance to settle down with Kris Kristofferson's decent local rancher, there is still the possibility she could follow her dream to the West Coast. Exactly where Scorsese had finally got his feet under the Hollywood table. Only he had a new obsession. New York called to him again.

Above left: *Backed by a healthy budget and studio marketing,* Alice Doesn't Live Here Anymore *is notable for being Scorsese's first genuine box office hit.*

Above right: *Lead actress Ellen Burstyn had instigated the choice of Scorsese as director, which proved a wise decision as the film would win her the Oscar for Best Actress.*

The film that still defines Martin Scorsese's career begins inside the yellow frame of a New York Checker cab, the kind now lost to the modern streets, left to myth and movies. It emerges in slow motion from the West 57th Street garage, through a cloud of Stygian vapour, urged on by the anxious two-note phrase of the score. A distorted vision of Broadway pours in through the rain-smeared windscreen. It is the start of the night shift. It could easily be the beginning of a horror movie. Maybe it is.

'This yellow, rectangular coffin, a metal coffin, floating through the open sewers of a metropolis,' recalled screenwriter Paul Schrader, the imagery, the story, this cab a product of his own demons. 'Inside that coffin is trapped a young man. And it looks like he's surrounded by life, but in fact he's absolutely alone.'[1]

Scorsese took to describing his film as 'New York Gothic.'[2]

The frame is repeatedly filled with the eyes of the driver in widescreen close-up, the same ratio as the rear-view mirror. They flicker left and right to the metronome of the wipers, bathed in hot red light. Maybe neon, maybe Hell. He is less a man looking for fares than a soldier on patrol.

Before any semblance of story begins, we know *Taxi Driver* will be dominated by a single, subjective perspective. That of Robert De Niro's Travis Bickle, unmistakable now from a thousand bedroom wall posters, a warped icon, who drifts through Manhattan's electric night, his dark thoughts shared via an unsteady voice-over. Words, we discover, that are filling up his diary. 'Someday a real rain will come and wash all this scum off the streets,'[3] he preaches to the crowds in his head – effectively us. The darkness is threatening to overwhelm him.

Schrader always imagined directing the film himself. How could he not? The script was close to autobiographical. 'Travis Bickle was just me,'[4] he told interviewers in search of the headwaters for the character. Scorsese was one of the few directors he could stomach. One of the few he respected. 'I feel I deliver three things,' he

Opposite: *Robert De Niro as Travis Bickle, the dark heart of* Taxi Driver, *yet a character the actor, director Martin Scorsese, and writer Paul Schrader all felt they understood.*

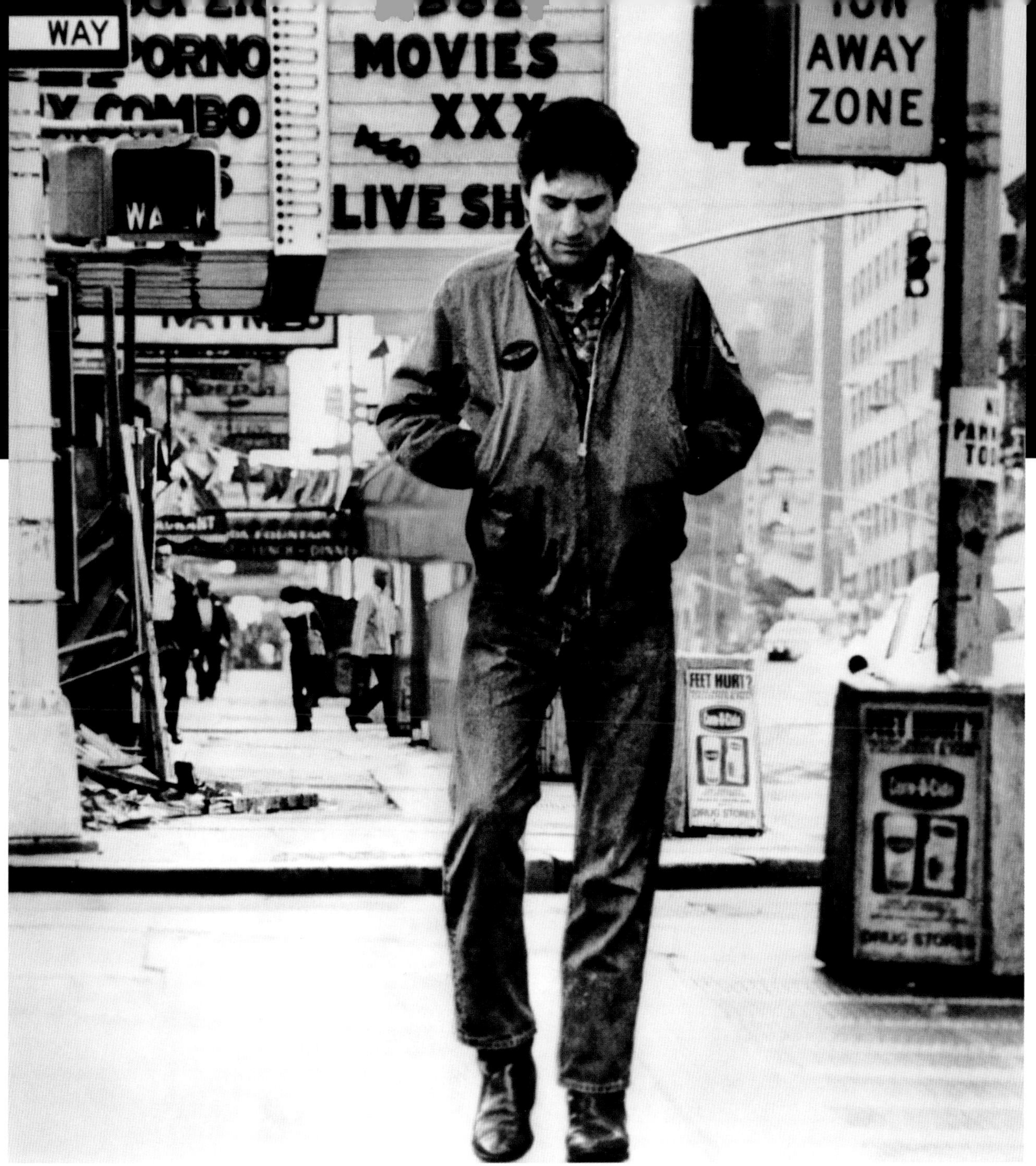

WAY
PORNO
MOVIES
XXX
AWAY
ZONE
FEET HURT?
DRUG STORES

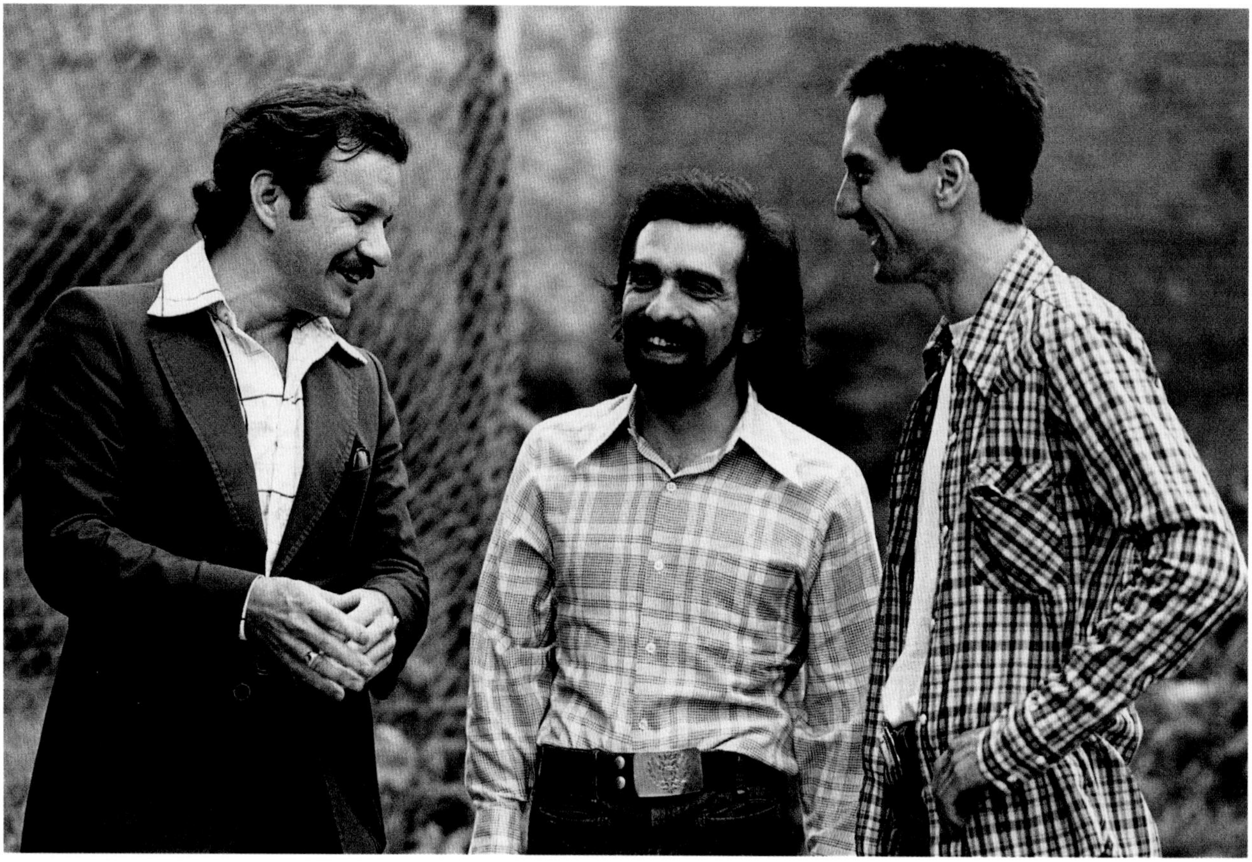

Above: *The unholy trinity – the meeting of minds between Paul Schrader, Martin Scorsese, and Robert De Niro evolved into this uncompromising look at America.*

told his friend, 'theme, character, structure. Bam, bam, bam. That's my job.'[5]

Nevertheless, a thrilling tension emerges between the prison-cell austerity of Schrader's intentions and the operatic expressionism that Scorsese brings to *Taxi Driver*. Neo-noir is the accepted classification, mixed with a raw tabloid sensationalism. But there's something deeper than genre going on here.

'Every film should look the way I feel,'[6] insisted Scorsese, capturing an entire career in a single sentence.

The film hovers elusively in a no-man's land between reality and a movie reality. Call it Travis reality. Scorsese never thought the film would make a dime, but it won the Palme d'Or in Cannes, transformed his career (making nearly $29 million, in fact), and changed the course of American movies, American art, maybe American life. *Taxi Driver* forced a country to stare at itself in the mirror.

'*Taxi Driver* is a great film,' wrote critic David Thomson, 'in which there was a clear and willing glimpse of disorder at the heart of America.'[7]

After the film came out, Schrader found a stranger standing in his office, his face intent. 'Who told you about me?'[8] he demanded. The screenwriter managed to talk him down, but it was a stark premonition. 'We had created the real thing,'[9] rued Schrader. Then in

1981 came John Hinckley Jr., the dropout who attempted to shoot Ronald Reagan, obsessed with Jodie Foster and *Taxi Driver.* 'I felt like I was walking into a movie,'[10] he confessed. Such pathologies were ordained by deeper afflictions, but there is no doubt the film touched a nerve.

It speaks volumes about the necessity of human partnership that *Taxi Driver* – this parable of isolation – would be the result of the collaboration of three souls, a holy trinity, all of whom saw themselves in the haunted eyes of Travis Bickle: Schrader, Scorsese, and De Niro. They all felt that loneliness. That rage. But they got lucky. They found the movies.

Schrader had been sleeping with a loaded Smith & Wesson .38 on his bedside table. That was when he wasn't spending the night in his Chevy Nova. It was late 1972 and he had left his wife, then the girl he left her for had fled, leaving him in her abandoned apartment in Silver Lake with no heating. Schrader was drawn toward death like a flame. There was a history of suicide on his father's side. He liked how the gun felt in his hand, and claimed to have come close to pulling the trigger. As a director, he would specialize in 'man alone in his room'[11] stories: *American Gigolo, Light Sleeper, First Reformed, The Card Counter.*

The fine print of Schrader's life is relevant. He didn't see a movie until he was seventeen. Born in Grand Rapids, Michigan, his was the opposite to Scorsese's asphyxiated childhood. Schrader's parents belonged to the Christian Reformed Church, a breakaway Protestant sect of the already fanatical Dutch Calvinist movement, ready to beat Satan out of their two sons. Like Scorsese, he was a younger brother. Like Scorsese, he had planned to be a minister, but the taste of cinema changed everything. Movies were the forbidden fruit in his cold Eden.

By 1966, he was in Los Angeles and a protégé of cultural figurehead Pauline Kael. She saw talent, getting him a job on the *Los Angeles Free Press,* then a precious place at UCLA. He wrote two classics of modern American film studies: *Transcendental Style in Film: Ozu, Bresson, Dreyer* and *Notes on Film Noir.* Film noir was not a genre, he espoused, but was defined by 'qualities of tone and mood.'[12] By 1972, the work had dried up, his personal life had collapsed, and the darkness was

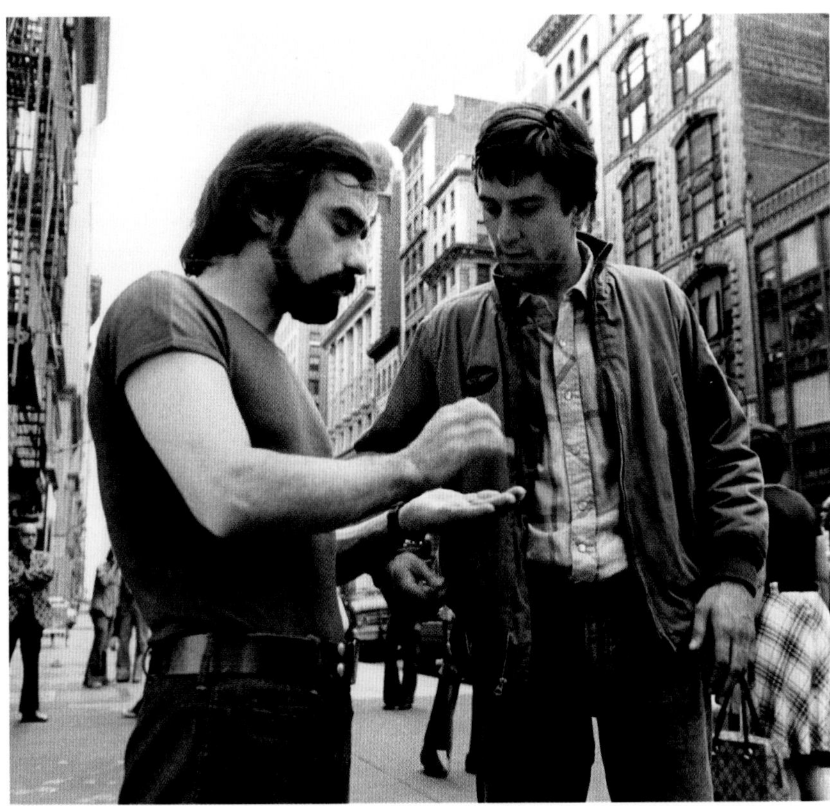

Left: *Not only was the film set in the pressure cooker of New York, it was effectively shot amid the same pressure-cooker environment – all Scorsese had to do was let his camera drink it in.*

> This yellow, rectangular coffin … floating through the open sewers of a metropolis. Inside that coffin is trapped a young man. And it looks like he's surrounded by life, but in fact he's absolutely alone.
>
> PAUL SCHRADER

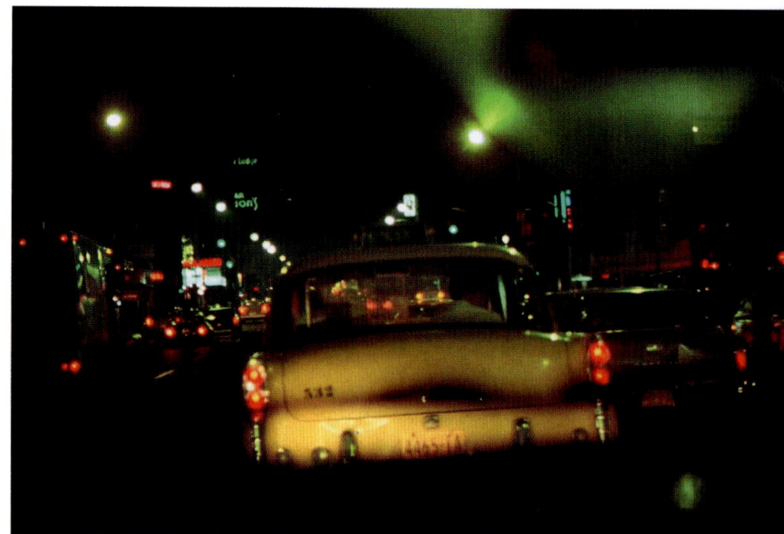

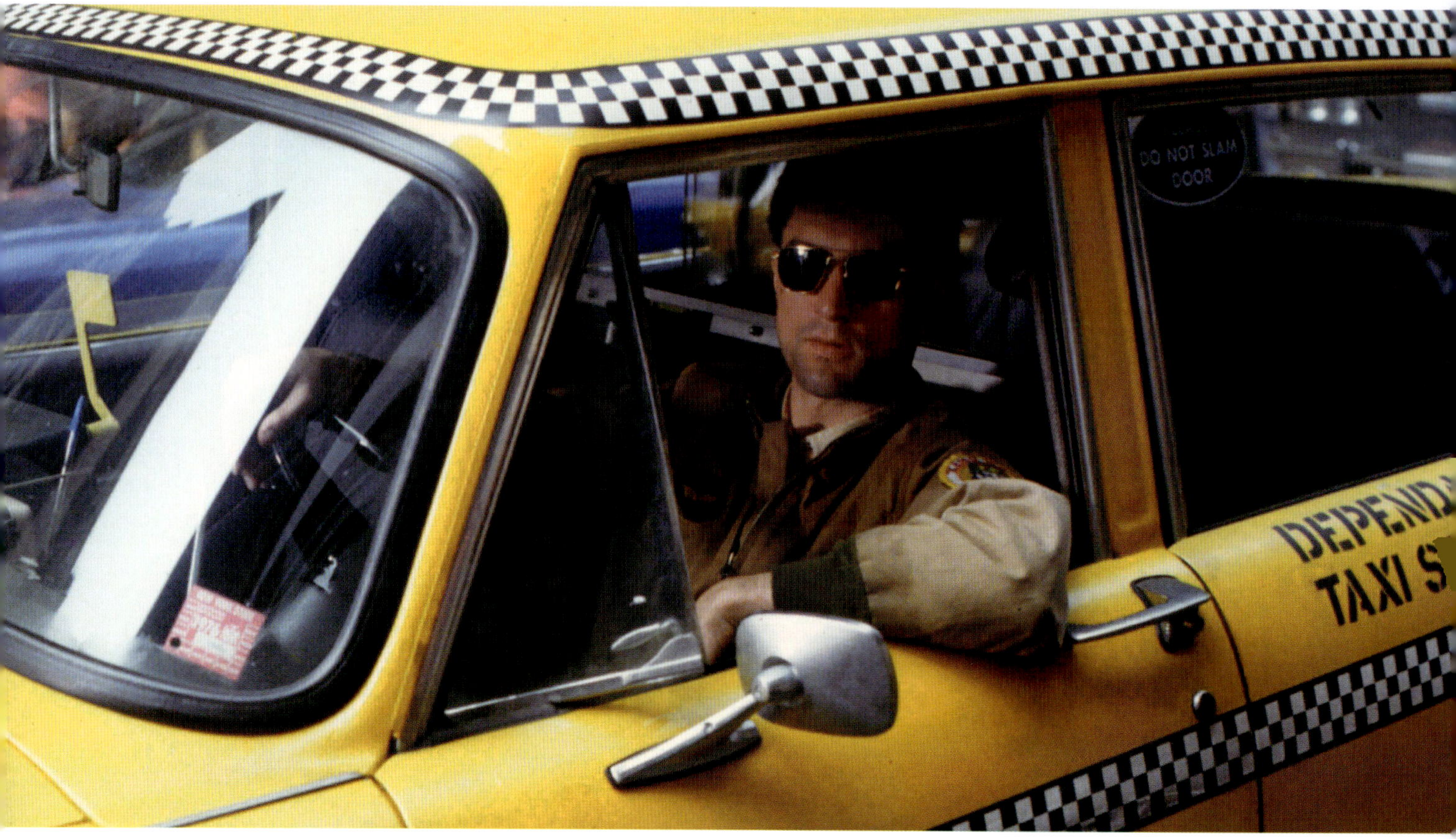

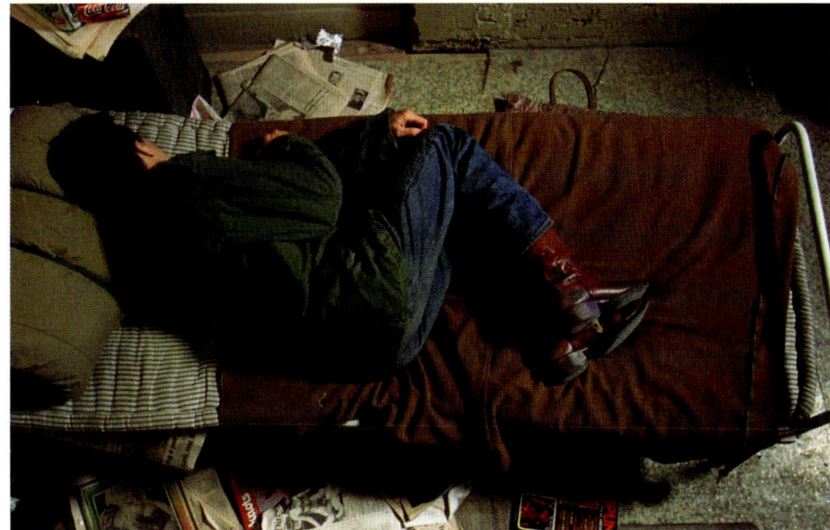

Opposite: *It would be a city observed from the hermetic world of the cab, so Martin Scorsese would place his camera on the back seat and simply have Robert De Niro drive him around Manhattan.*

Right: *De Niro as the sleepless antihero, lying in his rundown apartment. Paul Schrader's screenplay drew as much from his own insomnia as from the literary and real-life sources of anomie.*

catching up with him. 'These violent, self-destructive fantasies that one normally holds at bay started to prey upon me,'[13] he said. He drove around at night, drinking Scotch and slipping into peep shows, beyond the reach of gratification. When he was rushed into an emergency room, stricken with a gastric ulcer, the nurse was the first person he had spoken to in weeks. And in hospital, it came to him.

'I had this idea of the taxi driver, this anonymous angry person,' he recalled. 'It jumped out of me like an animal.'[14] In order to get the demons out of his head he would write a script. Finished in ten days, he called it an 'exorcism.'[15]

Schrader drew inspiration from Dostoevsky's *Notes from Underground*, Sartre's *Nausea*, and French director Robert Bresson's meditations on isolation *Pickpocket* and *Diary of a Country Priest*. Over the years, he would mention novelist Thomas Wolfe's autobiographical essay *God's Lonely Man*, in which loneliness figures as the 'central and inevitable fact of human existence.'[16] And the telling influence of Arthur Bremer's diary. In 1972, living out of his car, this Midwestern drop-out attempted to assassinate Alabama governor George Wallace, only to leave him paralysed from the waist down. Bremer's primary motivation was simply to be noticed.

The plot of *Taxi Driver* floats like a wraith at the fringes of our perception. Travis Bickle (De Niro), a Vietnam vet from somewhere in the Midwest (backstory remains sketchy), is a pathological loner adrift in what Schrader called the 'pressure cooker'[17] of New York. Unable to sleep, he drives a cab at night. Struggling to make connections with his fellow drivers, or anyone, he fixates on two women: beautiful campaign worker Betsy (Cybill Shepherd) and child sex worker Iris (Jodie Foster). Fixations that will slowly manifest themselves into homicidal intent, directed toward their perceived father figures: Leonard Harris's smarmy presidential candidate Palantine (echoing Bremer's pathology) and Harvey Keitel as Iris's malicious, oily pimp Sport. In each case, a path he considers righteous. There are intimations of a religious background.

'I almost felt I wrote it myself,' Scorsese told Schrader. 'Not that I could write that way, but I felt everything. I was burning inside my fucking skin; I had to make it.'[18]

Scorsese would trail producer Julia Phillips around Hollywood parties, begging her to let him make *Taxi Driver*. Or give chase to her producing partner and husband Michael Phillips. But who was Scorsese in 1973? ... just a guy who had just made a Roger Corman film.

The Movie Brat legend goes that Brian De Palma had been playing chess with Schrader when the young film critic mentioned a script. The young director groaned inwardly. These critics always had a screenplay lurking in their shoulder bags. But De Palma did get round to reading it and knew *Taxi Driver* to be a genuine piece of work, as did Phillips, who optioned it for $1,000.

For two years the film had very little chance of being made at all: studios were impressed by Schrader's daring, but this wasn't something they could actually *back*, for heaven's sake. Iterations were discussed, which never gained traction: absurdly,

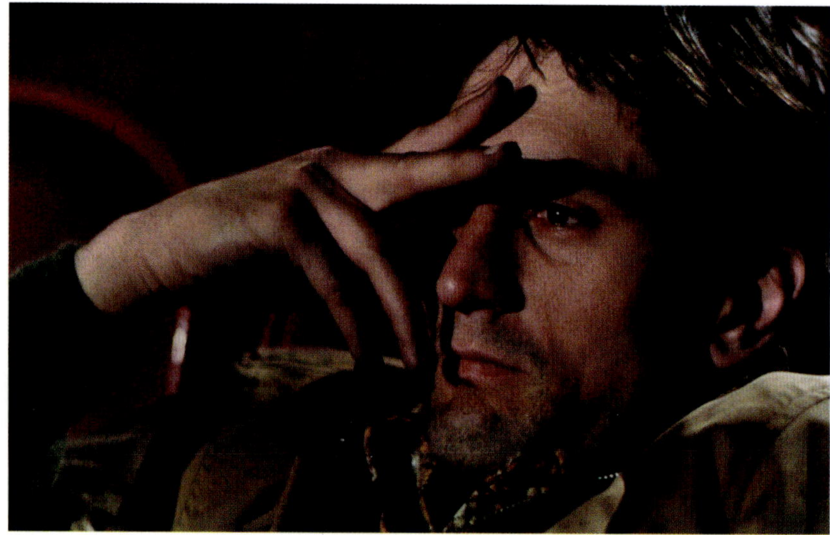

Right: *Travis Bickle is left unstirred by a porn film – is he making the shape of a gun with his fingers or framing a shot?*

Neil Diamond (looking to break into movies) was interested in playing Travis, and at one stage Robert Mulligan wanted to direct Jeff Bridges as the antihero. De Palma had thought to direct it himself, but couldn't see how it was going to make money, so he passed it onto Scorsese.

Taxi Driver is the Movie Brat era's defining film. Scorsese saw it as part of an evolution in Hollywood violence from *Psycho* to *Bonnie and Clyde* to *The Wild Bunch* to *Taxi Driver*; upping the ante, rattling studio and societal norms, shaking America out of its stupor, spurred on by the news reports spilling onto TV sets from Vietnam. Besides, he understood the isolation, the world viewed through a window, in this case the window of a cab, transformed into a movie in which you never take a role. There is a shot of Travis frequenting a grubby porn theatre (the Show and Tell on 8th Avenue). His fingers shield his face, appalled, but he could as easily be framing a shot.

The truth is the film got lucky. While *Taxi Driver* stalled, Schrader sold a thriller called *The Yakuza* to Warner Brothers and Sydney Pollack for a staggering $300,000 (his reputation had soared). Michael and Julia Phillips had produced *The Sting*, which was about to win over the Academy. De Niro had won an Oscar for *The Godfather Part II*. And Scorsese had a hit with *Alice Doesn't Live Here Anymore*, which had also landed Ellen Burstyn a Best Actress Oscar. He was already in pre-production on *New York, New York* with United Artists.

It was David Begelman, president of Columbia, who caved. He detested the script, but the Phillipses were developing *Close Encounters of the Third Kind* for him, the next from the young punk who had made *Jaws* (to which Schrader had contributed), and they assured him that if Scorsese didn't work out, Spielberg could step in (curious fact: during the tense edit of *Taxi Driver*, Spielberg dropped in to see Scorsese and indeed helped edit sections of the shoot-out). On the promise of De Niro as Travis, Begelman agreed to a contemptible budget of $1.3 million (Spielberg's UFOs ended up costing him $19 million), but the filmmakers grabbed their chance.

'The process of making that film for me was more important than the final result,' recalled Scorsese. 'And you know the second week I threatened to stop. I loved it so much I wanted to kill it. If it was not going to be done the right way, kill it.'[19]

The physical act of filmmaking was Scorsese's obsession, his mania, the holy fire that threatened to consume him. It was a way of channelling his rage: to lay it onto celluloid, bathed in a neo-noir gleam, as unsettling as a fever. Relationships were scorned, studios resisted, producers ignored, his own health pushed to the limit in order to capture that feeling. He was crusading like Travis, but with a camera not a gun.

'Scorsese got something out of his asthma; he knows how to make us experience the terror of suffocation,'[20] wrote Kael in the *New Yorker*, witnessing her sponsorship of Schrader bear dark fruit. At times the film is unbearable to watch, but we cannot look away. Travis is a coiled spring, we see it in the rope-like cords of his muscles, the set of his jaw,

Right: *Jodie Foster's young sex worker Iris is the only character with whom Travis can form any kind of connection. De Niro would take Foster out to local diners, and make sure she knew her lines, so she would be ready to improvise.*

Below: *Harvey Keitel pressed to play wiry pimp Sport, basing his expressive body language and hip-cat speech on a real pimp he had got to know.*

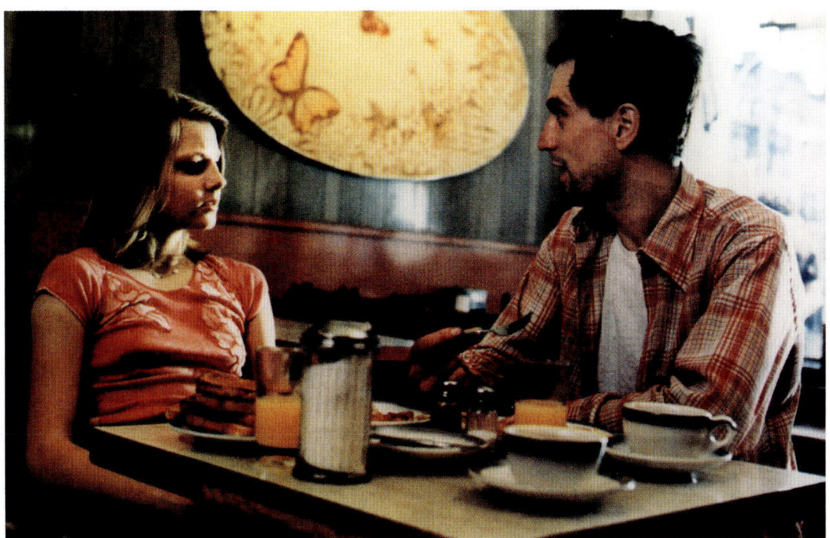

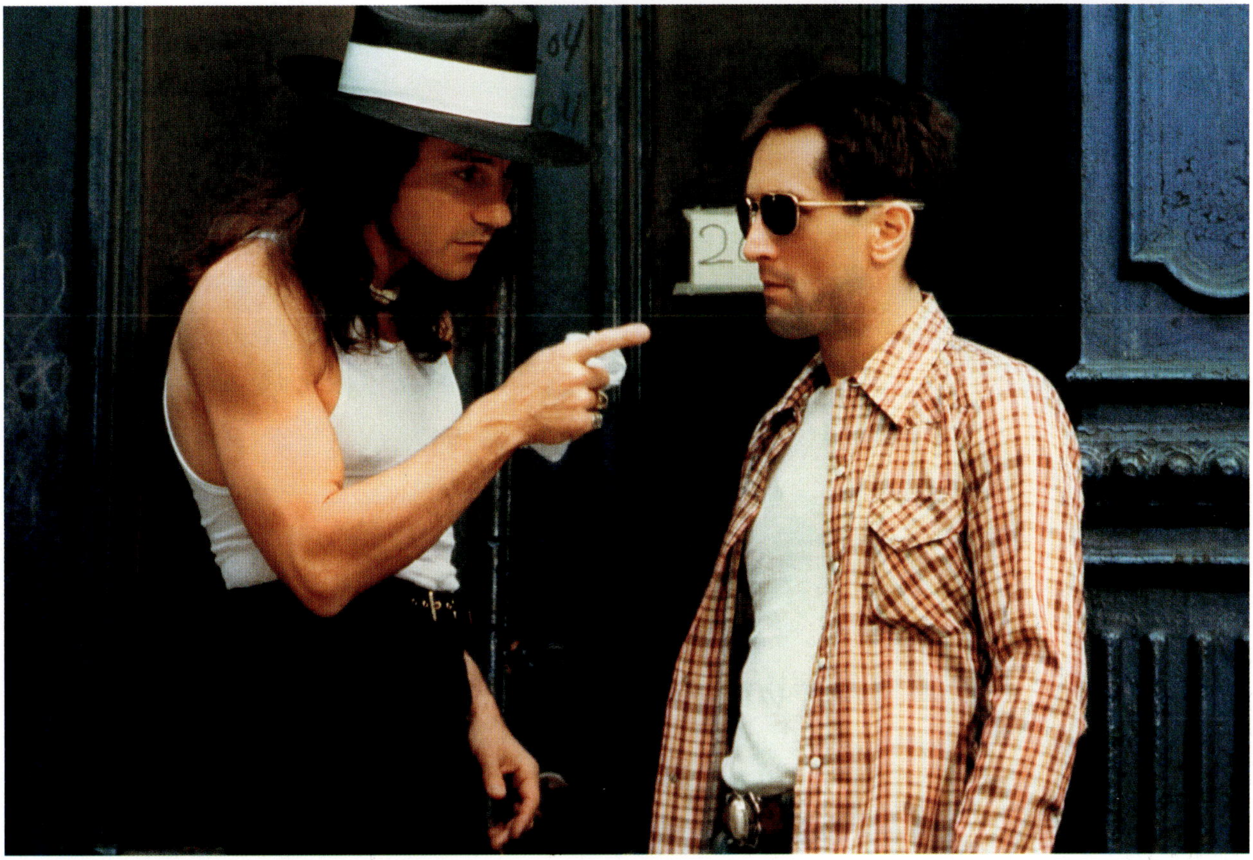

Below: *Much of the genius of* Taxi Driver *springs from Martin Scorsese's highly subjective style. The camera is infused with Travis Bickle's fraying mental state. For instance, in this famous mirror shot effectively splitting the personality of his leading man.*

the gleam in those eyes as he stares at himself in his apartment mirror (a moment famously born out of improvisation). We watch him flail – blowing it with Betsy by taking her to a porno, jousting with Sport, De Niro taking each scene to breaking point, woundingly intense toward his co-stars during production.

These were the doctrines of young artists, actor, director, and screenwriter: to give films a psychic charge, to peer beneath the skin of the characters without moral judgment, to be truthful to human experience.

Shooting through the sweltering summer of 1975, the city fouled by a garbage strike, Scorsese spoke of 'forty days, forty nights'[21] of filming. A Biblical test of nerve. Money was tight and the schedule at breaking point. Out of

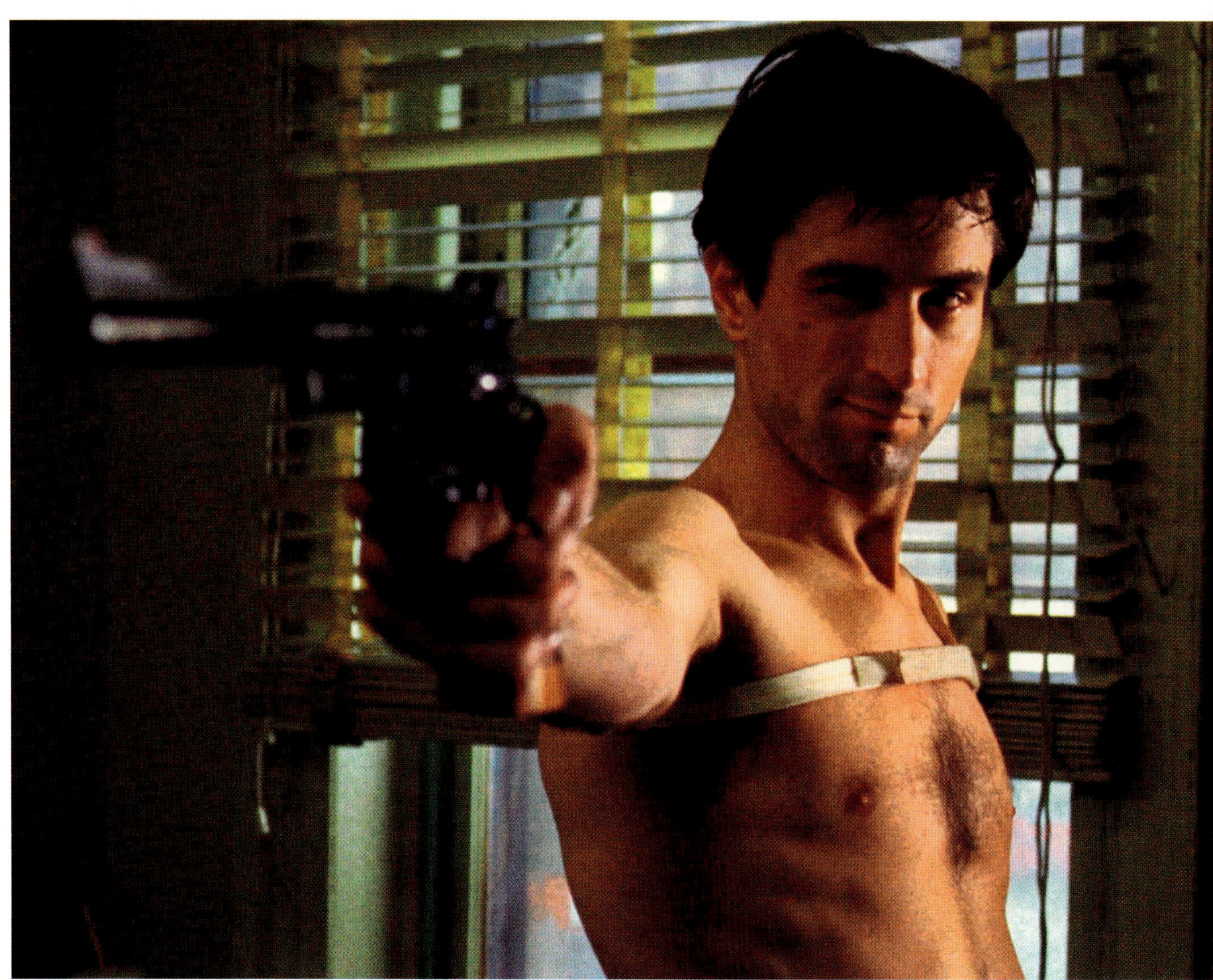

Right: *The rearview mirror in Travis' cab takes on a widescreen ratio of its own, reflecting back the empty eyes of the driver.*

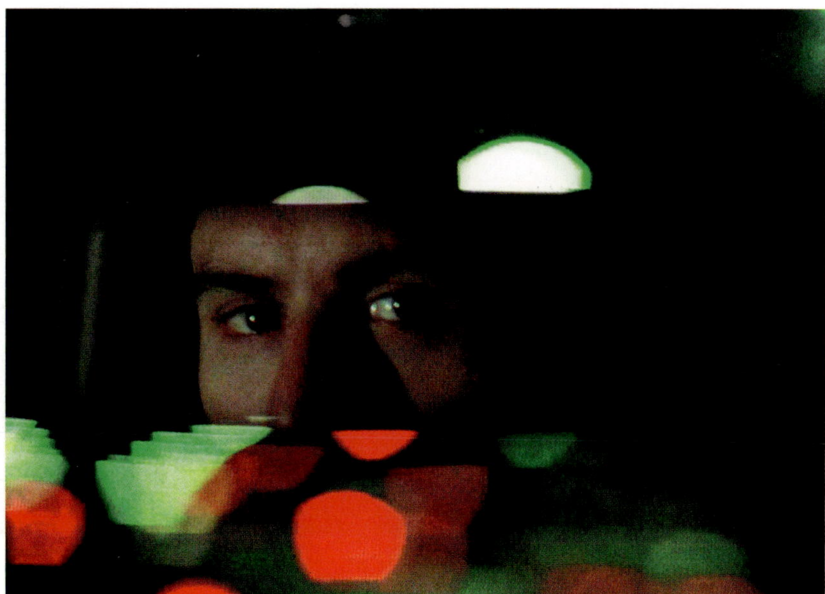

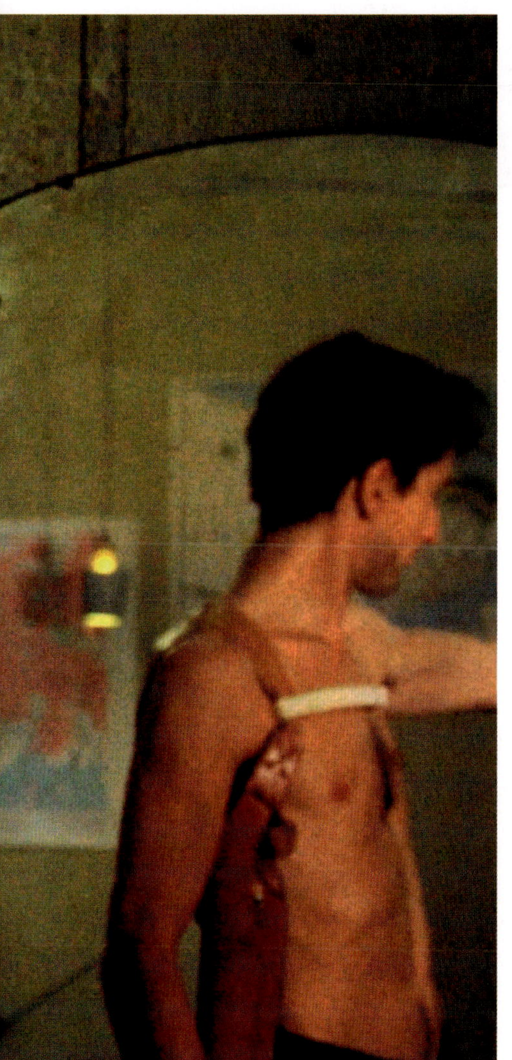

necessity, he storyboarded every shot, manic cartoons of never-before-seen camera moves. At night, unable to sleep, he would draw more shots.

After *Mean Streets, Taxi Driver* crystallized New York not simply as a setting, but as the root of Scorsese's art. In 1975, the city was on the verge of bankruptcy, financial and moral. Infrastructure was crumbling, drugs and prostitution rife, the air hot and heavy. 'You could see it in *The French Connection*. You could see it in *Taxi Driver*,' said Scorsese. 'Those two films, I think, give a real sense of what it was like. You can almost smell it through the screen.'[22]

These are the real streets, real bystanders, genuine porn theatres, dive bars, and the all-night Belmore Cafeteria where the cabbies gather to smoke and unwind, except for the one they call 'Killer'[23] sitting apart from them at the end of the table. He was only wound tighter.

At the heart of the film is the seedy, sinful Times Square district the priests had instructed the young Scorsese to resist. But he would venture uptown on the Subway to watch Westerns and double-bills on 42nd Street, slipping anonymously between hookers and dealers.

The city is less a character (that old cliché) than a state of mind, a nightmare projection of fear and loathing and unsettling desires. Scorsese's hometown. There was an atmosphere at night, he said, 'that is like a seeping kind of virus.'[24] And yet, through cinematographer Michael Chapman's subjective lens and beneath the sultry saxophone provided by composer Bernard Herrmann in his final score (he died the night he completed his task), it is a strangely glamorous world too.

'Much of *Taxi Driver* arose from my feeling that movies are really a kind of dream-state, or like taking dope,'[25] noted Scorsese. *Taxi Driver* is the apotheosis of the Scorsesean paradox – a highly stylized slice-of-life. He understood that verisimilitude and truth are not the same thing. With more intensity

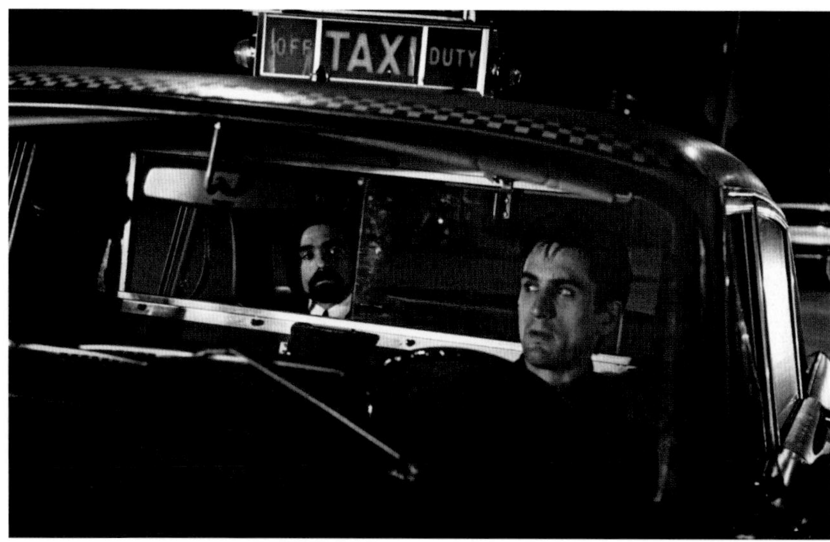

Right: *Backseat director – Martin Scorsese himself would play the cuckolded husband talking about killing his wife. A largely improvised scene, controlled and effectively directed by Robert De Niro.*

than ever, he riffed on Jean-Luc Godard. That freedom of expression, moving the camera in confounding directions, leaving Travis to pan around the taxi depot before catching up with him again. 'It was as if we were saying, "Don't follow this guy, but look at the world he lives in,"'[26] explained Chapman.

When Betsy gives Travis the brush-off on the phone, the camera leaves his side to stare down an empty, grey hallway. It was the first shot Scorsese thought of and the last he filmed. There is a constant commingling of objective reality, Travis's fragmenting mind, and the hand of the artist-director. The film plays temporal games, dissolving as Travis walks up a street; holding onto shots, an Alka-Seltzer fizzing in a glass, for long enough that an unnerved viewer starts to perceive meaning; or peering down from above as if Travis's disassociating mind had flown up to the ceiling to observe his own body.

It also has what New York-based critic Amy Taubin classifies as a 'hybrid iconography.'[27] Scorsese wasn't only feeding on the European radicals, but the power of American film. He examined Hitchcock's most paranoid piece, *The Wrong Man*, and Jack Hazan's *A Bigger Splash* for its head-on framing. Classic noir had captured the disillusionment among GIs returning from the Second World War; here it is the after-effects of Vietnam.

Both Scorsese and Schrader spoke of the fatalistic myths of the Western. Particularly the influence of John Wayne's Ethan Edwards in *The Searchers*, the Civil War veteran unable ever to access the comforts of hearth and home. Mirroring Edwards' search for his niece, abducted by Comanche, Travis will take it upon himself to rescue Iris from the clutches of Sport, depicted with long hair (Keitel had insisted on the wig) and native beads. The name 'Travis' was designed as an ironic echo to the folksy heroism of William Travis at the Alamo, with its bloody last stand.

De Niro got off the plane from Bertolucci's *1900*, got himself a New York cab licence (known as a hack licence), and started to prowl the streets for real. This was his process, his Method: to be consumed by a part to the point where distinctions between actor and role became obscure. He wanted every detail. He had spent weeks on the voice (Midwestern, though without a fixed source), but it was a bodily thing, every part of him conveyed emotion. Travis was in his bones.

He spent two weeks picking up fares, anonymous beside the meter. Scorsese went out with him for a few nights. 'It was like he didn't exist,'[28] he marvelled. People would say anything, do anything on the back seat, oblivious. That was until a former actor got in, saw De Niro's name on the licence, and laughed. 'Jesus, last year you won an Oscar and now you're driving a cab.'[29]

After *Mean Streets* and the exuberant, holy fool of Johnny Boy, De Niro allowed Scorsese to express his dark side. But he had his own connection to Travis. De Niro had told Schrader that he had considered writing a script about a man wandering about New York with a gun. The actor would sit in the General Assembly of the United Nations and think about what it would take to assassinate a diplomat. For all the solidarity of the movie set, acting remained (and remains) a lonely vigil for

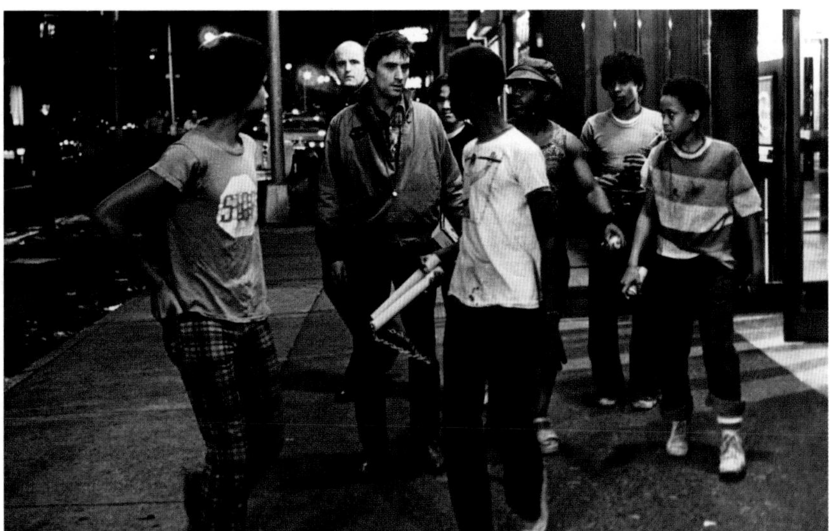

Left: *Most of the passers-by were real New Yorkers, bringing the film close to a form of docudrama. Something that would become integral to Scorsese's method.*

Below: *Funny how? Art director Herbert F. Mulligan implements some knowing humour in the signage of the West 57th Street garage where they shot.*

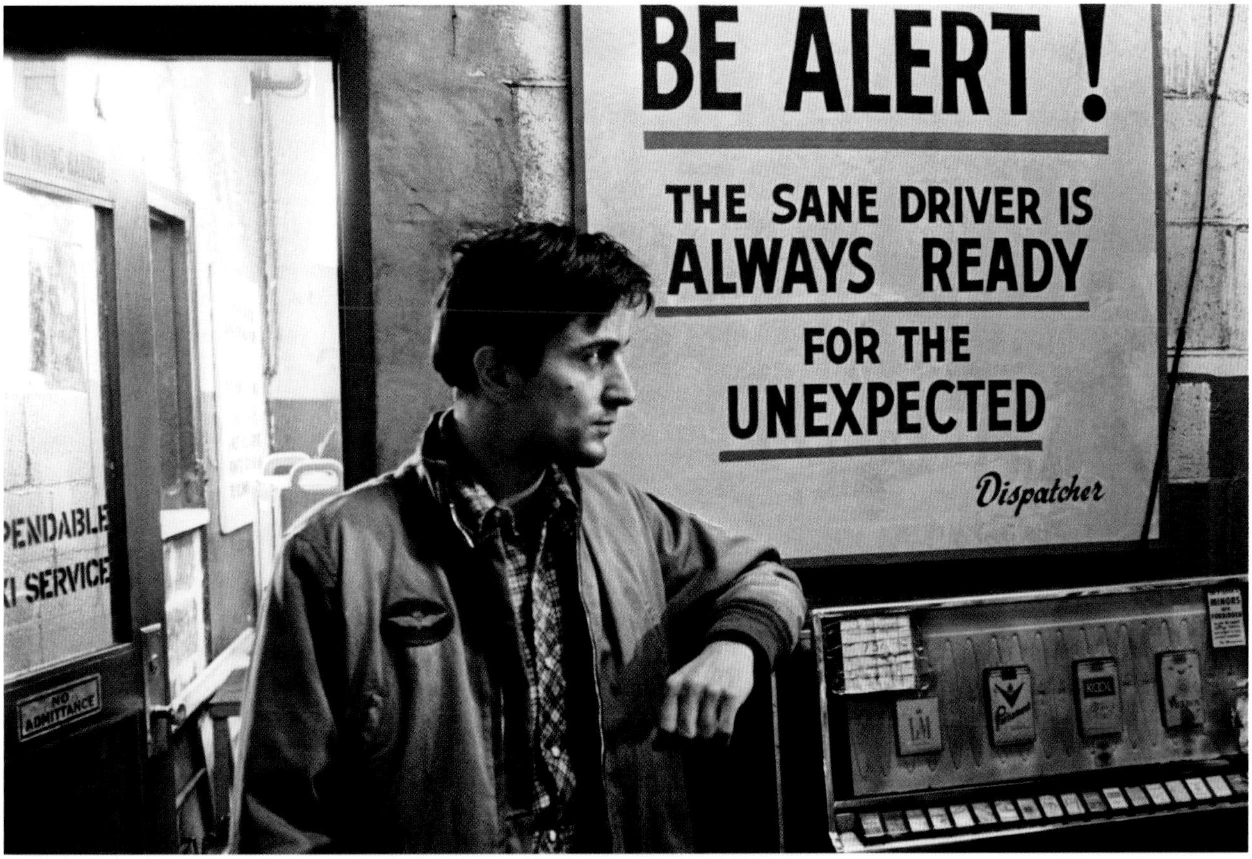

De Niro, a transformative process it pains him to explain, even to Scorsese. When they collude on set it is often in whispers.

De Niro lost thirty pounds, he wanted to be gaunt. The jacket and boots belonged to Schrader. The cab was rigged with multiple cameras to capture Travis's view of the streets, but it was never towed. De Niro drove through the night, with Scorsese and Chapman crammed onto the back seat. The Mohawk that Travis sports once he's stirred into violence in the final act was a chance discovery. Victor Magnotta, an old friend of Scorsese's from their NYU days who plays the Secret Service photographer, had served in Vietnam. Certain soldiers enlisted into special ops, he told director and star, would shave their heads into Mohawks as a sign they were ready to kill. The practicalities of schedule prevented De Niro from literally shaving his head. Makeup specialist Dick Smith designed a replaceable latex cap with painted-on stubble, which the actor would inspect thoroughly each day before putting it on.

Whatever happened to Travis in Vietnam, civilization has made him more paranoid. 'It's held in him and then it explodes,'[30] said Scorsese. The director maintained that this wasn't a political film as such, but the political can't help but seethe to the surface: the lost war in Southeast Asia, the fallen state of the homeland, Nixon's White House malfeasance. 'You can't make movies anymore in which the whole country seems to make sense. After Vietnam, after Watergate, it's not just a temporary thing...'[31]

Travis has come to stand for multitudes. He is the zombie representative of the failure of sixties liberalism, the forgotten outcast from the American Dream, the embodiment of the crisis in white masculinity in the face of the Civil Rights and Feminist movements.

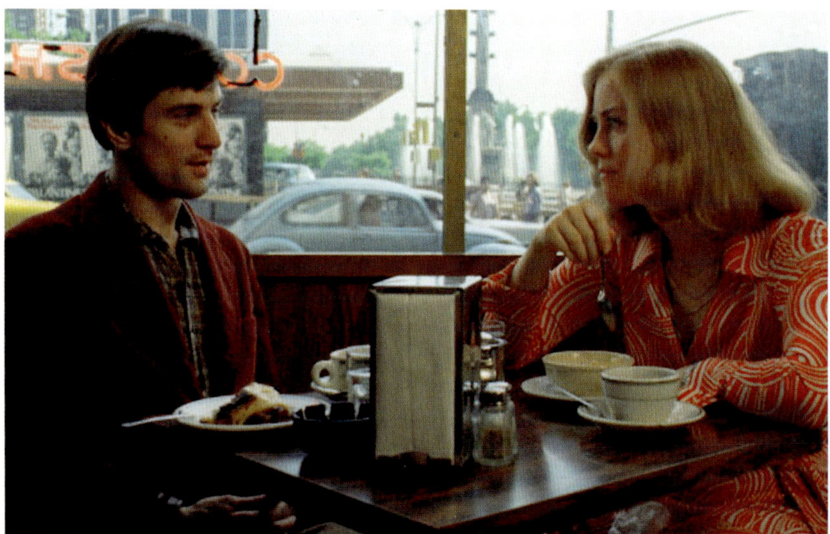

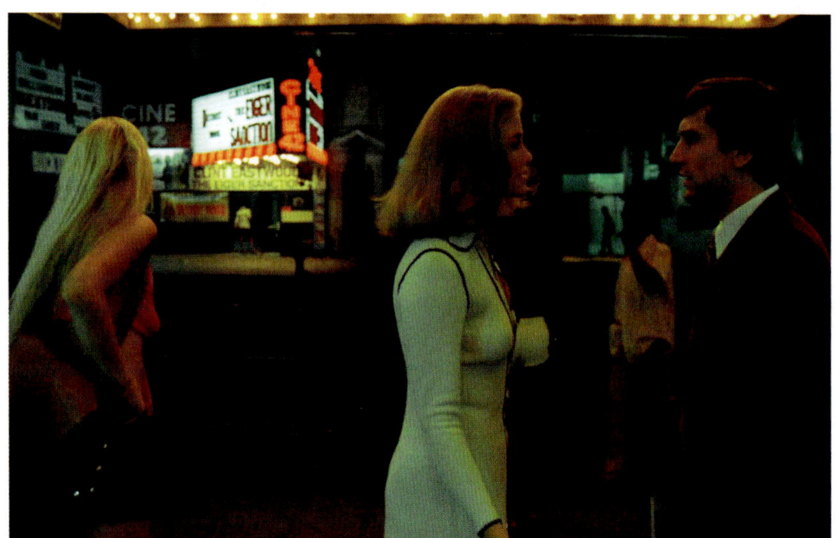

Top: *When Travis Bickle first takes political campaigner Betsy (Cybill Shepherd, perfect for the required Cybill Shepherd type) for a coffee there are hopes that he might find salvation...*

Above: *...only for these to be crushed in his misguided decision to take Betsy to see a porn film for their date – reminding the audience of how far gone he truly is.*

Below: *Below: Saviour complex – after Betsy abandons him, Travis Bickle obsesses about saving Iris from the hands of Sport. For Foster, the makeup and platforms took a lot of getting used to.*

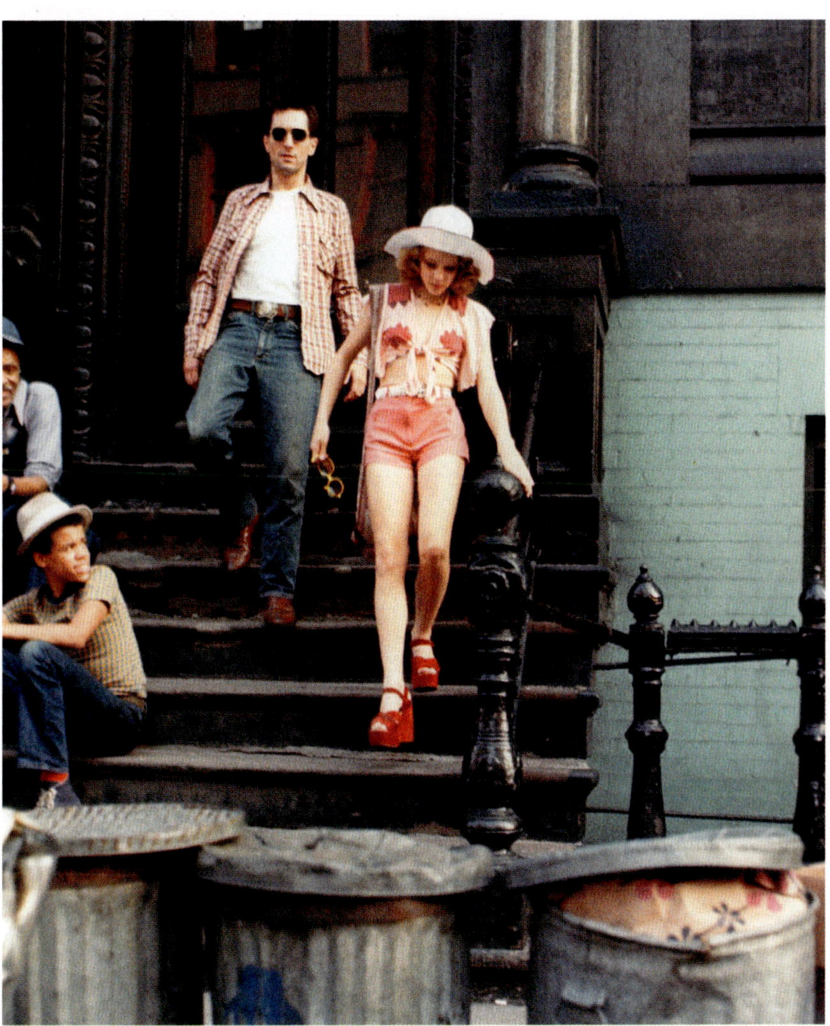

When it came to upwardly mobile Betsy, the initial object of Travis's projections, who even deigns to go for a coffee with him, and on that doomed date to the movies, Schrader had been clear in the script that she was a 'Cybill Shepherd type.'[32] Shepherd had blazed into focus at the beginning of the seventies in *The Last Picture Show* and *The Heartbreak Kid*, then just as abruptly hit the skids with two flops in a row: *Daisy Miller* and *At Long Last Love*. Studios were giving her a wide berth.

So the agent who represented the erstwhile American sweetheart called. 'Well, what about Cybill Shepherd?'[33] he asked. She would do it for whatever was offered, they were assured. She needed the work. Once on set, Scorsese and Schrader began to fret that there might be a significant difference between 'a Cybill Shepherd type' and Cybill Shepherd. She struggled the most, intimidated by De Niro and frustrated by a freewheeling Albert Brooks as her co-worker (Brooks largely improvised his lines).

In her discomfort Shepherd provides a sharp performance, with hints of dislocation and disappointment (maybe her own frustrations at Hollywood's dismissal). There is a connection with Travis, though their wires are completely crossed.

When costume designer Ruth Morley took Jodie Foster shopping for her costume, the young actress wept with embarrassment. The hotpants and platforms and doll-like makeup were a radical shift from the Disney films she had been making, but Scorsese saw a maturity that would transform her into one of the most lauded actresses of her generation. There were concerns from the Board of Education over her age, twelve and a half, and the sexualized content of her role, and it was agreed that her older sister Connie, her senior by eight years but with a similar build, would stand in for her when things turned provocative (it is hard to see where they weren't). An amused Foster recalled that she was required to see a psychiatrist beforehand – to check she was sane enough to play a hooker.

Reality was never far away. Iris had a real-life counterpart. In his research, Schrader had found this sex worker, no more than fifteen, and paid her simply to talk to him. He had slipped a note under Scorsese's hotel door: 'I have met Iris.'[34]

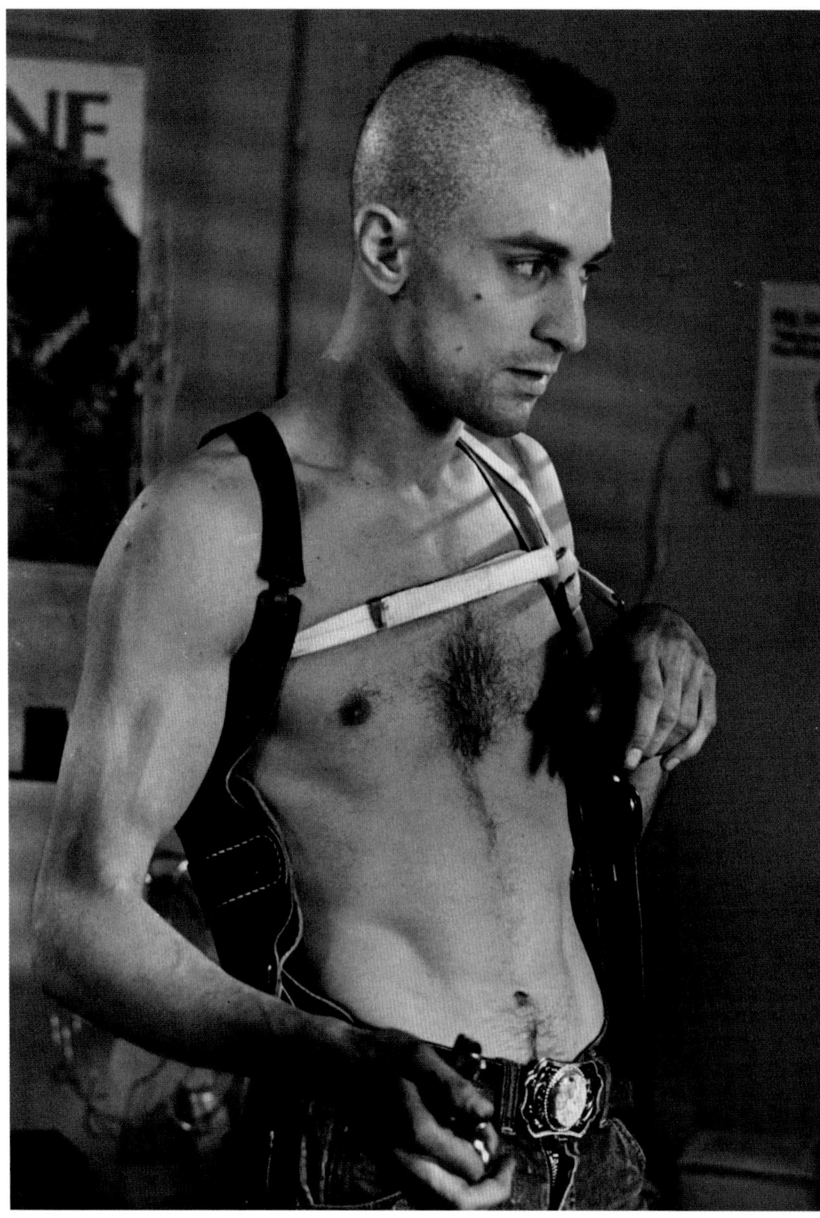

Above: *Madness in his Method – Robert De Niro got his wire-thin frame through a fitness regime matched by his onscreen persona. The Mohican was a Vietnam reference to the black ops agents who shaved their heads before a mission.*

She even appears in the movie as the slender companion to Foster's character.

Looking back, we can detect a three-act structure – a slow descent toward a full psychotic break. In the first act, the rage is more diffused and Travis numbly patrols the city, making his forlorn bids for human contact. In the second, plans are made, a noble cause established in a fraying mind. Having almost comically failed in his attempts to shoot Palantine, Betsy's boss, Iris becomes Travis's Holy Grail. He will attempt to save the child sex worker from Sport's malevolent clutches. And, with the third, comes an eruption of violence, as Taubin described it, 'as voluptuous as anything in American movies.'[35]

A brief mention is deserved at this stage for Steven Prince, the subject of an unreleased Scorsese documentary, *American Boy: A Profile of Steven Prince*, itself a Holy Grail for fans. Prince was a former Neil Diamond roadie, a drug addict, and close friend of the director. Among his many wild stories was one of plunging a syringe of adrenaline through the breast plate of a girl overdosing on heroin, an anecdote put to great use by Tarantino in *Pulp Fiction*.

And so to a brief word on influence. Tarantino constantly cites *Taxi Driver* as an inspiration (a film he recalls as a comedy). Travis's reach is long: *Reservoir Dogs, La Haine, Unforgiven* (turning back toward those Western myths), *The Limey, Nightcrawler, Joker*. There are too many films to mention. But more tellingly, Scorsese has never truly been able to shake Travis. He reoccurs in his work in different guises, the director's shadow twin. To put something on film doesn't mean you're rid of it, Scorsese once confessed. 'I was crazier when I finished *Taxi Driver* than when I began.'[36]

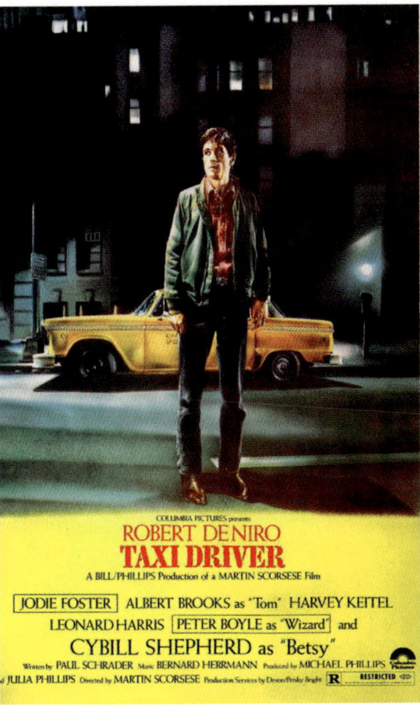

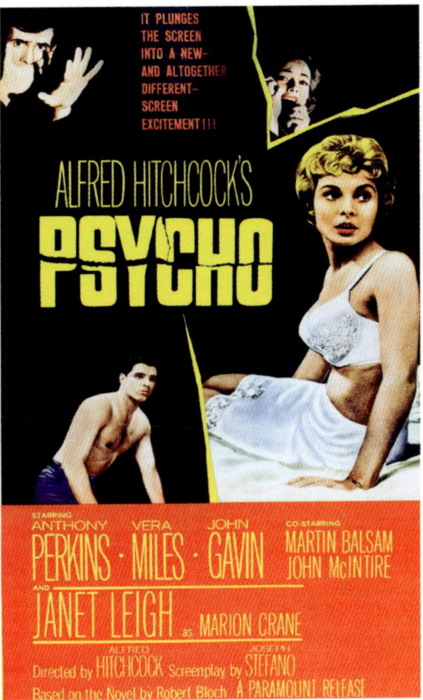

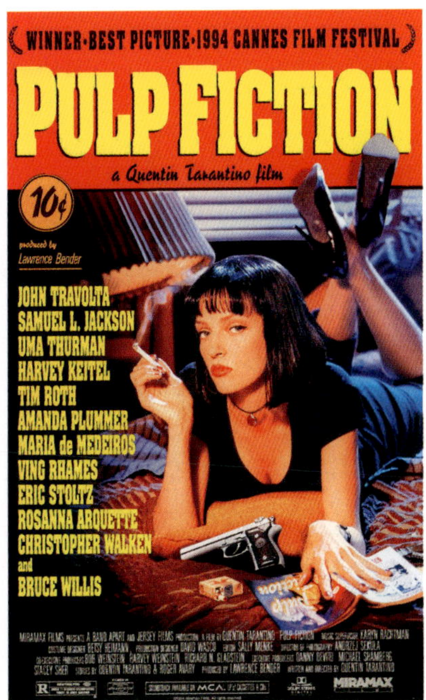

Above: *Cycles of violence –* Taxi Driver *picks up on the exploration of psychosis handed down by Hitchcock's* Psycho*, just as Scorsese's self-aware style would be bequeathed to Quentin Tarantino's* Pulp Fiction.

Returning to the point, it is Prince who plays Easy Andy, the dapper crook who sells guns to Travis, laying them out on the bed, 'like arranging the altar during Mass,'[37] said Scorsese.

The calm before the storm.

Taxi Driver is not a consciously religious film, not in the way *Mean Streets* is stalked by Catholic guilt. But there is a feeling of purification for Travis before he sets out on his crusade, the avenging angel, God's lonely man. Scorsese termed the film's eruption of violence as Travis's 'coming into glory,'[38] from the Nicene Creed. Freudian takes call it 'orgasmic.'[39] For a film so notorious for its violence, the carnage is concentrated in a near seven-minute outburst as Travis blasts his way through Sport and his cronies. A bloody tableau all the more shocking for how inevitable it feels. 'It's suddenly clear that the entire film has existed for the purpose of this sudden change in register,'[40] wrote Taubin. Scorsese pointed to the slow-motion, art-of-death crescendo in Peckinpah's *The Wild Bunch*; that Western corollary again, those hail-of-bullet myths. His carefully storyboarded compendium of 'shots' was technically the production's biggest challenge. He needed it to be visceral, a real world of cause and effect, with hands blown off, faces puckered with bloody spouts, the walls sprayed with blood and brain matter like a Samurai film. Simultaneously, the film's hallucinatory quality only intensifies, as if Travis has stepped into the movie in his head – acting out his fantasy.

They filmed in a condemned brownstone on 89th and Columbus Avenue, where the narrowness of the house was difficult to negotiate. Makeup effects had to be sprung by fishing line, wrenching out fake flesh, limiting takes. The air was filled with the sweet, syrupy smell of fake blood. De Niro recalled the strange good

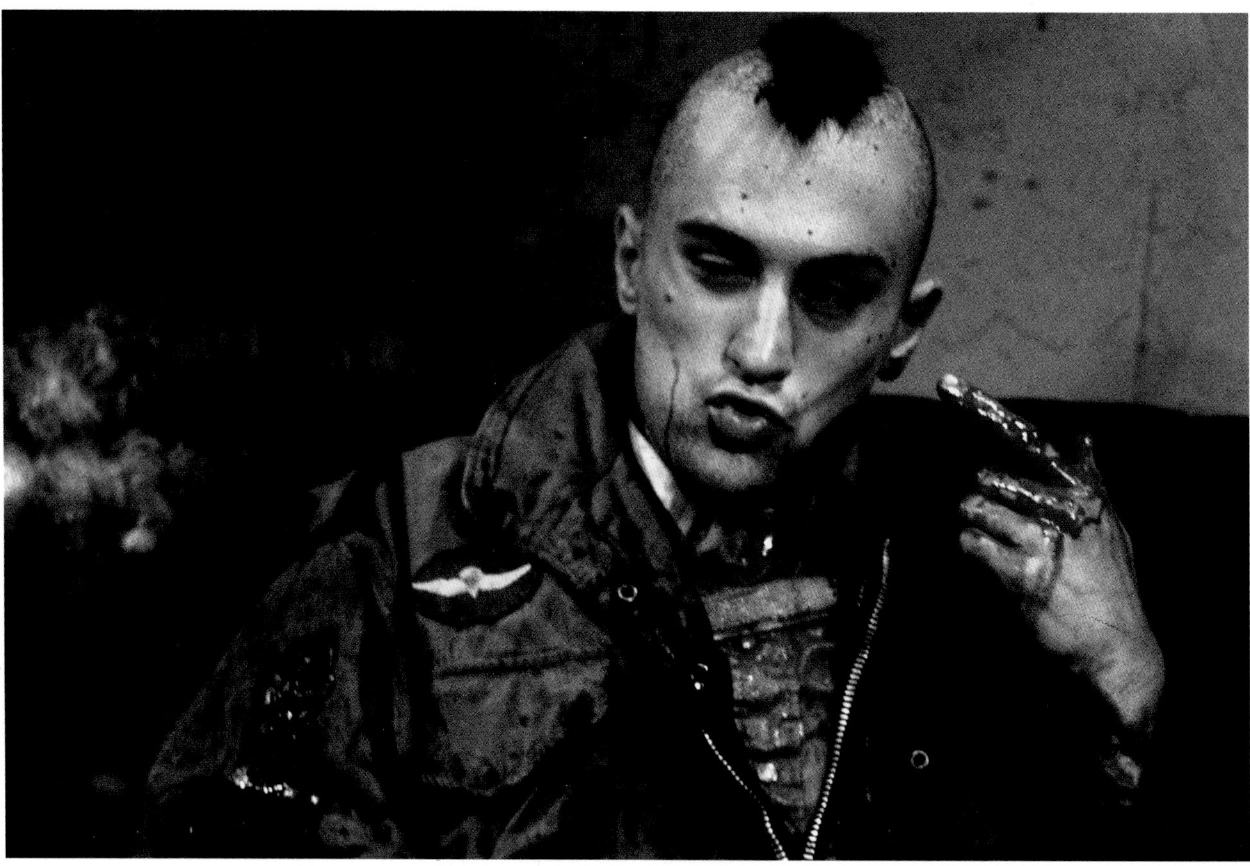

humour among cast and crew – a need to decompress. The sequence ends with the camera tracking back over the devastation from above, with Travis slumped on a sofa bleeding. What we assume is an out-of-body experience as he succumbs to death, a finger pointed to his brain. The only way to pull it off was literally to rip out the ceiling. After which, due to child labour laws and Foster being central to the scene, they had twenty minutes to complete the shot. The MPA later refused an R rating unless the ending was toned down. So Scorsese took them at their word and desaturated the film into a grubby monochrome as grainy as tabloid print, the blood crimson like communion wine.

And what of the very ending – this absurdly happy ending – with Travis contentedly back behind the wheel of his cab? Declared a hero for saving Iris, seeing Betsy on his back seat, is Travis saved? Not so fast. Some take this to be a dream sequence, a moment of serenity in a dying man's head, as he slumps on the sofa after the gunfight. Scorsese preferred to emphasize the sudden flash of those paranoid eyes in the rear-view mirror, a horror movie motif, and Herrmann's music borrows three notes from his score for *Psycho*. The cycle is beginning again.

Above: *The ending of* Taxi Driver *remains ambiguous to this day – for many this moment signals that Travis Bickle is dying, and the rest of the film is no more than a final dream.*

SAVED BY CINEMA

Martin Scorsese the cinéaste

As a child, Martin Scorsese consumed film as if gasping for air. It was as if the play of light across a screen soothed his asthmatic lungs. Prevented from partaking in normal life, cinema became reality. At the age of three he dreamed of being a cowboy, but somewhere amid all the images, he knew he really wanted to be a director.

'The first name that I remember being associated with films I really responded to, was Ford, John Ford,'[1] he recalled, but it was Elia Kazan who reflected the world he knew outside of his window.

Scorsese's vocal appreciation of the medium has elevated him to the station of America's leading cinéaste, ready to wax lyrical on behalf of obscurities and classics. 'He's onto himself. He knows he's an obsessive,'[2] said Richard Schickel, introducing a collection of conversations with the director. Any interview with Scorsese becomes a fervent, discursive voyage into cinema history, with names, dates and pithy summaries delivered without pausing for breath.

His obsession has been channelled not only into every film he has made, but into two remarkable, four-hour testaments. *A Personal Journey with Martin Scorsese Through American Movies* and *My Voyage to Italy* pay tribute to the two national cinemas that run in his veins. 'Scorsese's thesis, for lack of a better word,' appreciated Nicholas Laskin in *IndieWire*, 'seems to be that if we study and appreciate the art of the past, it will help us in creating beautiful, sustainable art for future generations.'[3]

Co-directed by Kent Jones (previously Scorsese's video archivist), *A Personal Journey* is like a map to the beginning of his career, setting out from the primal effect of seeing *Duel in the Sun* aged only four. 'To a child it was sort of a puzzle,' he recalls in the documentary. 'How could the heroine fall for a villain?'[4]

It is his grasp of a genre, like the gangster movie, musical or film noir, that allows him to reinvent traditional forms. 'The face of John Garfield, a lawyer for the mob, was a landscape of moral conflicts,'[5] he relishes, discussing a supposedly minor noir in *Force of Evil*. And he homes in on the directors, 'smugglers'[6] he calls them, from Erich von Stroheim to Stanley Kubrick, who instil entertainment with bigger ideas.

It's an ongoing pursuit. In 2010, he co-directed (with Jones) *A Letter to Elia*, exploring the life and career of that influential New York director.

Above: *The personal touch – the logo for Scorsese's cinematic documentary uses his sketch and his handwriting.*

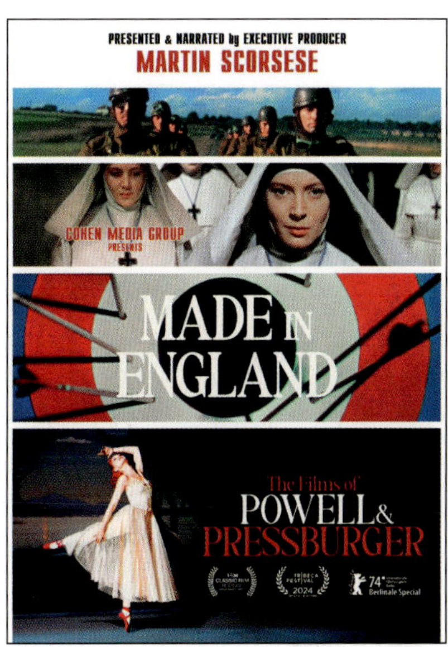

Above: *Scorsese's detailed reflections on the British-based filmmakers who are among his greatest influences.*

And in 2024, served as chief guide in David Hinton's love song to Powell and Pressburger, *Made in England*.

Furthermore, alongside his scholarly reflections, Scorsese champions the restoration, preservation, and exhibition of old prints, through The Film Foundation. This non-profit organization was founded by Scorsese in 1990, enrolling fellow directors (including Spielberg, Coppola, and Kubrick) into fighting for film heritage. The studio vaults were in a sorry state. It was a quest to make everyone aware, he said, 'of the value in this artform.'[7]

THE DARK ARTS

New York, New York (1977), *Raging Bull* (1980), *The King of Comedy* (1982)

When citing the greatness of Martin Scorsese, *Taxi Driver* and *Goodfellas* may spring to the lips, but it is the trio of unnerving masterworks made between 1977 and 1982 that form the strange, dark, thrillingly experimental heart of his career. Three films made amid chaos both personal and professional (as if there was a difference). Each one pressed against the boundaries of genre, each one featured the towering methodology of Robert De Niro, and each one was a flop, pushing Scorsese closer to the artistic brink. Each has since been considered, and reconsidered, a seminal work that established our expectations forevermore.

If you truly want to make the case for Scorsese, heedless and headlong in his pursuit of a singular art, then try his take of an MGM-style musical (who else would dare that in 1977?) *New York, New York,* where the Expressionist cityscapes and song and dance numbers are a cover for the story of a fragmenting marriage. Or *Raging Bull,* cloaked in haunting black and white, the harrowing biopic of Italian-American middleweight Jake La Motta whose psyche rested permanently on the brink, voted the greatest film of the eighties by both *Premiere* and *Sight and Sound*. *The King of Comedy* offers little relief, a devastating satire of celebrity, with De Niro as the disturbed stand-up ravenous for fame.

Scorsese's best work is marked by its opposition to the consolation of happy endings. We depart less sure of the world. And this uneasy trilogy is the apotheosis of such dark arts. Cinema has never felt so alive and brutalizing. Like a priest testing his faith, he pushes the medium, and himself, to the limit, yet without ever losing his belief in the transporting power of cinema.

'It was fun, it was crazy, it was upsetting, it was terrific,'[1] he reminisced, and he nearly died doing it.

Here is an irony the size of a billboard. Scorsese shot a film called *New York, New York* in Hollywood. Which was the whole point. It was a big studio production by design. Arriving on the West Coast, he had searched in vain for the glamour that

Opposite: *Martin Scorsese in a different key* – New York, New York's *troubled lovers Francine (Liza Minnelli) and Jimmy (Robert De Niro) find some solace in music.*

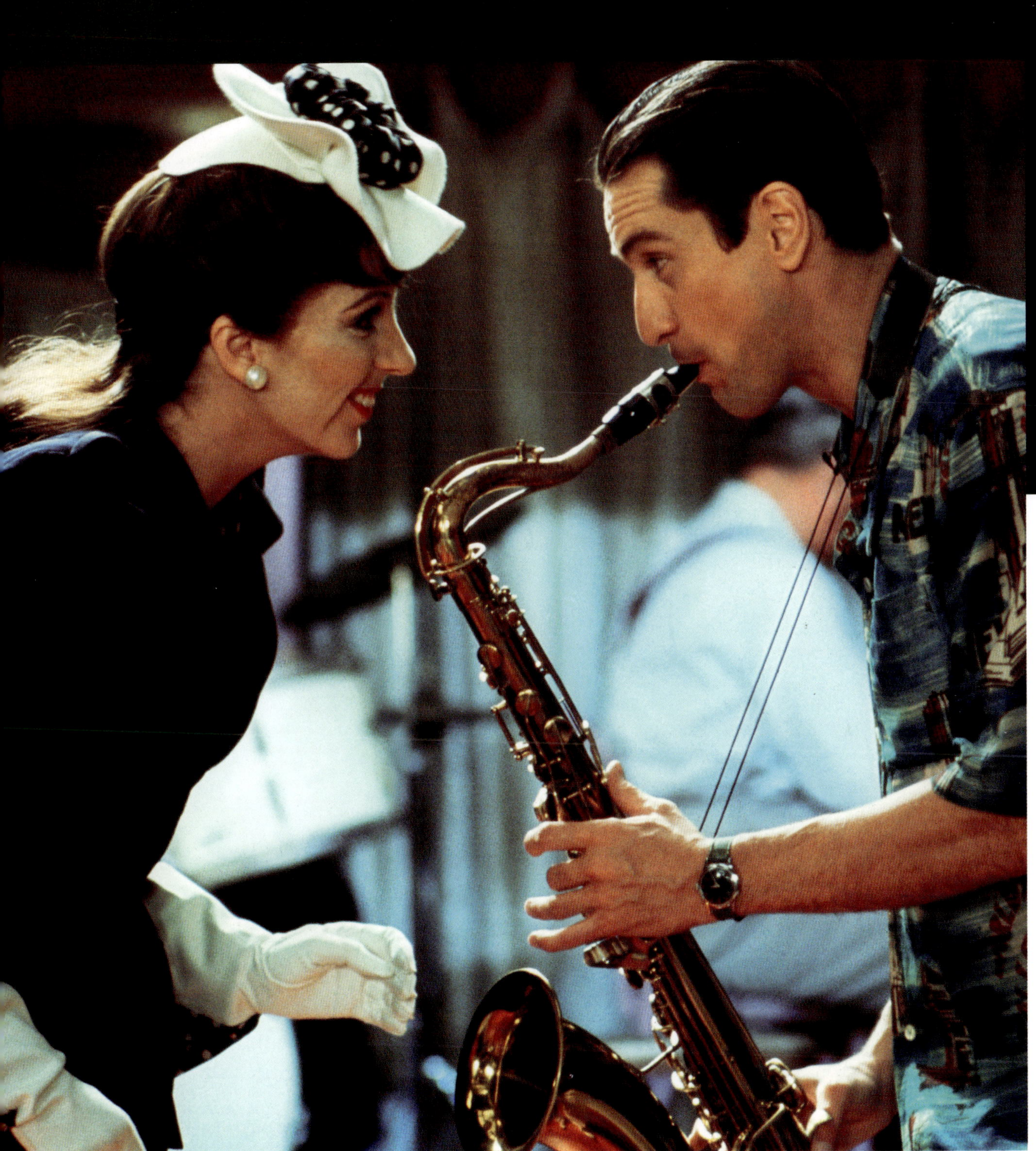

had filled his youth, only to be met by a ghost town. So he attempted an act of resurrection. Hearing of a script called *New York, New York* being developed by producers Irwin Winkler and Robert Chartoff, he got his agent to put in a call. Earl Mac Rauch's screenplay was a straight attempt to revive the big-band musical exuberance of the 1940s and 1950s, when Scorsese fell in love with movies. It centred on the romance between a wannabe singer and struggling saxophone player who meet on V-J Day.

Scorsese had in mind a more radical form of homage. In a sense, *New York, New York* (with its already doubled title) defines his philosophy. This was a conscious attempt to marry the Kazan-Cassavetes school of naturalism, the river that had swept him up as a student and now coursed beneath New Hollywood, with the polished artifice of the old studio pictures, the films he knew by heart. 'To see what happens,'[2] he said, with an impish shrug. He was effectively seeking to marry the opposing sides of his nature: historian and revolutionary.

Even the leads represent the different camps: De Niro (without whom Scorsese could barely function) and Liza Minnelli, daughter of Golden Era darling Judy Garland and director Vincente Minnelli – whose fabulous musicals Scorsese was attempting to imitate.

New York, New York isn't pastiche so much as a visual essay on film form that cost $14 million to make.

Welcome to the 1970s.

Here's the thing, Scorsese was onto something. Each approach illuminates the other. As he said, 'the artifice of the old has a truth to it.'[3] Musicals expressed deeper emotions in a 'codified' form, which he made explicit. Likewise, all the firebrand realism of his earlier films was still

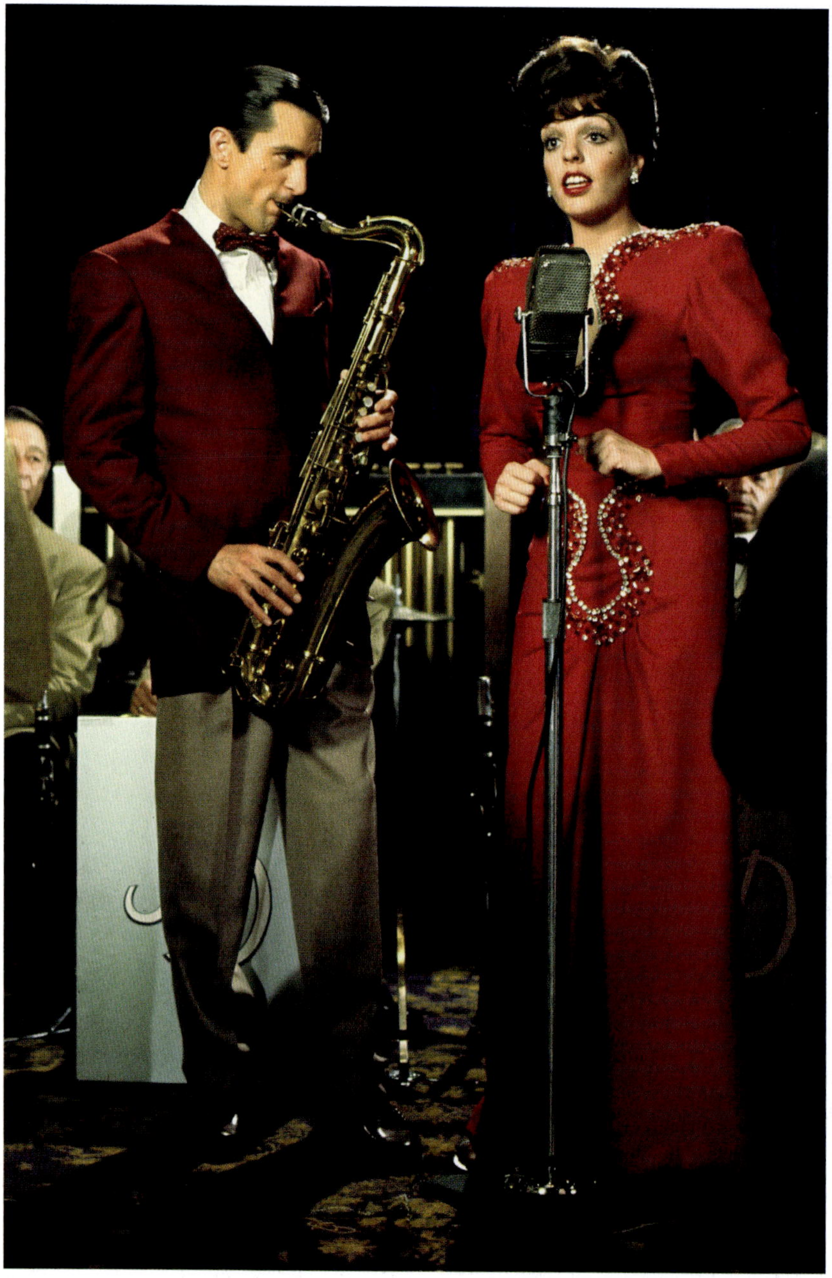

Above: *A musical set in the late 1940s,* New York, New York *(1977) demonstrated that periodic yearning in Martin Scorsese to experiment with classic Hollywood genres.*

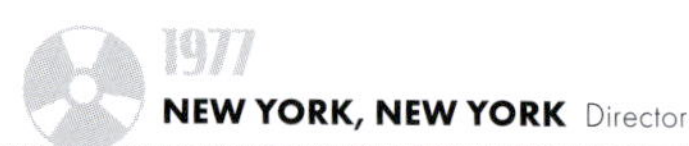

NEW YORK, NEW YORK Director

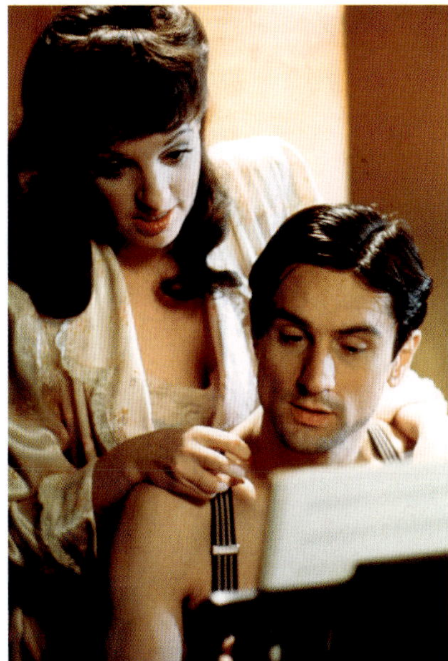

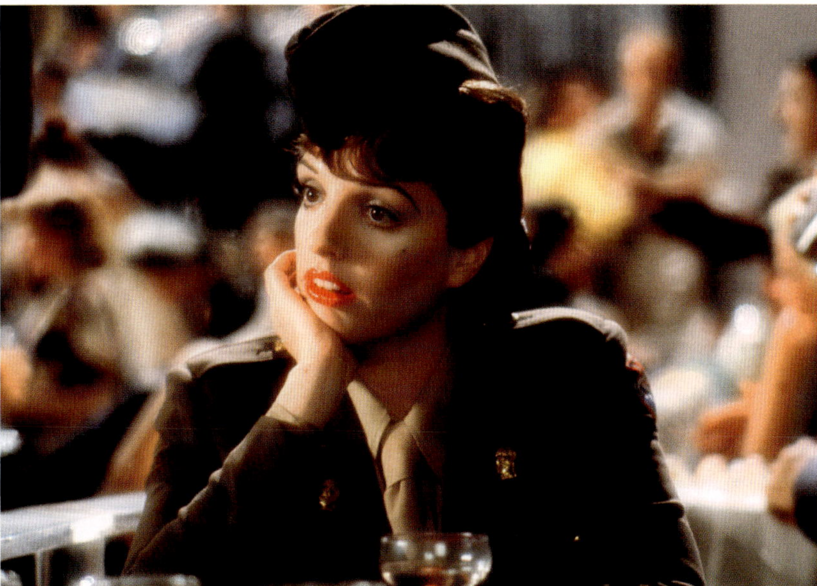

Above left: *The act of creation – Francine (Liza Minnelli) and Jimmy (Robert De Niro) collaborate on the titular song.*

Above right: *Scorsese does 'meet cute' – or his variation on it, as Francine resists Jimmy's romantic overtures for a full twenty minutes in the film's elaborate opening.*

beholden to style, only now conspicuously. There is something doubly moving when Minnelli's Francine Evans breaks into song (with the musical numbers purely diegetic), or De Niro's Jimmy Doyle loses himself to jazz. It's as if they can only truly communicate through music.

Scorsese 101 – art is to be found in the tension between opposing forces: the allure of the immoral, the violence within heroes, the destructive force at the heart of creativity. The pursuit of art can destroy a marriage.

'I got my entire performance by looking at Marty's eyes,' recalled Minnelli. 'I think Marty understands the struggle between feelings and thought – that intellect and emotion are always at war in people.'[4]

Amid the voluminous splendour of the MGM soundstages at Culver City, Scorsese was set on improvising entire scenes. Tough to pull off when grandiose sets, lighting, period costumes, musical cues, and crowds of extras called for strict planning and indeed plotting. Scorsese insisted cinematographer László Kovács use no modern techniques, and for the scenery to pointedly resemble backdrops. The entire production was moving in two directions at once. The opening sequence, where the couple 'meet cute' against the milling celebrations of the end of the war, is both fabulous and interminable, with Jimmy finally wearing Francine down. Minnelli says little more than 'no' for twenty minutes. It took them eight days to shoot.

Was De Niro's portrayal too much for the confines of genre, caught in the maelstrom of what *Slant* dubbed his 'seventies-era weirdo mode'[5]? There is an unsettling recklessness to Jimmy, as if he's trying Abbott and Costello routines, only without the punchlines. Travis Bickle haunts his steps. Witnessing the actor's edgy performance, wrote Vincent Canby in the *New York Times*, 'is to watch a man running to catch a train, only to pass right by it.'[6]

Scorsese's mood swings didn't help. Jimmy was his avatar, trying to prove worthy of Minnelli's Francine, the avatar of Hollywood. He was using drugs heavily and given to manic surges and deep insecurity. He would disappear to talk to his shrink. Production slowed to a crawl. At the end of twenty-two weeks, they were over schedule, over budget, and overwrought. He spent $350,000 on a razzle-dazzling and ironic number called *Happy Endings*, which he then decided to cut (though it was, winningly, reinstated for a 1981 re-release). It was a better picture than the original script, he reflected, 'but if I had known what I had wanted from the very beginning, it would have been much stronger.'[7]

True, the first Jimmy-led half of the film is unwieldy, with scenes left to drift. But in the second half, it's as if it comes into focus. For now the film belongs to Francine, as she emerges from beneath the shadow of Jimmy's womanizing, drug taking, tantrums, and ultimate desertion of wife and child. *A Star Is Born* was a touchstone for Scorsese, as *New York, New York* is the source code for Damien Chazelle's *La La Land*.

Minnelli's performance of the title song, which the couple have composed together (the child of their artistic union, in fact written for the film by Fred Ebb and John Kander), is among Scorsese's most inspired moments – and everything he was seeking with the film. Her expression of triumph and survival, with Jimmy gazing in wonder from the audience, is magnified by the dark journey we have taken with Francine. As

Below: *Drive-by shooting – Martin Scorsese conducts De Niro's Jimmy from the interior of a period car.*

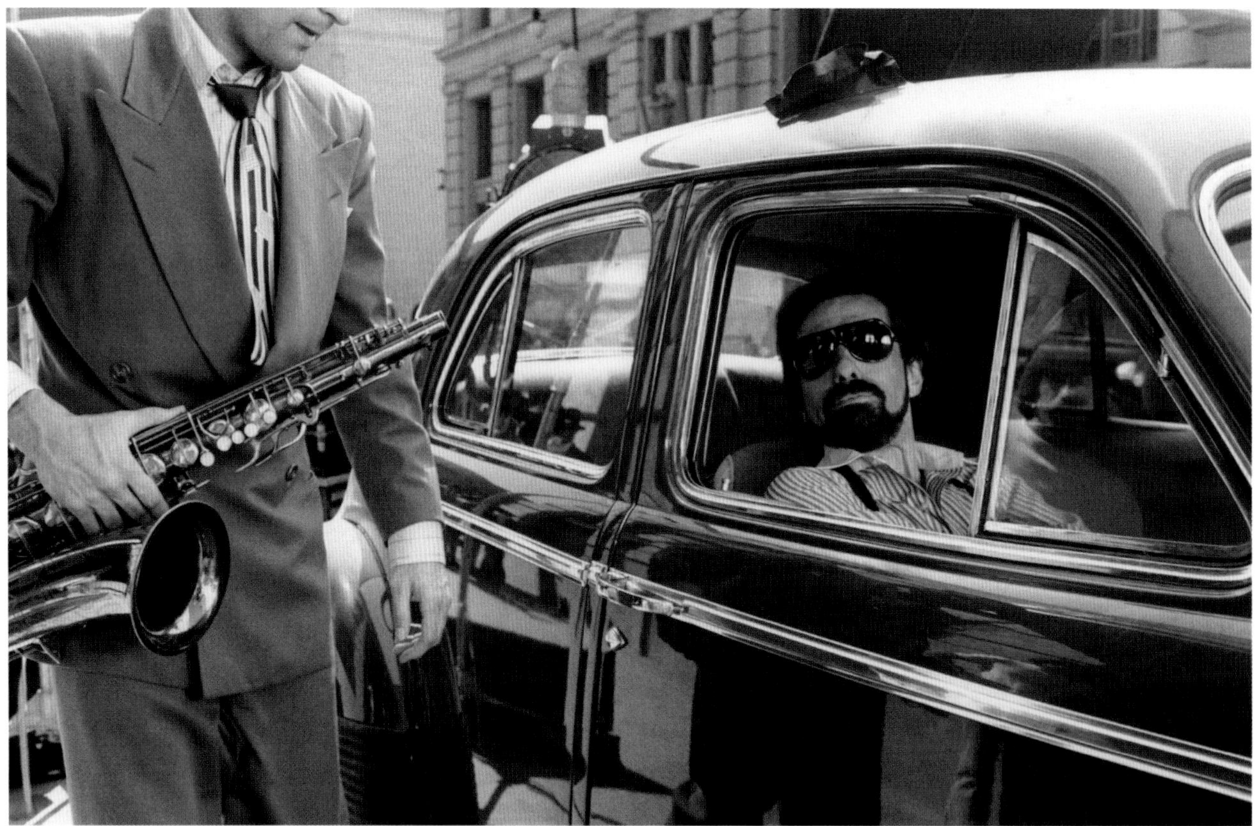

Minnelli said, 'It was hurt that made her a star.'[8] Winkler would rue that the song wasn't even nominated for an Academy Award, but re-recorded two years later by Frank Sinatra it soared into legend.

Post-production was even more tumultuous. Scorsese worked his way through three different editors to find a film within the reams of footage (Winkler claimed an unreleasable four-hour-twenty-nine-minute version really worked). Among the editors was again Marcia Lucas, who split her time with her husband's more upbeat spin on tradition, *Star Wars*. George dropped by to take a look at this realistic musical, informing his friend that if the couple walked off into the sunset he would add $10 million to the box office.

'When I heard him say that I knew I was doomed, that I cannot make it in this business, that I cannot make entertainment pictures, I cannot be a director of Hollywood films,'[9] lamented Scorsese. After all the characters had gone through in the film, all he had gone through in life, he wouldn't be able to face himself if he gave in to a happy ending.

As predicted, the film was a disaster, making $16 million worldwide. 'In 1977, a week or so after we opened, *Star Wars* opened. The whole industry went another way,'[10] he sighed.

All these years later, with the film reassessed and prized, the ending is perfect. It is now Francine who abandons Jimmy for the sake of her career, leaving him standing alone on a snowy New York street, which deliberately looks like the set it is, but the regret is real.

With the failure of his musical, Scorsese took flight from depression. Filming *The Last Waltz*, which documented The Band's final concert, released in 1978, he began house-hopping through LA with lead singer Robbie Robertson (miraculously,

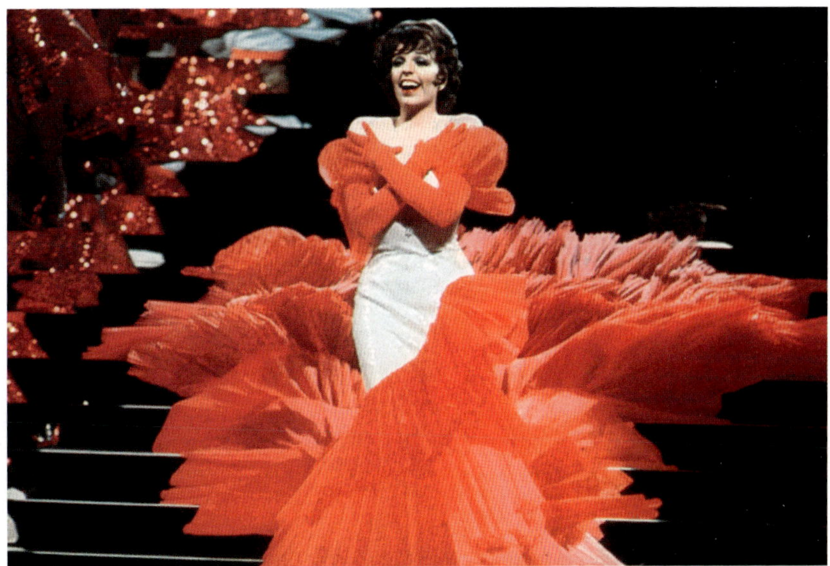

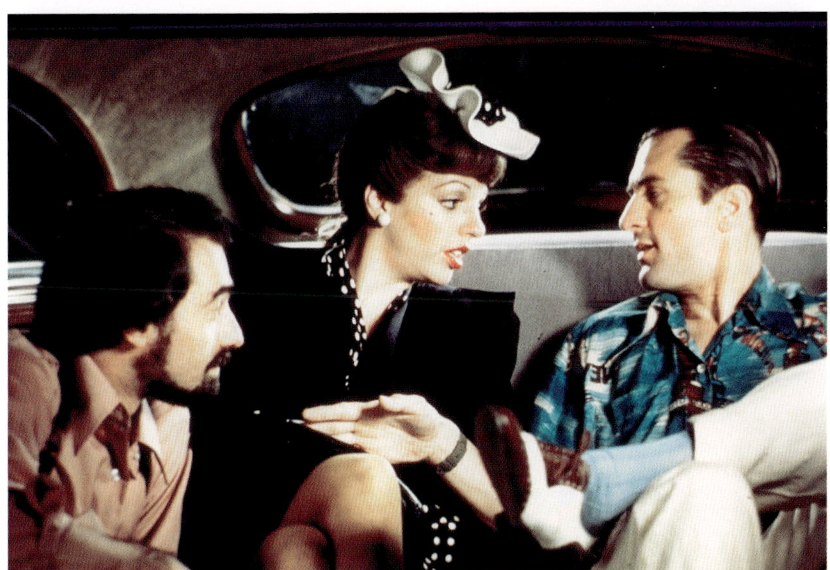

Top: *The ironically entitled, but still dazzling musical number* Happy Endings *took ten days to film – only to be left out of the original cut of* New York, New York. *It has since been restored.*

Above: *The two sides of Scorsese are represented by old Hollywood progeny Liza Minnelli and New Hollywood prince Robert De Niro.*

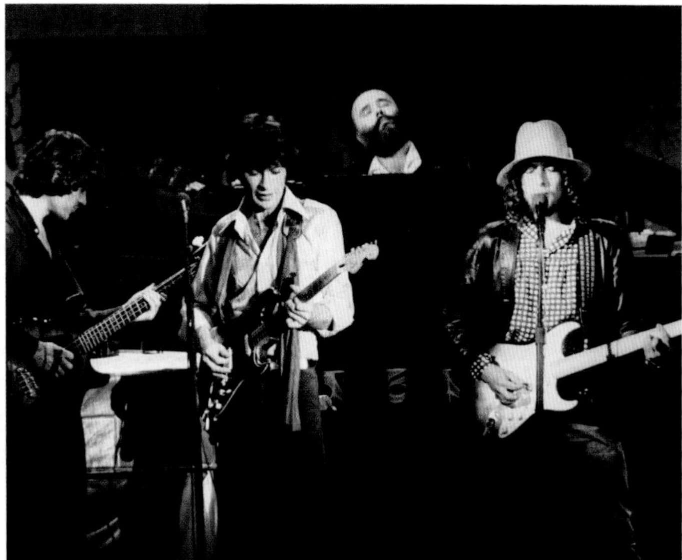

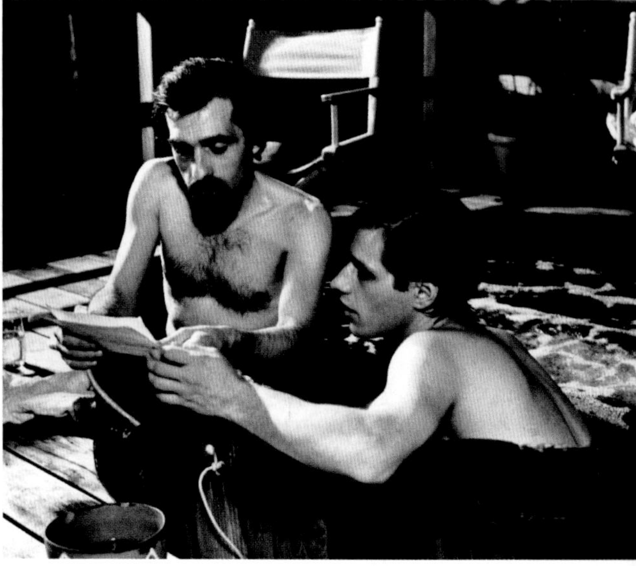

Above left: *Documentary vibes Part 1 – Bob Dylan (right) takes a turn with The Band in Martin Scorsese's celebrated account of the rock outfit's final concert,* The Last Waltz *(1978).*

Above right: *Documentary vibes Part 2 – Scorsese consults his notes while in the hot tub with his subject during the shooting of* American Boy: A Profile of Steven Prince *(1978).*

a lifelong collaborator), living it high, pushing his body hard. They were bingeing, womanizing, barely sleeping at all. The insistence of cocaine had taken hold of Scorsese's life. He grew as paranoid and unpredictable as his antiheroes.

'I was always angry, throwing glasses, provoking people, really unpleasant to be around,'[11] he recalled, ruefully.

There were prospective projects, but he wouldn't commit. De Niro was obsessed with a biopic of that old Lower East Side slugger La Motta. The actor carried a battered copy of the boxer's biography, by Peter Savage and Joseph Carter, everywhere he went on *New York, New York*, eventually getting Winkler and Chartoff interested, they offered it to United Artists, but De Niro insisted it could only be made by Scorsese.

The director resisted. What did he know of boxing? His friend pushed again and again – there was so much here. La Motta's talent was to soak up punishment and then mete it out, but his brutality spilled out of the ring into an abusive marriage, where the blows he delivered caused his pregnant wife to abort. And into his relationship with his brother Joey – who managed his career, and whom Jake, in his deluded, destructive fury, accused of sleeping with his wife. After the bloody trials of boxing, La Motta grew fat and melancholic, washed up and estranged from his family. De Niro insisting all the while that this was a study in humanity.

Scripts were developed, wrestling with the duality of the man: the pugilist as lithe as a cat and the loveless has-been mumbling platitudes in cramped clubs. The first to try was Mardik Martin, who got his old pal at least curious with an image of the boxer's blood raining down on the fur coats in the front row. Then came Paul Schrader, who fought with De Niro over a closing soliloquy in which a guilt-stricken La Motta tries to masturbate in a prison cell (De Niro won). But still Scorsese kept his distance.

'I knew what I wanted to say in *Mean Streets*, like I knew what I wanted to say in *Taxi Driver*, I even knew what I wanted

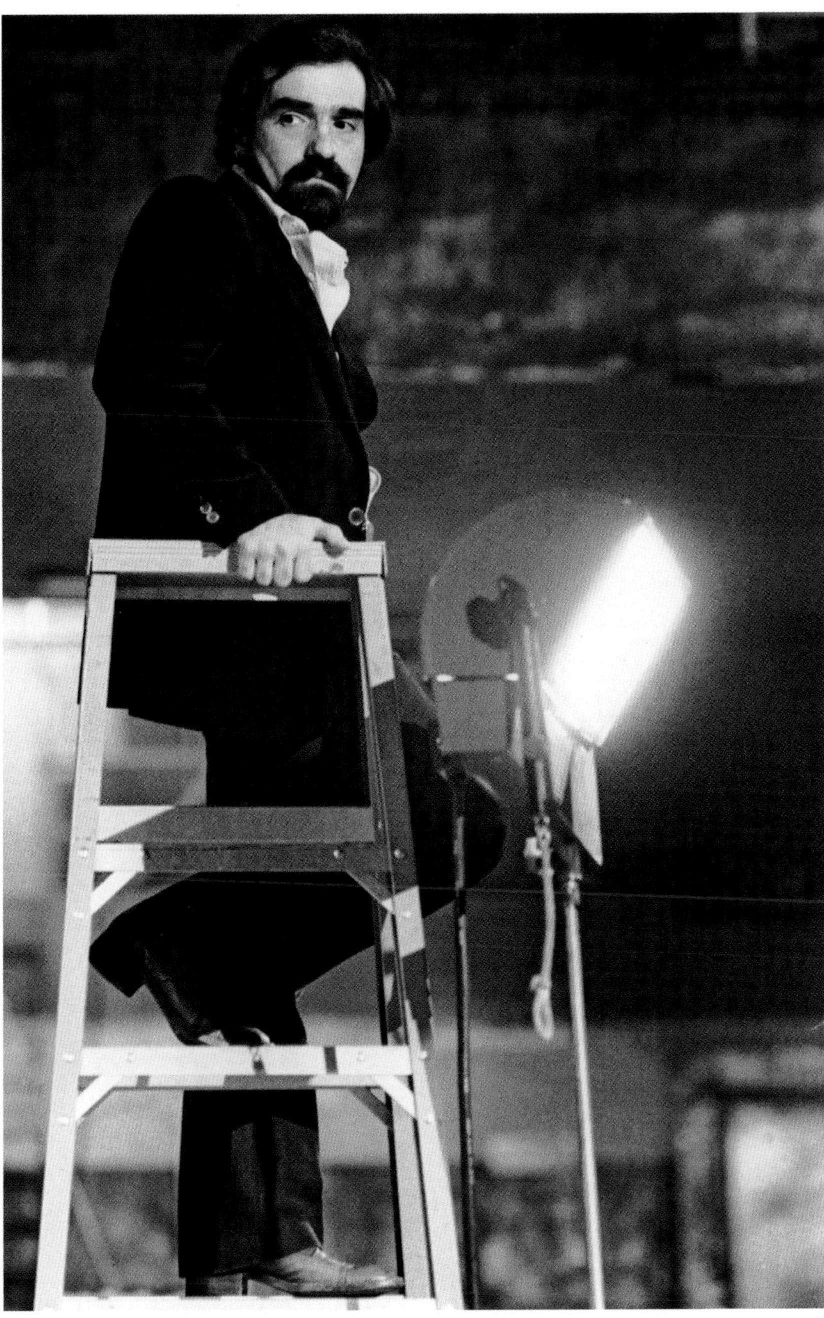

Above: *At the top of his game – after a brush with death, Scorsese came back with the film that many still consider his masterpiece,* Raging Bull *(1980).*

to say in *New York, New York*. But I didn't know what the hell *Raging Bull* was about.'[12] The thought of making any movie exhausted him.

On Labour Day weekend in 1978, Scorsese came close to a knock-out blow. A bad batch of coke playing havoc with his asthma medicine, he began coughing up blood. Steven Prince, the gun seller in *Taxi Driver* and Scorsese's guardian angel, rushed him to the New York Hospital (memories of the emergency resound in *Bringing Out the Dead*). He had no platelets in his blood. 'Basically, I was dying,' said Scorsese. 'I was bleeding internally all over, and I didn't know it. My eyes were bleeding, my hands, everything except my brain and my liver.'[13]

Unable to sleep, he lay in his hospital room watching old movies, the 1931 *Dr. Jekyll and Mr. Hyde* among them. De Niro came to see him. Stunned at the sight of his ailing friend, down to 109 pounds, he made his final entreaty – direct me in *Raging Bull*. Wearily, Scorsese acceded: 'Yeah.'[14] The only way to make sense of anything, even being alive, was to make a movie. A film not about boxing, but self-destruction.

'It was about me,'[15] he said.

United Artists were having misgivings. *Rocky* may have been a blockbusting hit for them in 1976, also produced by Winkler and Chartoff, but this was very different. How could even De Niro and Scorsese make us care for such a repellent character? A meeting was called at Scorsese's apartment, with executives Steven Bach and David Field, who didn't like Schrader's script one bit. There was a sum total of twelve minutes of boxing. Why would anyone stay for the second act?

'It's this man,'[16] said Field, beneath the frozen gaze of Scorsese. La Motta was so full of demons, what else was there? He was a Neanderthal. 'A cockroach,'[17] he concluded, perhaps goading the director into softening his approach.

'He's *not* a cockroach,'[18] retorted De Niro, until then as silent as a statue, and Scorsese contends that his defiance got the film a greenlight. Using his dark arts, Winkler also threatened to halt a *Rocky* sequel if the studio blocked *Raging Bull*. Through an uncredited rewrite by Scorsese and De Niro, and indeed through the volumes written on the actor's face, a human dimension emerged. Late in the film, La Motta is imprisoned in Dade County, shot in bars of Damascene light and glutinous shadow, a man fighting with himself, slamming his fists into the (rubber) wall, howling, 'I am *not* an animal!'[19] Despite everything we know, the scene is heart-rending.

Scorsese still claims not to understand what fuelled La Motta's self-immolating rages, and his film refuses judgment. 'That guilt, please understand this, doesn't come from a specific act, but is part and parcel of the character,'[20] he said. He was given an old folk painting of La Motta, on which the caption read: 'Jake fought like he didn't deserve to live.'[21] That was the whole picture, he thought, right there.

This is a story of brotherly love tested, shattered, and maybe redeemed. A film about inadequacy and violence, in the ring and out of it. This Scorsese knew - violence is a symptom of the world. Structured as a recollection (the ebb and flow of memory becoming central to his storytelling), the film crosses timelines: the corpulent old man, the wraithlike visions of prowess, and the clarity of the lives he destroyed, including his own.

The casting of Joey was pivotal and career-changing for both director and newcomer Joe Pesci, who had given up acting to run a restaurant in the Bronx.

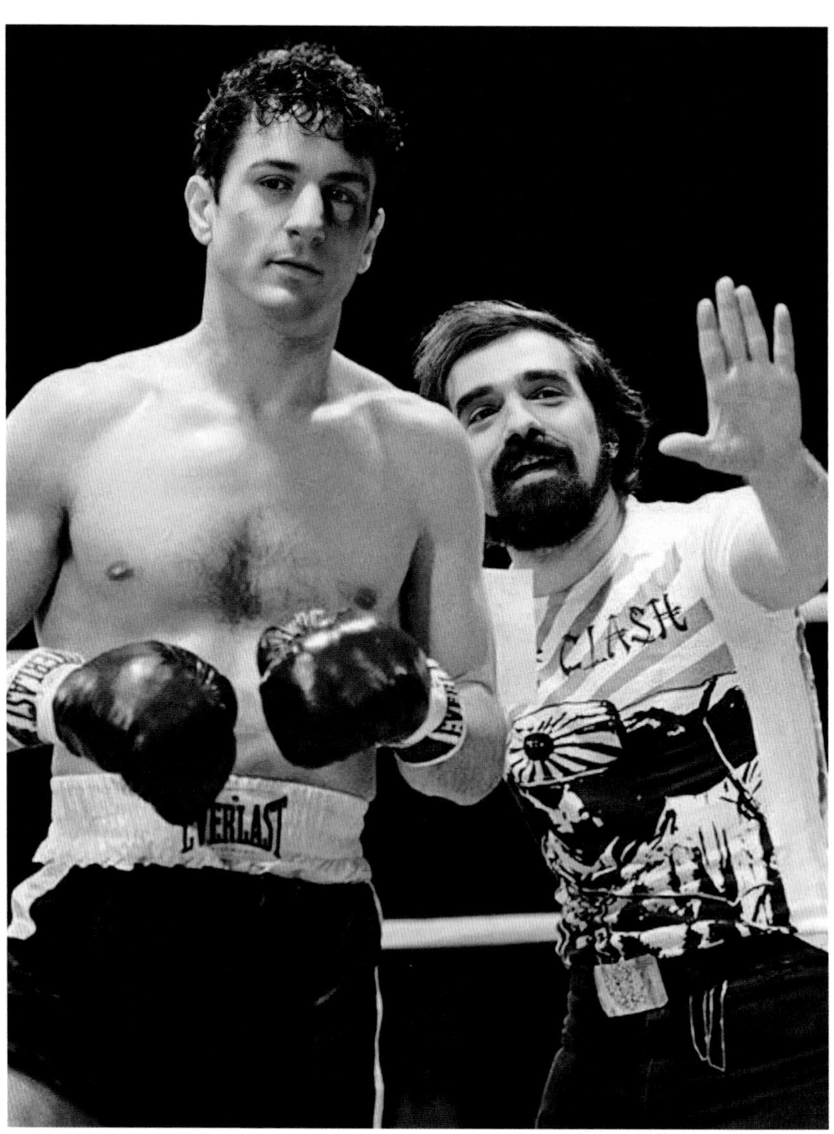

Above: *Actor and auteur – Martin Scorsese frames his shot as Robert De Niro channels middleweight Jake La Motta in* Raging Bull. *In case of confusion, outside of the film, the boxer's surname is often spelled LaMotta.*

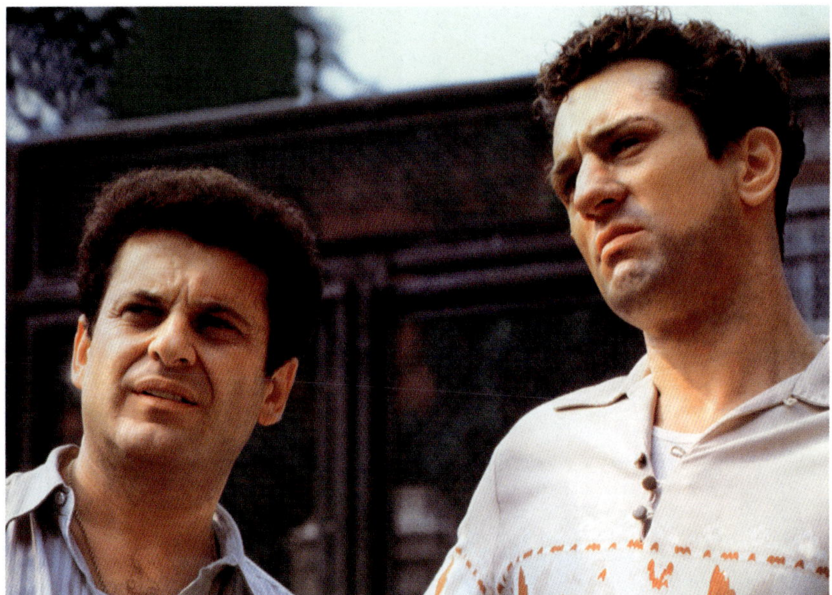

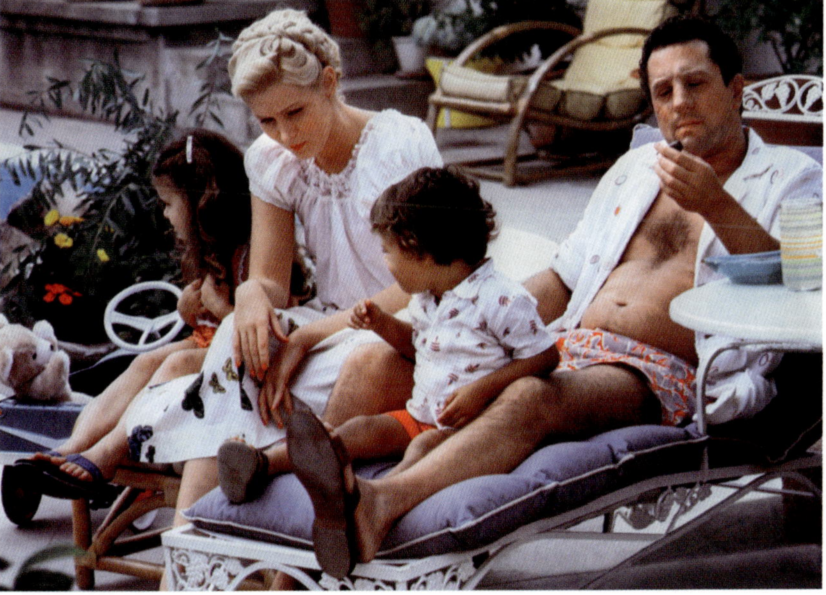

Top: *Brotherly love and hate – cast as Joey La Motta, who served as Jake's manager, Joe Pesci entered the Scorsese fold as the perfect foil for De Niro.*

Above: *Cathy Moriarty was a complete unknown when she was cast as Jake's wife Vikki, but she more than stands up to the test, and the film becomes as much a portrayal of a destructive marriage as of a fading champion.*

And still he had to be convinced. Spotted by De Niro, Pesci had this way with words, which he delivered in agitated gusts, his small body wired with a comedian's energy. Like Scorsese, he drew from life, imbuing his performance with memories of a tough Italian-American upbringing, recruited into the director's circle to be the funny guy to De Niro's straight man. The film is also the story of a marriage, a vision of love's endurance and fatal blows, with the wonderful, resilient, unknown Cathy Moriarty – recommended by Pesci, who'd seen her photo in a nightclub, a beauty contest winner who looked just like the real Vikki La Motta.

Scorsese was getting back to reality – his reality. He and La Motta came from the same working streets, whose urban aggression he had transcribed into *Mean Streets* and *Taxi Driver*. There are dalliances with the mob. For La Motta, the American Dream has gone sour. What good are you when you become good for nothing?

Shooting from 16 April 1979, Scorsese called it 'kamikaze'[22] filmmaking, throwing everything he had into it. 'I thought *Raging Bull* would be my last film,'[23] he insisted. After which, he would depart for Rome, where he had a personal life, and make documentaries on the lives of the saints. He would cut himself off from American movies, like kicking the coke. Rid himself of the urge in one last binge.

He, De Niro, and Schrader must have watched every boxing picture. Scorsese wanted something more hard-nosed, like the bitter crime flicks about doomed men from the era when La Motta fought: *Force of Evil*, *Kiss of Death*, Cagney in *The Public Enemy*. *Raging Bull* is the sports movie as film noir, soaking up the genre's moral eclipse, Expressionist look, and lyrical reading of human darkness. The demand for black and white would set the pulses racing

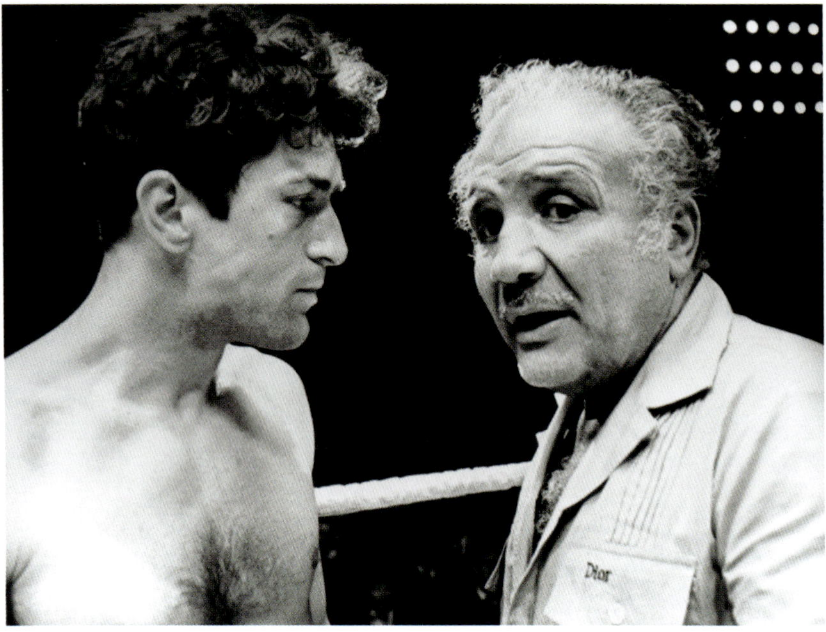

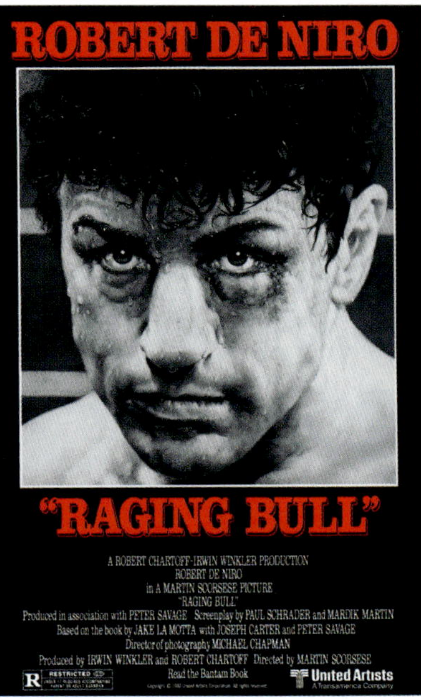

at United Artists again. Scorsese adored colour, but he wanted noir's chiaroscuro, mixed with the frankness of Weegee's street scenes and old newsreels of bouts.

Dualities are everywhere. The contrast of an old and young man, life inside and outside of the ring, the play of light and shadow in Michael Chapman's cinematography, and a production split between LA and New York.

Shot on a soundstage in LA, the first ten weeks were committed to boxing. The poetry of the ring! Scorsese had been taken to fights at Madison Square Garden, felt the heat of the crowd, but recalled only single images: the blood pouring from the sponge across the fighter's back, or congealed and dripping from the ropes. They used the syrup from Hershey bars, which looked so much better in black and white (Hitchcock taught him that, with chocolate draining away in *Psycho*).

Scorsese storyboarded every blow. 'It's very much like staging a dance to music,'[24] he explained. It was all choreography: fifteen punches, say, then a tracking shot, then close in for the final punch. They smashed melons for the sound effect. Every day a director's instruction to his leading man was the same: 'In this shot, you get hit.'[25] He used only one camera, a fighter's-eye view. Visual tricks romanticize our perception: different-sized rings, flames placed beneath the lens for the fingers of heat, smoke contained within the frame as if the boxer was fighting through a fog.

'It's not just the camera moves,' said Chapman, 'it was the emotion that it shows.'[26] Long before the Copa in *Goodfellas*, there is a tracking shot from dressing room to ring, a rapturous Scorsesean introduction to the furnace of the arena. The aged, bent-nosed real La Motta was there every day until they left the ring for home.

The editing is magical, with the film's zones of interest clearly defined: the majesty of the boxing, serenaded by Pietro Mascagni's *Cavalleria rusticana*; the listless

Above left: *The real Jake La Motta served as an adviser for the boxing sequences, but kept away during the filming of the darker, home-life scenes.*

Above right: *Neglected by a troubled studio,* Raging Bull *was only a moderate hit at the box office, but acclaimed by critics. For Scorsese it was a rebirth into the potential of film.*

Opposite: *Martin Scorsese knew nothing about boxing, but approached the fights, which are among the greatest expressions of his visual talent, as operatic arias.*

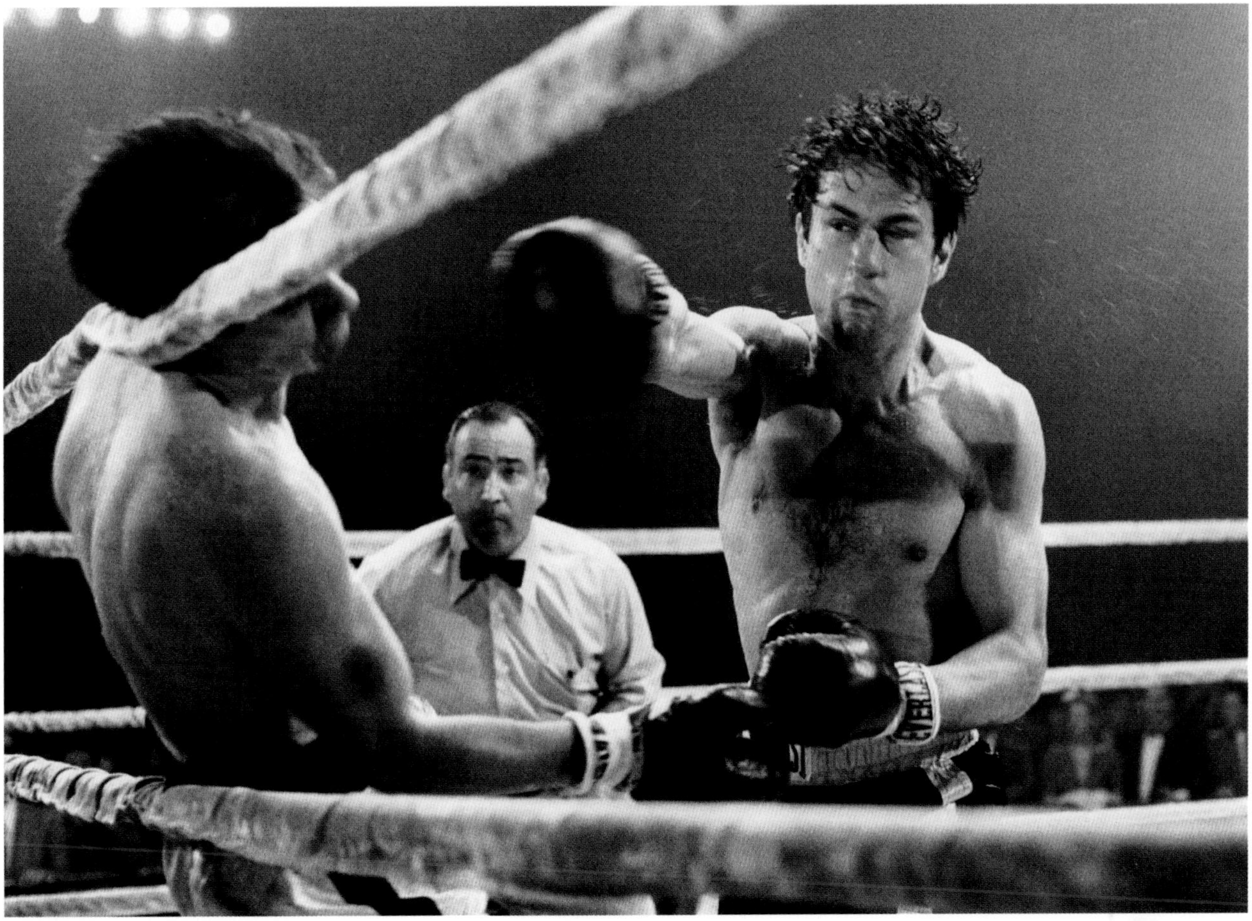

claustrophobia of La Motta's life; and the debris of the ex-pro doing one-man shows, a life story among snatches of Shakespeare, Tennessee Williams, and *On the Waterfront*. This was Thelma Schoonmaker's first full feature with Scorsese, and it gained her an Oscar. They got away from the biopic cliché of a life told in order, undercut the potential stunt of De Niro getting fat. Prosthetics would never do, the actor had to know what it was like be heavy, physically and psychically. So the shoot had paused for four months while he mainlined pasta and ice cream, returning unrecognizable beneath a swollen face. He looked beaten up. Scorsese was minded to shoot the bloated La Motta at a quicker pace, as De Niro's breathing had become as laboured as his own.

It made a respectable-at-best $23 million (having cost $18 million), but the reviews were rapturous, singling out the leading man's Oscar-winning transformation. Though, beneath an arched eyebrow, the *New Yorker's* Pauline Kael suspected the entire film was predicated on 'the metamorphosis of De Niro.'[27]

Raging Bull has become an emblem and an epitaph for an era. Peter Biskind's celebrated history of the rise and fall

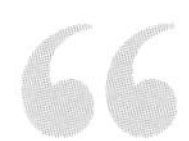

It's not just the camera moves, it was the emotion that it shows.

MICHAEL CHAPMAN

Right: *Double act – Jerry Lewis and Robert De Niro pose for the camera on the set of* The King of Comedy *(1982).*

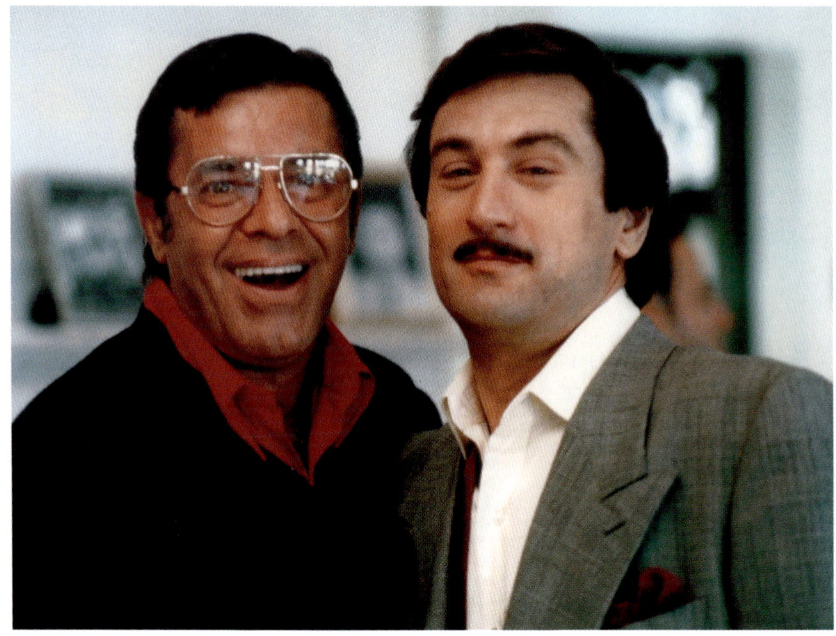

of the Movie Brat generation is entitled *Easy Riders, Raging Bulls*, and Scorsese's beautiful yet formidable film, intimate and epic, reverential yet revolutionary, is a 1970s masterpiece released in 1980. The party was over, but Scorsese was still toiling, out of step with his times, but in tune with posterity.

'I must say, that was painful,' he mourned of his next project. 'Because the film came out and died in four weeks, and they were right – the picture was a bomb. It's called *The King of Comedy*, it's Jerry Lewis, and it's not a comedy. I mean, already, it's a problem.'[28]

Weeks into a production languishing in a boiling New York summer of 1981, he wasn't sure why he was making this strange parable of celebrity. It was another De Niro-inspired joint, rushed into production to get ahead of the imminent directors' strike. Scorsese had never felt up to it, his asthma was raging. He was working slowly, painfully, with the film dragging on almost as long as *New York, New York*. Even he was blinded to the caustic marvel that emerged from the mists of failure.

De Niro had been sitting on Paul D. Zimmerman's script. The *Newsweek* critic had passed it on at Cannes, when such a thing was conceivable, and the actor was initially taken with its satire of fame. At its clotted heart is Rupert Pupkin (De Niro), a seriously deluded man who believes he is destined to be a great stand-up if only he can catch a break. In his sights is late-night television host Jerry Langford (Jerry Lewis) – modelled on Dick Calvert – as the answer to his overdue good fortune. If he lands a slot on Langford's show then the world will catch on. What begins with leaping, by chance, into the celebrity's limo, metastasizes into full-scale house invasion and kidnap, with fellow stalker Masha (Sandra Bernhard) as a more outwardly deranged accomplice.

By 1981, the obsessive nature of fans had reached the headlines, adoration fuelling psychosis. John Lennon had been shot by soured devotee Mark David Chapman in 1980, followed by the attempt on Ronald Reagan's life by the loner John Hinkley, who had openly cited *Taxi Driver* as an inspiration. De Niro was increasingly uneasy with his own celebrity, a quiet man who sought cover in outrageous parts. He also understood that this obsessive stand-up was a warped reflection of his own artistic pursuits.

Together, he and Scorsese made the characters far more unsympathetic. With Pupkin it was almost like a dare. How over the top could they go, laughed Scorsese, 'and still remain in a realistic framework?'[29]

Pupkin is on a spectrum with Johnny Boy and Travis Bickle, infected by a fever only New York brings. *The King of Comedy* is read as a companion to *Taxi Driver*. But Pupkin also inverts De Niro's studies in human darkness. Living in an unseen mother's basement, Pupkin is a voyage

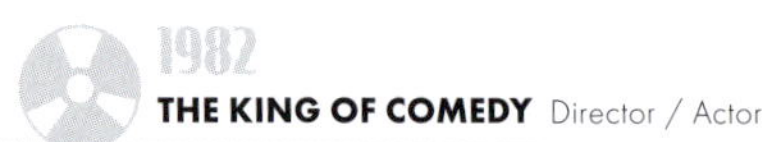

away from the curdled machismo toward a desperately single-minded geek, the terrain of a Dustin Hoffman or Jack Nicholson.

De Niro toured the stand-up circuit, met with Robin Williams, and took counsel from the real autograph hunters who jostled at the stage doors of New York's studios. The sky-blue suit and scarlet tie, neat but hideous, were waiting for them wrapped around a mannequin in a forgotten Broadway clothes store – it even sported a moustache. 'That's him!'[30] cried Scorsese, and nothing needed changing.

You can see the thought process that went into the ideal calibration of real-life celebrity for Langford. When Johnny Carson turned him down (the talk show legend fretted about life imitating art already imitating life), Scorsese tried Orson Welles, then Frank Sinatra, then Dean Martin, and finally Jerry Lewis, who agreed (being a fan of Scorsese's work). Lewis brought with him another ironic dimension, effectively playing the embittered straight man, having been the king of Pupkin-like weasels. He was the model of professionalism, doing all that was asked of him, turning that elastic face immobile with disdain.

With the third of his trilogy studying dark artists, Scorsese's great experiment was to go against himself, dropping style almost entirely. The camera tricks and edit-suite shadow-boxing are replaced with a silent-movie-inspired stateliness and a sickly, soap-opera gleam.

It was a tough shoot. Scorsese was still recovering from pneumonia, his body not yet fully restored after his breakdown, and would punctuate his instructions

Below left: *As the truly warped celebrity stalker Masha, stand-up Sandra Bernhard unleashed an improvisational mayhem on the film.*

Below right: *De Niro's delusional Rupert Pupkin presented a new avenue for the actor's pursuit of human extremes. Gone was the dark machismo, to be replaced with a geeky mania.*

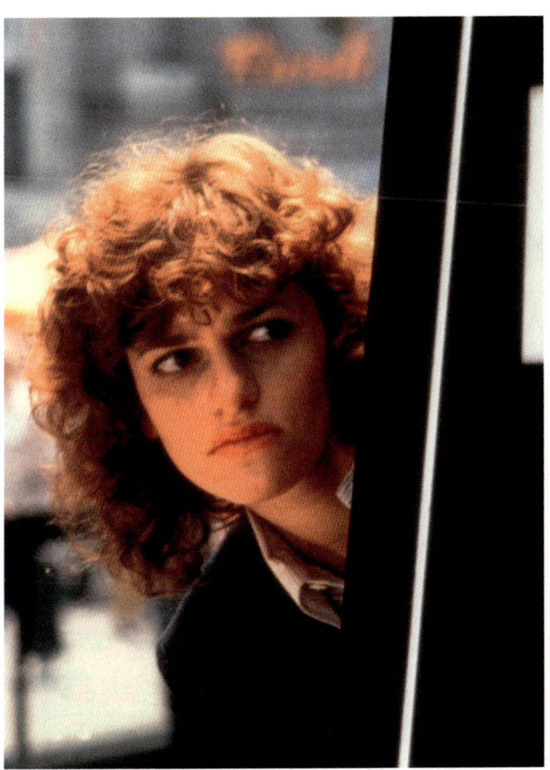

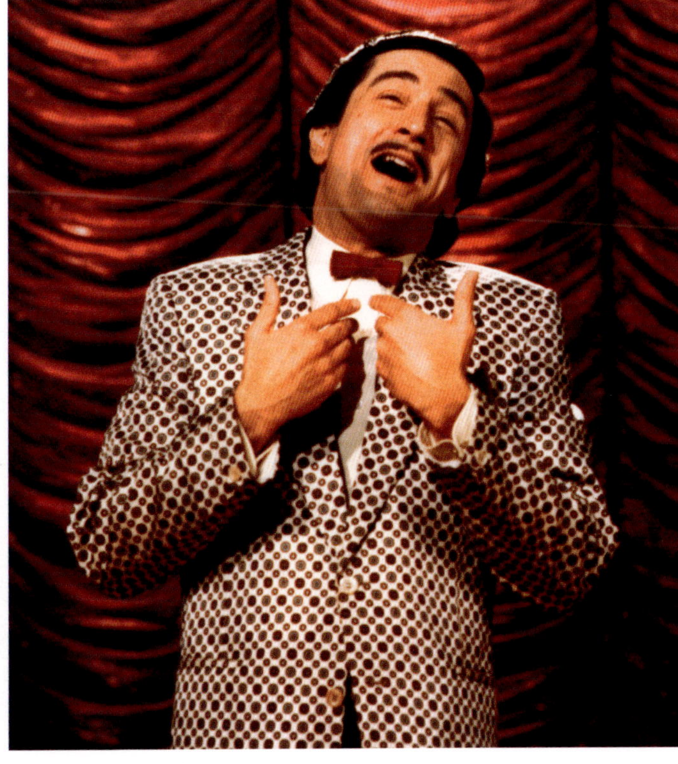

with lengthy coughing fits. Lewis's comic routines off-camera left him gasping. 'We discovered it as we made it,'[31] he reflected. If he was apathetic on the surface, his subconscious was stirring. This was the story about a fantasist who conjures up another life like a director; about a vampiric need as strong as addiction; about that porous line between love and hate. Scorsese wondered if Pupkin, below the inane grin, was 'more violent'[32] than Travis Bickle. He saw it as a scathing 'comedy of manners,'[33] with New York as a heady backdrop – a comedy that makes you stop laughing.

Moreover, he became obsessed with finding the right tone, going to Kubrickian lengths, with simple scenes running to twenty or thirty takes, keeping Pupkin's asinine fantasies on repeat play. Entire sequences were improvised, the whole film set on edge – with Lewis and Bernhard, veterans of the comedy circuit, more than a match for De Niro's constant needling. Scorsese would hand over the reins for certain scenes to Lewis, former director and a master of timing. Such as the jolting moment when Langford is stopped by an old woman on a payphone and refuses to speak to her nephew. 'I hope you catch cancer,'[34] she squawks. That had happened to him.

For a so-called smaller, more contained film, backed by independent producer Arnon Milchan, and picked up for distribution by 20th Century Fox, it ended up costing $20 million.

By post, Scorsese was blocked, unable to bring himself to sift through one million feet of uncertain footage, the studio going crazy. It was as if he could foresee the failure to come. Finally released in February 1983, it died an ignominious death, making only $23 million worldwide. Fan turned foe, Pauline Kael led a chorus of disapproval against this bitter film with a 'grossly insensitive, coldhearted deadhead'[35] at its centre.

Below left: *On its release,* The King of Comedy *confounded audiences, who expected to be laughing, only to be left horrified. The film has since been re-discovered as a kind of horror movie, which indeed now stirs dark laughter.*

Below right: *A consummate pro, Jerry Lewis answered all of his director's needs, though his wisecracking routines between takes were liable to set off Martin Scorsese's asthma.*

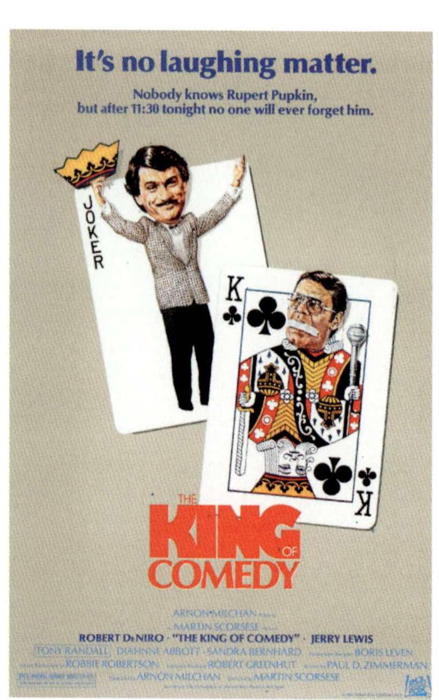

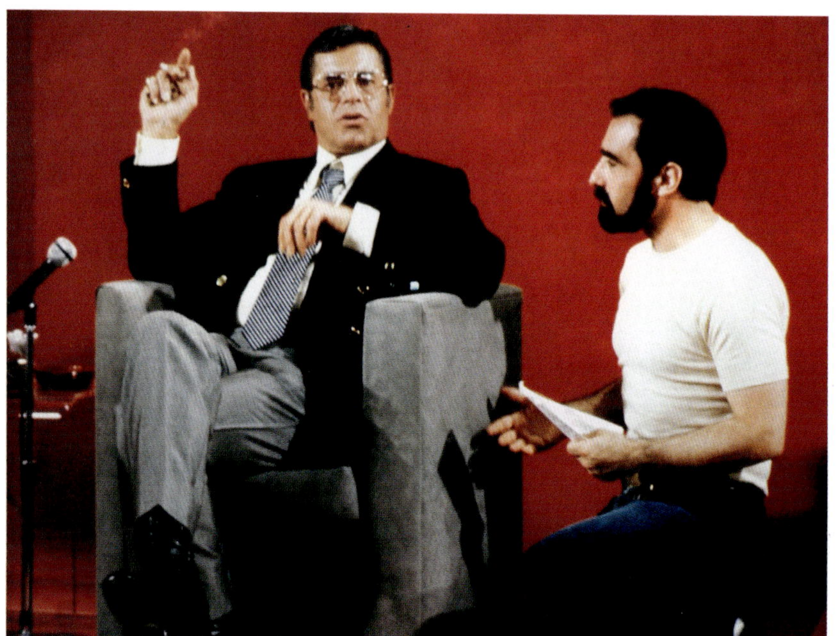

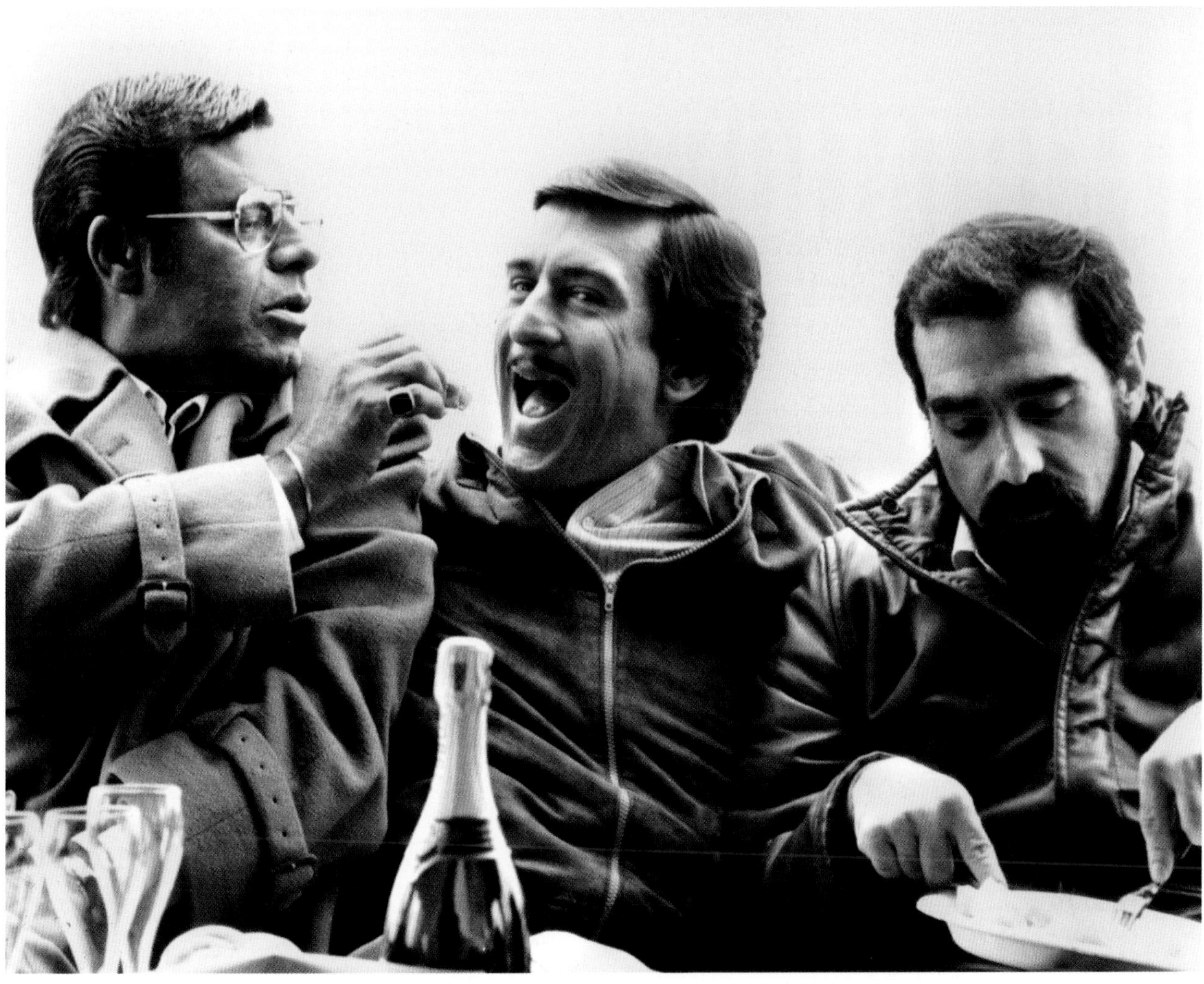

Above: *A close collaboration – Lewis and De Niro goof around during lunch, while Scorsese concentrates on refuelling himself. The champagne could be a Method thing.*

Like a hall of ironic mirrors, and the first hint of a meta-ingredient in Scorsese's work, *The King of Comedy* was reborn as a masterpiece (and source code for *The Joker*). As *Collider* believed that Pupkin, unravelling beneath the surface, is 'the most dangerous threat to society that Scorsese has ever put on screen.'[36] By the end, his crime has made him famous, with his own talk show and an offer for a film adaptation of his life. Or is this, like the disconcerting happy ending of *Taxi Driver*, potentially another product of an unstable mind? Either way, Pupkin is the herald for the insane celebrity culture of modern times.

The scene simply required Griffin Dunne to request his keys back from the bartender. But by now we are deep into an endless night, lost in an *Alice in Wonderland* Manhattan, with Martin Scorsese pursuing the dystopia of an anxiety dream. Keys prove key – jangling and jarring (how the sound edit rides our nerves), tossed from windows and left behind bars, keys are the central motif of *After Hours*: a symbol of both the unattainable safety of home and passage to the next instalment of peril awaiting Dunne's strung-out hero Paul Hackett.

Here's how it goes on set. Scorsese doesn't call cut. The scene just keeps going, with Dunne growing more and more desperate and John Heard's barkeep really getting into things, thumping and kicking an uncooperative till. After an eon, the director's voice is heard from the darkness behind the camera: 'I'm not going to stop shooting until you convince me you *want* those keys.'[1]

To be fair, Dunne had willingly employed all of Scorsese's suggestions in the pursuit of character, chief of which was to abstain from sex for weeks. *IndieWire* succinctly described his nebbish computer programmer as a 'desperately unlaid Freudian creature.'[2] Scorsese wanted that 'look of hunger,'[3] recalled his actor. The character's terrifying adventures through a New York underworld – part Kafka, part Dante, part Bickle – are driven by sexual impulse. Catholic punishments will be meted out on the horny sinner.

Dunne recalled *After Hours* as an epiphany for his director, 'because it brought him back to the urgency and passion he had when he made *Mean Streets* and *Taxi Driver*.'[4]

The when is important. In 1983, Scorsese's career was itself a succession of trials. Four days before cameras were due to turn on his $12 million passion project, *The Last Temptation of Christ*, based on the controversial novel by Nikos Kazantzakis, Paramount had pulled the plug. He was set to shoot in Israel, with Aidan Quinn as Christ. Sets were built, military helicopters placed at his disposal, Harvey Keitel had

Opposite: *Brief encounters – Griffin Dunne's hero Paul Hackett attempts a relaxing massage on Linda Fiorentino's sculptress Kiki in Martin Scorsese's ode to anxiety* After Hours *(1985).*

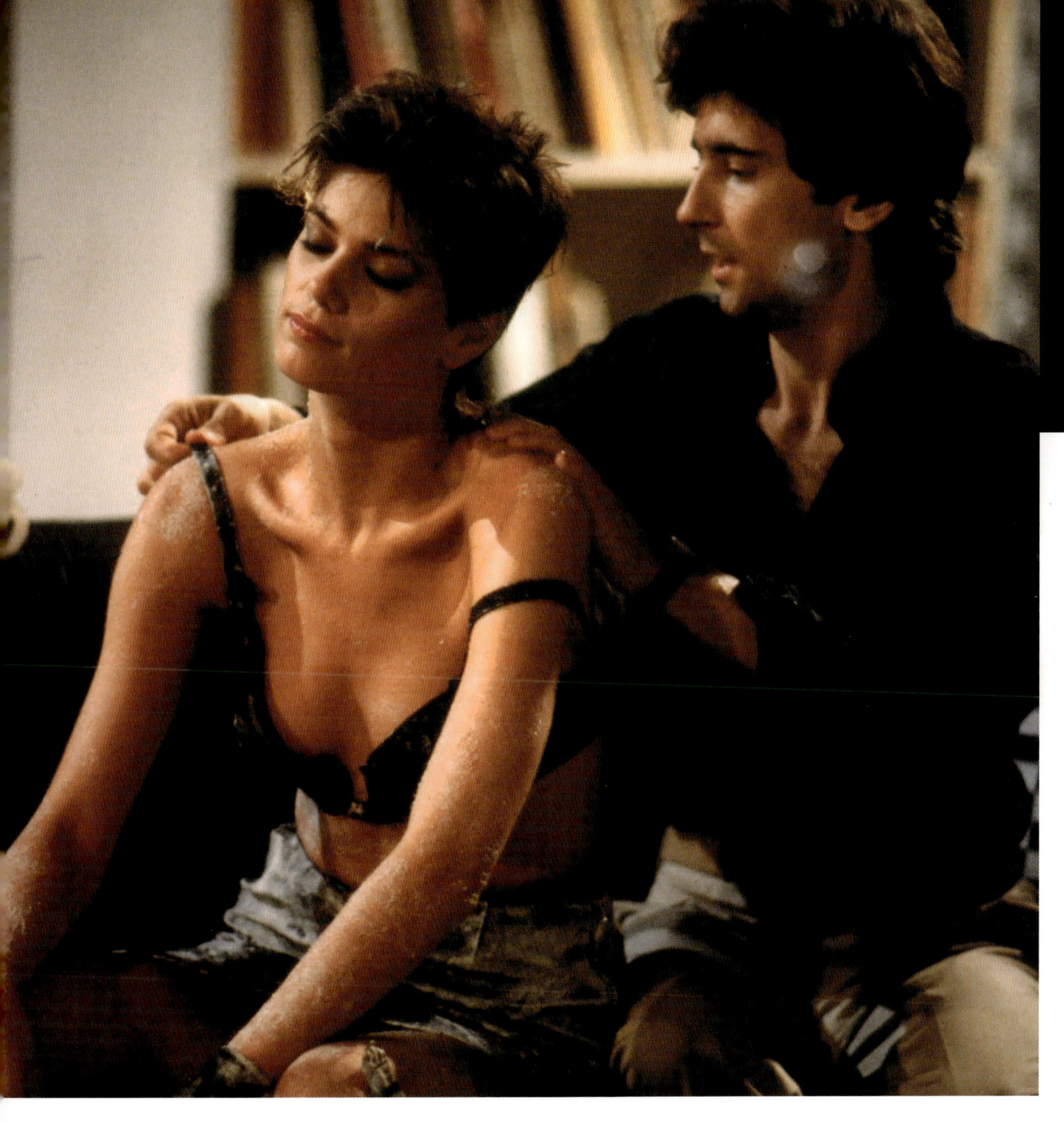

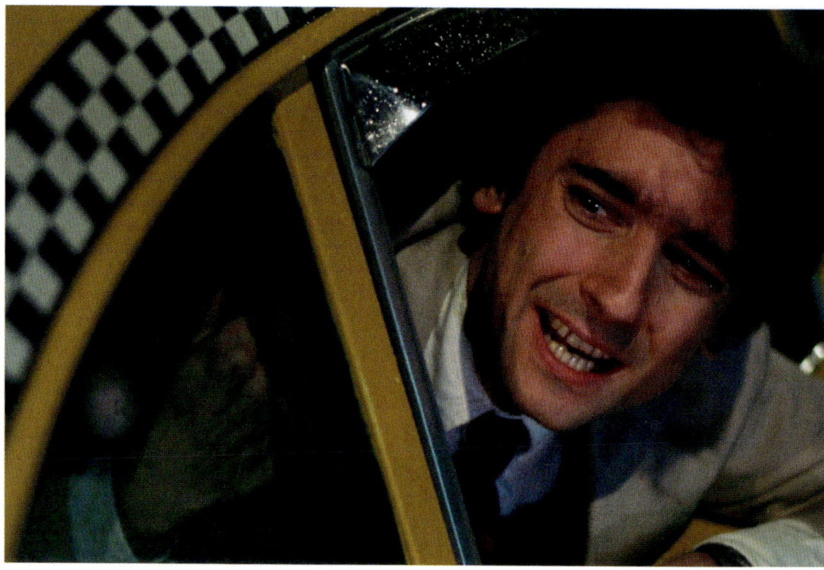

Right: *The Wimp of Wall Street – following his libido south, everyman Paul Hackett (Griffin Dunne) descends into a nightmare version of Manhattan. In its way,* After Hours *was a reflection of Martin Scorsese's endless struggles with Hollywood.*

dyed his hair red for Judas. Had there ever been a greenlight? The studio had been so evasive. We're fighting for your picture, he kept being told.

'Paramount's policy at the time was to be wary of "name" directors going way over budget,'[5] rued Scorsese. The *Heaven's Gate* affair had got everyone spooked, and filming in the Middle East was fraught with unknowns. He tried slashing the budget, halving the shooting schedule, but to no avail. The final straw came with the religious right, prophesying pure blasphemy in a depiction of Christ's human impulses, putting in furious calls to head office. Studio chief Barry Diller placed the irrevocable call to the director.

'We just don't want to make it.'[6]

Scorsese was knocked flat. His entire career was falling apart. After *The King of Comedy* had been lambasted as Flop of the Year by *Entertainment Tonight*, his commercial credibility was at an all-time low. It was as if his very talent spelled trouble. There were vague offers, but for production-line movies designated to restrain his passion: like *Beverly Hills Cop* (then a thriller to star Sylvester Stallone) or *Witness*. He genuinely didn't know if he was going to be able to get another film made. Not on his terms.

Could he ever just take a job, pay his way? 'Yes, I think I could,' he once mused, 'but then I would be taking the role of a real director. And I really don't want to be a director... I just want to be a filmmaker. An American filmmaker.'[7]

The script for *After Hours* had arrived a few weeks earlier via his lawyer. Known first as *Lies* and then *A Night in SoHo*, it was written by Joe Minion as his film school thesis at Columbia (gaining him an A), based in part on the radio monologue by Joe Frank. The rights had been picked up by Dunne in partnership with Amy Robinson (Teresa in *Mean Streets*), two actors-turned-producers determined to develop their own material. Scorsese was intrigued – it was a screwball comedy, black as a used match, but with this strangeness that felt real. He loved the initial encounter in the coffee shop between Paul and the kooky Marcy (Rosanna Arquette, first and most confounding of four blondes the hero will encounter), as he ostentatiously reads Henry Miller's *Tropic of Cancer* (the first signal that artistic pretension is a fool's errand) – the innocent (seeming) moment of attraction that propels him into the night. Scorsese was halfway through reading the scene before pausing to go upstairs in his apartment, attending to some forgotten chore. 'And I kept wandering about upstairs, wondering what was going on downstairs.'[8]

Paul will follow Marcy's temptation south of Hudson to the moonscape of SoHo and a spiralling nightmare where nothing and no one makes sense, his last $20 bill having been swept out of the cab window. An odyssey by no means limited to an S&M-leaning sculptress named Kiki (an icy Linda Fiorentino, who beat Madonna to the part), Heard's volatile barman (and Marcy's ex), an emotionally unstable blonde waitress (Teri Garr), Biblical downpours, flooded toilets, two jaunty burglars (Cheech Marin and Tommy Chong),

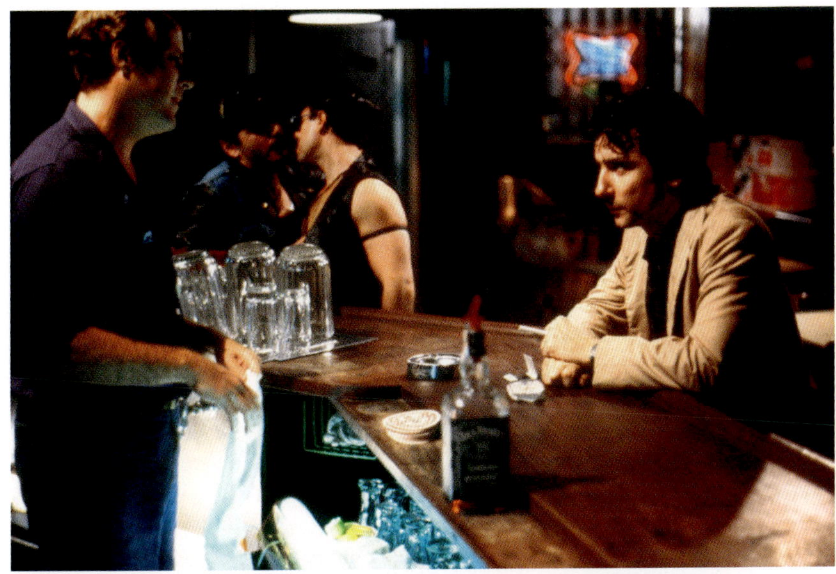

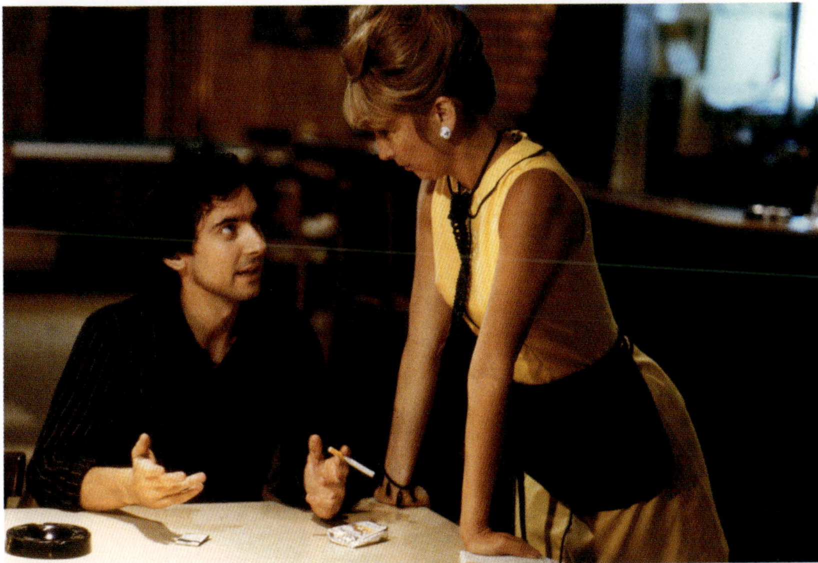

Top: *Paul finds temporary respite in The Terminal Bar, until John Heard's bartender proves that he is another part of the madness. For Scorsese the film spoke to a universal sense of panic – that the world is against us.*

Above: *Teri Garr's initially sweet-natured waitress Julie is one of four consciously Hitchcockian blondes tempting the hero out of his comfortable life.*

a malicious blonde ice cream vendor (Catherine O'Hara), and Marcy switching grooves from dream girl to femme fatale to corpse. Paul ends up hounded by a mob of vigilante homosexuals, and finally encased in plaster, driven away at daybreak as a living statue.

'If *Taxi Driver* was a paranoid man who believed that the city had turned against him, then *After Hours* is about an ordinary man to whom it is proved that the city has indeed done that very thing,'[9] declared Chris Peachment in *Time Out*.

At the time, with Christ's sufferings still occupying his attention Scorsese had, regretfully, passed, leaving a fledgling Tim Burton to sign on – and you can see how the story might thrive within his comic-horror mode. That was not to be. When Scorsese came sprinting back around the street corner, Burton gracefully bowed out.

Having been cast out of paradise, in desperation (he needed to get creatively laid, so to speak), Scorsese returned to the possibilities of *After Hours*: here was an independent film promising next to no budget ($4.5 million), returning him to the heartland of Manhattan. He would have to shoot fast, think on his feet. He recognized that his films had been taking too long, *he* was taking too long. He needed to free himself from his artistic pretensions. And quite frankly, he needed the money. Besides which, he saw his own studio predicaments writ large in Paul's phantasmagoria: the film is equally comedy and 'cri de cœur'[10] from a stranded artist. Dunne even resembled a handsome younger Scorsese.

'I actually kinda identified with the character at that point,'[11] confirmed the director. He was living in a converted shoe factory in the Tribeca branch of SoHo. The sound of the streets was comforting. As was the clicking of fifteen VCRs, recording a comprehensive list of films from the television schedule. Scorsese also recognized that this script spoke to an existential panic in all of us. Forty years later, it remains his last original story. One that was neither an adaptation, remake, sequel, or variation on a biopic. It was born purely as a movie.

Production got underway on 19 July 1984, roving at speed through the chilly SoHo of the early eighties, this ghost ship of Lower Manhattan. Scorsese decreed they would shoot entirely between dusk and dawn – even the interiors. Dunne remembered 'living like a vampire.'[12] German cinematographer Michael Ballhaus was chosen for his speed and European idiosyncrasy. He had been Rainer Fassbinder's man (and was Max Ophüls' nephew), with a gift for enhancing existing light sources. They were up to seventeen set-ups a day – the effect is a neurotic reality. Production designer Jeffrey Townsend emphasized hidden parts of the frame, a labyrinth of doorways, stairwells, and fire escapes. At the heart of the maze, The Terminal Bar has the fish-tank timelessness of the joints in *Mean Streets*.

Yuppie-in-peril movies were all the rage (a trajectory from *Miracle Mile* to *Something Wild*), but Scorsese naturally finds a deeper, edgier, more personal way to go, a breath away from film noir. Anxiety

Below: *Rosanna Arquette stars as Marcy, whose slippery allure first encourages Paul to venture to SoHo. Everything in the film is framed through the prism of his anxiety.*

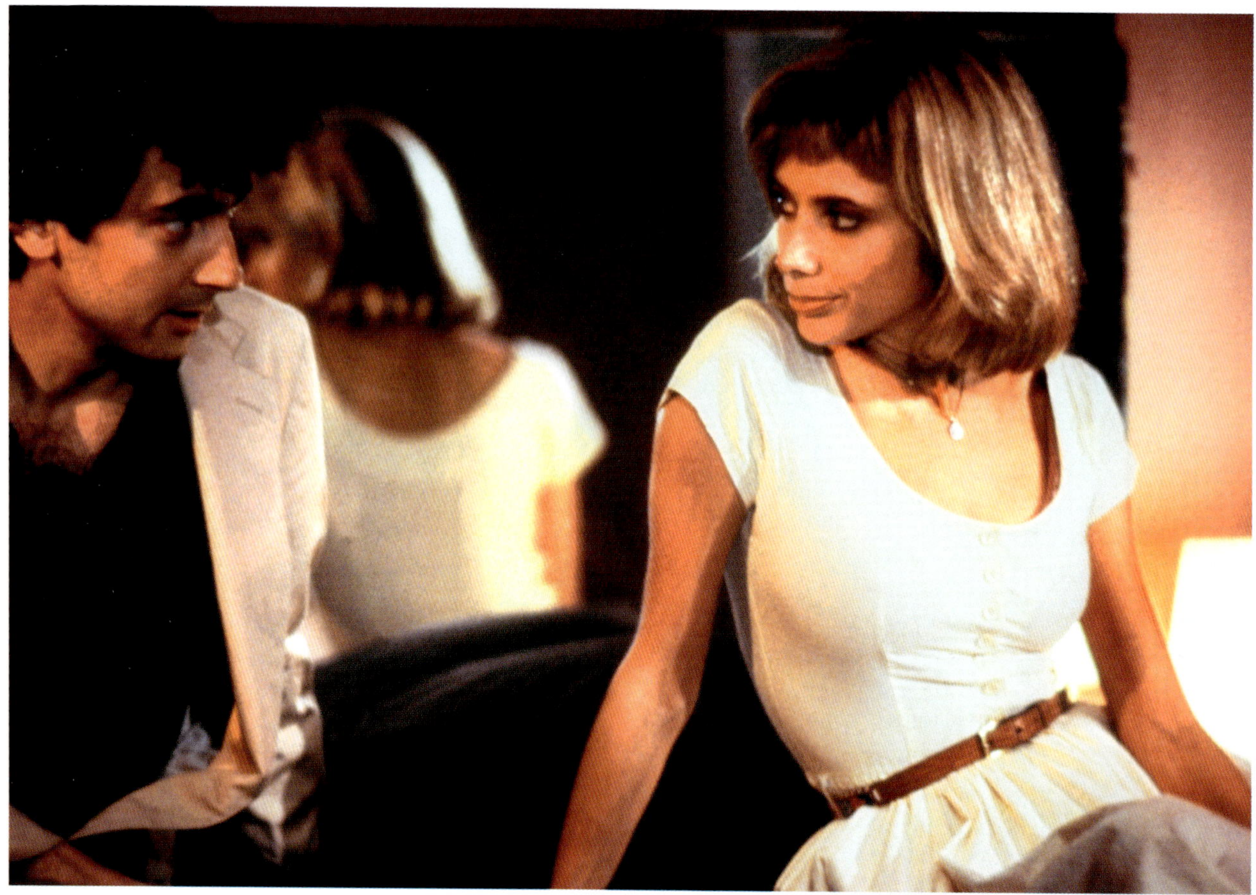

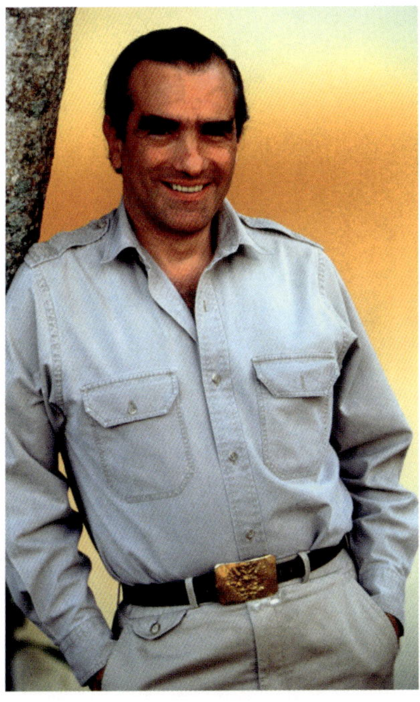

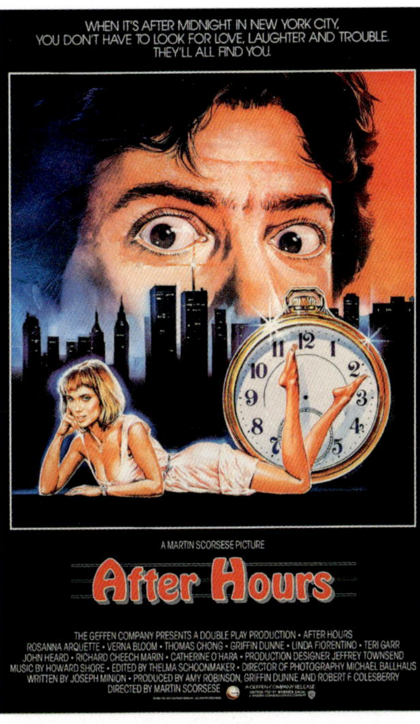

Far left: *Working with limited means, and back on the streets of New York, Martin Scorsese found making* After Hours *a cathartic experience.*

Left: *The black comedy was a moderate hit on its release, but has since developed a cult following, and even become a sub-genre of New York nightmares.*

becomes style, a reflection of character, director, and a New York caught between the neon criminality of the seventies and the yuppie insurgence and arty influx of the new decade. Scorsese would have glass boxes made with a brick to hand; the shattering sound had the actors reeling. The worse things got for Paul, the more the director laughed. Dunne recalled dashing round the block, into a real bar, buying the house a drink, dashing out again before paying (the ADs would settle his bill), then sprinting back *into* the scene. Bereft of backstory, he tunes his performance to borderline hysteria, constantly out of breath, a rational man confronting the irrational. Is this what it is like to go mad?

Scorsese called upon the screwball operatics of Preston Sturges, the feisty brio of Howard Hawks, the gleaming streets of *The Third Man*, and – not for the last time – the tricks Hitchcock played with keys, watches, telephones, and light switches filling the frame. Objects become sentient things, the world tactile. Can we spy a mirage of Scorsese's three failed marriages (to date) in the trio of Hitchcockian blondes (most notably Arquette's quicksilver Marcy), before a final mother figure, with Verna Bloom's June, who offers Paul sanctuary?

He added the direct reference to Kafka, lifting dialogue from *Before the Law*, the short story embedded in *The Trial*, about a man who seeks the law but is consistently denied by a doorkeeper. Entry is possible, he is told, but it is just not the right time. Welcome to Hollywood. Furthering the Mitteleuropean chill, such Kafka rhetoric comes from the bouncer of the Club Berlin wearing a Checkpoint Charlie t-shirt. Inside, amid a frenzy of Mohawks (another tribe to which Paul does not belong), Scorsese cameos in a real Russian officer's uniform sweeping the dance-floor with a spotlight.

'*After Hours* could be called a "hypertext" film,' decided Roger Ebert in the *Chicago Sun-Times*, 'in which disparate elements of the plot are associated in an occult way.'[13]

The symbolic possibilities of classical storytelling are let loose among the avenues of New York. Kiki's statue of a tormented man, cowering like a Pompeiian victim, becomes Paul's spiritual double. The hero is buffeted from Siren call to baying mob. It's all here in Scorsese's divine comedy: the poet Orpheus venturing into the Underworld, Joyce's Nighttown, Dante's rings of Hell (Marcy's bedtime reading is a book of burn scars). Paul finally falls to his knees in the street and cries out to the God who has abandoned him. 'I'm just a word processor, for Christ's sake.'[14]

Here too is Scorsesean mythology. That is the same King Kong Cabs emblem from Travis Bickle's jacket on the sleeve of O'Hara's deranged purveyor of Mister

1986
AMAZING STORIES (TV Series, 1 episode) Director

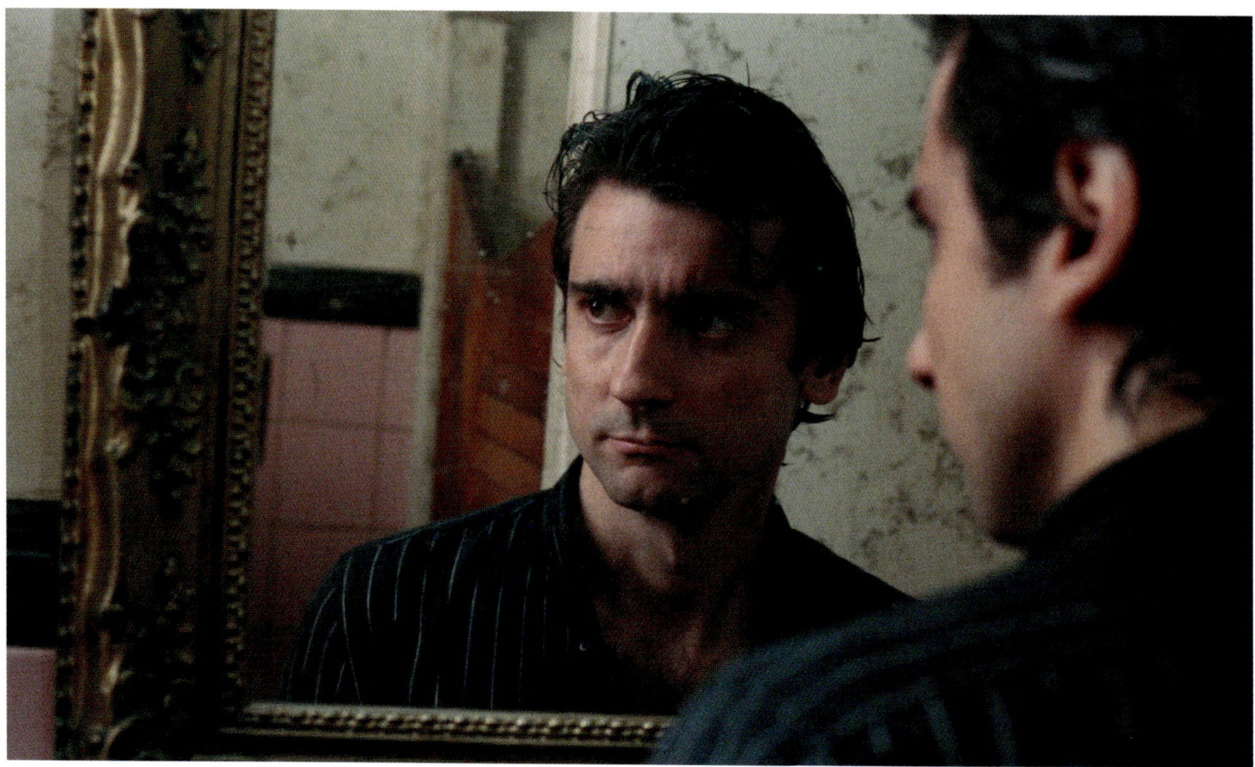

Above: *Mirror, mirror – in* After Hours, *Griffin Dunne's Paul effectively embarks on a journey to discover his identity, one of the central themes of the Martin Scorsese canon.*

Softee. Yellow and black dominate the film's colour code, beginning with the cab that has ferried Paul with furious haste to his doom, the driver a scowling Charon. A hyper-real gamesmanship that will return in *The Departed* and *Shutter Island*.

Ideas circulated for how to draw the nightmare to a fitting close. Scorsese was in favour of Paul remaining in the thieves' van, stuck fast in plaster (a man trapped in art), but that infuriated the test audience. An alternative, storyboarded ending in which Paul literally hides within June's expanded womb had producer David Geffen wondering if the director had lost his mind. It was friend and adviser Michael Powell who suggested the symmetry of Paul simply returning to work, where it all began, smeared in deathly plaster, the gates opening to let him in once more.

'That's the key thing to me – the idea of being a pawn, that the gods really don't care and we've got to make a life in spite of that,'[15] concluded Scorsese. We keep going.

After Hours would win him Best Director in Cannes, and the returns were modest but, on this budget, modestly successful. Pauline Kael may have denounced Dunne as a 'second-rate Dudley Moore,'[16] but an avid cult has swelled around Scorsese's dark night of the soul. We see its funny-scary bandwidth replayed in the Safdie brothers' *Good Time* and Ari Aster's *Beau Is Afraid*. Scorsese was invigorated. Reborn you might say, with a new sense of purpose and discipline. And with that, a new day dawned in Hollywood. It was a case, he laughed philosophically, of 'you can let him in the room again.'[17]

And so they did. *The Color of Money* is Scorsese's first and arguably only true star vehicle, originating with Paul Newman, who would receive an overdue Best Actor Oscar for his part. Alongside him is an ascendant Tom Cruise, and this mentor-pupil partnership delivered a considerable hit ($52 million in America alone). Scorsese's presence often gets forgotten. It was a new way of working, going toe-to-toe with a heavyweight like Newman. With Scorsese, we don't tend to think in terms of actors, we think about characters. With De Niro it was almost symbiotic; the shared New York DNA. This was different.

A fan of *Raging Bull*, Newman had put in a call. His pitch was a sequel, of sorts, to Robert Rossen's *The Hustler*, picking up twenty-five years later with Newman's iconic pool shark 'Fast Eddie' Felson. As far as Newman was concerned, Eddie was a perfect fit for Scorsese's realm of flawed heroes. He had a script ready in which the ageing Eddie runs a pool hall and meditates on an ill-spent past in flashback. As far as Scorsese was concerned, as much as he adored the black-and-white original, he would rather stick to his own material. 'I had a lot of reservations about it,' he recalled. 'I felt that it was a literal sequel.'[18]

The only way he could generate the right measure of enthusiasm was to begin again from scratch, bringing in streetwise novelist Richard Price (*Bloodbrothers*) to develop the script. It was a three-way process, with director, star, and writer meeting at Newman's Malibu beach house, waves crashing against the shore as they imagined the hardscrabble gambits of the Midwestern pool scene. Between sessions, Price would hang out with real hustlers, getting a feel for their closed-circuit subculture and snake-oil argot. For Scorsese, it was all about getting the character of Eddie to work: he needed the old meanness, a sense of loss, but remain likeable. They were writing a film to fit the wizened glamour of Newman.

Below left: *The fame game – Paul Newman and Tom Cruise provided two generations of stardom for* The Color of Money *(1986). This is arguably the film least synonymous with Scorsese.*

Below right: *Scorsese resisted making what he saw as a plain sequel to* The Hustler *(1961), instead exploring ideas about age and American life.*

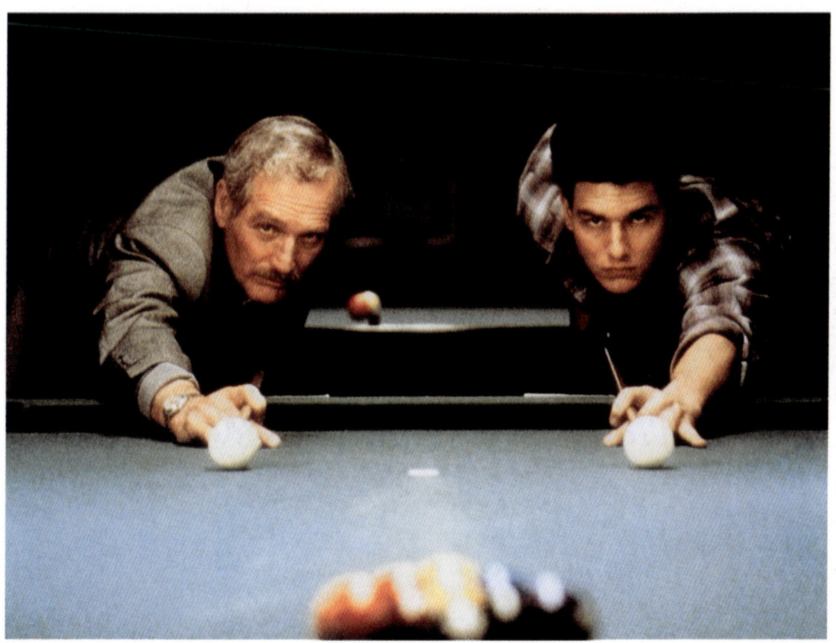

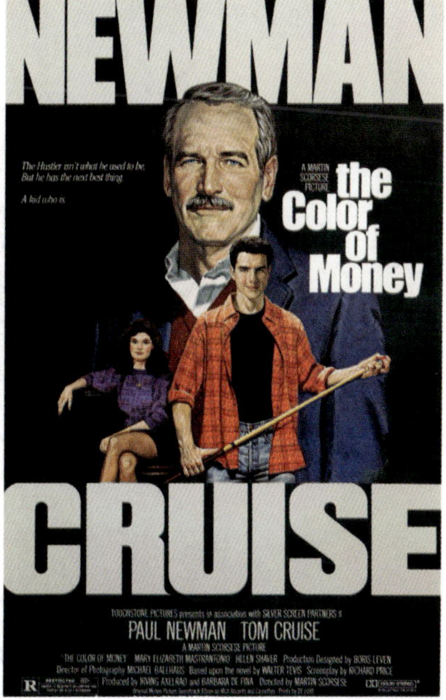

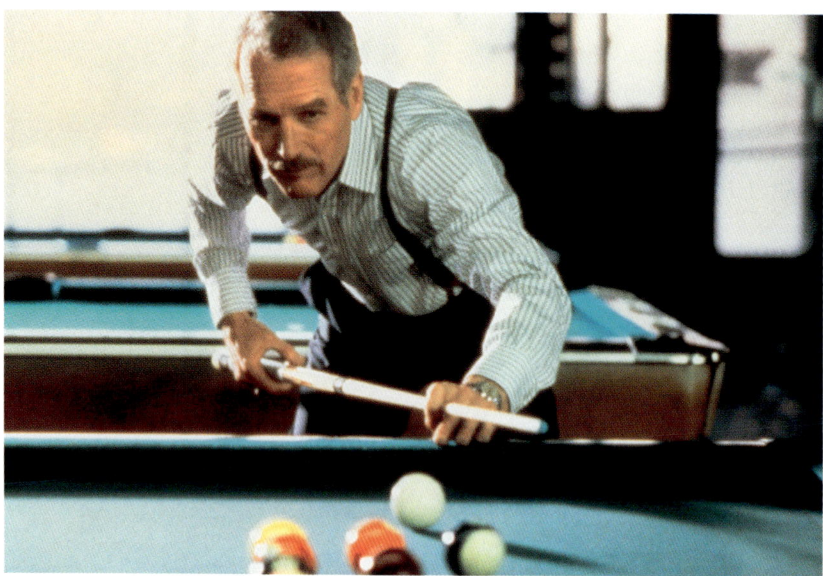

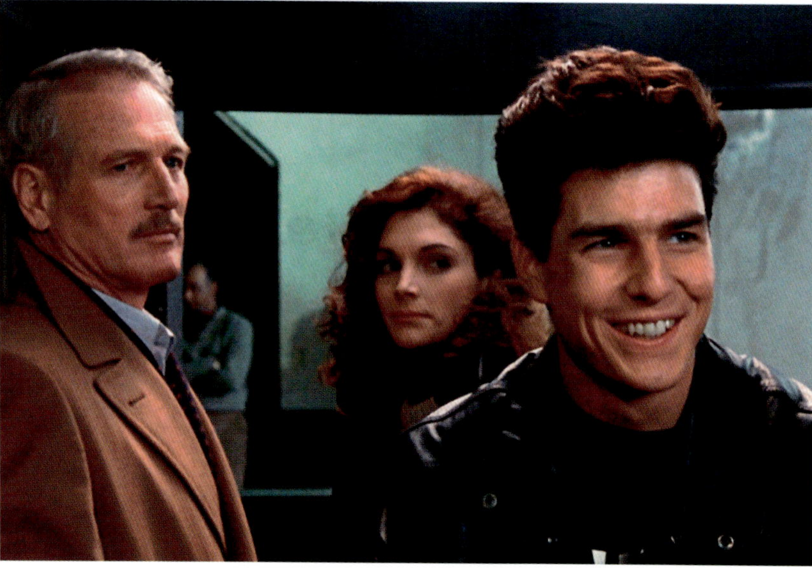

Top: *Paul Newman had specifically sought out Martin Scorsese to direct* The Color of Money, *certain he would understand the texture of edgy characters like Eddie Felson...*

Above: *...a feeling borne out in Scorsese approaching this as a film as much about the relationships between Eddie (Newman), Vincent (Tom Cruise), and Vincent's girlfriend Carmen (Mary Elizabeth Mastrantonio), as playing pool.*

'We're making a three-piece suit for the man,' Scorsese told Price. 'He's the main character and the reason we're involved in this thing. He's got to look a certain way and the words have to come through his vocal cords.'[19]

The title was taken from another book by Walter Tevis, author of *The Hustler*, but the plot was left behind. It was a sequel at a slant. The only common ground with the original was Eddie, now out of the game, making a decent living dealing booze from his white Cadillac. Then he spies a young, cocky talent, and the opportunity that comes with him.

This was an older man's search for redemption – a familiar theme. Eddie sees himself through the prism of Cruise's Vincent, brash with ability, but naïve. Eddie sets about educating the kid, corrupting him to turn the posturing on or off at will and put the making of money above every other temptation. What Scorsese made is a dark-hearted *Rocky*. At some point this taut apprenticeship will come to a boil, a situation made more complex by the presence of Carmen, Vincent's savvy, older girlfriend (Mary Elizabeth Mastrantonio quietly giving the performance of the film).

If Newman was the steely-eyed glower of classicism, then Cruise was the future. He had *Risky Business* behind him (Scorsese cited *All the Right Moves*), and *Top Gun* in the can. The uncorked smile, pompadour hair, and the sheer vivacious strut of a young man on the cusp of superstardom elevated Scorsese to an unusual place. The *Color of Money* may be the first of his films that a studio understood.

Not that it was smooth sailing: the project bounced from Fox to Columbia to Disney, where it was picked up by Michael Eisner and Jeffrey Katzenberg, formerly of Paramount and two of the

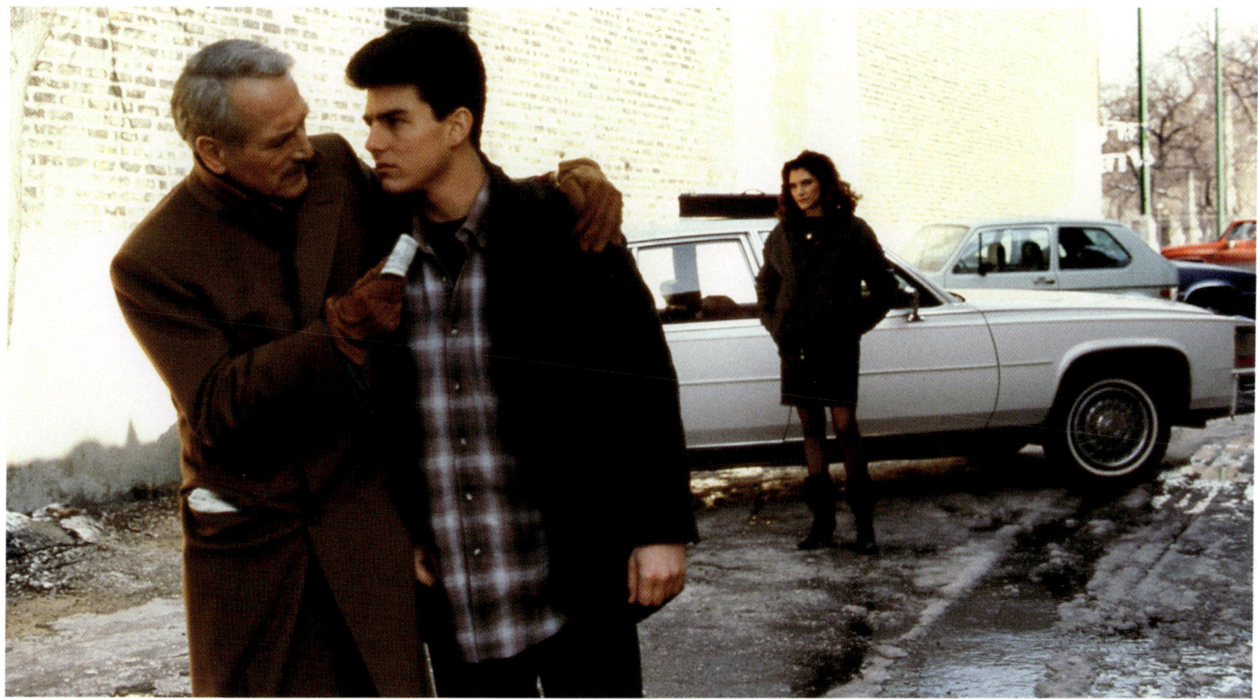

executives who had led him a merry dance with *The Last Temptation of Christ*. Production was a relative breeze. Following two weeks of rehearsal (at Newman's behest, unnerving Scorsese), they shot through a mild Chicago winter, where the pool halls carried an authentic timbre. Such was Scorsese's newfound discipline that they came in a week ahead of schedule and a million under budget. 'That's the stuff sainthood is made of in Hollywood,'[20] he laughed.

The pool scenes were choreographed and covered in three days flat. They had top players to advise on trick shots and tactics, with Newman and Cruise good enough to pull off the action before the lens (only the ball-leaping trick was executed by Michael Sigel to save on time). There is a gleeful counterpoint to the drama in the way Scorsese and Thelma Schoonmaker edit the montages – a sense of cutting loose, like the rush of a dance number, Cruise howling along to the needle drop of Warren Zevon's *Werewolves of London* (is it playing in the venue or in Vincent's head?) intercut with Newman's Easter Island scowl. They are surges of talent, camera and pool cue, just as the ring scenes were the arias of *Raging Bull*.

'It doesn't have the electricity, the wound-up tension, of his best work,'[21] grumbled Roger Ebert, for once nonplussed by his friend's latest. The word generic was bandied about by critics. Perhaps so, but *The Color of Money* is the definitive film on pool as a way of life, and another American underworld peeled open by Scorsese's perspicacious eye. The only lesson he drew from his first outright hit since *Taxi Driver*, ten years before, was that he must remain true to himself and return to that career-threatening itch, *The Last Temptation of Christ*.

Above: *The film was shot during an unseasonably mild winter in Chicago, venturing into the authentic pool halls, and striving for that trademark Scorsesean candour.*

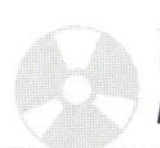

1987

MICHAEL JACKSON: BAD (Music Video) Director

Where did it come from, this obsession with portraying the last days of Christ on the big screen? Was it simply the mirror it held to his inner turmoil - the failed priest who yearned for the movies? He had imagined making 'a black and white *cinéma vérité* version of the Gospels.'[22] That was until he caught Pier Pasolini's 'wonderful,'[23] almost newsreel-styled *Gospel According to St Matthew*, and knew he must tack a different course.

The answer came with Kazantzakis' 600-page novel, given to him by Barbara Hershey while shooting *Boxcar Bertha*. He took six years to finish it, savouring every word, deeply moved by its daring. That the Greek writer approached the substance of Christ from two vantage points: 'Jesus as human and Jesus as divine.'[24]

Scorsese and Kazantzakis were kindred spirits in their way: the writer had been excommunicated from the Greek Orthodox Church, and his novel forbidden by the Vatican as heretical, because it imagined a Christ with human hungers, not least sexual. *The Last Temptation* of the title has Satan offering him the chance to come down from the Cross, marry Mary Magdalene (to be played by Hershey in the adaptation) and live as an ordinary man.

While this is the first of Scorsese's faith pictures, his signature remains the same: find the reality in the mythical and the transcendent in the worldly. His Christ is as rough-hewn and anguished as Charlie from *Mean Streets* or Travis Bickle. The film's introduction also makes it abundantly clear that this is a 'fictional exploration.'[25] Which placated exactly no one.

Scorsese's saviour was the unlikely figure of Michael Ovitz, head of the massive Hollywood agency CAA, who had brokered the deals for *The Color of Money* and was now representing the director.

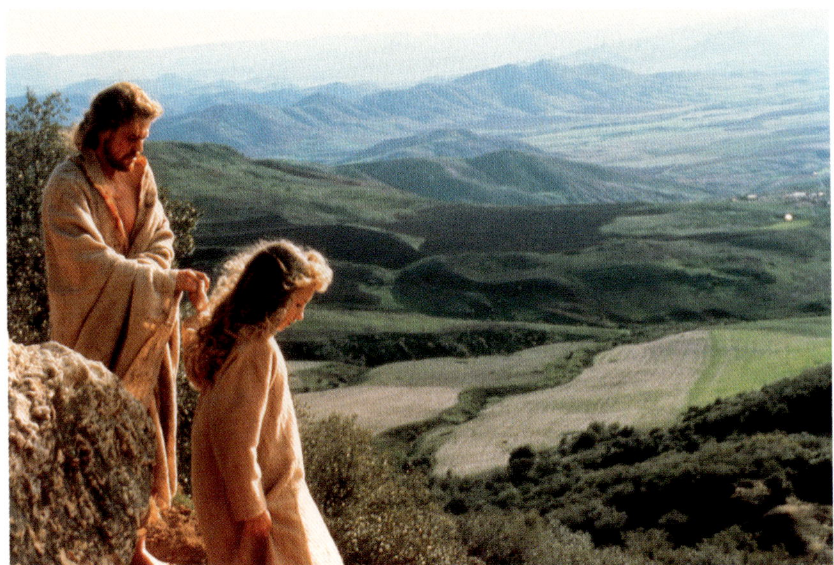

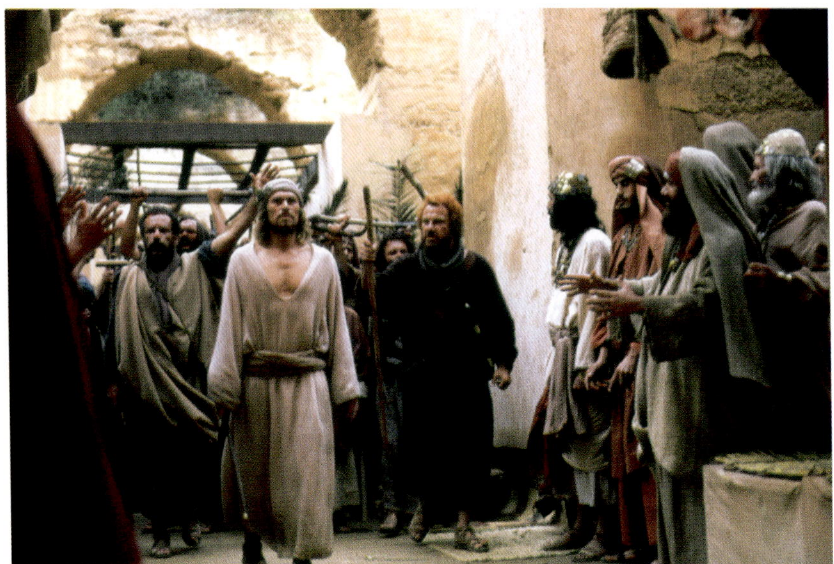

Top: The Last Temptation of Christ *was both a passion project and a millstone for Martin Scorsese, something he had to get made and out of his system, despite Hollywood's trepidations.*

Above: *Willem Dafoe replaced Aidan Quinn in the lead role, after Scorsese became enamoured with the timelessness of his face.*

They had met at the agent's sprawling neo-Georgian in Brentwood Park.

'What do you want to do the most?' enquired Ovitz.

Scorsese looked him in the eye and replied, '*The Last Temptation of Christ*.'

Ovitz didn't blink. 'I'll get that made for you.'[26]

He returned with a potential deal at Universal, though Scorsese still had to pitch to studio head Tom Pollock.

The script had been evolving. It is credited to Paul Schrader, who wrote the Paramount-era drafts (he and Scorsese had discussed the novel as early as *Taxi Driver*), paring the book down to ninety pages and straightening the portentous dialogue. Still fraying against his Calvinist upbringing, Schrader included descriptions of an erotic kiss with John the Baptist and Christ's disciples literally drinking his blood. Even as he toned things down, he knew they were going to have trouble.

As permutations came and went, and potential backers disappeared, Jay Cocks helped the director rewrite the film with a more indie-movie inflection – the life of Christ on a street level. Scorsese looked to be more immediate, 'so people have a sense of who these guys were, not out of a book or a painting, but as if they lived and spoke right now.'[27]

Allowing the actors to keep their accents proved a distracting choice. The apostles are tough guys who worked with their hands, protested Scorsese, but there

Below: *Bible class – Victor Argo as Peter, Dafoe as Jesus, and Harvey Keitel as Judas attempt to humanize venerated (and not-so-venerated) names.*

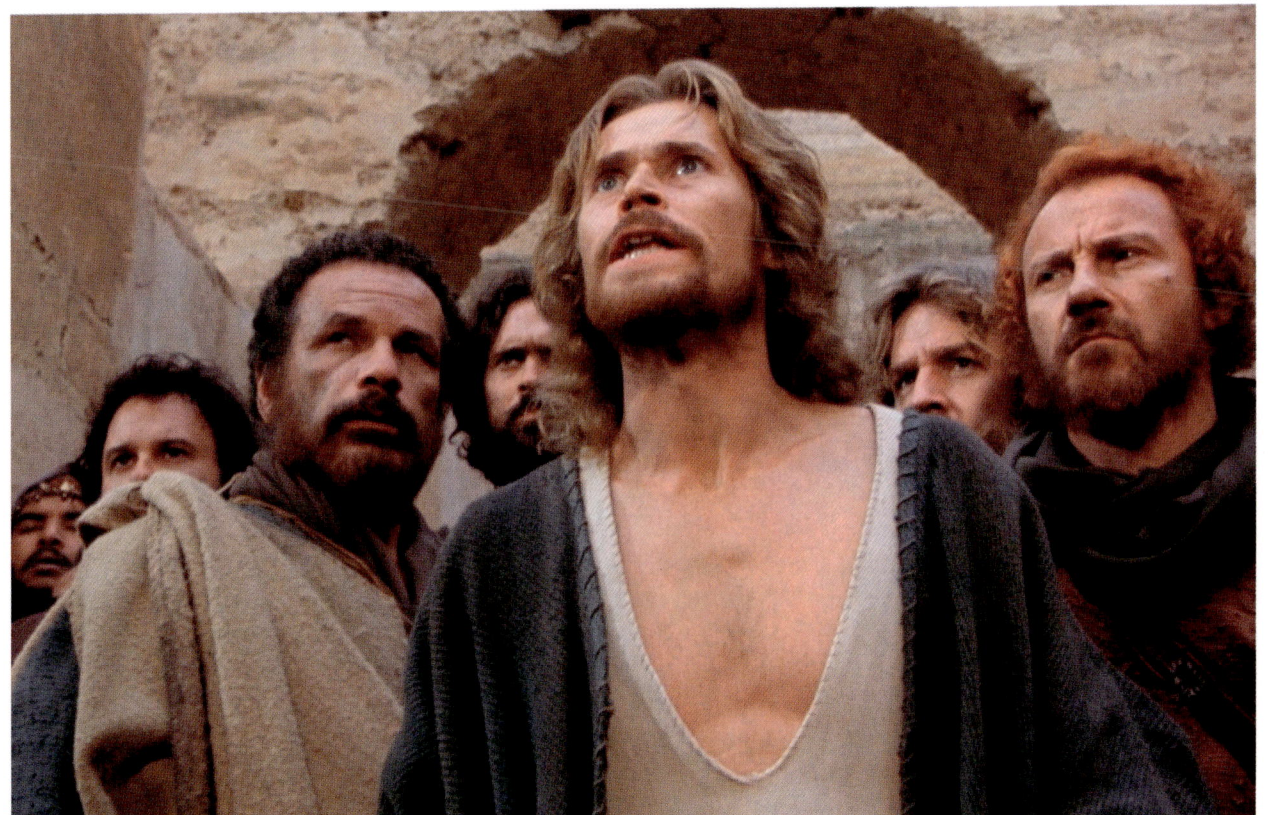

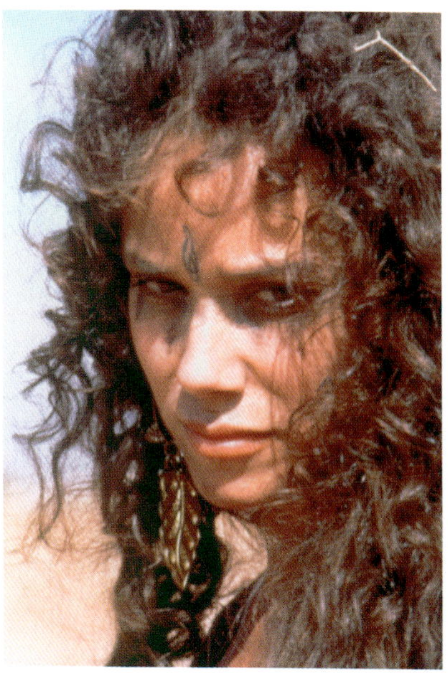

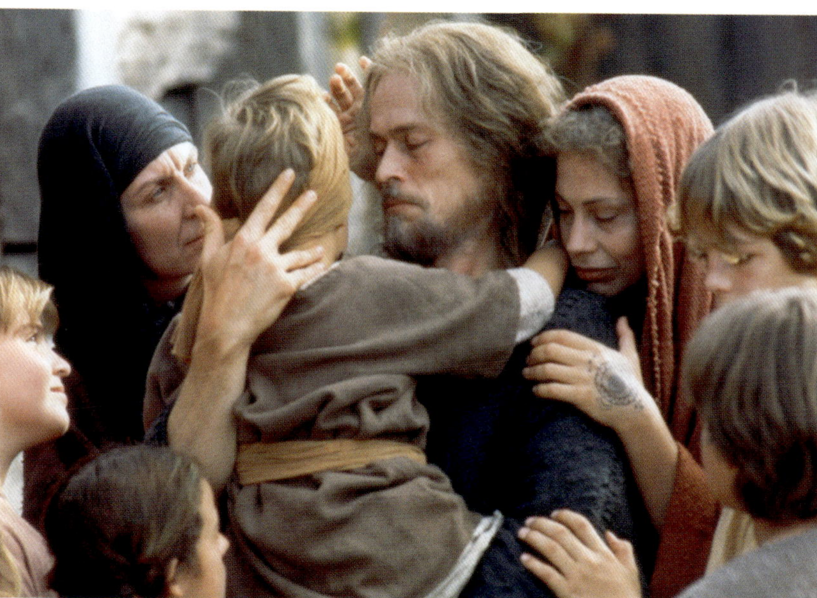

is something inescapably goofy about the thick Brooklyn accent on Victor Argo's Peter. He would walk about set with a stogie between his teeth, griping when Scorsese called for him to join the scene: 'I have to lose the cigar, right?'[28] The overall feel is surprisingly uneven, with David Bowie (replacing Sting) especially mannered as Pontius Pilate.

Keitel is more reliable, beneath his copper thatch, another villain given a heartbeat. Of course, betrayal is a classic Scorsese riff, and he rises to the chance to portray the parallel journey of the revolutionary Judas, and the contradiction (the lifeblood of Scorsesean drama) that he was necessary. 'Nobody's to be blamed, nobody's to be cursed,'[29] insisted Scorsese. Judas is part of the sacrificial plan.

With Quinn detained making *Crusoe* for Caleb Deschanel, Scorsese turned to Willem Dafoe (over Christopher Walken and Eric Roberts) as his lead, impressed by his performance in *Platoon*, drawn to that Renaissance face. The actor remembered the call from his agent with the news that Martin Scorsese wanted him for *The Last Temptation of Christ*.

'Really?' he replied. 'What role?'[30]

He had thought they were mad, but when he read the script it made sense. This human slant. 'I'm the guy to do this,'[31] he said. In *The Spectator*, Hilary Mantel was sceptical about Dafoe's 'trance-like enunciation,'[32] but we begin to wonder if this is just a man losing his mind.

The start still comes as a shock, with Scorsese's prowling camera far from home, seeking out Christ asleep in the olive grove. The director filmed in Morocco (where tensions still circled the two-month production) from October 1987, and amid the dust and heat and in the shadow of the Atlas Mountains, imagined he was making a Western. Shots were borrowed from John Ford and Anthony Mann. While backed by Universal, at $7 million it remained a low-budget film. Scorsese had to move fast. They would set up before dawn, readying themselves for first light. The rushes were

Above left: *Barbara Hershey as Mary Magdalene – Martin Scorsese kept faith with the actress who had introduced him to the novel while shooting* Boxcar Bertha *in 1971.*

Above right: *The controversy, which began even before the film was made, surrounded the central concept of depicting Jesus as both the Son of God and a human being.*

Opposite: *After exploring the possibility of shooting in Israel, Scorsese opted to film* The Last Temptation of Christ *in Morocco, but still under intense scrutiny and threat.*

sent back to Schoonmaker in New York, with Scorsese demanding how things looked over long-distance calls.

Everything is contained within the nexus of magic and life. Michael Ballhaus' camerawork presents the Holy Land with the street-sharp insistence of Scorsese's early New York films. Peter Gabriel's score is a vibrant mix of mysticism and twanging guitars. The torture scenes are visceral. Scorsese is reaching for the sensory – agonies made real. They shot the Crucifixion in a tumult of sixty set-ups a day. Dafoe was raised on the cross (on an invisible stool) for five-minute spells. And in a flash it was done with – this forbidden film.

'I expected some controversy. But I expected it to be intelligent. I expected discussion and dialogue,'[33] said Scorsese.

With the film made, he was met with a howl of outrage and misinformation. Based on a leaked version of Schrader's early draft, headlines claimed the film depicted Christ as a homosexual. Religious groups took up their pitchforks again, demonstrations were mounted, and cinemas picketed all over the world. Republican senators called for the boycott of Universal. The Catholic Church called for its members to keep away. It was banned in Israel and in Kazantzakis' Greek homeland (alongside the novel). Four major American cinema chains refused to show it. Under increasing pressure, Universal stood by the film, craftily slipping it into cinemas a month early to fool the mob. Within its limited release, it made them no more than $8 million.

> “I expected some controversy. But I expected it to be intelligent. I expected discussion and dialogue.
>
> MARTIN SCORSESE

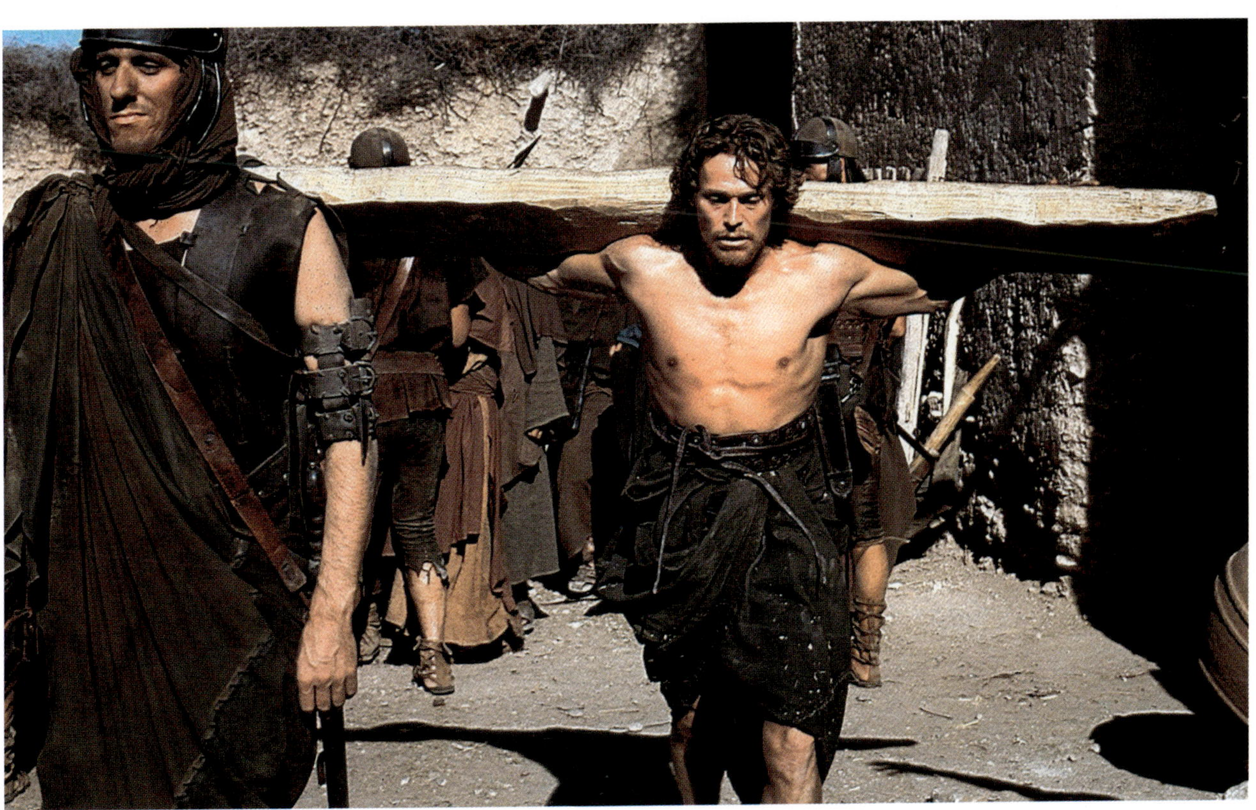

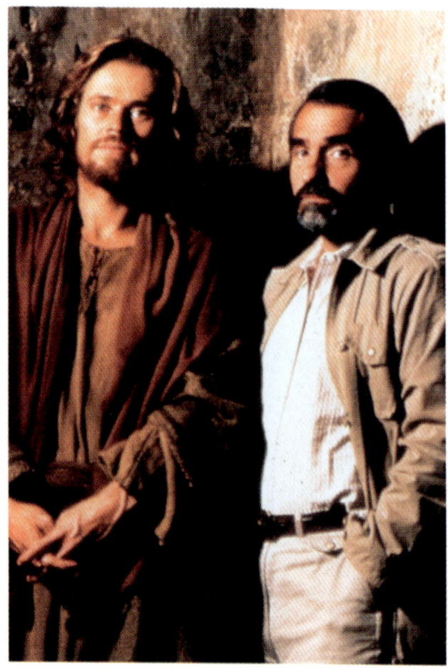

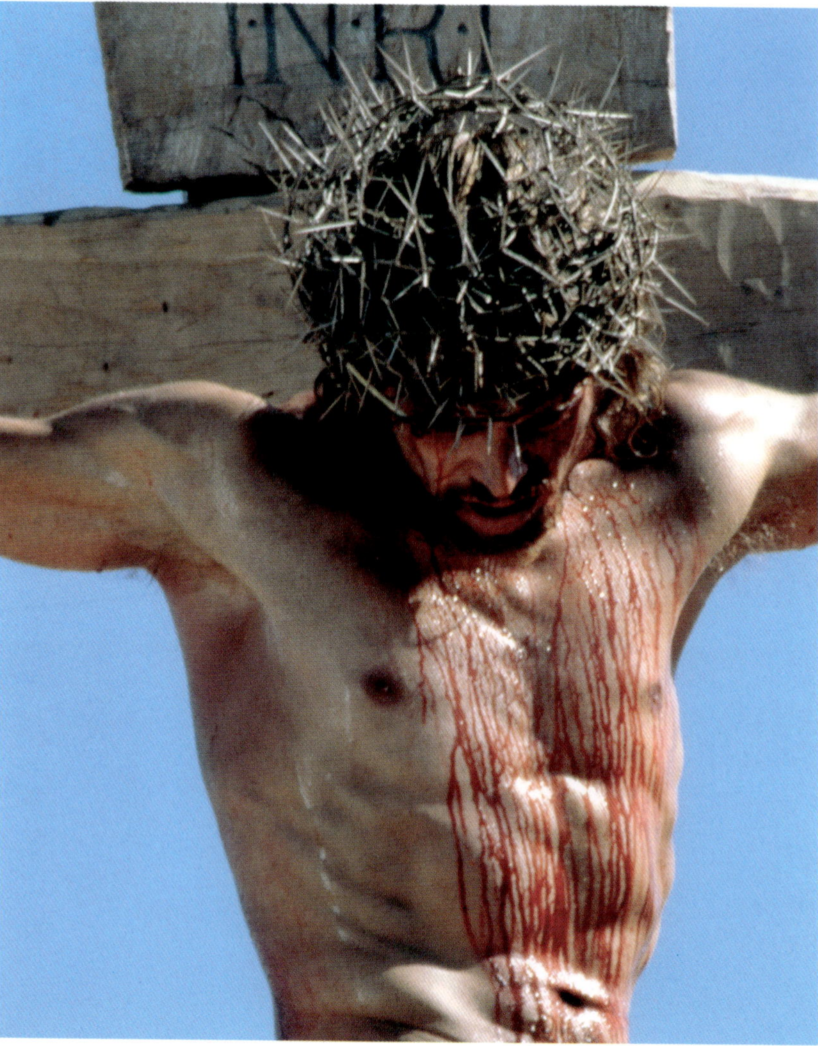

Above: *The nature of faith – Willem Dafoe and a tanned Martin Scorsese pose for a publicity shot on the set of* The Last Temptation of Christ.

Right: *A thorny subject – the Crucifixion was created through a flurry of set-ups, with Scorsese reaching for a mix of the almost supernatural and a visceral realism.*

Had it all been all worthwhile? Today, it's viewed as a lesser film in the canon. Critics made passionate defences of Scorsese's artistic freedom: 'At the bottom of the controversy is an intense, utterly sincere, frequently fascinating piece of art,'[34] asserted Sheila Benson in the *Los Angeles Times*. But there were equal snorts that this lengthy, humourless Biblical sojourn was not far off *The Life of Brian*. 'The movie has such an insistent, serious tone that you may get a bad case of church giggles,'[35] warned Michael Sragow in the *San Francisco Examiner*. Even Scorsese admitted that he might have laid the Catholic symbolism on a bit thick. According to biographer Tom Shone, there is something too obvious in the match of material and director, leaving subtext to wither in the desert sun. 'Scorsese didn't need to make a film about Christ – he had already made it, many times.'[36]

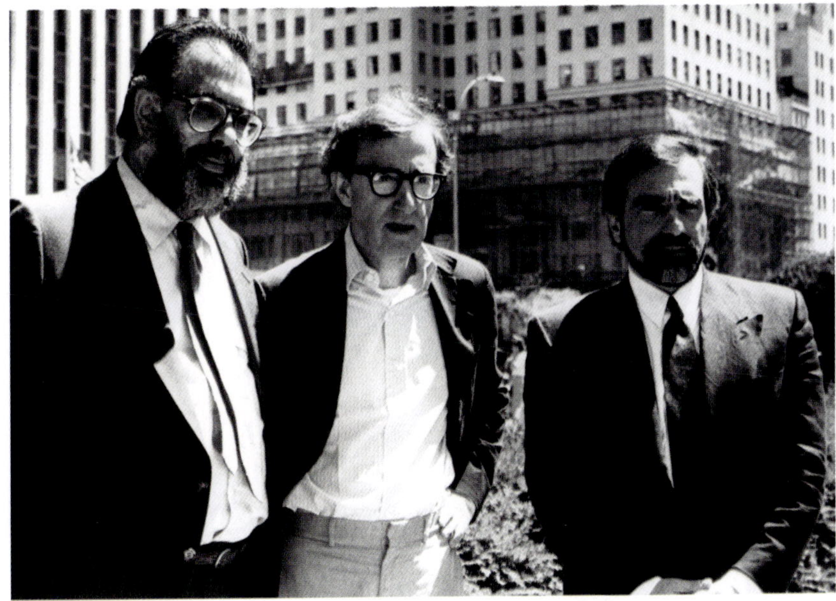

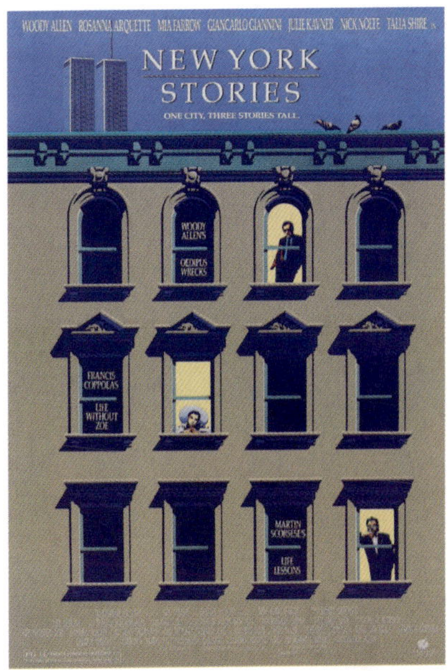

Above left: *A triptych of New Yorkers – Francis Ford Coppola, Woody Allen, and Martin Scorsese joined talents for the portmanteau of* New York Stories *(1989). The results were mixed.*

Above right: *The effect of the three short films was to dilute each director's reputation, with Scorsese's* Life Lessons *(relatively speaking) the most admired.*

Finally, a brief word on *New York Stories*, the tri-part, tri-director curiosity thought up by Woody Allen, based on the Italian portmanteau films like *Boccaccio '70*. Allen had called: the plan was that he, Scorsese, and Steven Spielberg would each provide a short, united by the theme of New York. Spielberg soon dropped out to be replaced by Francis Ford Coppola, a more pertinent choice given he was another native, though his coming-of-age entry, *Life Without Zoë*, is derided. The results are indeed mixed (and met with indifference, making $11 million on a $15 million budget). There is an inescapable air of indulgence. Compared to Coppola, and Allen's mother-son dramedy *Oedipus Wrecks*, Scorsese's part in the game is the most successful. Written by Richard Price, *Life Lessons* charts the disintegration of the relationship between Nick Nolte's arrogant Manhattan artist Lionel Dobie and his assistant, lover, and muse Paulette (Rosanna Arquette).

The idea was based on Dostoevsky's *The Gambler* (based in turn on the Russian writer's troubled relationship with mistress Polina Suslova), and resonates with Scorsese's marital woes (with the added frisson that his wives often worked for him). It is a curious if brisk critique of the damage done to love by the creative process (returning to the central theme of *New York, New York*), four weeks in the making, forty minutes in length. 'What interested me was the pain of this situation,' recalled Scorsese, 'how much of it was needed for his kind of work, and how much he creates himself.'[37] Beware becoming an institution.

The most iconic shot of Martin Scorsese's career begins on the sidewalk outside the Copacabana. Books could be written on Scorsese's street scenes, but we don't dally for long. This is the early sixties in New York (naturally), and Henry Hill (Ray Liotta, as slick and radiant as Brylcreem) is trying to impress his date Karen Friedman (Lorraine Bracco, taking uncertain steps into a forbidden world), by passing through the restless queue and into a side entrance to the famous club.

Scorsese knew the Copa. The East 60th Street nightclub was legend. The father of a friend worked behind the bar and there were times when he too was invited to sample that world. This was where Frank Sinatra performed, and Dean Martin; on the night of Scorsese's graduation, he saw Bobby Darin sing at the Copa. And this was the nightspot where the mob puffed out their feathers, perched at the tightly-packed tables in their silk threads, sat beside their fancy women, craning to see who was closest to the stage.

This is the real Copa we are watching, returned to its pomp. The jukebox soundtrack delivers the shimmering dream-pop of *Then He Kissed Me* by The Crystals – the forty-three curated songs serve as rhythm, mood, chronology, and a caress of narrative; Scorsese would write their names in the margins as the script was being written. He could both see and hear the film in his head. We follow the couple's arrival for an unbroken three minutes and five seconds, a swaggering piece of direction to embody a swaggering wiseguy ritual. What we might call the incandescence of *Goodfellas* is distilled into Hill guiding his paramour from sidewalk to a front row seat via damask corridors and bustling kitchen, out onto the floor of the club like the headline act.

'What's so wonderful about this episode is not only the smoothly galvanized camera work…' relished David Denby in *New York* magazine, 'but the bits of exuberant detail that Scorsese shoehorns into the corners of the shot.'[1] The *storytelling* lies in Hill's familiar exchanges with off-duty waiters

Opposite: *Made to measure – a promotional shot of the leading men of* Goodfellas *(1990), Ray Liotta (as Henry Hill), Robert De Niro (as Jimmy Conway), Paul Sorvino (as Paulie Cicero), and Joe Pesci (as Tommy DeVito).*

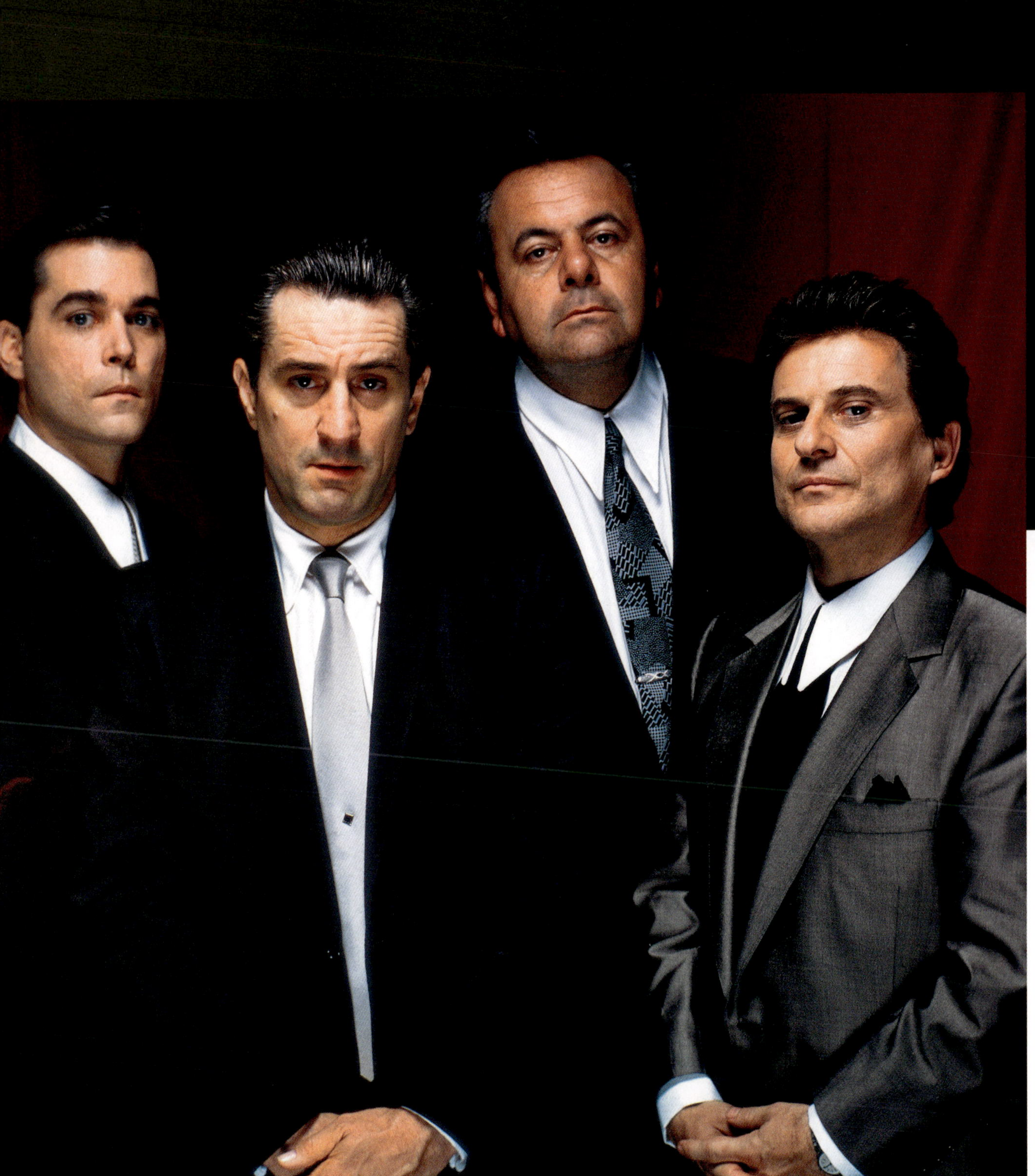

and cooks, the dollar bills he slips into eager hands, and the homage paid to him by gilded men at adjoining tables. There are 400 individual acting moments in the scene, and Liotta revels in it all, every smile, every tilt of the head oozing with Henry's snake-oil largesse.

The 'Copa Shot'[2] wasn't storyboarded, it was enacted. Scorsese simply walked them through the scene, a director entering his fictional world, swinging through the kitchen (the actors secretly walk out the same kitchen door they came in), trailing a phalanx of ADs, Liotta and Bracco, cinematographer Michael Ballhaus, and Steadicam operator Larry McConkey, on whose shoulders rested its mastery. Scorsese spun gold instinctually. Make sure you see the hand giving the money. The camera must pan over to see the table. Then he left his team to figure out the mechanics.

A part that is from the taped rehearsal, which caused Scorsese to take a gulp of oxygen – he had a tank to hand as his asthma was kicking up a storm. 'No, no, no!'[3] he gasped. It was the way Henry's table was lifted in from the wings to be placed in front of the stage. It had to be 'flying right out of nowhere,'[4] he insisted, the way he remembered, like a magic trick.

Six hours later, as evening fell, they were ready to shoot. The number of actual takes varies depending on the account (averaging at eight), but Scorsese began to notice that the extras playing the club's seated guests were starting to grouch.

Below: *The good life – Henry Hill (Ray Liotta) and wife Karen (Lorraine Bracco) enjoy the fruits of mob influence.*

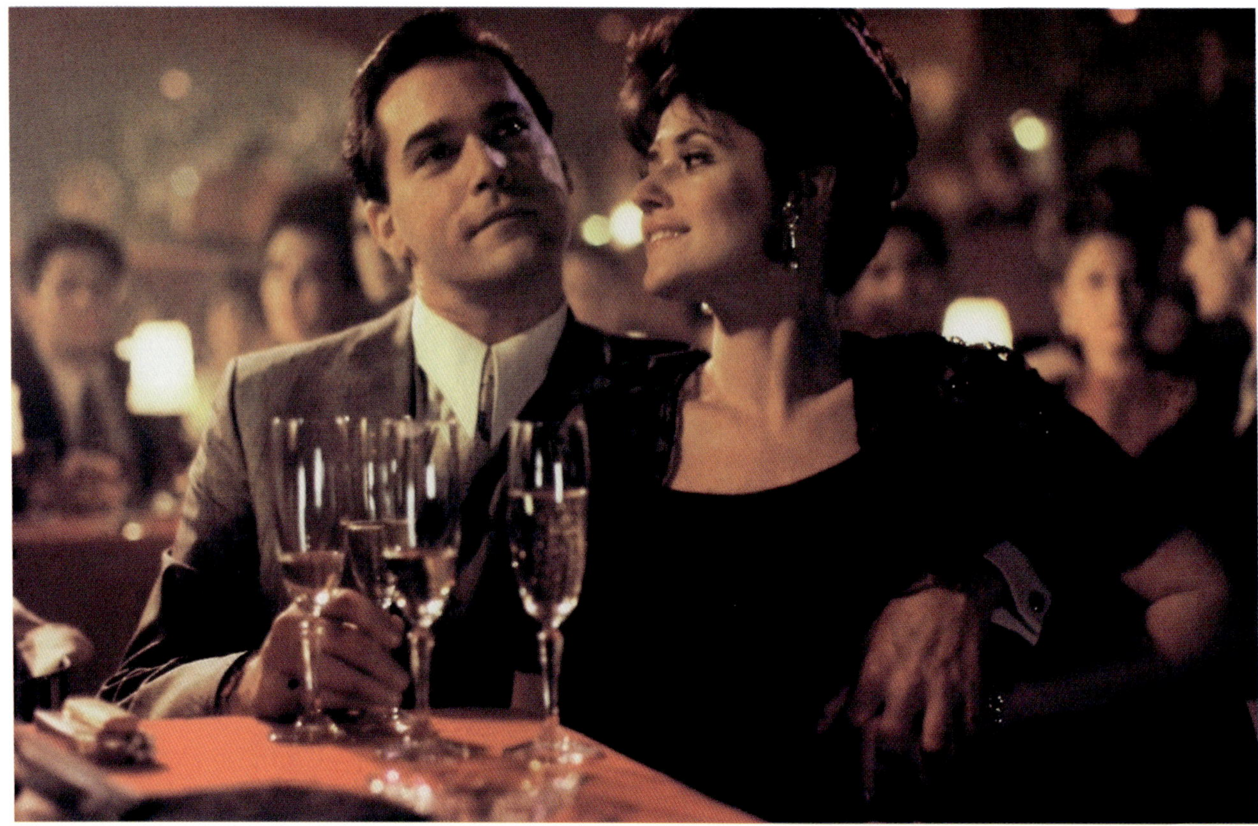

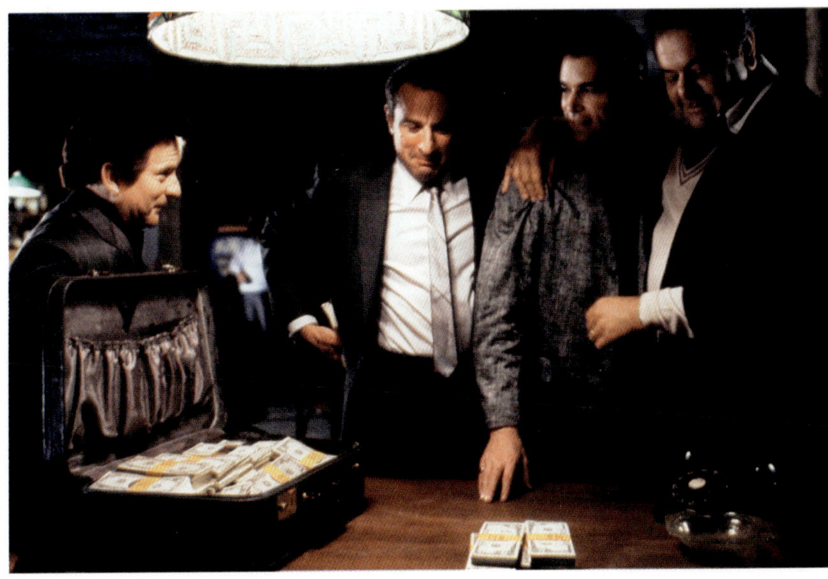

Left: *Mob anthropology – as Martin Scorsese illuminates, for the mob, money was a side-effect. It was really all about power.*

'What's the matter with them, they're sitting down, what's their problem?'[5] he whispered to his longtime assistant director Joe Reidy, who was largely responsible for managing the shot. Reidy confessed that as they were short on numbers, these were the same extras who were waiting in line outside. They had to sprint down the front stairs and get into place before the camera swept back into the room.

And they weren't really extras at all.

They had found them in Scorsese's old neighbourhood. Three of his regular guys, Frank Aquilino, Butchy (with the hat), and Johnny 'Cha Cha' Ciarcia (old friends turned performers who shored up the authenticity of his New York films) had gathered up all these guys and dolls with strong faces, offering them $10 a piece to be in a Scorsese movie.

'What do you do?' an incredulous Karen asks her date, setting up the punchline to the labyrinthine scene. 'I'm in construction,'[6] replies Hill, not meeting her eyes. She caresses hands that have never seen a day of labour in their life. She knows. Surely the most telling point of this microcosm of the *Goodfellas* effect is that she finds it thrilling. As do we. Then the camera whips round to the arrival of (real) comedian Henry Youngman and his dusty catchphrases.

For Scorsese this scene was the essence of the story. The allure of this world. 'He's the young American ready to take over the world and he's met a girl he likes.'[7] Hill has connections, he's on the rise in the mafia. His reward is not having to worry about getting a parking ticket, and to bypass the line at the Copa. 'So it had to be done in one sweeping shot, because it's his seduction of her and it's also the lifestyle seducing him.'[8]

Denby called *Goodfellas* the 'greatest film ever made about the sensual and monetary lure of crime.'[9] It was about murderous freedom. Stylistically, thematically, overwhelmingly this gangster masterpiece lies at the core of Scorsese's career. And this shot lies at the heart of our understanding of him. To subjectively show the real thing. To express what lies beneath the images. That this film is not about the experience of being in the mafia, divined critic Roger Ebert, 'but the *feeling*.'[10] Good and bad.

'That's the privileged moment they pay for in blood and death,'[11] said Scorsese.

Nicholas Pileggi loves to recall the phone call that changed his life. His book, *Wiseguy*, had begun as an article for *New York* magazine, the mesmerizing account of a Mafia foot soldier named Henry Hill, who in a flood of existential panic (and no little cocaine addiction, which would have struck a chord) turned FBI informer. Hill was hardly the biggest fish, being Irish-Italian he could never become a Made Man, the rank of untouchable only the pure achieved. Hill only climbed halfway up the mob ladder, but was willing to talk, still eager to be centre stage, despite now being buried on the witness protection scheme. His curdled nostalgia was enough to fill a book.

Then the phone rings.

'My name is Marty Scorsese,' the voice starts with that familiar Tommy gun clatter, 'and I'm a movie director.'[12]

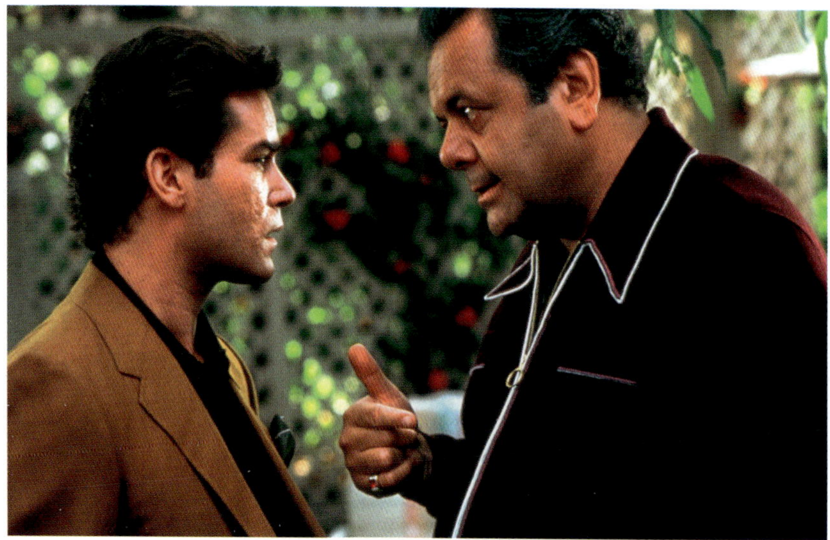

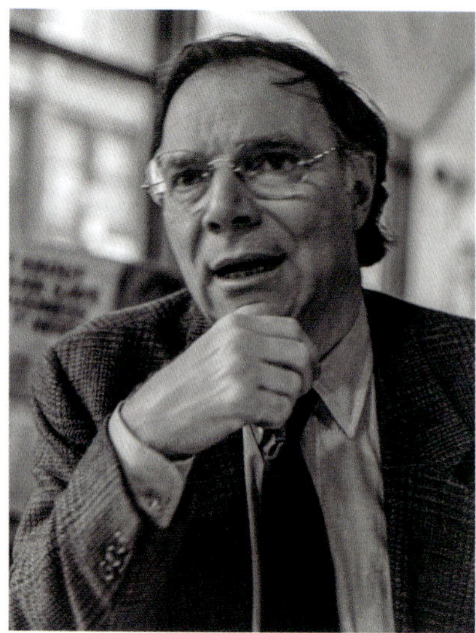

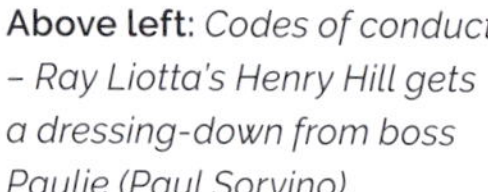

Above left: *Codes of conduct – Ray Liotta's Henry Hill gets a dressing-down from boss Paulie (Paul Sorvino).*

Above right: *Nicholas Pileggi, co-screenwriter and author of the original book* Wiseguy *on which* Goodfellas *is based.*

Did he always introduce himself that way? With such deafening understatement. Does he still? He goes on to say, at great length, that this is the kind of book he has been waiting for all his life. He wants to direct it.

There is a pause. The faint sound of the greatest living American director catching his breath.

Pileggi takes his chance to respond. 'To tell you the truth, I've been waiting for this phone call all my life. If you want to do it, you can do it.'[13]

Alerted by a review while shooting *The Color of Money*, as soon as Scorsese read the book, with its free-flowing style and wonderful arrogance, he was certain this was the way it must be. 'This was something I knew from my own experience,'[14] he said. The closed society of organized crime among the Neapolitans and Sicilians of Little Italy, the power these men wielded without lifting a finger. That was the root of the attraction, not money, though these mobsters were greedy. It was about respect, and how respect corresponded to power. It was there in *Mean Streets*, the first of what has since expanded into a six-film chronicle of organized crime taking America from the 19th century to modern times. And it was here fizzing from the pages of Pileggi's book.

It was about the *life*.

Pileggi mentioned to Scorsese that in reality Paul Sorvino's character, the local don Paulie Cicero (in real life: Paulie Vario), cold as stone, never went to the movies, never went out. But there was this one night the guys just grabbed him, bundled him into a car, and took him to see a film. 'It was *Mean Streets*,' laughed Scorsese. 'They loved it.'[15] That topped any rave review. He knew he was being accurate.

The power of the book lay in the fact that Hill had been involved with the mob since he was a boy, parking Cadillacs, running errands, collecting debts, stealing, informing, working his way up to be somebody, his suits as clean as his hands were dirty. Then committing the ultimate sin in the eyes of the 'family' – to turn rat.

The film Scorsese could see instantly in his head was effectively Hill's confession. To the FBI, to the court, to his kids, to the

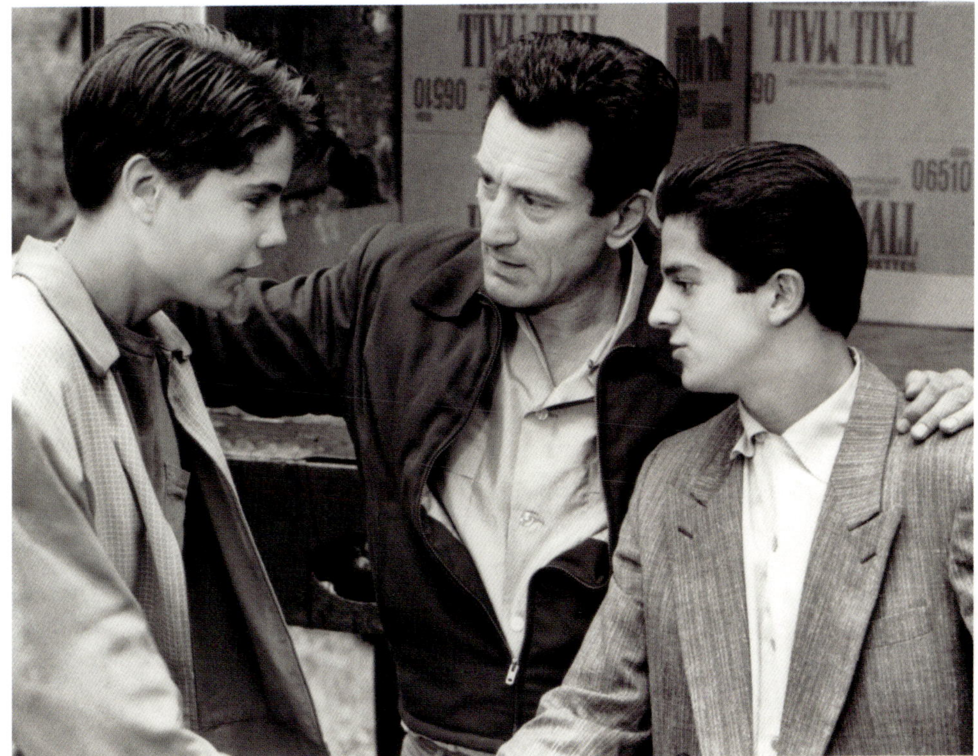

Right: *The young incarnations of Henry (Christopher Serrone, left) and Tommy (Joe D'Onofrio, right) fall under the tutelage of Jimmy Conway. Robert De Niro took the role of Jimmy knowing he was too old for Henry.*

Below: *The older manifestations of the* Goodfellas *characters – played by Liotta, De Niro, and Pesci. The question is, how far can you trust a friend?*

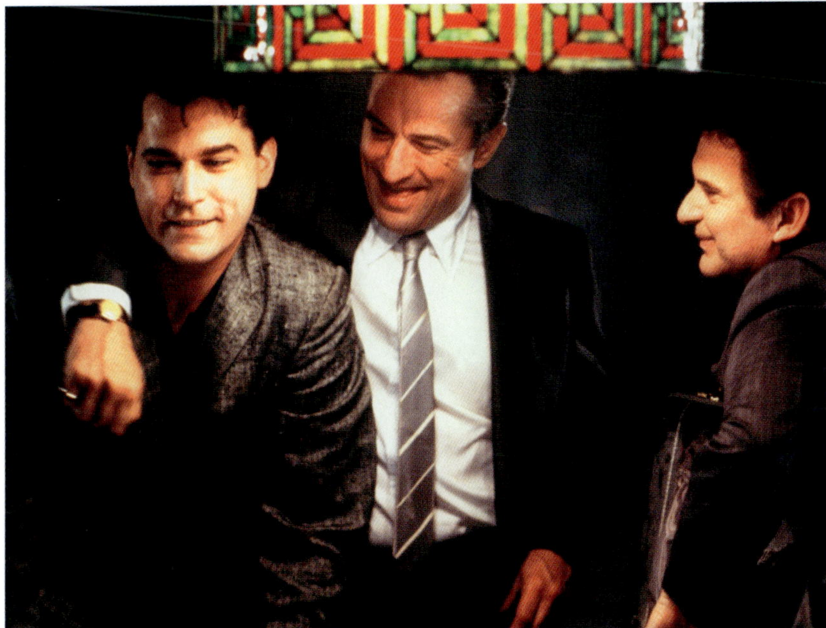

men he betrayed, to the world at large, to God, and to us, his hungry audience. And from the first line of the film it was clear that, despite everything, he had loved it all.

It's an immortal introduction, declared by Liotta's ever-present voice-over in a register of nasal glee: 'As far back as I can remember, I've always wanted to be a gangster... To me being a gangster was better than being President of the United States.'[16]

With *Goodfellas,* as it was retitled (another ironic epithet of the mob's own coinage), Scorsese was determined to raise a moral question. 'I knew it would make a fascinating film if we could just keep the same sense of a way of life that Nick had in the book – what Henry Hill had given him – and still have the audience care about these characters as human beings.'[17]

Was it possible to make the audience feel something for killers and their accomplices? The only way to achieve such a daring aim was not to make a gangster picture, embalmed in mythology, but to aim for a certain kind of reality. To get as close as possible, said Scorsese, 'to the spirit of a documentary.'[18]

At $25 million, it was the largest budget he had ever worked with, though still relatively conservative by Hollywood standards, especially those of his peers. 'Still doing low budget?'[19] quipped Steven Spielberg. Warner Brothers, who pioneered the gangster genre, classically speaking, were bankrolling the film.

Shooting began on a warm May night in 1989, and they sprawled across the boroughs until August. The list ran to forty-four locations, sometimes two or three in a day, chalking up Queens, Manhattan, Upstate, New Jersey, Long Island, JFK Airport, bars, restaurants, clubs, houses, warehouses, lock-ups, courthouses. Scorsese kept known 'associates' of the real characters on set to check on veracity, and they began to notice the counterfeit money going missing.

'Actors have a way of doing their best work – the work that lets us see them clearly – in a Scorsese film,'[20] declared Ebert. Which is true, but as Scorsese preferred to say, ninety percent of any movie is casting, and Hill was going to be the trickiest part to cast. A relatively reliable narrator of fact, slippery in terms of moral accountability, Scorsese knew they were very few actors who could capture that mix of wormy and sympathetic. De Niro and Keitel were now too old, DiCaprio still only fifteen. Tom Cruise had been discussed, as had Madonna for Karen. It took Scorsese a year to settle on Liotta. He had liked his nervy performance in *Something Wild*. Liotta was

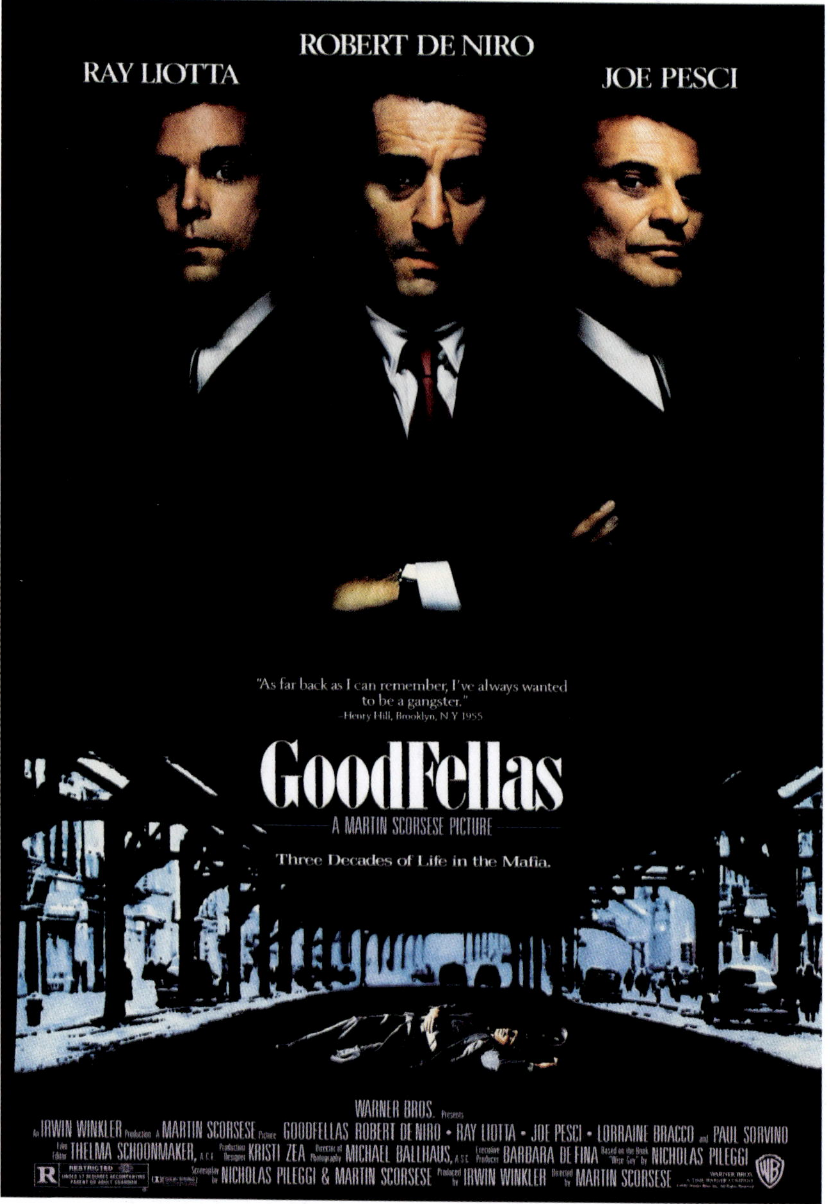

Above: Goodfellas *was not only a significant hit, landing six Oscar nominations, but has become a rite of passage – fans can recite its screenplay almost word for word.*

Opposite: *The three wise guys – Pesci and De Niro walked into their roles, but Henry was more elusive. Liotta would eventually confront Martin Scorsese, demanding he get his chance. Which was a very Hill-like way of going about things.*

determined, though he had been told the studio were fixed on having a star (he had done three movies at this stage).

Then at the Venice Film Festival, Scorsese was walking across the lobby of his hotel with a formation of bodyguards – there had been death threats following *The Last Temptation of Christ* – when Liotta approached, and the men in black stepped forward to intercept the actor. What impressed Scorsese was the 'interesting way'[21] he reacted. 'Which was he held his ground, but made them understand he was no threat.'[22] He had Hill's instincts, he didn't lose his cool.

Of course, three faces stare out at us from the famous poster, not only Liotta's Hill, but his two accomplices, compatriots, brothers in arms, and friends willing to have him whacked. Unannounced, as per the code. Loyalty is always conditional. This trio, funny and terrifying, is the chain that holds the necklace of events in place.

After John Malkovich turned down the role, Bobby simply called Marty and professed a keenness to play Jimmy Conway, Hill's mentor, a born thief, organized, ruthless, pathological. De Niro was always on the phone to the real Hill (the real Conway, né Jimmy 'the Gent' Burke, was

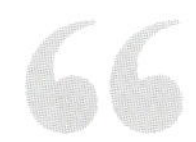

Actors have a way of doing their best work – the work that lets us see them clearly – in a Scorsese film.

ROGER EBERT

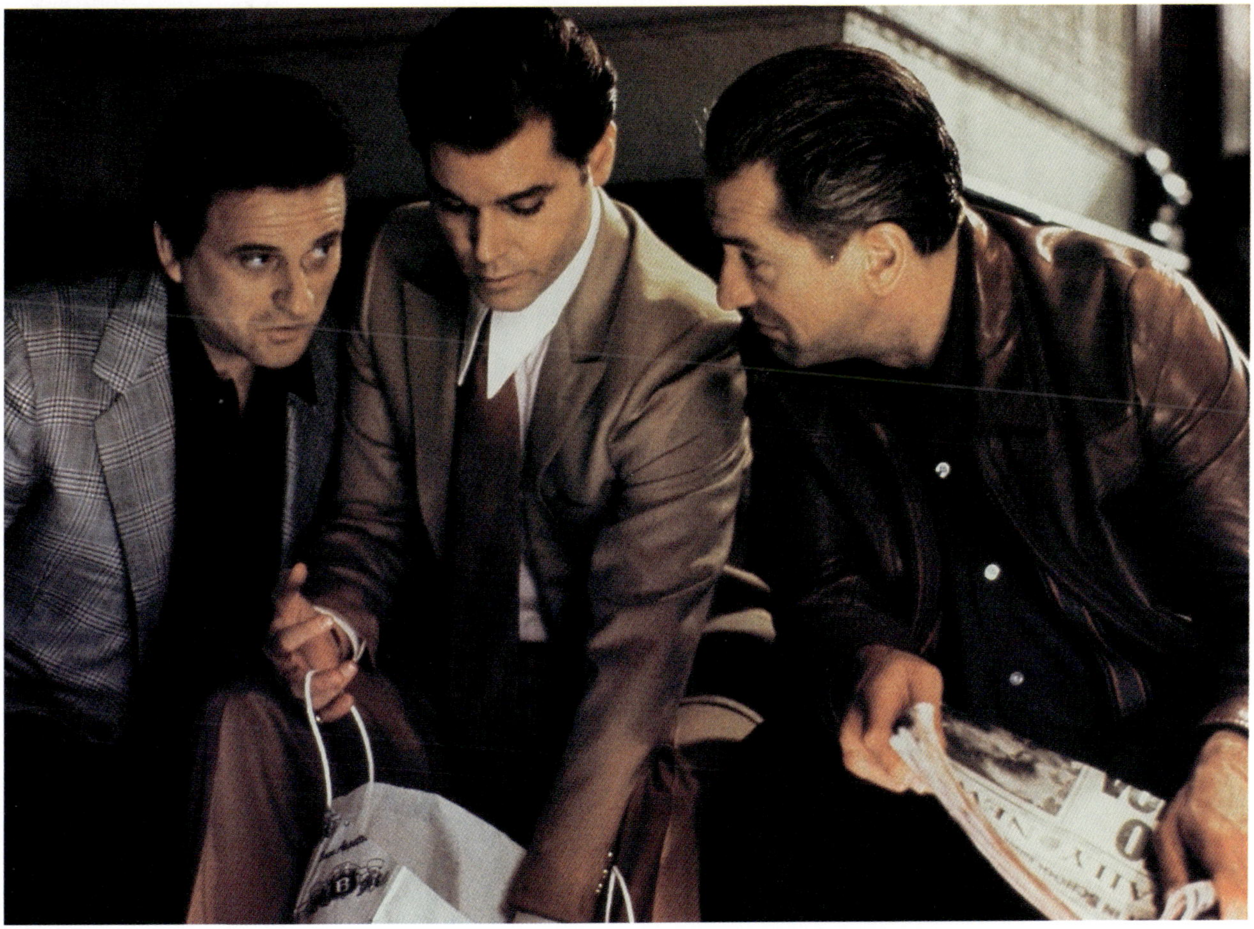

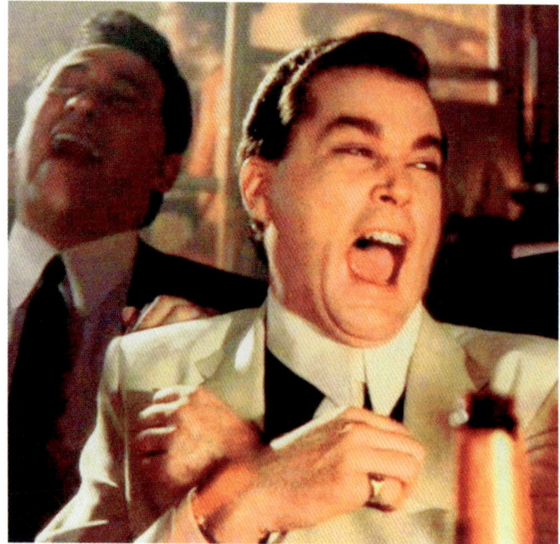

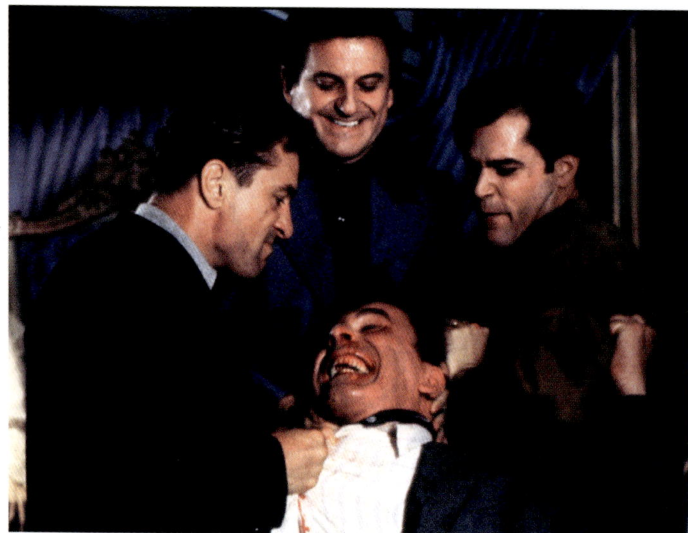

Above left: *The unforgettable 'funny how' scene in* Goodfellas *swings on a pendulum, between Joe Pesci's improvisations and Ray Liotta's nervous reactions. Even Liotta wasn't sure of the outcome.*

Above right: *As the film progresses, the cause and effect of mob violence rises to the surface, a stark reminder of how the good life can be short-lived.*

serving time in a New York State prison for murder): he wanted details, the thread that made up the suit. He insisted on carrying real cash, a roll of notes (mafia didn't carry wallets), up to $5,000, throwing them around, these $50 and $20 bills. The ADs had to scurry to reclaim them when the scene was done. De Niro and Joe Pesci went to the same Italian tailor to have their suits made from imported Italian cloth. Every day, Scorsese would personally tie Liotta's tie. 'There was a certain way he wanted it done,'[23] the actor said.

For the part of trigger-happy, motor-mouthed Tommy DeVito, pure of blood and black of soul, Pesci had also turned Scorsese down. But they got talking, sharing stories. Pesci had his New Jersey experience of the mob life. Tales Scorsese promised to invest into the film, which swung him round. Pesci is unforgettable as the showman psychopath who becomes a liability (and Hill insisted the film went easy on him), and would receive the film's solitary Oscar. Symbolically beating Andy García for *The Godfather Part III* and Al Pacino in *Dick Tracy*, Pesci's acceptance speech was as politely succinct as Tommy had been a foul-mouthed torrent: 'It's my privilege. Thank you.'[24]

Like Scorsese, the process meant so much more to him. The way the director encouraged his actors to improvise during rehearsal. Once the camera was moving things were more disciplined; the director's designs fixed. Though he had this habit of giving the cast contrasting instructions to keep things unexpected.

The film's second most celebrated scene was not to be found in the script. Tommy's 'Do I amuse you?'[25] response to Hill's throwaway compliment was inspired by a specific memory of a mobster unnerving a young Pesci. The guys are huddled together at a table in the Bamboo Lounge, collars like blades, when Tommy seemingly (big *seemingly*) takes exception to Hill calling him 'a funny guy.' 'Funny how?'[26] he presses, needling his so-called friend, stretching our nerves like harp strings.

'Medium shots, no close-ups, because the body language of the people around them was as important as their own,'[27] recalled Scorsese.

In all senses, we feel the performance, the put-on of the gangster persona, an attitude they wear like a suit, Tommy deciding internally which way events will fall. Is he showing off to the crowd, or is he genuinely willing to pull out a gun over an assumed slight? Or indeed a pendulum swinging between both? All of it sprang fully formed from Pesci's imagination, with Scorsese and editor Thelma Schoonmaker timing exactly when to break the tension. It is another example of the manic liminal zone between comedy and violence in which the film exists, never knowing which way it will fall. 'You may fold under questioning,'[28] Tommy finally quips to Hill, who of course will do just that.

In *Goodfellas*, style is story, fiction pulling up to the kerbside of fact. There is no conventional dramatic development, it is a 'mob home movie,'[29] the director would grin. The cumulative effect of all Scorsese's gifts is laid across the framework of another voice-over, that anthropological slant he adores. This is how it was.

Hill's voice-over would carry the distinctive voice of the book, contrasted on occasion with Karen's interior memories. Scorsese cited the tone set by Truffaut's *Jules et Jim*; the storm-the-gates audacity of the French New Wave always an inspiration. Stories told with the subjective vibrancy of personality. Funny how? The structure, figured out

Below: *Tommy DeVito (Joe Pesci) takes lethal exception to the waiter's attitude – Scorsese sees this as the exact moment things start to disintegrate for the trio.*

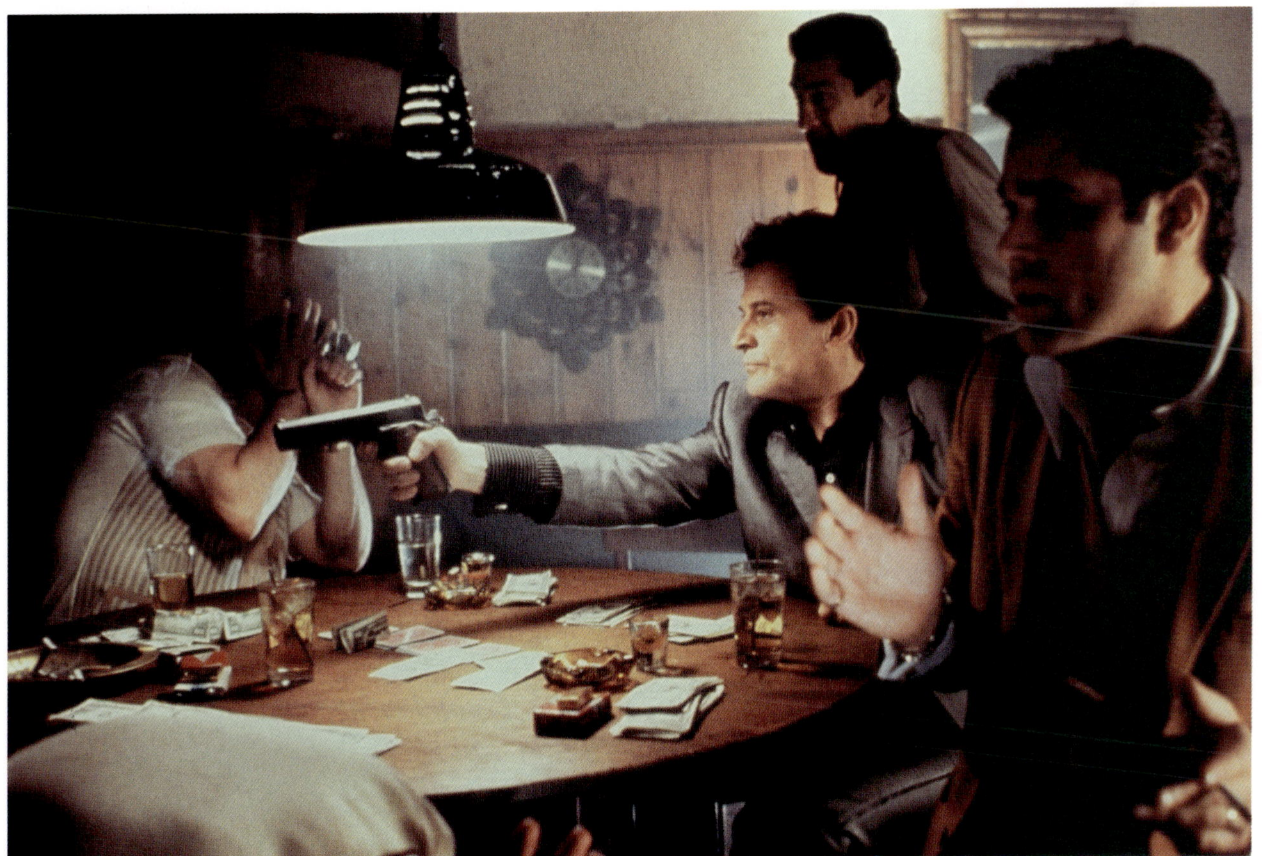

with Pileggi (they share the screenwriting credit), was a constant accumulation of incident. A life recalled in a can-you-believe-it gasp, but with wiseguy eloquence too. Often at tangents to what might be considered plot, or traditional drama, or even the point: heists go by unseen, murders are glimpsed in passing, the before and after of events so much more interesting to Scorsese. That's how memory works. With the filmmaking confidence to take control of time: to freeze-frame a moment, literally stop the picture, while Liotta's stream of lack-of-conscience savours the recollection, earnest and ironic all at once. It is like the film taking a breath.

Scorsese thought of it as going on 'some sort of crazed amusement park ride'[30] through the Underworld. A recklessness with Hollywood convention to match the attitudes of these gangsters. He wanted to overwhelm the audience with images. This constant, frenetic motion. Even when the characters are sat around the table, you can feel it in their pent-up bodies, or the camera lingering on De Niro's ice-cold eyes from across a bar as Cream's *Sunshine of Your Love* begins to play. In the edit, Scorsese kept shaving down scenes like Paulie's precious garlic shavings from his prison recipe.

This is how the great director talks, continually in flux, as if formulating his

Below: *Karen (Lorraine Bracco) accepts the ritual cheque from Paulie (Paul Sorvino), already seduced by the trappings of being married to the mob.*

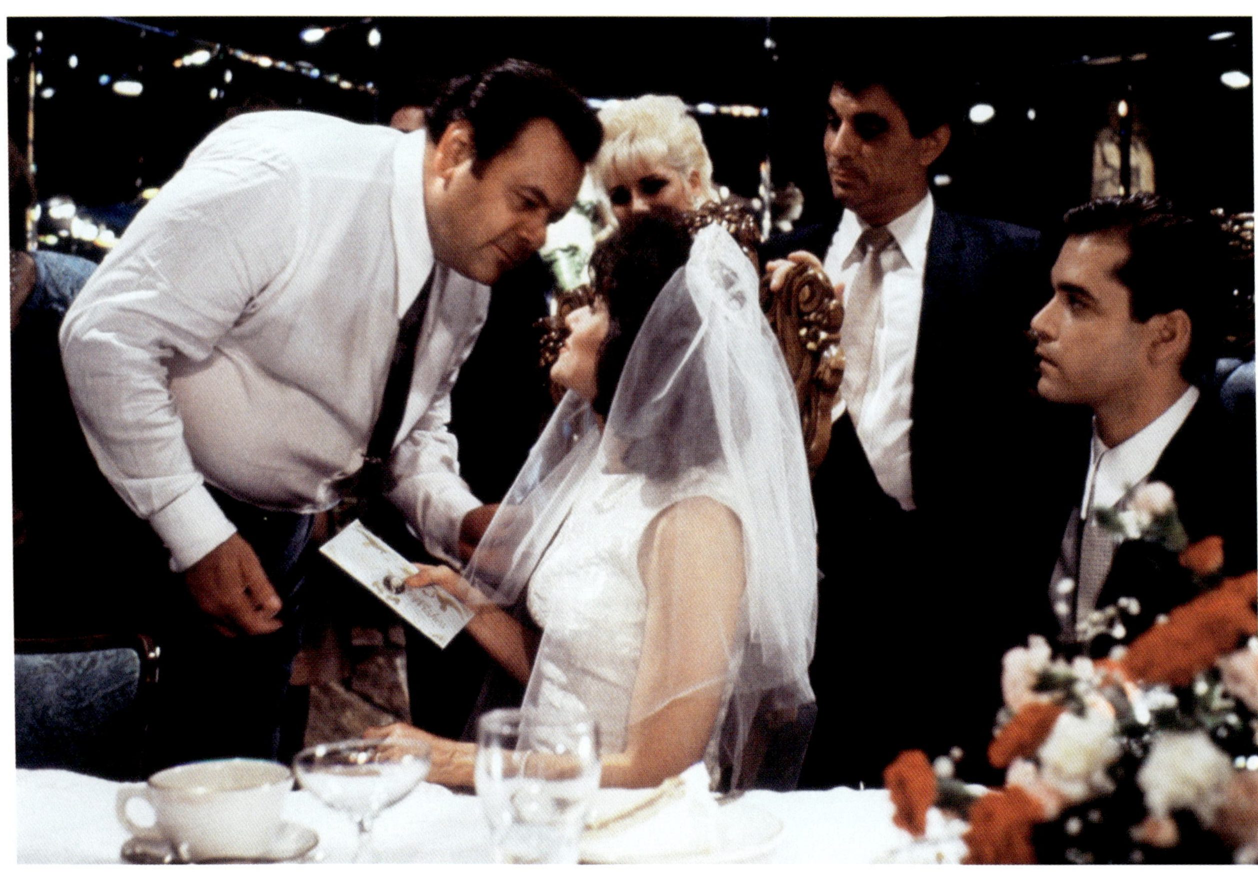

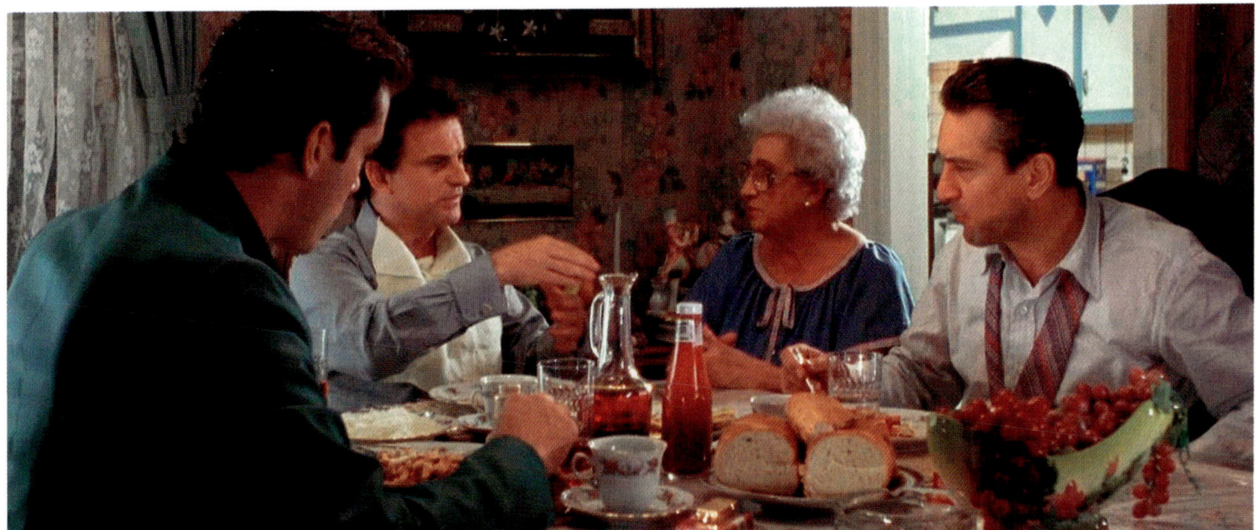

thoughts, something key that has occurred to him that instant, punctuated with hand gestures and wild bursts of laughter. Did Pesci model Tommy's explosive cackles on his boss?

'Then, of course, there were some scenes which would take longer,' explained Scorsese – the Copa Shot being one, 'because the exuberance, the exhilaration of the lifestyle carries you along, until they start having problems and it stops – and you have to deal with that.'[31]

The arc of *Goodfellas*, this unruly biopic, has taken us with increasing pace from 1955, when Hill first steps through the fateful door, through the idealized sixties, the violent seventies, to 1980 when things really turn sour. The film traces a rise-and-fall parabola, not moral, more inevitable. Scorsese said the life had a ten-year span at most, 'before they either get killed or go to jail...'[32] (not so different from most directors). The life also begins to wear you down. Hill never really had it in him to be a great villain – the guilt gnawed at him, the faintest echo of a conscience that begins when they dispose of Billy Batts

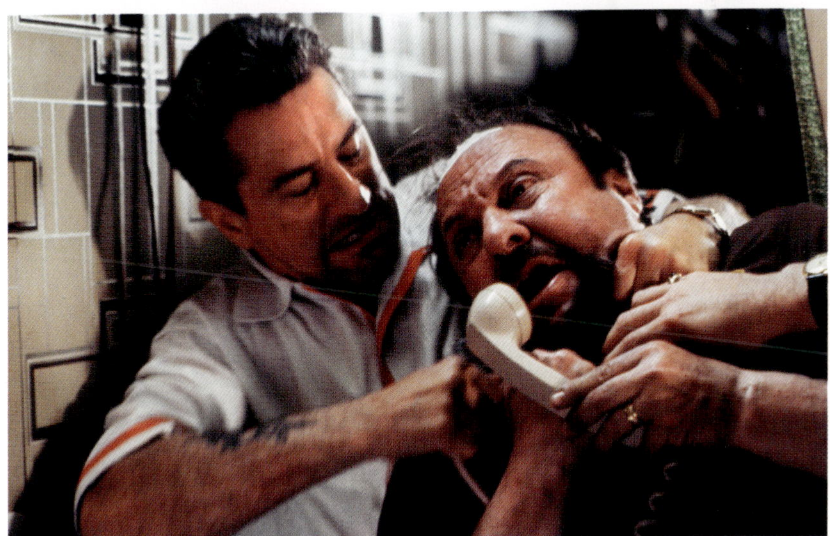

Top: *Keeping it in the family – Catherine Scorsese, Marty's mother, takes a cameo as Tommy's mother. Naturally, she presides over a hearty meal.*

Above: *Jimmy (Robert De Niro) ties up some loose ends – in this case big-mouthed wig salesman Morrie Kessler, played by Martin Scorsese regular Chuck Low, formerly De Niro's landlord.*

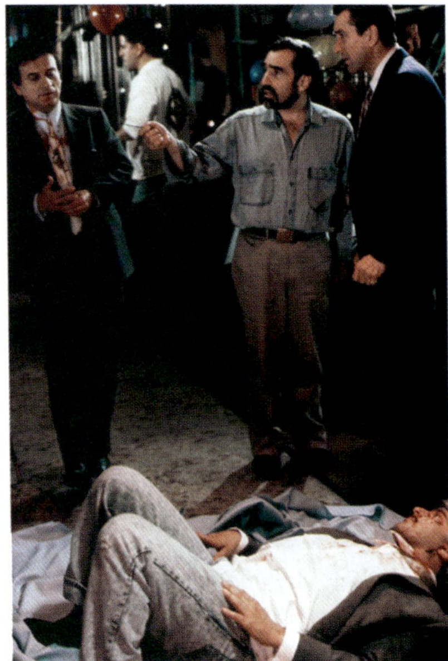

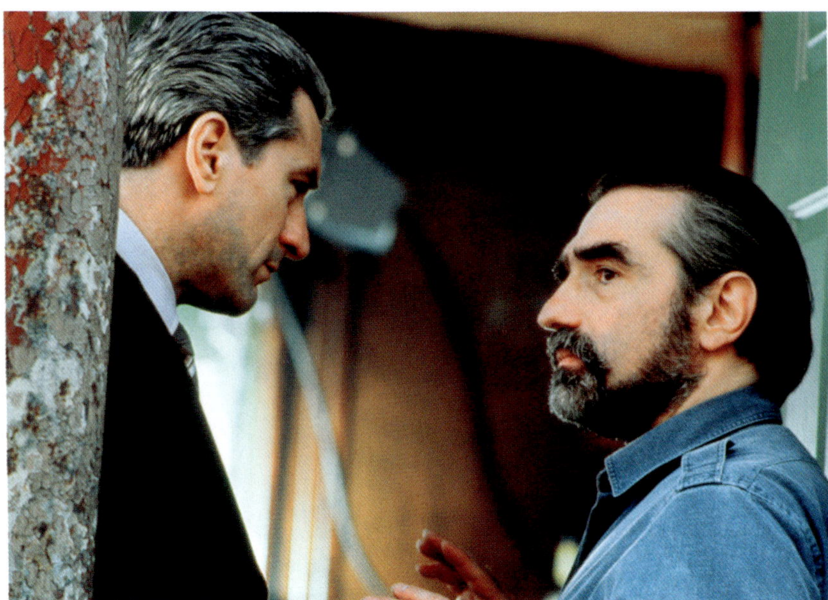

(Frank Vincent), battered to a pulp, but still banging on the trunk roof (not for long). He was a Made Man, which made it a bad move. The scene is bathed in a hellish red glow from the tail-lights.

'To a certain extent we pushed that idea, that they are like gods, and gods fall,'[33] said Scorsese. Behind all the good times, the action, lies an equal and opposite accumulation of dread, which eventually spills over. The final coruscating act encompasses Hill's last day as a wiseguy, strung out on drugs, wired on anxiety, attacked from all sides, knowing he is next on Jimmy's hit-list (one-by-one all the gang behind the Lufthansa heist), the infernal rotor whirl of a circling chopper. Under that kind of pressure, well, a man's loyalty can waver. 'They don't come to you like you usually see in the movies,'[34] retorts Hill on the voice-over, the irony red-raw like his eyes.

The style starts consciously to break down. 'So that by his last day as wiseguy, it's as if the whole picture would be out of control, give the impression that he's just going to spin off the edge and fly out,'[35] explained Scorsese. He and Schoonmaker kept urging each other to cut it faster, faster, faster, virtuosos free-forming with montage. The music keeps switching like a bad party: *Jump Into the Fire* by Harry Nilsson to *Memo From Turner* by Mick Jagger to the live recording of *Magic Bus* by The Who to *Monkey Man* by The Rolling Stones, the list goes on. This was the joyless sensation of a system overloaded with coke. Scorsese channelling personal experience. You couldn't edit like this if you didn't know.

The early nineties had seen a renaissance of the gangster movie with every take on the genre: *Bugsy, Miller's Crossing, Dick Tracy, State of Grace*, and Francis Ford Coppola had been talked into making *The Godfather Part III*. Scorsese resisted any competition between his work and Coppola's, which he compared to epic poetry. 'My stuff is like some guy on the street corner talking,'[36] he laughed.

Above left: *Martin Scorsese chose to tell the story in snapshots of memory, where the 'before' or 'after' of a crime prove more interesting than the deed itself.*

Above right: *Indeed with* Goodfellas, *he was extending a world he had begun to explore in* Mean Streets, *bringing a reality to the myth of the American gangster. These were men he had seen on the streets, and taking the front tables at the clubs.*

Opposite: *At the end of an exhilarating and exhausting production, Scorsese was determined that this was his last word on the mob. A promise that would last four years.*

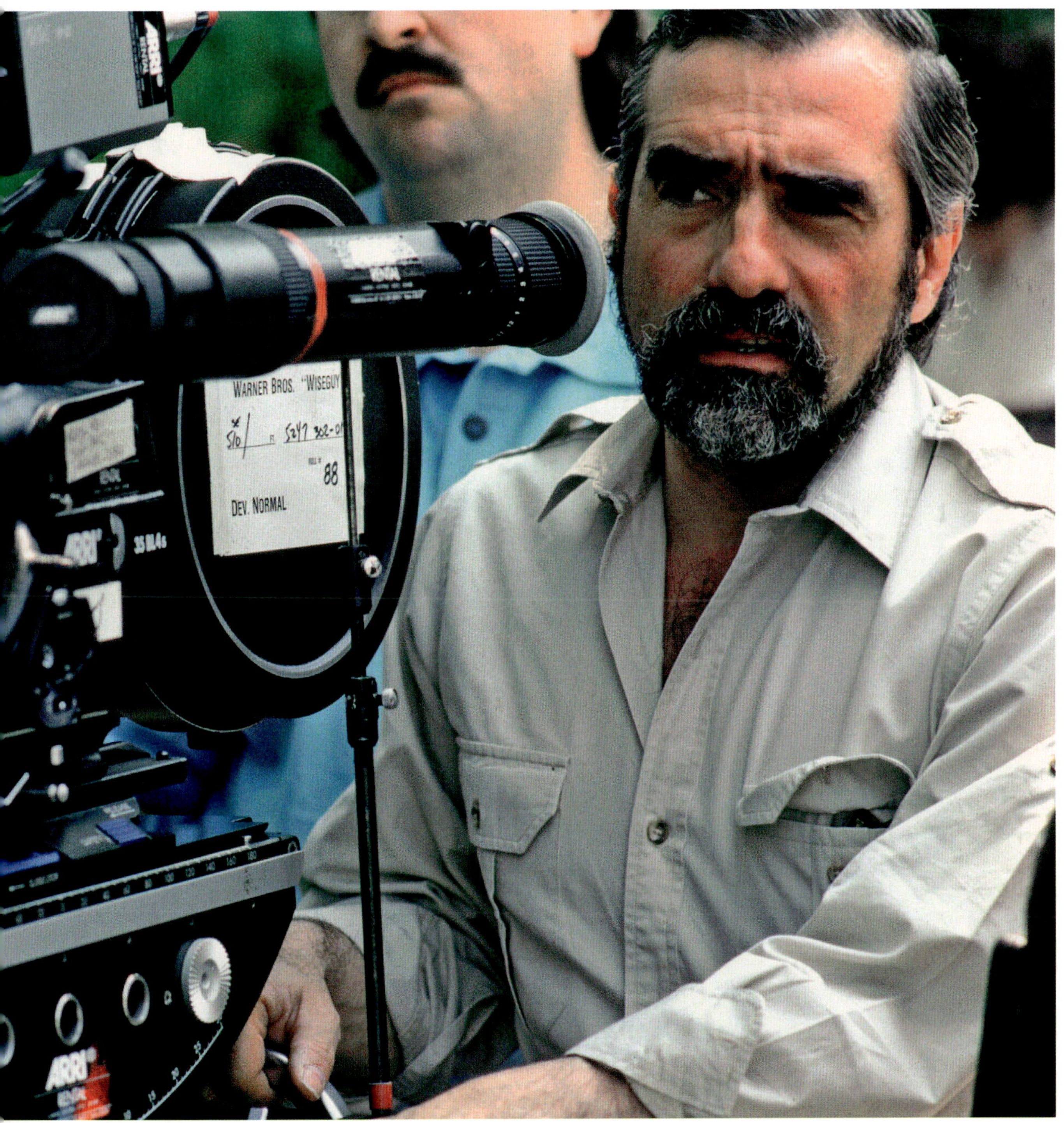
WARNER BROS. "WISEGUY
88
DEV. NORMAL
35 BL4s
ARRI

What is so inspired about his approach to the genre is what the *Evening Standard* called 'Scorsese's magisterial detachment.'[37] He stands aloof from moral judgment, withholding psychological insight, throwing us headlong into Hill's life. The moral friction lies in how much we find ourselves seduced.

Yet the studio thought *Goodfellas* was a bust. Relations had broken down during the shoot. 'We went over schedule, about fifteen days over, and the studio was furious,' recalled Scorsese. 'We were treated very badly; they even refused to give a little wrap party.'[38] With the director's nerves reaching a Hill-like state of agitation, his doctor advised him to give up coffee. Then the mandated test screenings went poorly. Audiences complained that they felt agitated by the switch in tone to the high anxiety of Hill's downfall. Scorsese insisted that was the point. There was a screening in Orange County where seventy people walked out. One wrote 'FUCK YOU'[39] on the comment card. Meanwhile, the ratings board began pushing for cuts. It always depressed him – this infringement of his artistic freedom. 'We go through this on every film,'[40] sighed Schoonmaker. After a decade of flops, Scorsese couldn't face another miss. He shaved a few more frames, Tommy's face getting blown off, tiny compromises, which still felt like pinpricks on his soul.

Then the reviews came in. Prestigious writers like Denby and Ebert took up the

Below: *Decline and fall – Karen (Lorraine Bracco) visits her husband Henry (Ray Liotta) taking his predictable spell in prison.*

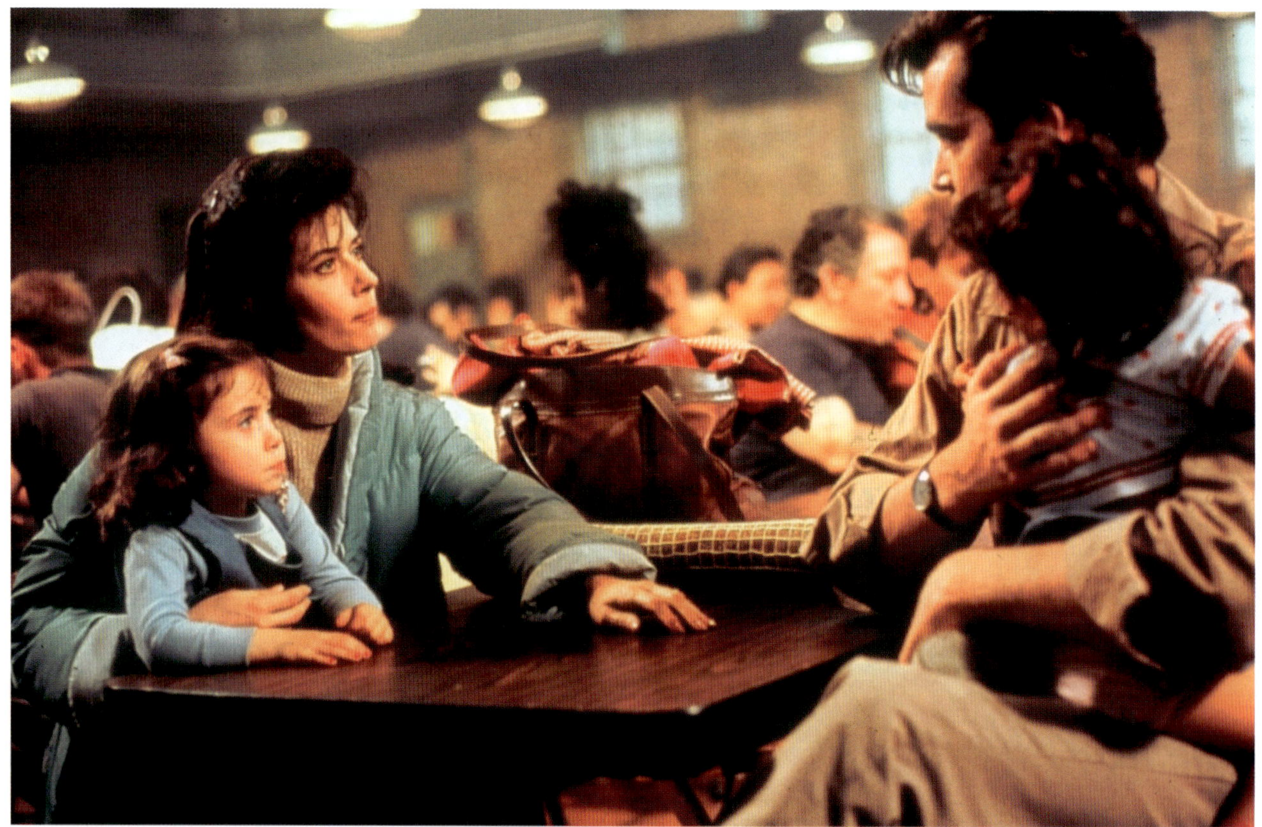

Right: *Hill's reverie ends as he turns rat on his mob brothers – another betrayal at the heart of a Scorsese film.*

Below: *Test audiences complained of feeling agitated by the final act of* Goodfellas, *as a drug-addled Henry (Liotta) feels the law getting closer and closer. Scorsese was pleased. That was exactly the reaction he wanted.*

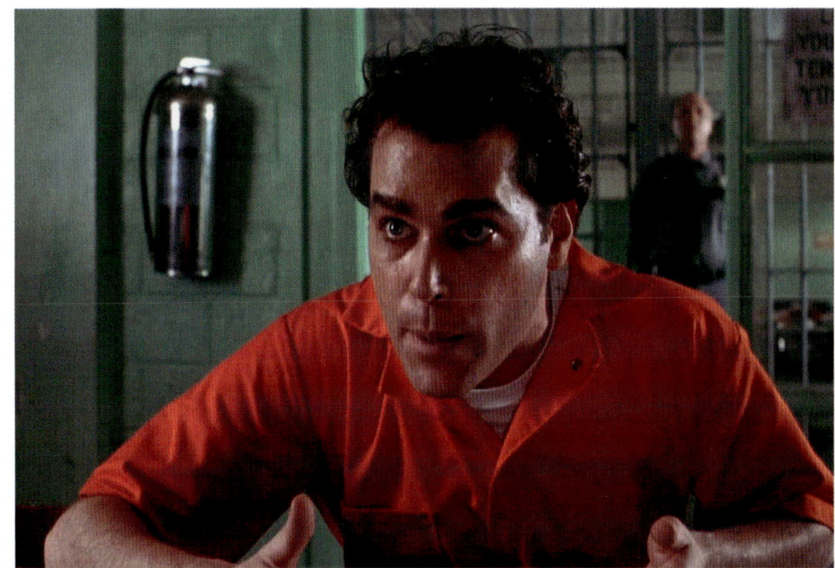

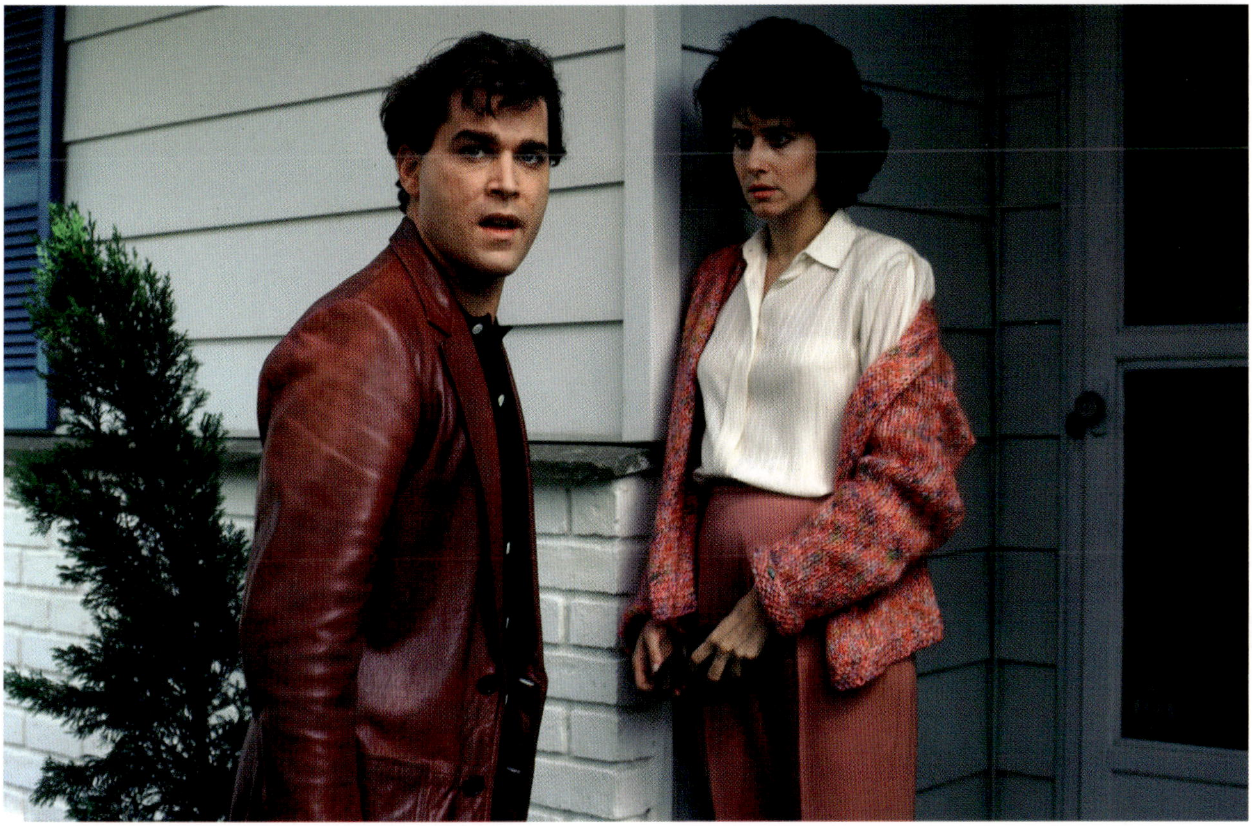

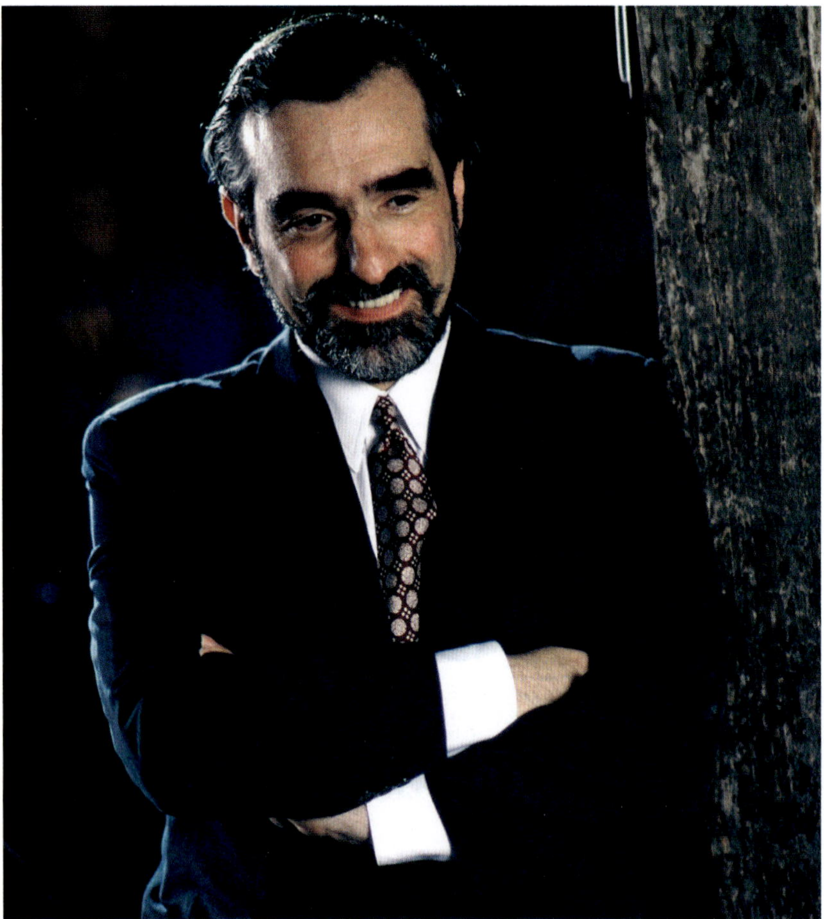

Left: *There can be no doubt that it was* Goodfellas *that finally lifted Scorsese to the top of the pantheon of living directors.*

film's cause with religious zeal. As *Film Comment* commented, 'we never doubt that a master at the top of his game is calling the shots.'[41] The response was rapturous. Okay, there were dissenting voices complaining of a lack of focus, a section squeamish over the violence and amorality, the lack of counterpoint, the good to go with the bad. And it still galls that *Goodfellas* lost out to *Dances with Wolves* at the Oscars. Another Academy injustice to add to the pile. 'Maybe he got what he deserves - exclusion from the mediocre,'[42] mused Keitel. But it was a much-needed hit, making $47 million.

Nearly forty years later, *Goodfellas* is part of the modern cultural conversation, a filmic right-of-passage. There was not a day for the rest of Liotta's life when he didn't hear somebody quote it to him on the street. It does not overstate the case to say that this film transformed a genre. Without Scorsese's up-close exploration of the life, so secure in its style, so rich, *The Sopranos* would not exist. That exalted series drew deep from Scorsese's well, casting among others Bracco, Vincent, Michael Imperioli, Chuck Low, Tony Sirico, and Johnny 'Cha Cha' Ciarcia. *The Wire* would never have happened, or *Boardwalk Empire*. The grand stature of modern television owes this movie a huge debt. And Scorsese was breaking the rules long before Quentin Tarantino.

Goodfellas was the first time that Scorsese could think of himself as an established director. In Hollywood terms, a Made Man, seated in the front row, not that that was any guarantee of survival.

1990
MADE IN MILAN (Documentary) Director

ACTING UP

Ten significant Martin Scorsese performances

Like Hitchcock, Scorsese enjoys taking a cameo in his films, extending the potential for personal expression. Such is his charisma on screen, he has regularly been called upon as an actor in his own right.

1. Jimmy Shorts in *Mean Streets* (1973)
The young director can be seen as the assassin, Jimmy Shorts, firing at Charlie and Johnny Boy from the back of the mobster's car – a literal version of the shooter.

2. The Passenger in *Taxi Driver* (1976)
His most memorable cameo came by chance. When the actor due to play the homicidal husband in the back of Travis Bickle's cab was injured on another film, De Niro convinced his director to step in. Scorsese recalled improvising 'something a little more outrageous… I was getting him crazy.'[1]

3. Mafioso in *Cannonball* (1976)
The first appearance outside of his own work came in this illegal road race B-movie. Star David Carradine had appeared in *Boxcar Bertha* and *Mean Streets*, and Scorsese returned the favour with a walk-on as, of course, a mafioso.

4. Giulio Gatti-Casazza in *Anna Pavlova* (1983)
In this elaborate European biopic of the Russian ballerina, Scorsese gets more to work with as the Italian opera manager who ran La Scala in Milan.

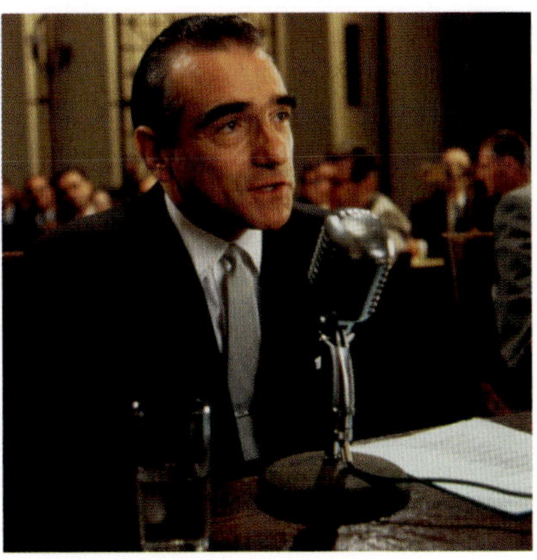

Above: *Scorsese proves as charismatic in front of the camera as behind it in Robert Redford's* Quiz Show *(1994).*

5. R.W. Goodley in *Round Midnight* (1986)
This story of a troubled jazz saxophonist was born as a spiritual sequel to *New York, New York*. As a gift, director Bertrand Tavernier offered him the chance to portray R.W. Goodley, real-life manager of Manhattan's Birdland joint. Every time Scorsese opened his mouth, Tavernier had told him, 'it's New York!'[2] Which saved on a lot of establishing shots.

6. Vincent van Gogh in *Dreams* (1990)
Japanese maestro Akira Kurosawa had written Scorsese a letter requesting he bring his trademark intensity to the legendary Dutch artist in this magical realist anthology. Scorsese was still finishing *Goodfellas*, but could hardly say no. After three hours in make-up, he did four takes and was done.

7. Joe Lesser in *Guilty by Suspicion* (1991)
Scorsese appeared in this McCarthy-era drama as a favour to the director, his former producer Irwin Winkler. His small role resonates, as he plays a director loosely based on the great Joseph Losey, who was blacklisted and exiled from Hollywood.

8. Martin Rittenhome in *Quiz Show* (1994)
In an ironic flourish, Scorsese plays the icily convivial corporate overlord in this riveting account of a fixed 1950s television quiz show, directed by Robert Redford.

9. Sykes in *Shark Tale* (2004)
You can't fault his sense of humour. In this animated tale of a fish caught up with the undersea mob, Scorsese voices a pufferfish who happens to be a loan shark. Meanwhile, De Niro voices Don Lino, a Great White.

10. Elderly Sage in *In the Hand of Dante* (2025)
Shot in Italy in 2024, Scorsese was enlisted in Julian Schnabel's era-spanning epic about the discovery of a handwritten manuscript of *The Divine Comedy*. Scorsese plays a wise adviser to Dante in matters of poetry. 'You can't take your eyes off him,'[3] reported Schnabel.

Overall the nineties were good to Martin Scorsese. Which was unusual in itself. After the blazing reaffirmation of *Goodfellas* came a quartet of contrasting films that spoke of confidence, brio, the smartest man in the game at play, and a refusal to be pigeonholed. Ball gowns and ultra-violence! Gambling etiquette and sexual deviance! Nutball Max Cady and the Dalai Lama! The great paradox of Scorsese's talent was writ large through this mid-career stretch.

He had even signed a six-picture pact with Universal, contemplating the studio life as the way forward. Could he make films within the gilded cage where Steven Spielberg thrived? After all, he was a cultural institution, honoured with degrees, documentaries, and career awards. Film historian Ian Christie drily noted that Scorsese's artistry 'helps the studios feel like occasional patrons of the art they daily prostitute.'[1] But could his gifts be spun into box office gold?

At the heart of Scorsese's process remained an irresistible urge to be unpredictable, with every film, every scene, every shot. 'I've always said the way I learned to make movies was by being a wise guy in the theater when I was a kid,' he recalled. 'We were merciless, my friends and I. You know, picking out clichés, saying the line before the actor said it.'[2] It was another obsession. He test-screened his own muse, selecting safer projects then making them treacherous.

'He wants to make big personal pictures,' said Richard Price, who had served as his writer on that previous swerve toward the mainstream *The Color of Money*: 'the best actors he can get, the biggest audience he can get, to make the smallest films he can make.'[3]

What was it F. Scott Fitzgerald famously said? 'The test of a first-rate intelligence is the ability to hold two opposed ideas in mind at the same time, and still retain the ability to function.'[4] Scorsese was taking the chance to be that paradox – the artist inside the studio system. There is a voluptuous pleasure in the sheer possibility of film. As his budgets soar, so does his

Opposite: *Badfellas – the psychotic Max Cady (Robert De Niro) confronts philandering husband and dubious lawyer Sam Bowden (Nick Nolte) in Martin Scorsese's heady thriller* Cape Fear *(1991).*

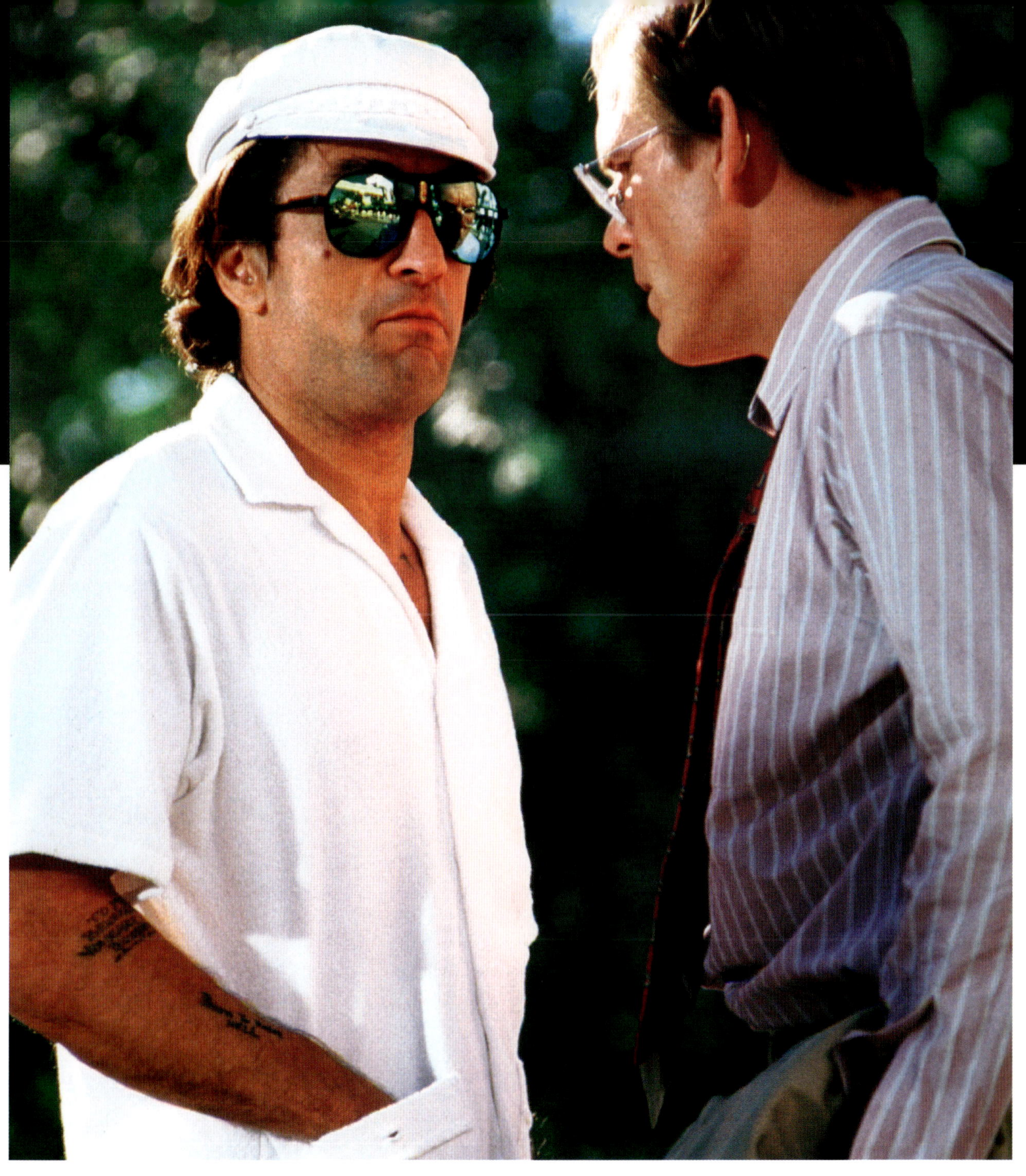

sense of adventure. There are remakes, literary adaptions; a gangster movie, for sure, but set in Las Vegas; and a portrait of the young Dalai Lama. Intimate character studies delivered in bold cinematic strokes.

Naturally, he had no intention of making *Cape Fear*, despite the urging of Spielberg, who was producing, and Robert De Niro, who was keen to star. He had read the script three times while editing *Goodfellas*. 'And three times I hated it,'[5] he retorted. The thriller had been stewing away at Universal for years: Stephen Frears had been attached before moving onto excellent neo-noir *The Grifters* (produced by Scorsese in 1990, giving him a taste of genre), then Spielberg (going through a mid-career crisis after *Hook*) had commissioned a script from Wesley Strick, with half an idea of directing it himself.

As far as Scorsese was concerned, this was merely a contemporary reworking of J. Lee Thompson's hot-headed Hitchcockian yarn from 1962 – itself based on John D. MacDonald's novel *The Executioners* – in which recently released rapist Max Cady (Robert Mitchum, Hollywood's heavy of choice) stalks Sam Bowden (Gregory Peck, Hollywood's beacon of decency), the attorney who testified against him. Against a sweaty Georgia backdrop, Bowden and his young family are drawn into a life-and-death battle for survival against a deranged, vengeful Cady. Strick's script still took its cues from Thompson's melodramatics. The morality was black and white: Cady was a bogeyman and Bowden this improbably virtuous father figure. 'They were like Martians to me. I was rooting for Max to get them,'[6] grumbled Scorsese.

Besides, he was leaning toward another offering from Spielberg's table in historical drama *Schindler's List*, the story of the German industrialist who saved his Jewish workforce from Auschwitz. Then in the throes of an awakening, Spielberg pleaded for the return of his lost child, and Scorsese, understanding his friend's need to make *Schindler's List* was far more personal than his (he was fascinated by the ambiguity of Schindler), accepted *Cape Fear* in return.

So they traded films like baseball cards, and Spielberg turned to the project that would win him Oscars, while Scorsese made the thriller which set the critics carping about a short-stop experiment in genre mechanics. *Newsweek* called it 'violent pulp.'[7] Another paradox: how Scorsese's oft-declared greatness is only perceived in hindsight. *Cape Fear* is far more interesting than its reputation might suggest.

Shooting across the winter of 1990-1991, with Fort Lauderdale, Florida doubling for Georgia, what had changed Scorsese's mind was the chance to inject something desperately human into the material. Indeed the recalibration of *Cape Fear* is an object lesson in what defines Scorsese as a filmmaker. Following a serious rewrite from Strick, a forthright horror-thriller (in theory, this is Scorsese's slasher movie) became a parable of sexual guilt and punishment. His version is another pathology of a broken marriage, a story where no one is clean. 'That's the Scorsese touch,'[8] savoured Roger Ebert.

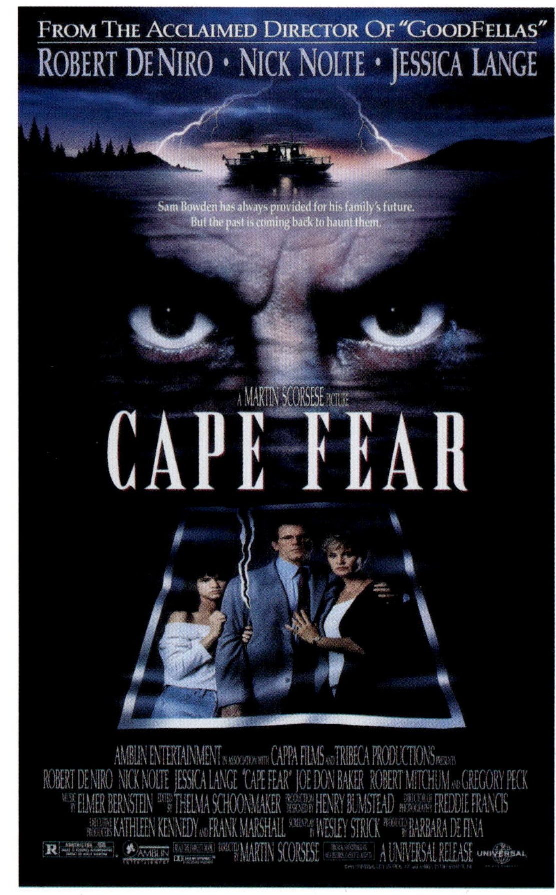

Right: *Produced by Universal,* Cape Fear *was a conscious attempt by Martin Scorsese to work within a Hollywood framework.*

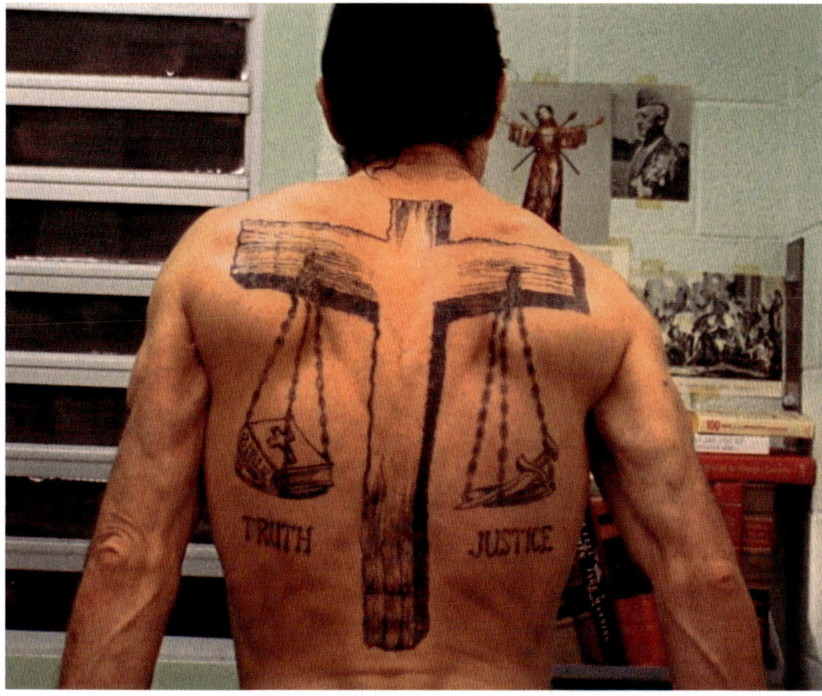

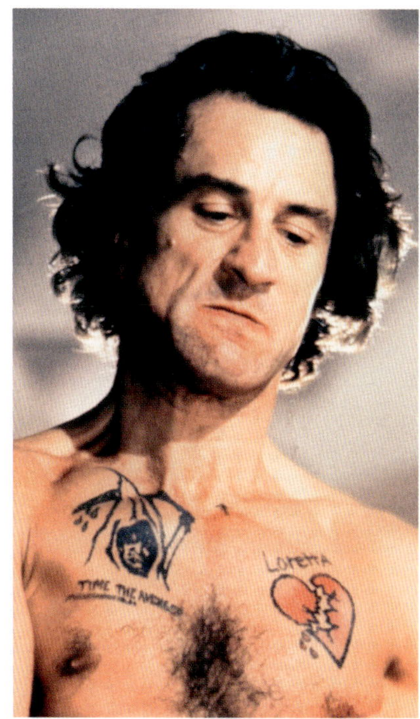

Slender and bespectacled, Nick Nolte's Sam Bowden is a deeply flawed man trying in vain to set things right. He's well cast, as it's so hard to respond to him as a hero. Nolte could easily have played Cady. Bowden is slippery and desperate. We learn that as Cady's former defence lawyer (another change instituted by Scorsese), he deliberately suppressed evidence. Themes bubble to the surface: the malleability of the law, the deception of civilized life, a sneering across class divides.

Bowden's wife Leigh (Jessica Lange) seethes with bottled-up rage over her husband's infidelities; dabbling in Method, Lange and Nolte would needle each other between takes. Sixteen-year-old Danielle (a remarkable Juliette Lewis) is crumbling beneath the squalls of her parents' marriage, while negotiating a sexual awakening. It's not precisely reality, but there is an agitation in the air to set our teeth on edge.

'Cady was sort of the malignant spirit of guilt, in a way, of the family - the avenging angel,' explained Scorsese. 'Punishment for everything you ever felt sexually.'[9]

Departing prison with furious purpose, Cady strides straight for the camera (Thelma Schoonmaker's brilliant cut is a whisker ahead of him, and you picture the tripod clattering to the ground). De Niro spent months returning his body to the taut muscularity of Travis Bickle, smothering his torso in specially designed tattoos of Biblical cant, the scales of justice imprinted on his back, a prison cell full of Nietzsche and law tomes behind him. His motivation is written all over him.

De Niro read Cady as an embodiment of pure evil, with a touch of the Terminator in his relentlessness and Popeye in his lurid squint. The director wasn't quite so sure. He saw the film in a similar vein to *The King of Comedy*, about the 'violence of

Above left: *Written on his skin – Max Cady is the most externalized of Robert De Niro's great Scorsesean weirdos, taut with months of training, tattooed with the scales of justice, his cell adorned with the signature of his obsession with vengeance.*

Above right: *De Niro had pushed Scorsese to make the film, fascinated with playing this embodiment of evil. Scorsese pushed back for something more human.*

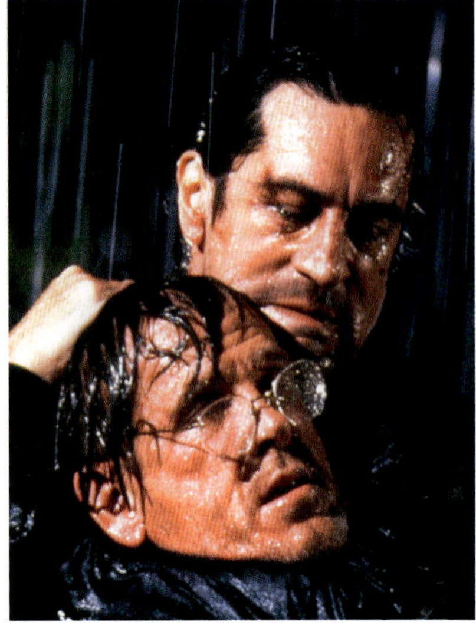

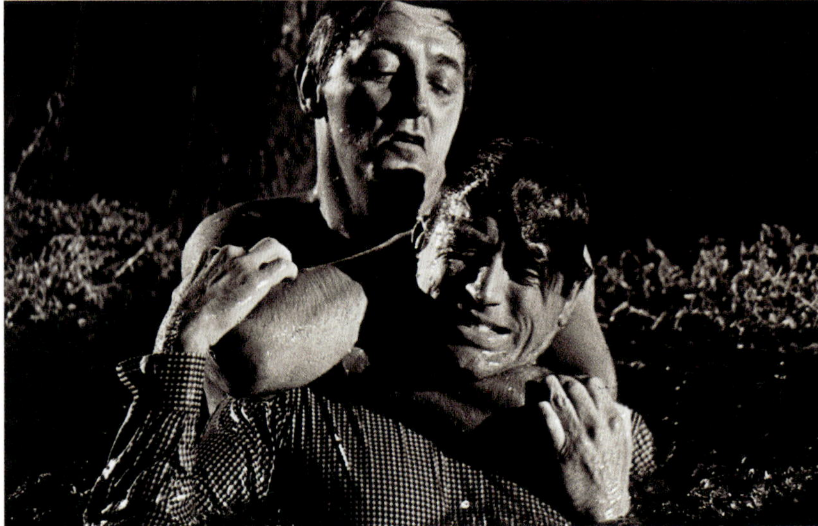

Above left: *Martin Scorsese never shied away from the fact that this was a remake of the 1962* Cape Fear, *replicating shots…*

Above right: *… such as the original's Robert Mitchum and Gregory Peck wrestling in the action-packed, river-bound finale.*

intrusion.'[10] Cady is both a force of nature disrupting the white-bread American family unit and a distorted reflection of Bowden in the ripples of oily Georgia water.

Crucial to the director's schemes (and daring) is Cady's mesmerising verbal seduction of Danielle in the school theatre, amid what looks like a production of Oz. What in Strick's first draft had been a visceral chase through the school, becomes a charged moment of Danielle betraying her father, drawn to this man she knows to be a psychopath, with Lewis holding her own against De Niro's Southern-tongued improvisations.

'I said that, I'd like to make that scene about the violation of the kid,' said Scorsese, recalling an early debate with Spielberg. 'It should be quiet.'[11]

As with *Boxcar Bertha* years earlier, he was driven by the possibility of inserting himself between the lines of an exploitation movie, only one that came with a budget of $35 million. *Cape Fear* is so self-consciously derivative it deconstructs the concept of the popular thriller. What Scorsese called its 'Hollywood theatricality.'[12]

From the very start, as Lewis delivers a haunting homily straight to camera (this is her reminiscence), Scorsese is evoking the cadences of Charles Laughton's lullaby noir *The Night of the Hunter* (featuring Mitchum as a killer dolled up as a priest), forewarning us that this is fairy-tale territory. The casting of an antique Mitchum and Peck – reversing their moral poles as a wry cop and smarmy attorney – makes explicit this is a remake. As does the music, by having Elmer Bernstein rework Bernard Herrmann's original Hitchcock-styled score, including the signature F C B F horn blast.

There is a radiant display of Hitchcockian tricks, gleeful lifts from *Vertigo, Marnie, Psycho,* and *Torn Curtain* (on the effort it takes to kill a man). The film is cock-a-hoop with symbolism: negative images for moral distortion, the bold colours and Panavision for that movie gleam, split diopters to warp reality. Cinematographer Freddie Francis was a veteran of Hammer Horror. Schoonmaker's hyperbolic editing pumps the film with anxiety, blinds are snapped shut and doors locked like percussive blows, ringing phones jar the nerves like an electric shock. This is the most present tense of all Scorsese films.

The third act fully embraces the watery tableau of *The Night of the Hunter* as the Bowdens flee to their houseboat on the titular river ahead of a mythically-minded storm and Cady in full spate. Scorsese was consciously testing himself with the brute mechanics of action. It took seven wearying weeks to shoot the gripping (if formulaic) showdown with Cady, utilizing a tank at Shepperton Studios near London.

Cady disappears into the drink babbling in tongues. Bowden is left to wash the blood from his hands. Danielle's dream-like reminiscence returns. 'The end,' she announces. Scorsese decided this was likely the end of the Bowdens' marriage too. How could it survive such wreckage? Inevitably, *Cape Fear* became his biggest hit to date, making $182 million.

What followed was another act of thrilling trespass. This time onto the hallowed ground of the literary adaptation in Edith Wharton's *The Age of Innocence*. First published in 1920, the Pulitzer Prize-winning depiction of New York high society in the 1870s sails close to satire. It is itself an act of archaeology, a survivor's memoir like Henry Hill's account in *Goodfellas*. Wharton describes a labyrinth of social codes and poised

Below: *Central to Scorsese's take was a study in family dysfunction, with the woes of daughter (Juliette Lewis), mother (Jessica Lange), and father (Nick Nolte) almost conjuring up this force of nature in their midst.*

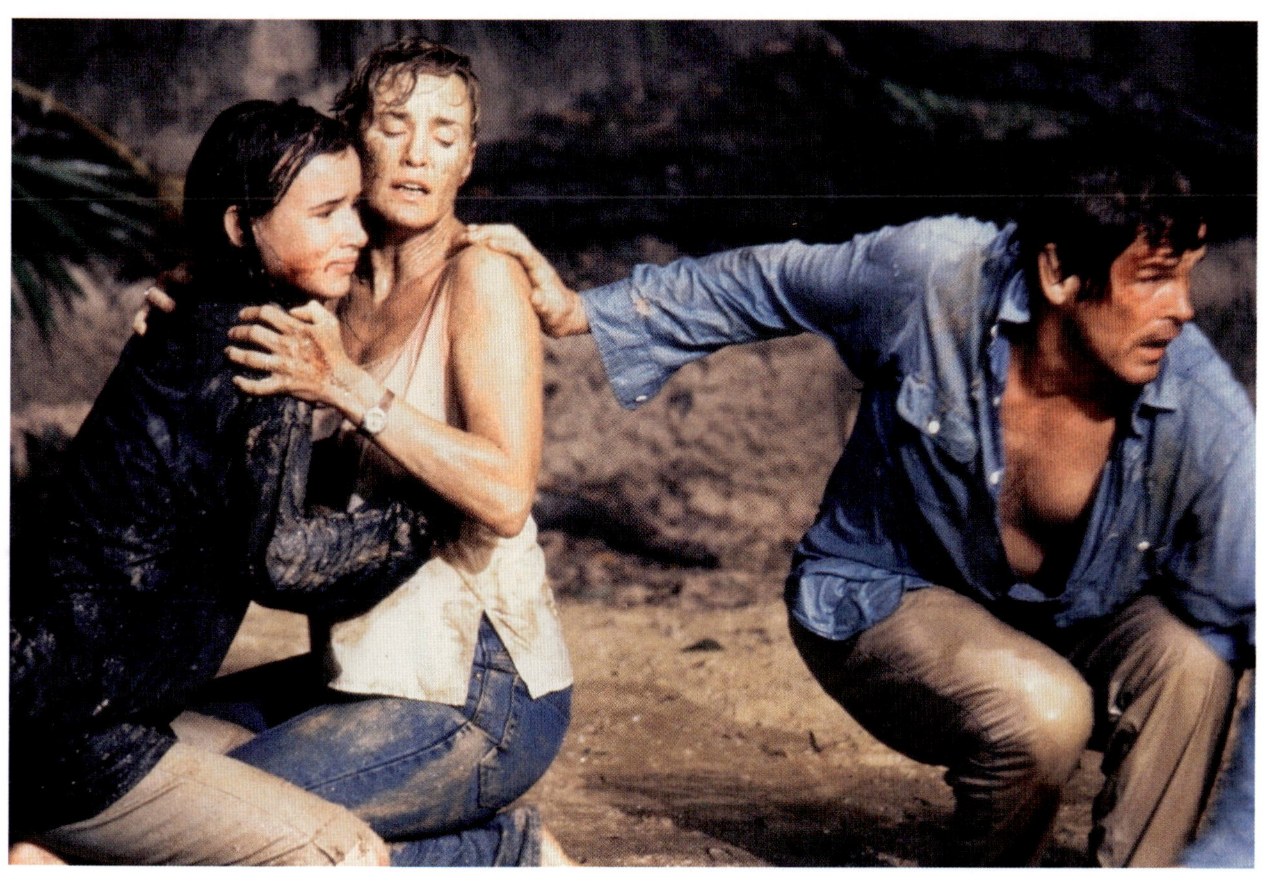

1991
THE KING OF ADS Director (segment Armani, *eau pour homme* commercial)

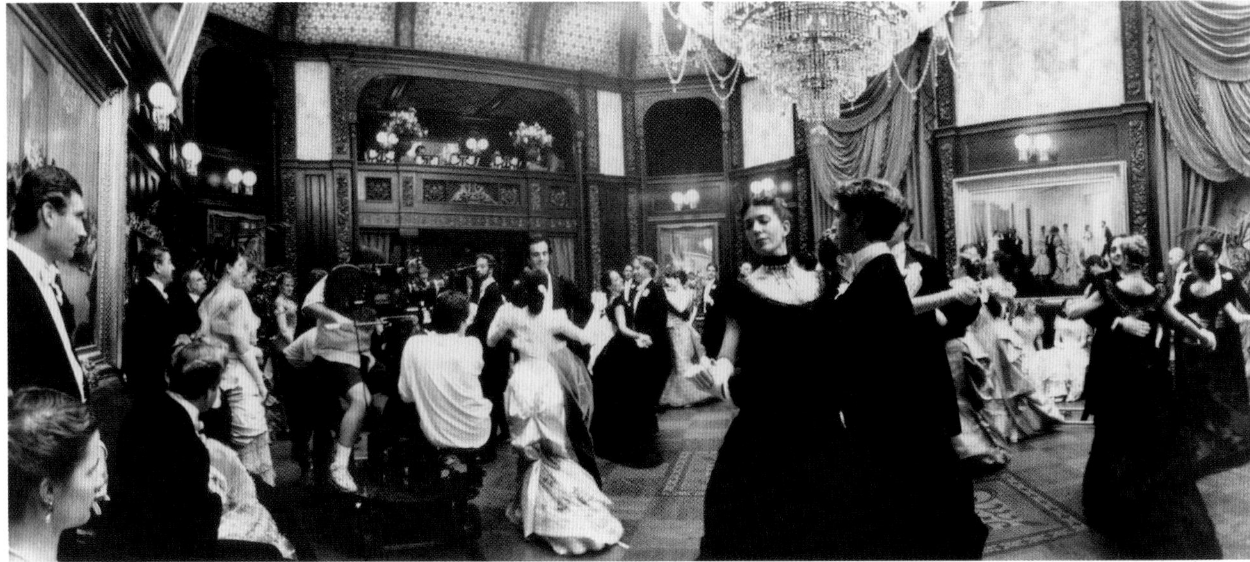

tribalism upheld by the great American families, the Roosevelts, the Astors, and the Vanderbilts. Step out of line, and you face disgrace and exile.

Film critic Jay Cocks had presented Scorsese with a copy of the novel in 1980. Close friends and collaborators since 1968, their bond was founded on a *bel esprits'* love of discussing film, often deep into the night. Scorsese spoke of wanting to attempt new genres. A Western or a revisionist gangster movie – together they had approached Philip K. Dick in 1969 about adapting *Do Androids Dream of Electric Sheep?* (later to become *Blade Runner*). He even talked of trying a romantic piece.

'You want to do a romantic piece, a costume piece,' Cocks had informed him, book in hand, 'well, this is the one, because this is you.'[13]

Wharton's story is a love triangle sealed in aspic. Newland Archer (Daniel Day-Lewis, that master time traveller) is about to announce his engagement to May Welland (Winona Ryder, who unveils a glance as loaded and terrible as De Niro's

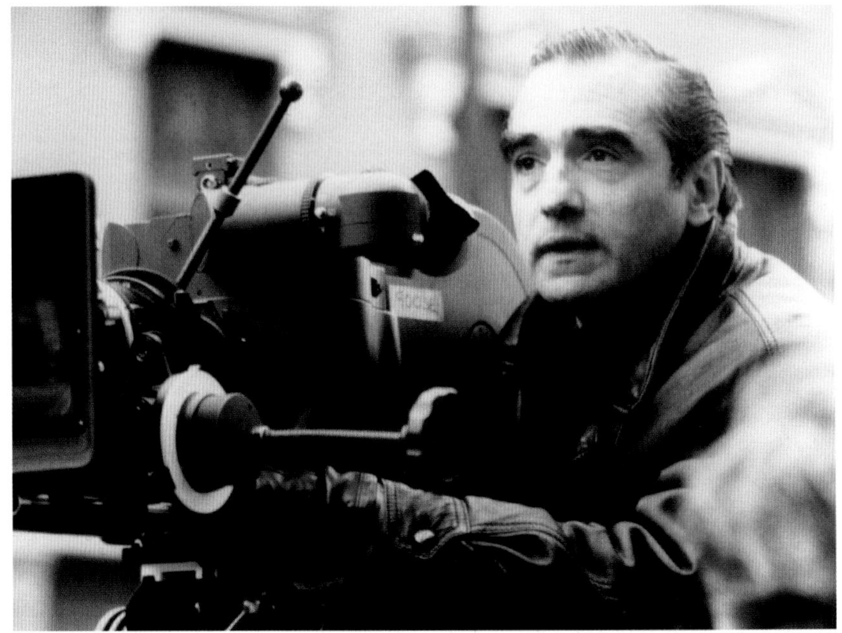

Top: *The dance of time – Martin Scorsese modelled the intricate ball sequence in* The Age of Innocence *(1993) on Luchino Visconti's* The Leopard *(1963).*

Above: *With* The Age of Innocence, *Scorsese was fascinated by the challenge of depicting purely emotional violence, welling beneath a pristine surface.*

death-dealing eyes in *Goodfellas*), of the influential Welland clan. A natural order threatened when Archer encounters May's fallen cousin, Ellen Olenska (Michelle Pfeiffer, as pale and anguished as a David Lean heroine), who has fled a scandalously unfaithful husband in Europe and dares to wear crimson to the opera. Channelling Wharton, Ellen is a doomed realist in a world of androids. 'It seems stupid to have discovered America only to make it a copy of another country,'[14] she retorts. They will fall passionately in love, but the ranks of society, May's cunning, and the self-sabotage of Archer's own breeding will force them tragically apart.

Swept up in his revisionist gangster movies, it wasn't until 1987 that Scorsese read the book and knew this was a film he had to make. In three weeks Cocks had delivered a first draft, and the intrepid director set out for Merchant Ivory territory (filmmakers he much admired), although production would be delayed for a further two and half years, lose and gain a studio (20th Century Fox lost patience and Columbia took over with an estimated budget of $34 million), before Scorsese was on set, his supple camera roving amid a panoply of ballgowns and top hats in search of chilling subtext.

When *The Age of Innocence* arrived in 1993, making a muted $32 million, critics and commentators took great pleasure in announcing how 'gorgeously uncharacteristic'[15] the film was of Scorsese. That was until you got beneath the place settings and double-talk, when they declared it to be entirely characteristic of his work. The rituals! The five-course dinners! Death by social exclusion! 'The refusals were more than a simple snubbing. They were an eradication,'[16] reports Joanne Woodward's voice-over (the voice-over!) in cut-crystal deadpan. 'This is a world run by the snob mob, the Goodfellas of Fifth Avenue,'[17] quipped the *New Yorker*.

Scorsese was well aware of all this, but it wasn't the point. Certainly, he wanted to try his hand at the literary genre. To this day, he remains troubled by the esteem in which literature is held compared to film. Can film ever attain a similar credibility? He was trying to break down the wall between the novelistic and the filmic. But

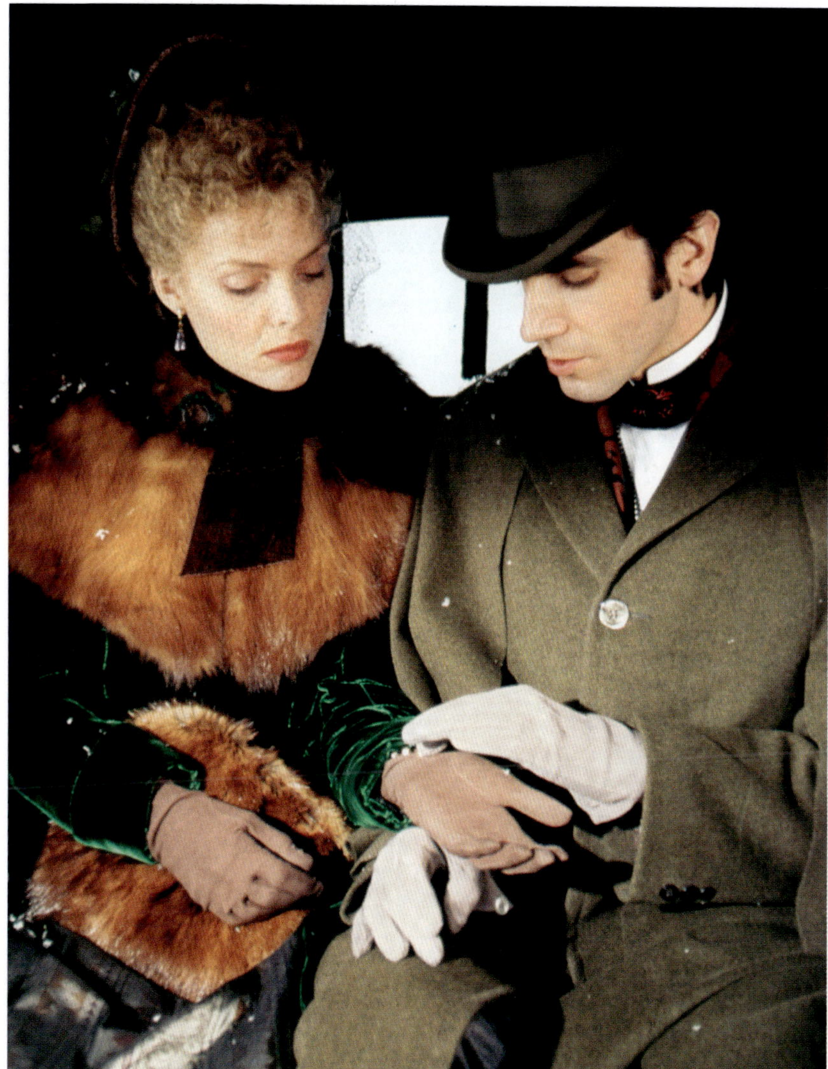

Above: *The lust temptation – Ellen Olenska (Michelle Pfeiffer) and Newland Archer (Daniel Day-Lewis) savour a momentary touch, though significantly with their gloves on.*

what truly fascinated him was a story about 'a passion that could not be expressed.'[18] Archer's love for Ellen is not unrequited, it is unconsummated. This was a film about a stifled rebellion. It echoed the guilt and repression of *Who's That Knocking at My Door* and the longing of *Taxi Driver*. There is an intense erotic tension between Archer and Ellen that can never be released – this is a Scorsese film that can't exhale.

He found locations fixed in time, such as Troy near Albany, with its impeccable brownstone exteriors, and the National Arts Club in Gramercy Park, for the hub of the Beaufort Mansion. Only three sets were built (including the pivotal ballroom). The centrepiece of the Beauforts' ball is a bewildering tableau of rehearsed movements, society in miniature, beneath a chandelier, commissioned for $25,000.

As he beheld the world of *Goodfellas*, Scorsese brings us into intense proximity with upper crust American society in the 19th century. Eighteen months of research accumulated twenty-five reference books, covering spoons to gowns to the looming portraits (ghosts at the dance). Where once Johnny 'Cha Cha' Ciarcia would drop by set to vouchsafe ethnic nuance, they hired an etiquette consultant named Lily Lodge, whose grandmother had known Wharton.

Suffused with ironic hauteur, Woodward's anonymous voice-over is essentially Wharton, recalling events. Or the voice of the book: a densely packed litany of artefacts, a dizzying stocktaking of an era we can barely take in. All of which is setting us up for the devastating fall of Archer's hopes. The studio were baffled.

'Who's the narrator?' they pressed.

'Who cares?'[19] replied Scorsese.

This is a world reassembled with the infinitesimal care and poise of the novel, a movie locked in a snow globe, through which his camera glides like an uninvited

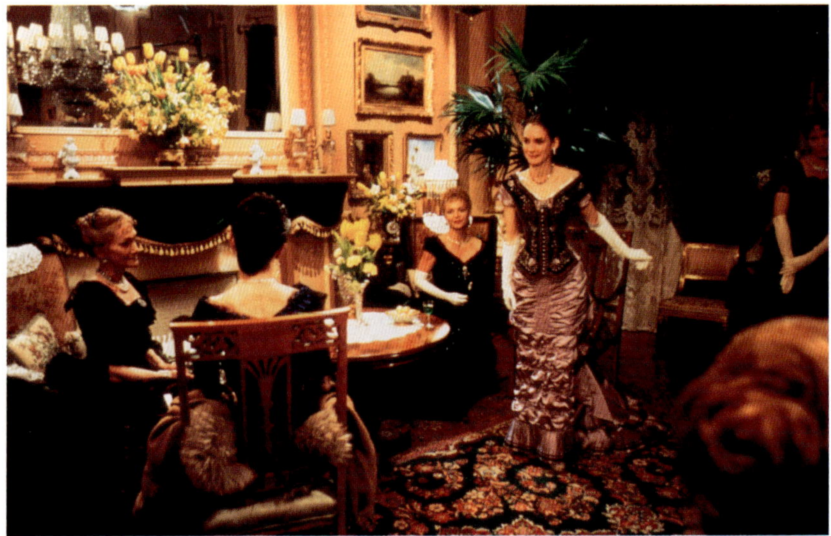

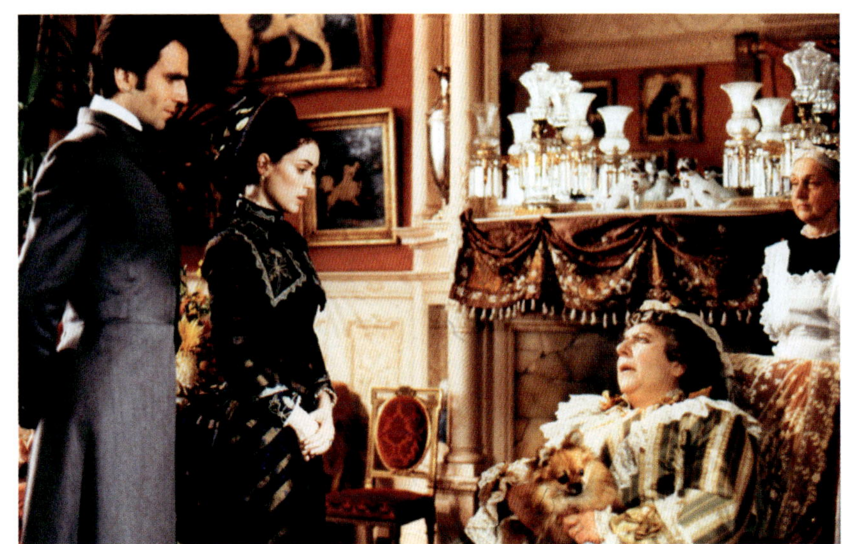

Top: *Winona Ryder's May Welland holds court in* The Age of Innocence *– design was everything, the world had to be dazzlingly full, a New York locked inside a snow globe.*

Above: *Newland (Daniel Day-Lewis) and May (Ryder) meet with her grandmother, Mrs Mingott (Miriam Margolyes) – the unconventional* grand dame *is the society equivalent of a mob boss.*

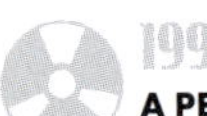

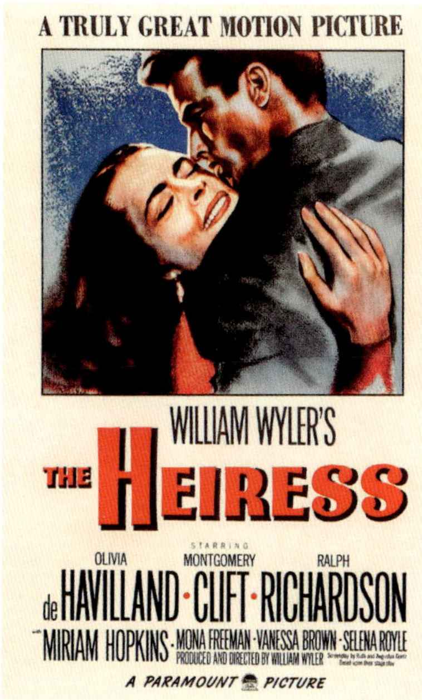

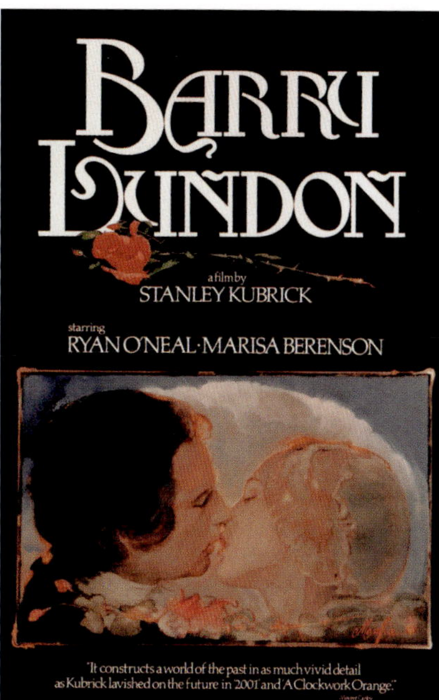

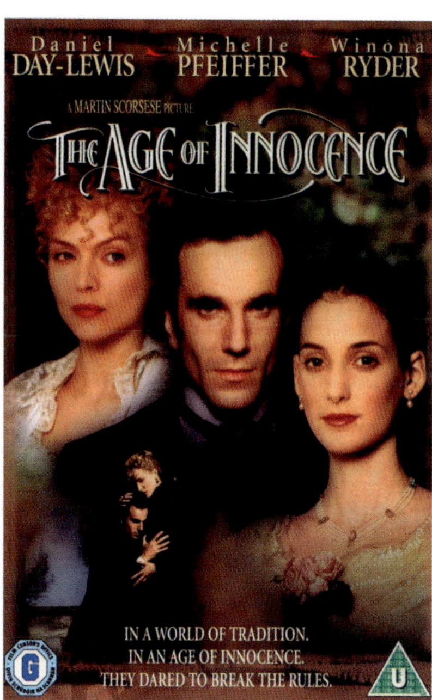

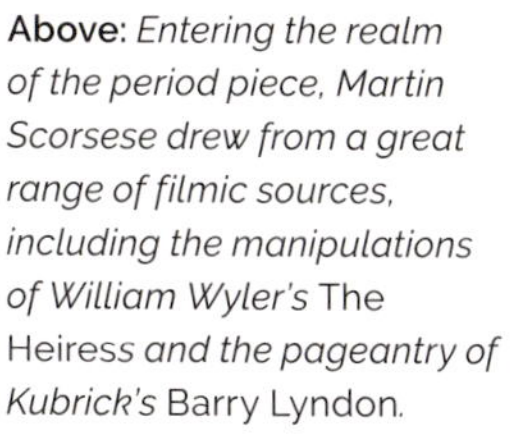

Above: *Entering the realm of the period piece, Martin Scorsese drew from a great range of filmic sources, including the manipulations of William Wyler's* The Heiress *and the pageantry of Kubrick's* Barry Lyndon.

but curious guest, where impossible passion is displaced onto the beauty of objects. It's an unconsummated world.

Meanwhile, Scorsese's cinematic quotations are true to the mood. Alongside Merchant Ivory, he used Visconti's trilogy *Senso*, *The Leopard* (with its extensive ball sequence), and *The Innocent*, as well as Kubrick's *Barry Lyndon* for the slow zooms. The clipped ecstasy of his beloved Powell and Pressburger is there in the florid richness of gold-plated New York; that feeling of a stage setting, or the backdrop to a fairy tale. Scorsese screened William Wyler's *The Heiress* and Orson Welles' *The Magnificent Ambersons* for his cast and crew to take in the textures of American wealth.

Cut to Vegas, somewhere in the seventies.

Ace Rothstein (De Niro keeping the furies bottled) certainly likes to look the part. The head of the Tangiers casino in all but name (the mob have coined the title 'PR Director'[20] to cut a few legal corners), his array of silk suits and gartered socks are as garish as the cascading neon beyond the revolving doors (Scorsese specifically chose every one of De Niro's fifty-two costume changes, a colour-coded path to damnation from steel blues to bloodbath scarlet). Ace reigns in the 'morality car wash'[21] of Las Vegas, patrolling the casino floor, fastidious eyes trained for anyone aiming to beat the system. He's the crime boss who abhors cheats.

In every gleaming frame (and Scorsese is rapturous with what he termed 'the blast of Vegas'[22]) it is clear this is another film about the lure of American wealth. There is a fascinating parallel between Ace's prescribed operation, keeping the coffers filled, and the nervous struggles of a studio boss.

With another local big shot in a Stetson looking for a favour, Ace rises from behind his desk in silk boxers and turquoise loafers to retrieve his trousers from the closet. Sitting in them would only ruin the crease.

It's a comical image, but for Scorsese it revealed Ace's precariousness - nothing can get out of line. 'The small moves are what I'm interested in.'[23]

Why did Scorsese make *Casino*? Hadn't *Goodfellas* been his final word on the mob? Hadn't he claimed that he no longer wanted to be the Italian-American guy who made fast-talking gangster films like home movies with bodies in the trunk? Then again, hadn't he made the same claim after *Mean Streets*? History just has this habit of repeating.

Goodfellas writer Nicholas Pileggi had shown him a newspaper article about a domestic fight on a Vegas lawn one Sunday morning. The husband turned out to be Frank 'Lefty' Rosenthal, the mob's man in Vegas; the wife was Geri McGee, former showgirl and erstwhile hustler, the wrong side of the booze and drugs that were eating her up. Writer and director followed the thread back into the maze: this marital spat was the final act of a ten-year odyssey that charted the collapse of mob rule among the fountains and roulette wheels. Real Fall of the Roman Empire stuff. The article led them to Lefty's car being bombed (the perfect framing device), and how by a stroke of luck the dapper mobster lived to tell (he advised both Pileggi and De Niro). That led them to the love triangle between Lefty, Geri, and his best friend, a real live wire named Nicky, useful when it came to collecting overdue debts but eventually beaten to death by a chorus of baseball bats. Scorsese was hooked.

'I just thought it would make a terrific story,'[24] he said, and Pileggi set about transforming the real figures into the volatile trio of Ace, Ginger (Sharon Stone), and Nicky Santoro (Joe Pesci). The next chapter in Scorsese's career-spanning mob saga unfurled before him.

More prosaically, he owed Universal another picture. And they were offering $52 million for a crime biopic in a familiar guise: alongside De Niro and Pesci are a

Below left: *Familiar faces, new city – Robert De Niro and Joe Pesci return for* Casino *(1995), Martin Scorsese's Fall of the Roman Empire-style take on the mob in Las Vegas.*

Below right: *Sharon Stone excels as Ginger, the untrustworthy wife of De Niro's casino boss Ace Rothstein.*

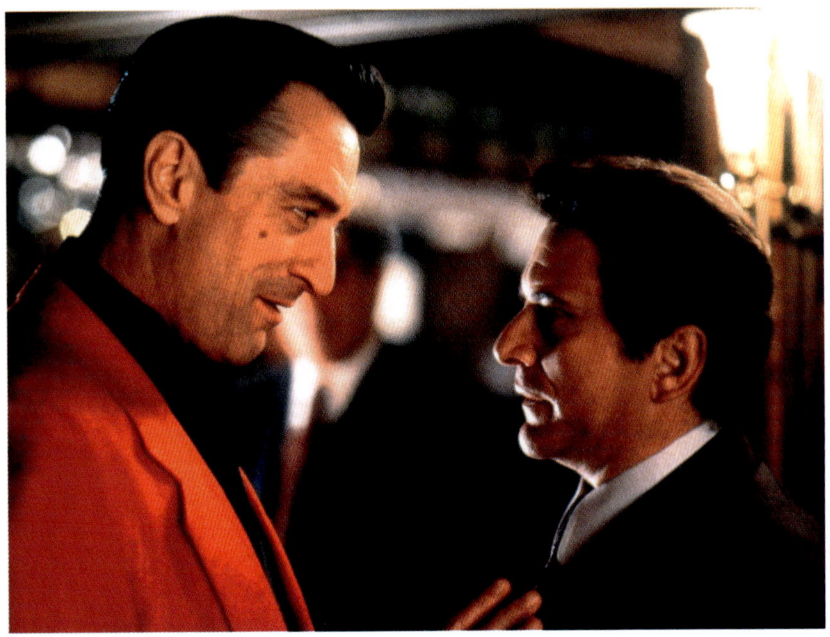

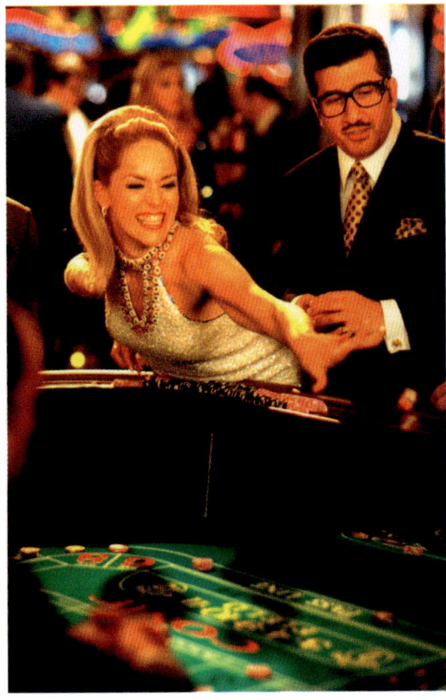

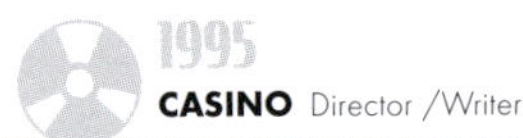

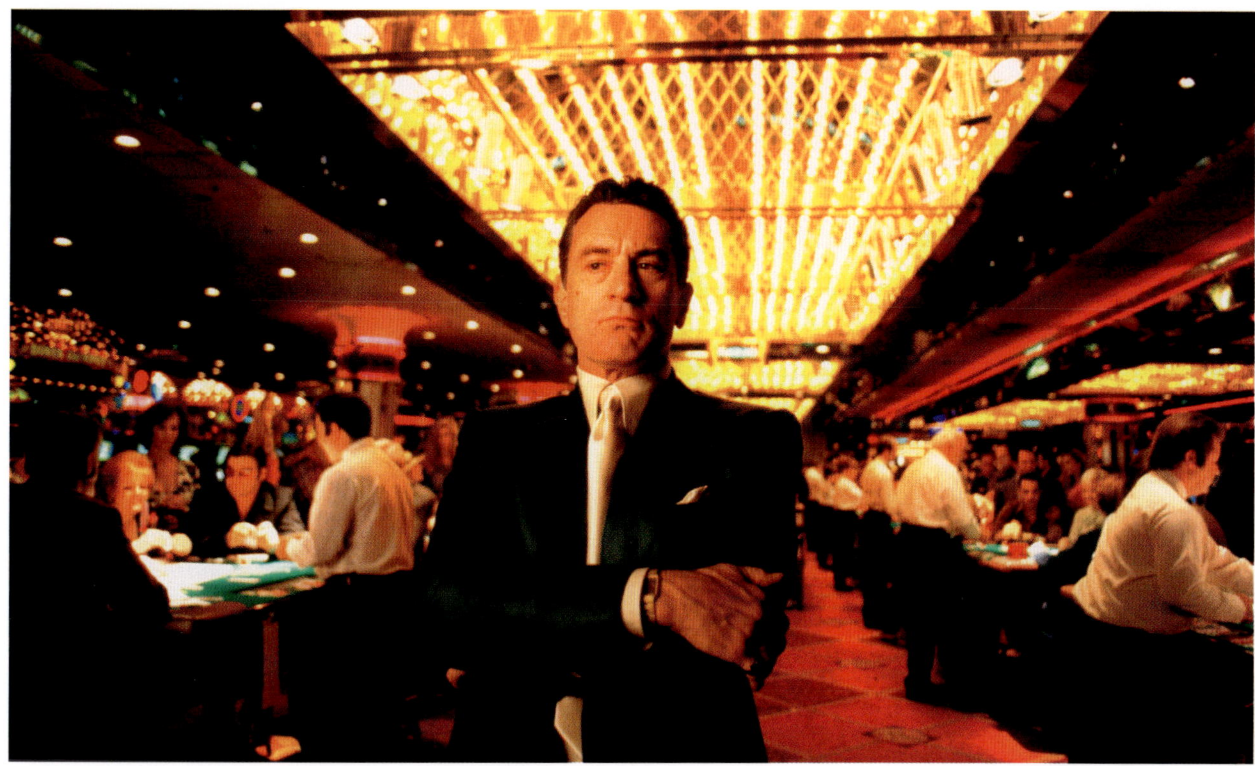

host of regular Scorsese players to cover the statutory tableau of foot soldiers and made men and all the lickspittle fronts for the business, every minor figure beautifully drawn. We even get Scorsese's mother cooking meatballs.

Shooting from September 1994, with the Riviera used for the Tangiers (there was no need to build a single set when they could haunt real Vegas tables by night), Scorsese is consciously playing to old strengths. This is what happens when the goombahs of *Goodfellas* get big ideas. There is even a tracking shot pursuing the bag man across the casino floor, into the counting room (coins, bills, chips, jewellery: the camera revels in the very texture of money), and back out again into a waiting taxi. The bosses back in Kansas City, framed like Da Vinci's *Last Supper*, like to skim from the official profits. And don't take kindly to Nicky skimming from the skims.

Casino contains multitudes, three hours (Scorsese is growing plump with age) of the epic and personal, the documentarian nuance and violent spectacle (literally eye-popping when Nicky puts a vice into use) braided together. We are guided through the intricate workings of the bright-light city under mob management from 1973-1983 by a duet of nostalgic voice-overs: De Niro's edifying Ace and Pesci's retorts as Nicky, the best friend and made man who gets greedy, because that is his nature. There's a hint they are waxing wise from beyond the grave like William Holden in *Sunset Boulevard*, but that will prove to be only half true.

The first hour alone is devoted to the crisp, funny, authentic groove of Scorsese

Above: *Set a thief to catch a thief – De Niro's mobster Ace Rothstein scrutinizes the casino floor for any hint of cheating.*

> Scorsese certainly hasn't forgotten how to make a movie. What he appears to have forgotten is why...
>
> TERRENCE RAFFERTY

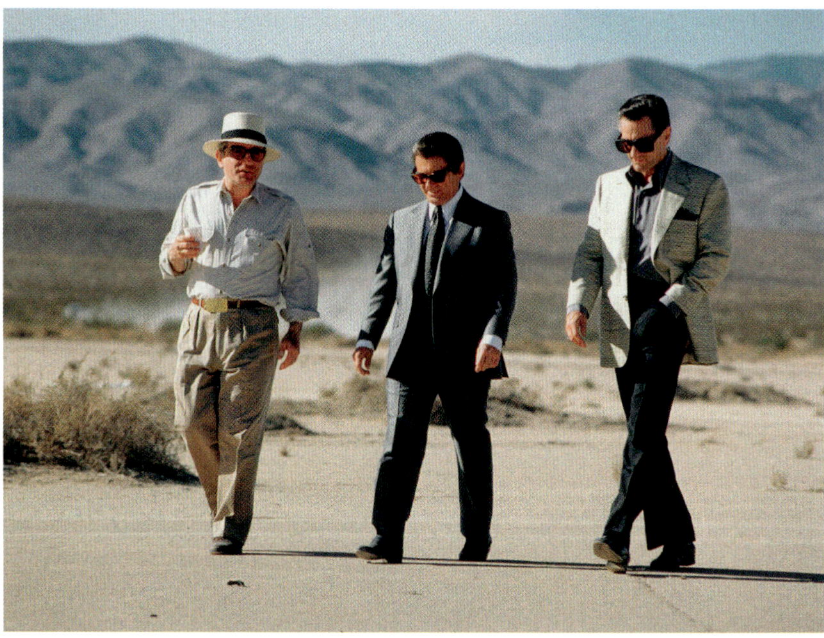

Above: *Out of their comfort zone – Martin Scorsese, Joe Pesci, and Robert De Niro plan a desert-set face-off in* Casino.

as mob historian. This is editing as symphony, fact stacked on fact, giving us the full fiscal breakdown of Ace's purring Vegas machine... The Age of Guilt. All of it building incrementally to the sight of Ginger, a vision in a pearl-white mini-dress, making a scene as she pilfers chips from a craps table, and Ace is in love.

Freeze frame.

Stone was the first actress Scorsese met with for Ginger, and ended up nominated for Best Actress (with Scorsese dutifully nominated as Best Director). Every potential Ginger was required to audition. Scorsese was in search of a particular energy; the frequency of her descent into addiction was something he understood from experience. Stone, he knew, had a 'determination to play this woman.'[25] And there was something in her screen presence that corresponded with seventies Vegas: she even resembled the real Geri.

Ace's downfall can be traced to the night he asks Ginger to marry him (it was the first scene Stone shot). Even she tries to dissuade him: 'You've got the wrong girl...'[26] As Dinah Washington's *What a Difference a Day Makes* serenades the wedding party, *Casino* becomes another tumultuous study in marriage, as bruising as *Raging Bull*.

Reviews were surprisingly cold. 'Scorsese certainly hasn't forgotten how to make a movie. What he appears to have forgotten is why...'[27] sneered Terrence Rafferty in the *New Yorker*. He was accused of coasting. But Oscar nominations followed and respectable box office ($116 million worldwide), and if the film is familiar, it's also a reminder of how good Scorsese is on home turf.

We depart with another montage. As the mob lost ground, the corporations moved in to turn Sin City into Disneyland. 'And that's that,'[28] shrugs Ace. Not quite, Scorsese would wheel back onto the theme with the same diagnostic eye in *The Wolf of Wall Street*, the moral much the same: the house always wins, until fate comes calling.

If we could be satisfied that we knew Scorsese in middle age, luxuriating in studio budgets, while smuggling his ideas into the multiplexes, he then chose to make a biopic of the young Dalai Lama set against the invasion of Tibet by communist China, just as Hollywood was making profitable inroads into the Chinese market. Universal refused to touch the film, and having backed the production Disney grew nervous, seeking the advice of Henry Kissinger on how to handle its release. Framed as an artistic whim, the film would be quietly smothered at birth, making less than $6 million.

What was on Scorsese's mind was less provocation than meditation. *Kundun* (the Tibetan name given to the reincarnated Dalai Lama) was a return to the spirituality of *The Last Temptation of Christ*, and equally to *The Age of Innocence* and the rituals of a closed world. 'I just know that I was burning to make it,'[29] said Scorsese.

Screenwriter Melissa Mathison had been on the fringes of the seventies scene, married Harrison Ford, and revealed a gift for fairy-tale-hued stories told from a child's perspective with *The Black Stallion* and *E.T. The Extra-Terrestrial*. Fuelled by a series of interviews with the Dalai Lama, in *Kundun* she depicted the life of the Tibetan spiritual leader from his discovery in a peasant family aged only two (Tenzin Yeshi Paichang), to leadership of a country at sixteen (the very moving Tenzin Thuthob Tsarong), before being confronted by an invading force intent on ridding the land of Buddhism, the very thing he embodied. The film ends as he escapes into exile in 1959.

Below: *A biopic of the Dalai Lama,* Kundun *(1997) would take Scorsese even further from his natural habitat, spiritually and geographically (Morocco stood in for Tibet).*

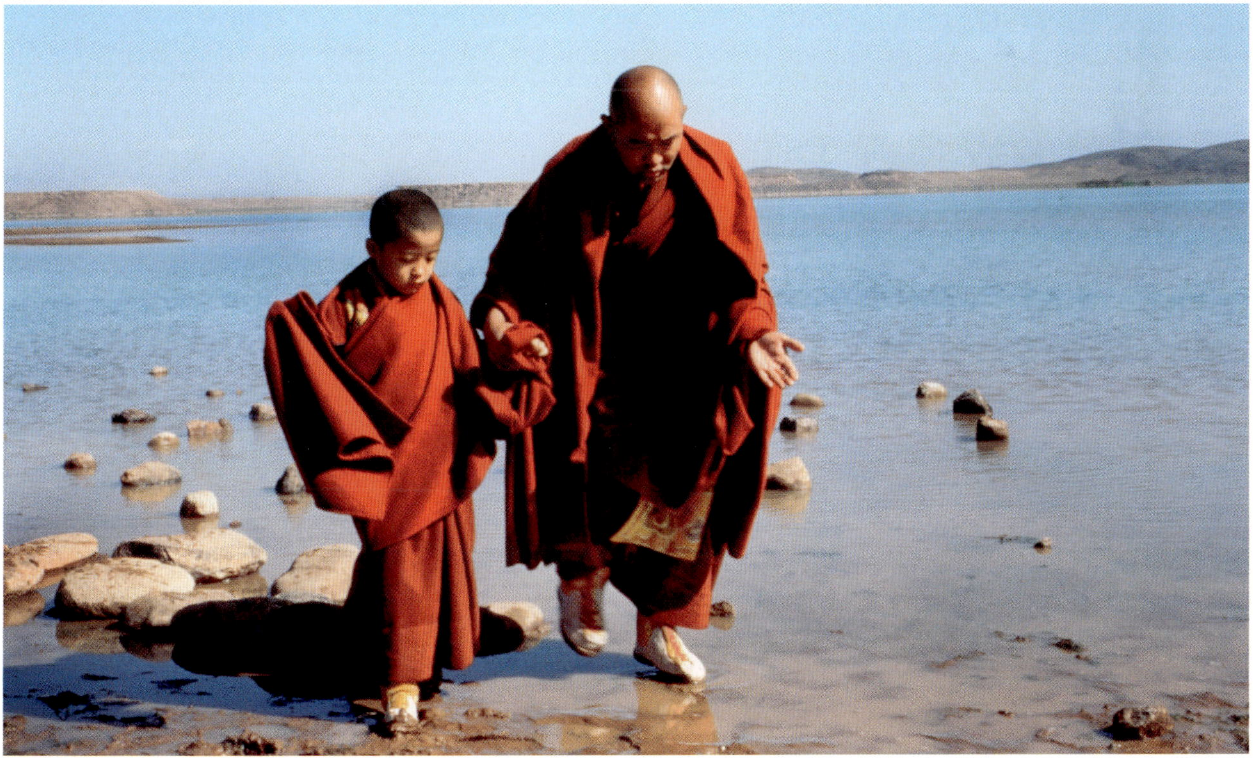

'I'm always interested in people who lose their world,' said Scorsese, 'like in *Mean Streets*, or *Goodfellas*, or *The Age of Innocence*.'[30]

At Mathison's behest, the script had been passed onto him by his agent. The director was immediately taken by its simplicity. How seismic historical events were viewed only from the child's perspective (court machinations are caught in whispers like the hidden gossip of Manhattan in *The Age of Innocence*). This was Spielbergian terrain – the savageries of growing up, but set against a grandiose backdrop both scenic and religious. It would take fourteen drafts before he was ready to shoot in Morocco in autumn 1996 (Tibet being well out of reach), with the Atlas Mountains doubling for the Himalayas.

Scorsese's choices were never solely about one thing, it was more a coming together of feelings, a sudden certainty about the material. There was a personal connection with *Kundun*: 'It has something to do with my own puffed up ideas of becoming a spiritual person and a priest.'[31] It was also about the desire to take film into the abstract, a realm of the senses, concomitant with a documentarian's dedication to depicting fact. He was attempting to bring together his religious and filmmaking sides.

Kundun offered a chance to work with new collaborators. Philip Glass provided what is for Scorsese a traditional score (the director was inspired by Glass's music for Paul Schrader's *Mishima*), and feted cinematographer Roger Deakins gave him timeless imagery. The result is a ravishing if distant epic, the camera soaking in the ancient fabric of Buddhism, down to the coloured grains of the great mandalas and vast, ancient landscape. After old New York and gaudy Vegas, these were the endless horizons of the Western. Scorsese was slipping into myth.

He pursued what he called 'dreamlike states rather than narrative states.'[32] He

Below left: *Martin Scorsese directs the five-year-old Tulku Jamyang Kunga Tenzin as an infant Dalai Lama.* Kundun *was the first time he had featured significant child performances since* Alice Doesn't Live Here Anymore *(1974).*

Below right: *The powerful Tibetan actor Tenzin Thuthob Tsarong as the adult Dalai Lama.*

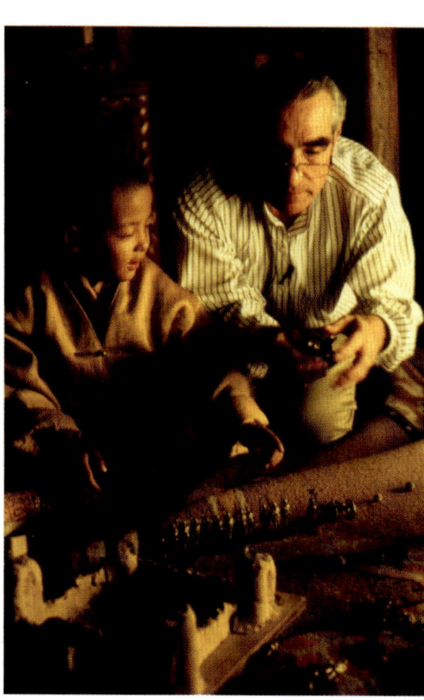

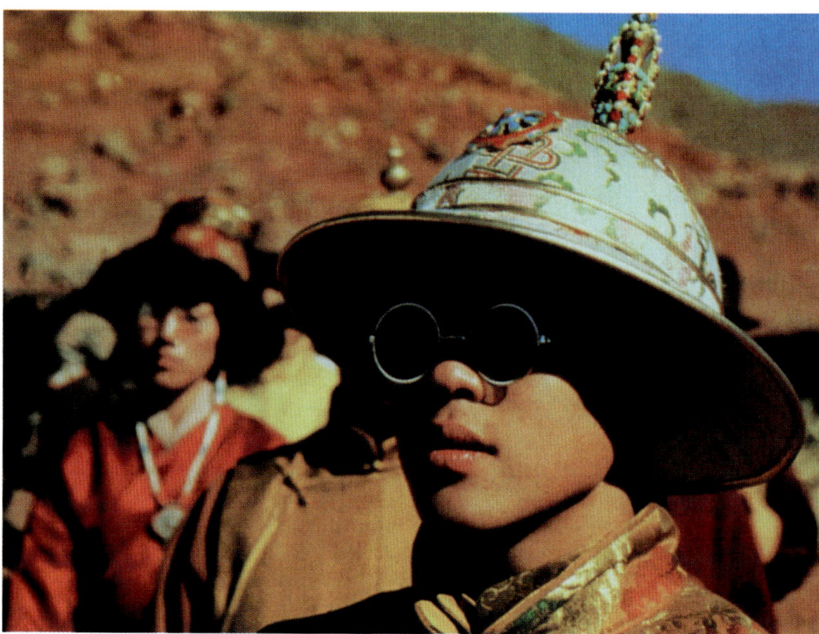

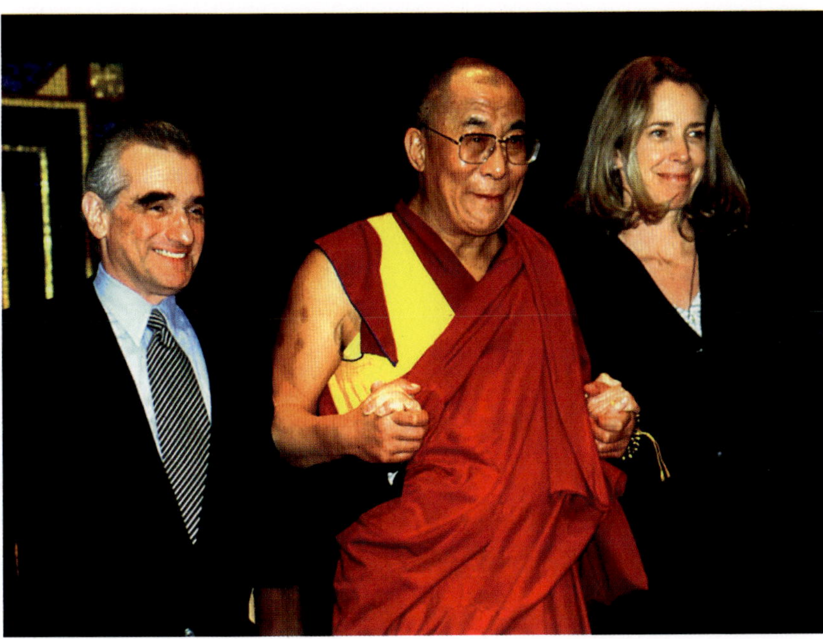

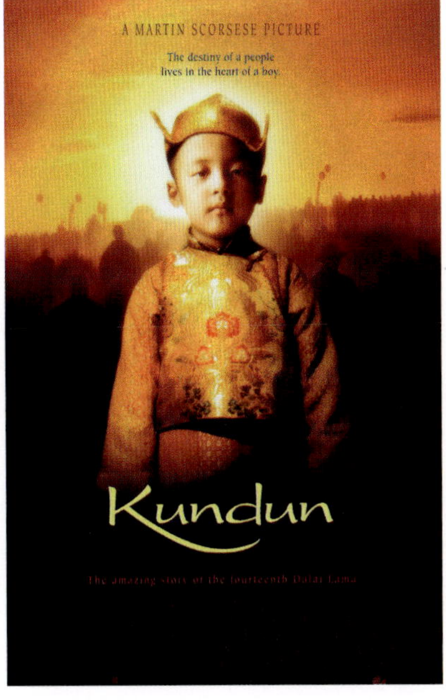

Above left: *Martin Scorsese and screenwriter Melissa Mathison accompany the fourteenth Dalai Lama, who had given his approval to the film, at an event to honour the release of* Kundun.

Above right: *Kundun was met with a muted response at the box office, a situation that wasn't helped by a nervous Disney not pushing the film's release.*

was testing himself, testing his medium, following the guide of Eastern cinema, artists such as Akira Kurosawa, Satyajit Ray, and Tian Zhuangzhuang. We observe the drama remotely, sometimes too remotely, as if through the old telescope through which Kundun gazes at the world.

The critics were split. The director's ambition couldn't be denied, he was in danger of disappearing into art. 'Scorsese devises a poem of textures and silences. Visions, nightmares and history blend in a tapestry,'[33] wrote Richard Corliss in *Time*. Whereas in *New York Magazine*, David Denby was blunt: 'It's an extremely beautiful, boring movie.'[34]

Some years later, Scorsese attended a ceremony in Washington with the Dalai Lama. One of the leader's retinue approached him. He was very small and encased in golden robes, with glasses on the bridge of his nose, evidentially a monk. He thanked Scorsese profusely for having made *Kundun*.

'I saw your other movie,' he went on to say, '*New York Gangs*. Violent violent.'[35]

Scorsese frowned.

'But it's alright,' the monk smiled. 'It's in your nature.'[36]

Was *Bringing Out the Dead* consciously a successor to *Taxi Driver?* This was the burning question when the film was released in October 1999, with the millennium looming and Martin Scorsese again patrolling the midnight streets of New York. He had been sent the galleys of Joe Connelly's semi-autobiographical novel by producer Scott Rudin while editing *Kundun*, and responded to its existential drift immediately. Working the graveyard shift, paramedic Frank Pierce (Nicolas Cage, plying his trademark mix of intensity and bolts of manic humour) rushes through the night, catching glimpses of those who died under his watch. Guilt threatens to consume him. He hasn't saved anyone for weeks. 'At the beginning of the story, he begins a three-day-and-night crack-up,'[1] relished Scorsese. Frank needs to quit, to get away like Charlie in *Mean Streets*. 'I just need a few slow nights,'[2] he sighs in voice-over, gloomier than Travis Bickle, more wounded. He will meet a girl, a drug addict named Mary (Cage's then-wife Patricia Arquette), whose estranged father lies dying in a hospital bed. The chaos of the E.R. will be created on a disused floor of Bellevue Hospital on First Avenue, real emergencies only a few storeys above. It goes by the name of Our Lady of Perpetual Mercy in the film – the drivers know it as 'Misery.'[3]

Even though they hadn't worked together for years, egos having clashed one too many times, Scorsese knew the man to do this character study justice was *Taxi Driver's* Paul Schrader. He wrote the first draft in three weeks, well aware they were coming full circle, but also sensing new ground.

Schrader divided the film into three consecutive, purgatorial nights, each featuring a different co-pilot for Frank: John Goodman, Ving Rhames, and Tom Sizemore provide a chorus of gallows humour – and coping mechanisms (food, religion, violence) – recalling the philosophical cabbies of 1976. The film opens with Frank's sleepless eyes in the rear-view mirror. We are embedded again in a subjective consciousness gripped by

Opposite: *Paramedical drama – John Goodman and a tormented Nicolas Cage attend at a scene of the scene of an accident. Martin Scorsese was quite open to* Bringing Out the Dead *(1999) being a spiritual successor to* Taxi Driver *(1976).*

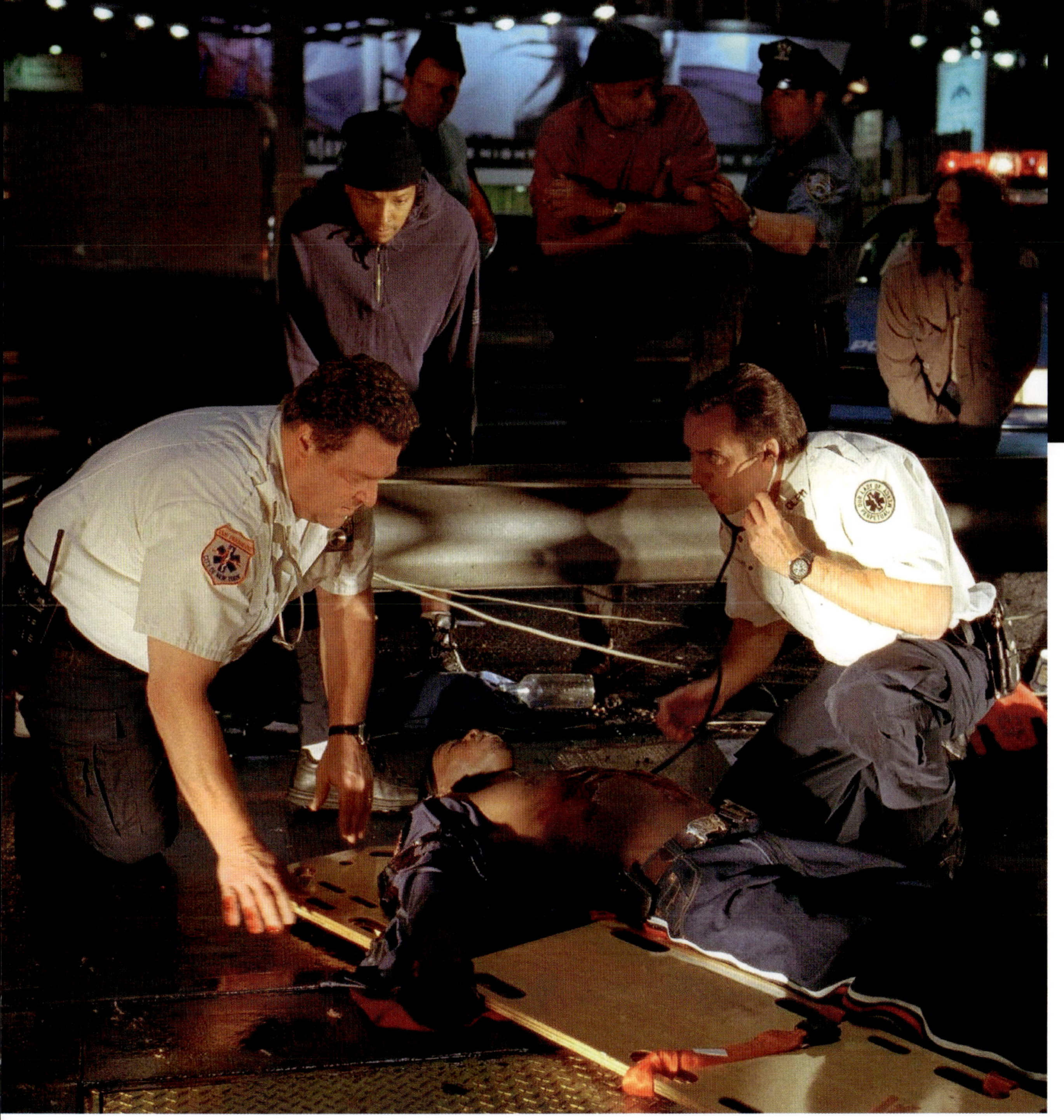

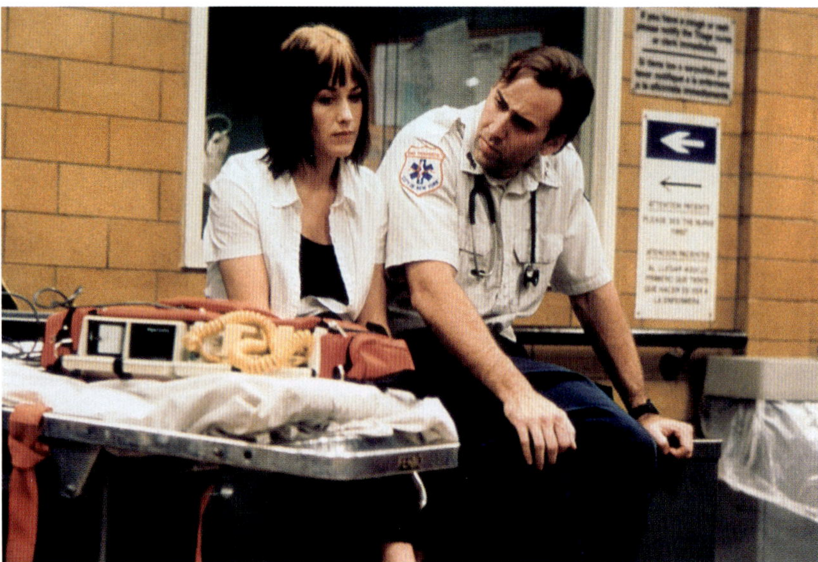

Left: *Old haunts – Patricia Arquette and Nicolas Cage star in Martin Scorsese's moody return to New York,* Bringing Out the Dead *(1999).*

crisis. Cliff Curtis' drug dealer Cy has the same jivey-menacing way about him as Harvey Keitel's Sport.

'The *Taxi Driver* comparison is there,' conceded Schrader, 'it's unavoidable.'[4]

'There's a correlation to *Taxi Driver*,' admitted Scorsese, '... Only it's twenty-five years later and we're a little mellower. Instead of killing people, our protagonist is trying to save people.'[5]

Themes of suffering and redemption, a phantasmagorical New York, classic Scorsese riffs, still coruscate across the screen, but the overriding note is compassion.

It's the flip side of the coin to *Taxi Driver*.

Like De Niro sampling life behind the wheel of a cab, Cage went out with real paramedic teams in New York and LA, startled to find himself wrapped in a bullet-proof jacket as they attended a drive-by. These guys don't necessarily arrive in the aftermath of incidents. Scorsese joined him, as he had De Niro, for a couple of New York shifts. 'As you speed down the streets, you start to imagine that you're seeing things in the blur of your peripheral vision,'[6] he noticed. He began conceiving ecstatic images. How to haunt his ghost story.

Bringing Out the Dead is in a sense a period piece, filmed in the winter months of 1998 but set in the early nineties, before Manhattan was cleansed of the past. Scorsese is vividly referencing Scorsese. Compelled by a jukebox of furious hits (Van Morrison, R.E.M., The Clash), the gyrating lights of the ambulance, hot reds and icy blues, melt into the electric blizzard of Hell's Kitchen, returned to its scummy glory. There is something of the delirious underworld of *After Hours* about it too, concluding a trilogy of Manhattan nightmares.

We are seeing through Frank's eyes, drowning in his tumbling thoughts, sharing his encounters with the dead. 'He is hallucinating, no doubt,'[7] insisted Scorsese. Madness can be so cinematic. The streets warp into blurs, the camera angles going haywire like the rush of a drug. Frank is another Scorsesean junkie, addicted to the high of saving lives. Across the helter-skelter nights of the script he is going cold turkey. 'None of us is God,'[8] warned the director.

Of any Scorsese, *Bringing Out the Dead* is the most forgotten. Paramount had done little to support its release and it disappeared from cinemas with undue haste, having made only $17 million and costing $55 million. Critics were a little taken aback. Why was the greatest active American director repeating himself? 'Though I hate to say so, it feels like a package,'[9] mused the *New Yorker*.

Isn't such zest and darkness a reaffirmation of style? A reminder that Scorsese could still dance with cinema like no other director alive. When Frank rushes to save Cy, impaled on an iron railing twenty storeys up after an altercation with a rival gang, Scorsese serenades his agonies, transforming acetylene sparks into a firework display in deft and dark homage to Woody Allen's transcendent *Manhattan*. 'I love this city!'[10] Cy cries out to the night.

Compare the end of *Gangs of New York* to its stirring beginning. The bookends – street battle to street battle, slain father to slain father – tell a tale of flawed potential. The beginning is extraordinary filmmaking, a master at his game, but in a transformative new context: deep underground, the doomed Priest Vallon (Liam Neeson, nobility personified) musters his immigrant Irish soldiers for a territorial dust-up with the despotic head of native-born rivals William Cutting, 'Bill the Butcher' by repute (a peerless, drainpipe-thin Daniel Day-Lewis, whose grin lurks close to a snarl). The martial drums of Howard Shore's score rattle the soundtrack, a call to arms, Natives versus Dead Rabbits. A tincture of customary voice-over is heard, Leonardo DiCaprio in reverie: 'Some I have remembered, the rest I built from dreams.'[11] The look is almost medieval: a bronzed montage of firelight and squalor, blades whetted at the wheel, cudgels snatched to hand, catacombs tracing a literal underworld beneath the streets. The set was a warren big enough to fill a soundstage at Cinecittà Studios in Rome, home to the grand formulations of the epic. In Scorsese's imagining, a door is finally kicked open, framing the snowy tableau of the Five Points in Lower Manhattan, 1846, as John Ford's fabled doorway framed the desert in *The Searchers*. It is tempting to call this an urban Western.

Religion carves its way through *Gangs of New York*, divisions sharp as a butcher's knife, taxonomies of immigrant and nativist that still sour the nation. This uncertain film grows more relevant. An almighty skirmish unfolds in a choreographed frenzy of Yugoslavian stunt men (communication was an issue) and

Below: *Shot at Cinecittà Studios in Rome,* Gangs of New York *(2002) saw Martin Scorsese moving fully into the epic mode.*

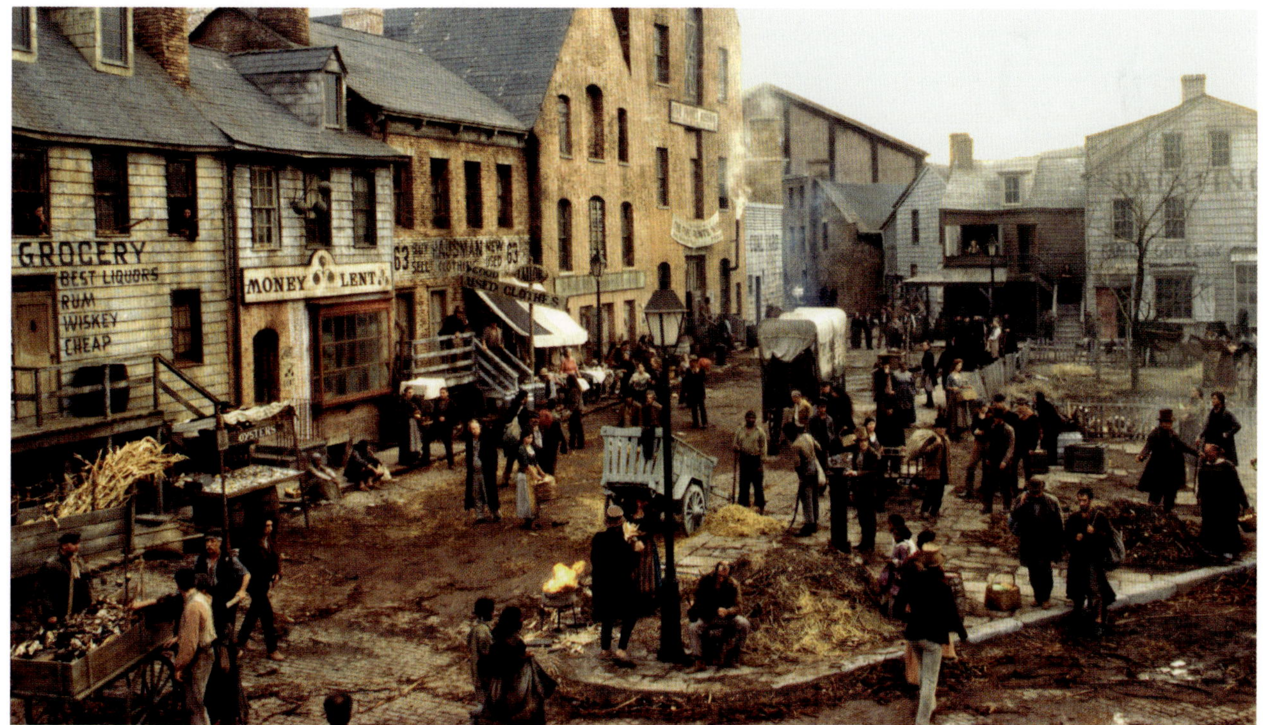

Below: *Street hassle – Bill the Butcher (Daniel Day-Lewis, centre-left in the waistcoat) faces off against his young rival Amsterdam Vallon (Leonardo DiCaprio, centre-right, raising his arms).*

character actors, among their number Brendan Gleeson, John C. Reilly, and Gary Lewis. The camera swoops like a bird into their midst. This is Scorsese, but on an unprecedented scale.

Whereas the ending. As the drama unfolds a decade or so later, Amsterdam Vallon (DiCaprio, never quite claiming his first Scorsese), at last revealed as Priest's son, exacts his long-harboured, *Hamlet*-hued revenge on Bill, his surrogate father, amid the Draft Riots that genuinely shook New York. Scorsese's sure hand trembles in the tumult of disconnected scenes that have fallen short of his ambitions. He is cramming in historical detail, but the

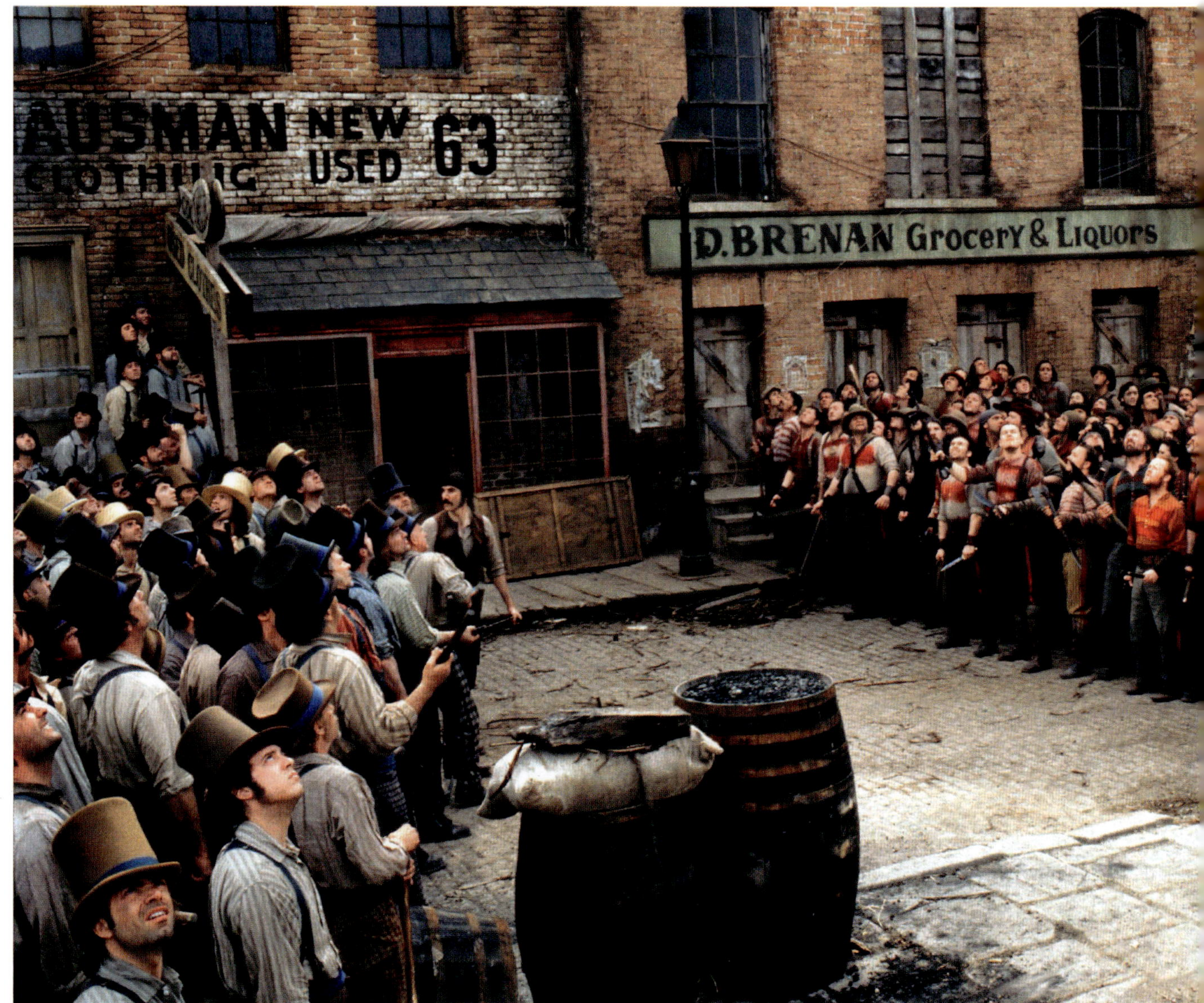

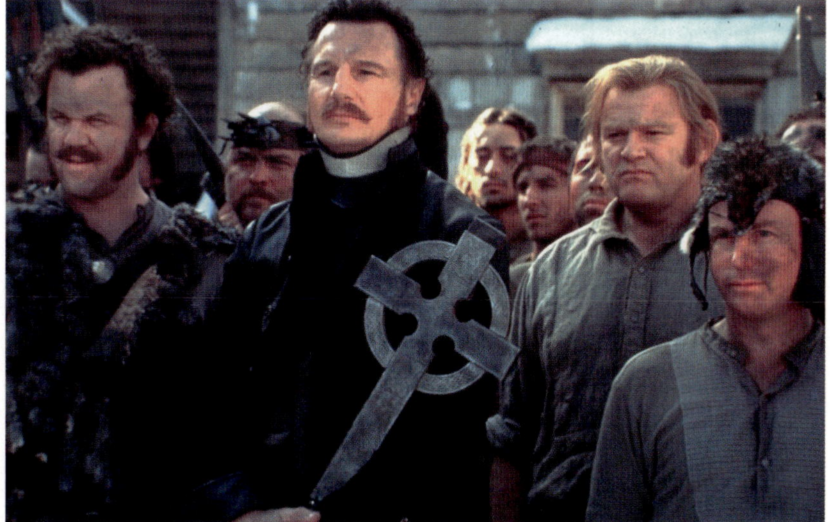

Right: *The gang's all here – John C. Reilly, Liam Neeson, Brendan Gleeson, and Gary Lewis feature among the restless Natives.*

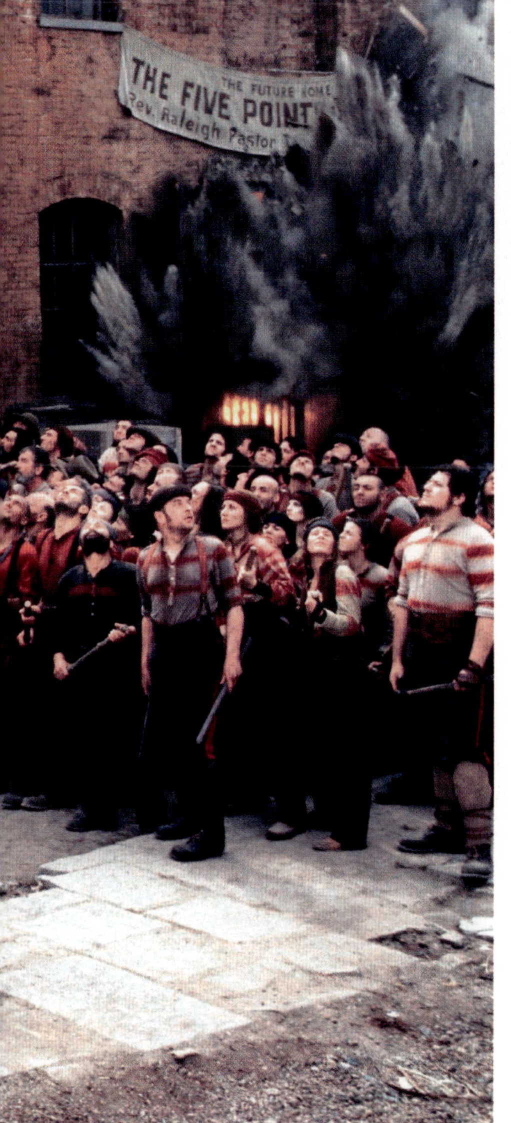

drama is diluted, the sequence of events confusing, the effect strangely ephemeral.

The film we see to this day is a winged beast, superlative in parts, compromised in others. Scorsese's preferred edit ran to three and a half hours, while it was released at two hours 48 minutes. He never really had the film he wanted. Half his salary went back into production, still shooting as extras were sent home, props packed, and sets dismantled. But there is no missing version, no director's cut. He simply ran out of time and money. As he and editor Thelma Schoonmaker tried to find a satisfying rhythm, the film was tested and tested again. How much history could the audience drink in?

Scorsese's vaunted spectacular had been on his mind for something like thirty years. Maybe too long. It took on legendary status, this monumental history of his home city, an excursion into melodrama, into the majesty of Lean, Leone, Visconti, and Shakespeare. Big sets, big shots, 1,200 extras. Was this really him? There was to be little of the 'dazzle of circumstance'[12] that enriches *Goodfellas* or the surging interiority of *Taxi Driver*; this was, he said, 'an opera not a documentary.'[13] Even so, these were still his mean streets.

Scorsese loves to play historian and anthropologist of New York, exploring the roots of *his* city, the violence that crosses class and city block alike. Run a finger along his filmography: it's there in *Mean Streets, Taxi Driver, After Hours, Bringing Out the Dead,* and in those preening gangsters of the outer boroughs in *Goodfellas*. And it is there in *The Age of Innocence*, uptown among the gentrified gangs. All of them intertwined with his own memories. 'I wanted to create that world,' he said, 'the foundation from which all my other films came from.'[14] These were the birth pangs of America.

He recalled tales from his father's youth, when the Irish were still found in the Bowery, not yet supplanted by the Italians. Back in the 1850s, the Italians had yet to arrive. He would roam the graveyard of St. Patrick's Cathedral, reading the gravestones. 'The cobblestones talked to me,'[15] he said. He haunted libraries, reading up on a history that didn't get taught. In

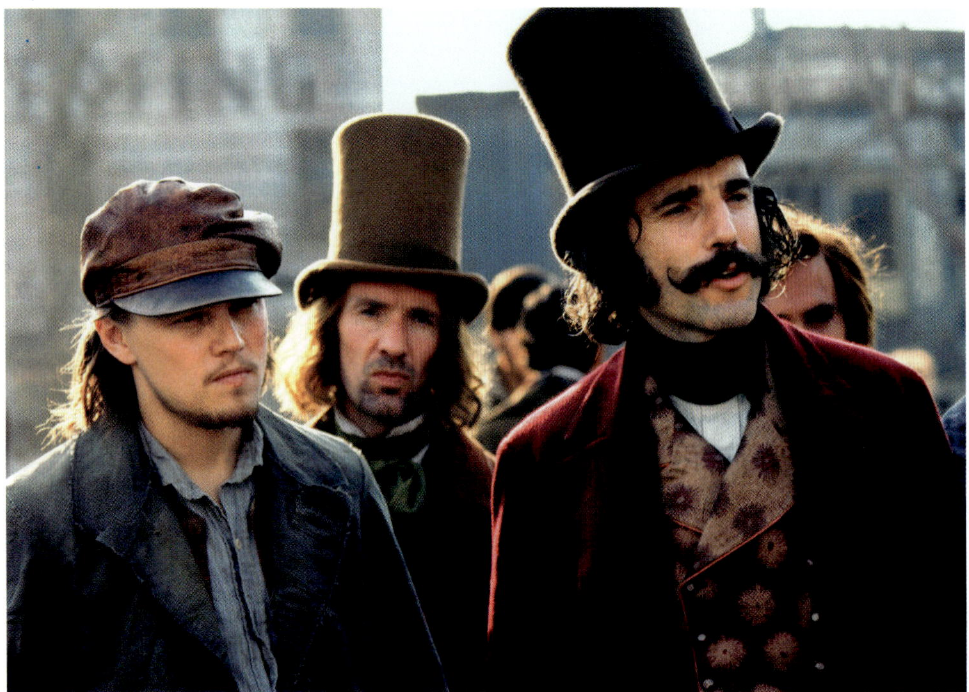

Left: *Hamlet in hats. The plot leans toward the classical as Leonardo DiCaprio's Amsterdam plans his revenge on Bill (Daniel Day-Lewis) for the murder of his father.*

1970, housesitting on Long Island, he came across Herbert Asbury's 1928 volume, *The Gangs of New York: An Informal History of the Underworld*, drawn to the section from the 1840s to the 1860s, when gang warfare had bloodied the very streets where he grew up. He and Jay Cocks began working on a script. It was 179 pages long and read like a novel.

In 1977, weeks after the release of *Taxi Driver*, Scorsese put a double-page ad in *Variety* announcing that *Gangs of New York* would be his next film. That didn't happen; it looked as if it would never happen. *Heaven's Gate* had curtailed any eagerness for the epic, and Scorsese had in mind the big-sky pictures of the fifties like *East of Eden* and *Giant*. Notice how DiCaprio resembles James Dean. It took until 1990 to establish Amsterdam and Bill, and their revenge-fuelled saga, culminating amid the Draft Riots. 'We knew we had to end with some sort of conflagration of the whole city,'[16] he recalled. He had ten incidents in mind, aswirl like the end of *Goodfellas*. The studio allowed him five.

Roger Ebert, Scorsese's old pal from the *Chicago Sun-Times*, could feel the struggle with 'more weight to overcome, more darkness.'[17] The film has a staged quality. Dante Ferretti's proliferating sets – including Five Points, Paradise Square, the Old Brewery, Broadway, Sparrow's Pagoda where Day-Lewis demonstrates his knife-throwing talents, and an entire cathedral – took six months to build across those famous soundstages and a backlot once home to Fellini (*Satyricon* was an influence), but the artifice of the world pokes through the veneer of authenticity. Shooting the film had been the best of times, and the worst.

The myth of the making of *Gangs of New York* has Scorsese hemmed in by money men, his vision thwarted. There is some truth to that. The violence was cauterized in search of a bigger audience. There were confrontations with notorious producer Harvey Weinstein, who was backing the project through Miramax with a tidy $100 million. But Scorsese was as much his own enemy. The shoot dragged on for nine months, everyone was exhausted. He knew he hadn't gotten the script right, then squandered the budget. The urge to linger over history's small print, lavishing us with luxuriant Scorsesean detail, allows the story to go slack. The quasi-Oedipal struggle between Amsterdam and Bill, supposedly charged with mythic resonance, becomes, according to the *New York Times*, 'the most conventional element in the picture.'[18] By its arrival in December 2002, steeped in industry *schadenfreude*, the film was almost preordained to fail. It made only $193 million. By the economics of Hollywood, a disaster.

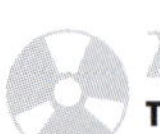

2003

THE BLUES: A MUSICAL JOURNEY (TV mini-series, 1 episode) Director / Executive Producer

Below left: *Amsterdam's love interest Jenny Everdeane (Cameron Diaz) has her own complicated past with Bill (Day-Lewis).*

Below right: Gangs of New York *never quite achieved what Scorsese had longed for, but still serves as a fascinating prelude to all his great New York pictures.*

Yet there is still power in the thickened stew of Scorsese's epic. DiCaprio, and Cameron Diaz as his streetwise paramour, the pickpocket Jenny Everdeane, are characters chiselled out of the strictures of story, but Bill is a marvel of menace – America's dark heart draping a Stars and Stripes across bony shoulders. While shooting *The Age of Innocence*, Cocks had suggested Day-Lewis for Bill. 'I *know*,'[19] responded Scorsese. He had to persuade the actor out of semi-retirement, certain he could summon the furies of this loquacious hoodlum. So he does, tapping a glass eye with the tip of his knife, a Dickensian grotesque in full spate assayed by an actor who stayed fully in character over the long months of production. No one has ever put such malice into a casual 'Whoopsie-daisy!'[20]

Bill the Butcher, killer and progressive, has a shrewd understanding that civilization is birthed in blood. Scorsese dwells on his testy arrangement with Jim Broadbent's Boss Tweed, Manhattan's snake-oil politico making periodic sorties south from Tammany Hall to buy or bully his way to votes. The cogs of democracy are viewed with cynicism and the message resonates. This is how crime got organized, and this is how America got organized.

'You know who looks uncannily like young Howard Hughes?' mused Scorsese, taking lunch with Ebert during the treadmill of promoting *Gangs of New York*. 'Leonardo DiCaprio.'[21]

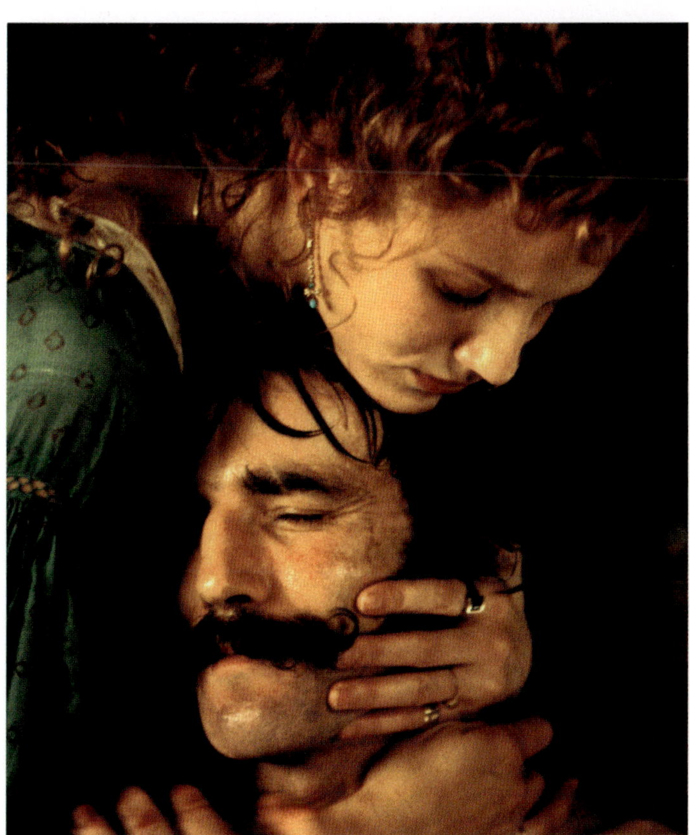

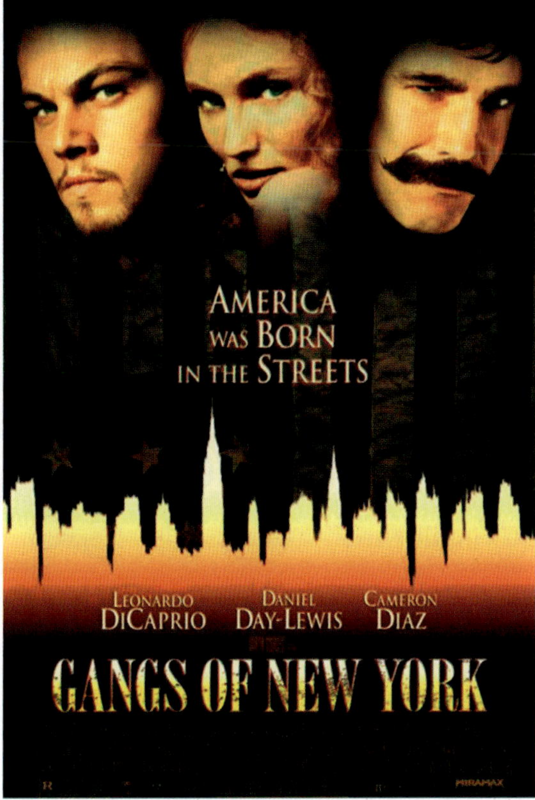

As America's most highly regarded cinéaste, for whom film has the aspect of a religion, there was a frisson in Scorsese turning to Hollywood history as an avenue for his art. *The Aviator* is the first in a self-referential duet on the subject of filmmaking itself, with *Hugo* to follow in 2011. They are arguably his two most enchanted films, certainly his glossiest, but *The Aviator* also presented the psychological enquiry we have come to expect from the companionship of Scorsese. *The Aviator*, the inward epic, has a lot on its mind. Maybe too much.

Pull back and we see a film akin to *Raging Bull*, a biopic of a real-life figure as tormented as Jake La Motta. Superficially, Howard Hughes (indeed a perfect fit for tortured cherub DiCaprio) was one of America's golden sons: the billionaire business titan of the twenties and thirties, handsome as the dawn, who surmounted those twin Californian peaks of moviemaking and aviation. Yet what piqued the Scorsesean muse was the dramatic contrast between his flights and his depths. Hughes was mentally fractured, suffering from an undiagnosed OCD and acute germaphobia, eventually derided as a pop-culture lunatic, cocooned from the world in a Las Vegas penthouse until his death in 1976.

'The movie is not an exposé of Hughes (what's left to expose?) but a rehabilitation and celebration,'[22] reflected David Denby in the *New Yorker*. Scorsese clearly admires this revolutionary capitalist coursing on instinct, focusing on his triumphal years from 1926 to 1946, producing *Hell's Angels* and *Scarface* (Scorsese could naturally hold forth on both), and pioneering air travel through TWA, the American ideal chipped by an untrustworthy mind. Imagine if Travis Bickle was sitting on millions, and for a

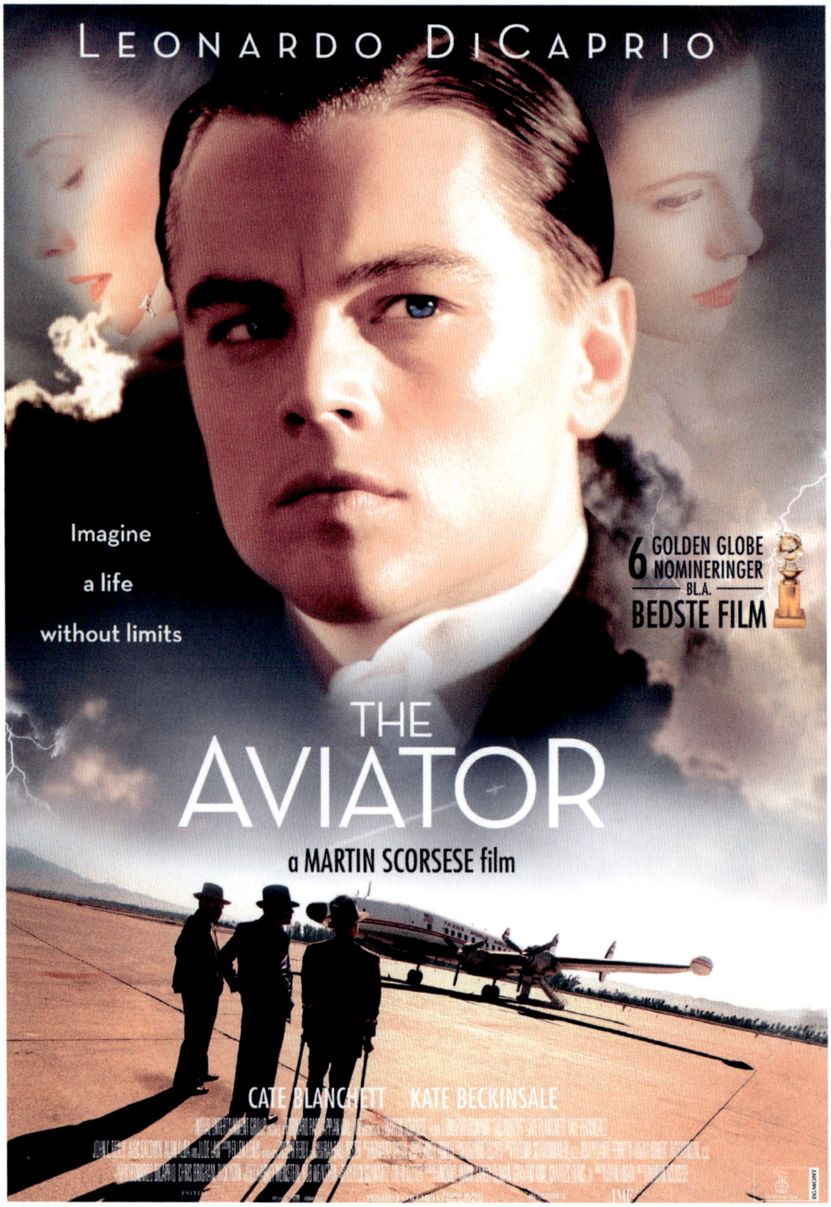

Above: *Hollywood epic* The Aviator *(2004) had been Leonardo DiCaprio's passion project, with Martin Scorsese relieved not to be undertaking another personal mission. But every film became personal.*

Opposite: *Hollywood producer, aircraft designer, playboy, and tormented man – Howard Hughes offered both DiCaprio and Scorsese the perfect subject.*

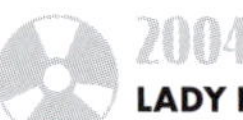

2004
LADY BY THE SEA: THE STATUE OF LIBERTY (Documentary) Director / Producer / Writer

while, money and daring and American individualism had Hughes soaring.

Once we do the calculus, *The Aviator* bears the hallmarks of classic Scorsese, but it came to him late. DiCaprio had been developing the idea with screenwriter John Logan, with Michael Mann keen to direct. They had hit a familiar roadblock: multiple Hughes projects were doing the circuit. Warren Beatty was longing to depict an older Hughes, which emerged indifferently as *Rules Don't Apply* in 2016. Christopher Nolan was developing a biopic with Jim Carrey in mind. Even Spielberg was talking about a potential Hughes story.

After the trials of *Gangs of New York*, Scorsese was quite prepared for something to fall in his lap. When DiCaprio passed on the script it was the title that he found inviting. The visions of Hughes flying over Beverly Hills in aircraft he invented, finding solace and romance in the beaming sky. And Scorsese hates to fly! Then he knew nothing about boxing before *Raging Bull*. And to sugar the deal, here was the chance to recreate the temple of Hollywood at which he had worshipped as a child.

'Scorsese places us in the world of 1930s Hollywood as though settling us into a stuffed chair, and then keeps attending to us,'[23] relished the *San Francisco Chronicle*. All the songs are specific, the mood Cole Porterish, featherlight jazz over the lurid glamour of Bernard Herrmann's *Taxi Driver* saxophone; cigarette girls have exactly the right bob; fabled A-list nightspot, the Cocoanut Grove, sprawls with champagne effervescence across the soundstage at Mel's Cité du Cinéma, Montreal (prewar Hollywood decadence was largely recreated in Canada).

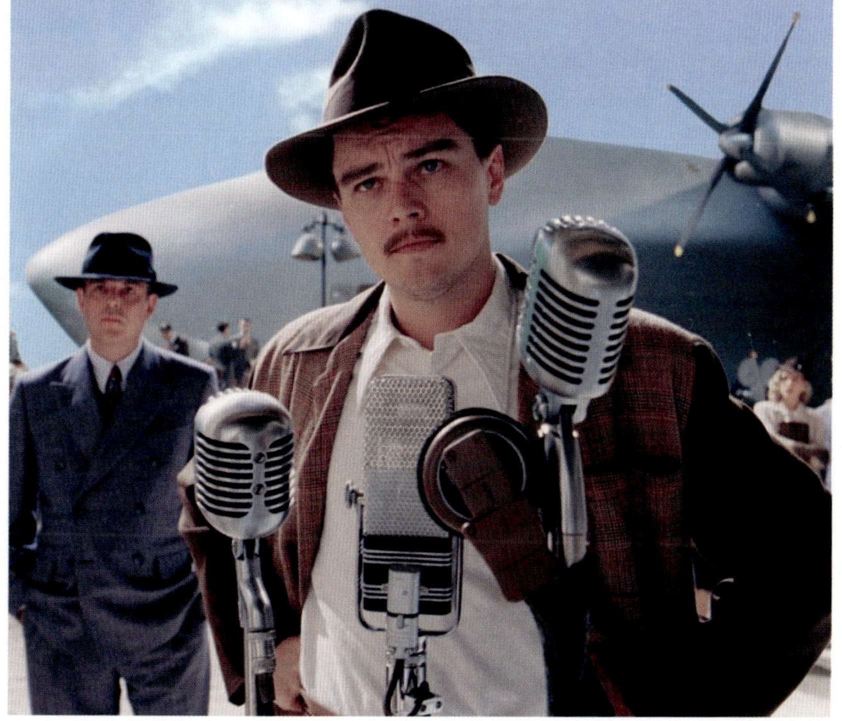

Drawn as ever to the possibilities of colour, Scorsese utilizes a startling era-specific tributary of Technicolor called bipack color, which brings out cyans and reds, so greens become blues. In one tranquil vision, Hughes and Katharine Hepburn (Cate Blanchett) putt and flirt their way across turquoise golfing greens in what appears to be Oz. The entire ambience is a shimmer of life and movies.

CGI was a relatively new brushstroke. Computers had extended his horizons on *Gangs of New York*, but they were now conjuring up literal flights of fancy, soaring over Beverly Hills, as well as a crash landing that nearly killed Hughes (one of four in his life). Scorsese was certain the damage to Hughes' frontal lobes contributed to his decline. Yet it was the performances that were the challenge. These were very real and distinctive historical figures: not only Hughes, but his great loves Hepburn and Ava Gardner (Kate Beckinsale), his business minder Noah Dietrich (John C. Reilly) and rival, Pan Am's slippery chairman Juan Trippe (Alec Baldwin).

DiCaprio called it catching a 'vibration.'[24] He read the biographies, watched the footage, met with an elderly Jane Russell, one of the many beauties Hughes had dated, and Terry Moore, who claimed to have been his second wife (she never provided proof) – they spoke of him fondly. He wanted to understand the contradiction of the control freak who risked millions on a whim. He consulted with doctors on the subject of OCD, and went some way to rewiring his own brain into the trapped clockwork of Hughes's spiralling compulsions. There is 'no real genius without obsession or compulsion,'[25] the actor concluded. Was he referencing Scorsese too?

Blanchett would pick up a Best Supporting Actress Oscar for her

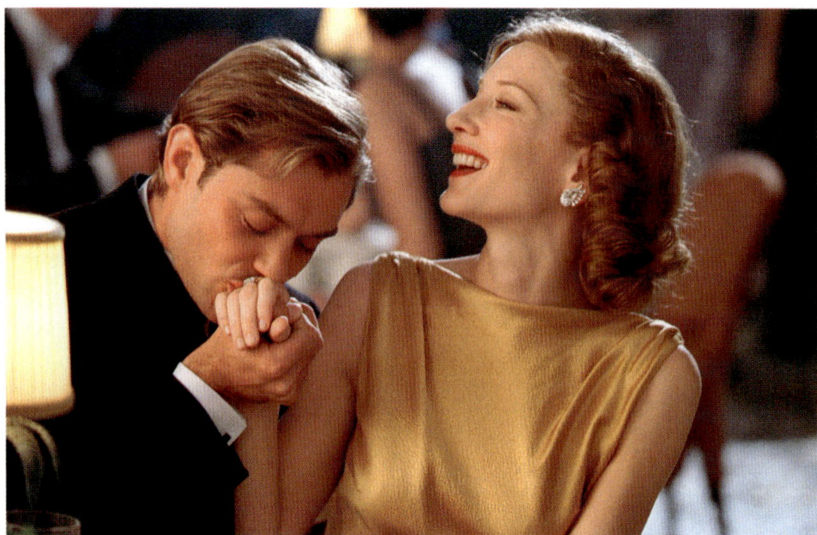

Left: *Art as life as art – Jude Law's Errol Flynn charms Cate Blanchett's Katharine Hepburn in* The Aviator *(2004).*

Below: *Grandstanding finished – Howard Hughes (Leonardo DiCaprio) gives as good as he gets at a trumped-up Senate hearing into his activities.*

wonderful take on Hepburn, closer than anyone to Hughes, and, in her own way, another control freak. Blanchett was walking an even finer line, the great actress's voice and mannerisms are folklore. To mimic her would be fatal, but she needed to be familiar. Scorsese put it to her that she was 'playing a character called Katharine Hepburn.'[26] Blanchett catches a fine balance between Hepburn's screwball screen persona and her fragile reality. She called it 'habitation.'[27]

The film surges along on the crest of its performances, its glamour, its widescreen polish. '*The Aviator* could be the quickest two hours and 50 minutes ever committed to celluloid,'[28] exalted the *Guardian*. This is another film about the shaping of America. How the West pulled at the American psyche. Scorsese had felt it himself, drawn to the shores of the Pacific in the seventies, where his own compulsions threatened to overwhelm him. Yet there is something assembled about the film, like one of Hughes's sleek aircraft. *The Aviator* never gains the gravity of *Goodfellas* or *Raging Bull*; there is none of their wildness.

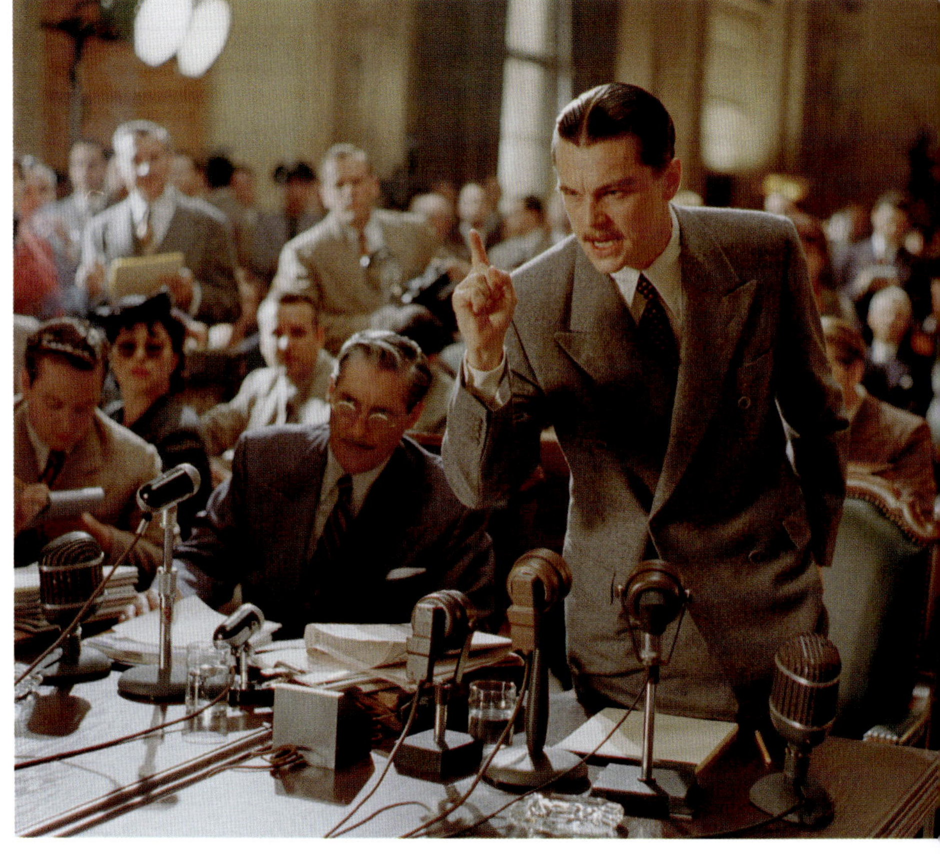

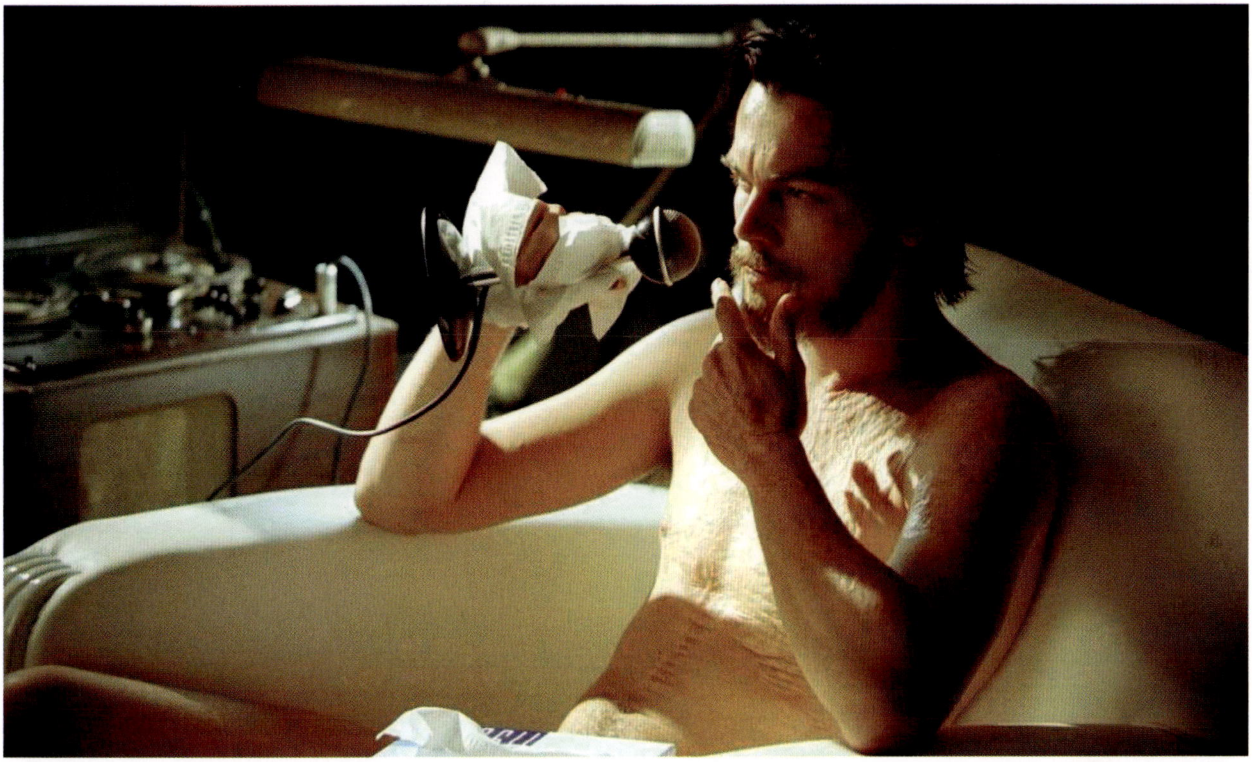

Scorsese's American fable ends in 1947, after Hughes bests corrupt Maine senator Ralph Owen Brewster (Alan Alda) in the cooked-up senate hearings against him. We have ventured into a courtroom drama, before his demons resurface to claim him, and you feel the real Scorsese film about to begin. *The Aviator* succeeded and failed, making $214 million, but on a budget of $110 million. Out of eleven Academy Award nominations, it won five: alongside Blanchett, there were statues for Cinematography, Art Direction, Costumes, and Editing. Scorsese went home empty-handed.

'Greatness in America is a cruel privilege that can turn on its recipient and ruin him,'[29] warned David Thomson, writing not of Howard Hughes but Martin Scorsese. The contradiction of being Scorsese in the noughties was that while he lived the impossible filmmaking dream, allowed the freedom to express himself, to be Scorsese, Hollywood still needed its pound of flesh. The stark truth was he hadn't made significant money since *Cape Fear*. In search of what might be deemed 'crowd-friendly Scorsese', he was losing something of himself. What kind of Marty did America want? What kind of Marty did the critics crave, to be placed in the legacy of film history? Which Marty did Scorsese want to be?

Writing in the *San Francisco Chronicle*, Mick LaSalle pondered a director 'who has been praised as America's greatest filmmaker ever since *Goodfellas*, and just about ever since, his films have taken on a heaviness – they're heavy with the attempt at greatness.'[30]

Above: *For all its glamour and spectacle,* The Aviator *follows the likes of* Taxi Driver *and* Raging Bull *in its close-up study of mental decline.*

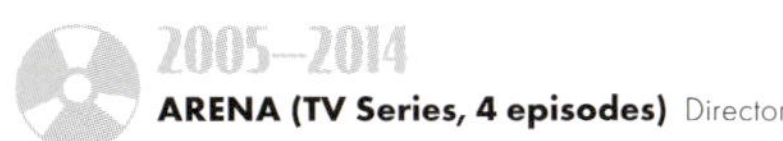

2005–2014
ARENA (TV Series, 4 episodes) Director

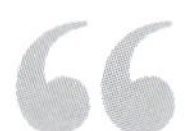

There's no attempt at greatness here, just a fabulously successful attempt at a good crime movie.

MICK LaSALLE

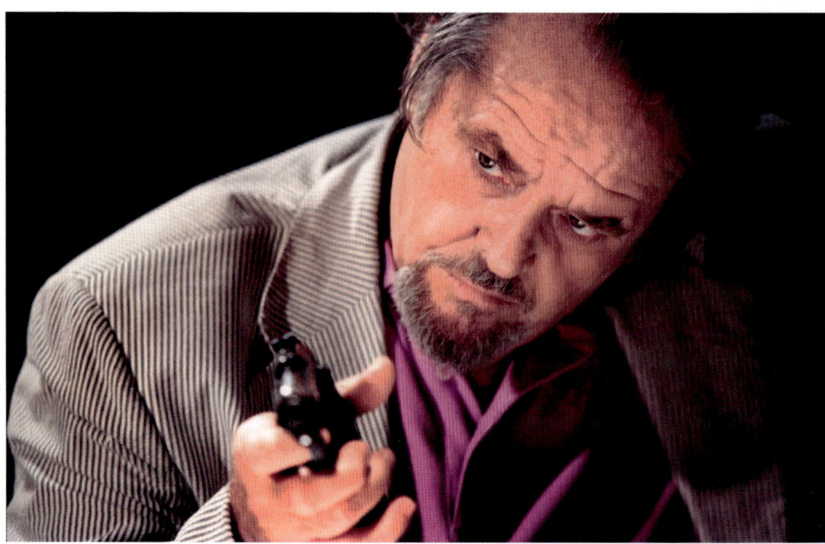

Then a twist. For we end this chapter with an image no one was quite prepared for, even though three of Scorsese's closest friends - Coppola, Spielberg, and Lucas, fluffing their prepared witticisms - were standing on the stage reading out his name. Frankly, it looked like a set-up. On 27 February 2007, Scorsese became the recipient of the Academy Award for Best Director. He was clearly moved, and out of breath, but there is something sheepish in his grin, maybe appreciating the irony that he was picking up not only Best Director but Best Picture for one of his least personal films. Carnally bloody and thrilling, *The Departed* was the exact opposite of Oscar bait. 'There's no attempt at greatness here,' said LaSalle, 'just a fabulously successful attempt at a good crime movie.'[31] The strange alchemy of Scorsese's career had landed him on the stage at the Kodak Pavilion for his most nakedly entertaining film. And his most successful, making $291 million, and having cost $90 million to make.

This is one hyperkinetic mob movie, even for the man who made *Goodfellas* (the film that should have won), conjoined with the tropes of the seventies policiers: cops and robbers, good and bad, the gritty films of Robert Aldrich and Don Siegel, a formula tossed in the air to land where it may. The mayhem of the ending, with A-listers dropping like flies, or being dropped from rooftops, is as tart and absurd as Jacobean tragedy.

The Departed was like a challenge to the Scorsese style - to make a film that was *all* plot. The tone verges on farce. Moreover, he really hadn't been convinced about making his Oscar-winning triumph at all. It was a remake of a trio of celebrated Japanese crime thrillers, the *Infernal Affairs* trilogy, directed by Andrew Lau and Alan Mak, though screenwriter William Monahan adds a seasoning of real-life crime in Boston's Winter Hill Gang. So wasn't even set in New York, but Boston, where the gangs were still Irish.

Hardly the respite of repute, a chance for Scorsese to kick back and have fun, it is surprising to learn what a struggle it had been to make this visceral black comedy. Then he suffered so much with every film.

Matt Damon and a returning DiCaprio are ostensibly the leads: Damon as the corrupt Colin Sullivan, the mob plant groomed to be recruited into the police and serve as a mole; DiCaprio as Billy Costigan, born on the working-class streets, who is sent undercover into the ranks of Boston mobster Frank Costello (Jack Nicholson). Each begins to suspect the presence of the other.

This was the third film in succession that paired DiCaprio and Scorsese. It was less favouritism than obsession. 'I'm thirty years older than him,' responded the director, 'but I think we see the world in the same way, meaning he feels comfortable with the characters I've dealt with over the years in movies - with Robert De Niro's films, with Keitel.'[32]

Away from the oppressed leads, crumbling beneath the weight of their deceptions, the effect is a roistering, macho ensemble. Alec Baldwin and a joyfully profane Mark Wahlberg (a true Bostonian) nearly steal the show as bullyboy officers. Warner Brothers fretted over the language (which stood at

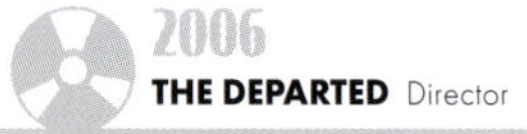

Opposite: *Jack Nicholson as Boston mobster Frank Costello in* The Departed *(2006). The legendary actor's habit of doing radically different versions of each take was a new experience for Martin Scorsese.*

Right: *Alec Baldwin and Mark Wahlberg bring a dose of profane black comedy to the film as two uncompromising cops.*

Below: *Scorsese confers with Leonardo DiCaprio (as the heroic Billy Costigan) and Matt Damon (as the conniving Colin Sullivan) on location in Boston.*

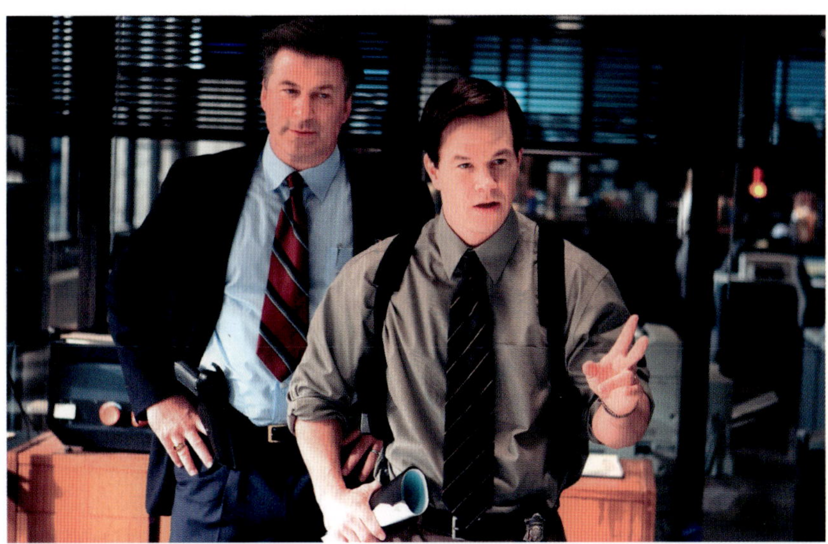

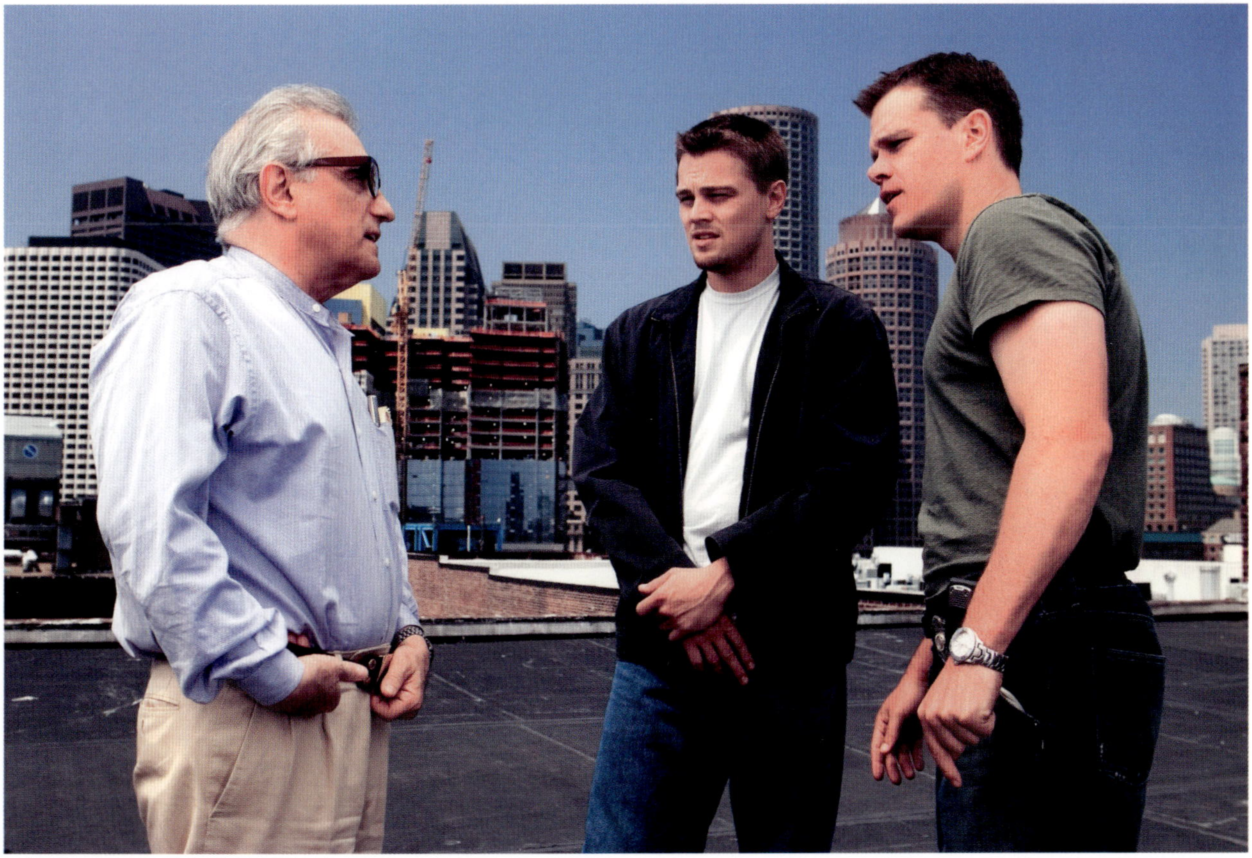

a conservative 237 F-bombs compared to *The Wolf of Wall Street's* 569), not to say the level of Costello's sexual violence. Scorsese found himself squirming in the studio's grip – caught on the wrong side.

He also only had Nicholson for twenty-five days, and the icon went about things his own way, creating a compelling if outrageous figure in the unkempt Costello. They had known each other for years, always looking for that film that might bring their reputations together. On set, Nicholson was a fountain of ideas, constantly wanting to come at things in different ways. So contrasting to the controlled rigour of De Niro or Day-Lewis, against the clock Scorsese had to embrace the flux of Nicholson's experimentation. 'That was very interesting to me, being in a situation where I didn't know what was going to happen,'[33] he said. The scene of Costello sniffing his brandy over the table from a twitchy Costigan, snarling 'I smell a rat'[34] before a revolver was sprung on both DiCaprio and Scorsese. The director grew to like the performance, Costello was King Lear, coming apart himself. His obscenity permeates the picture.

There was also Martin Sheen, Ray Winstone, Anthony Anderson, and James Badge Dale (they even had Brad Pitt as a producer). Poor Vera Farmiga struggles to establish a female presence as the shrink who inevitably ends up falling for

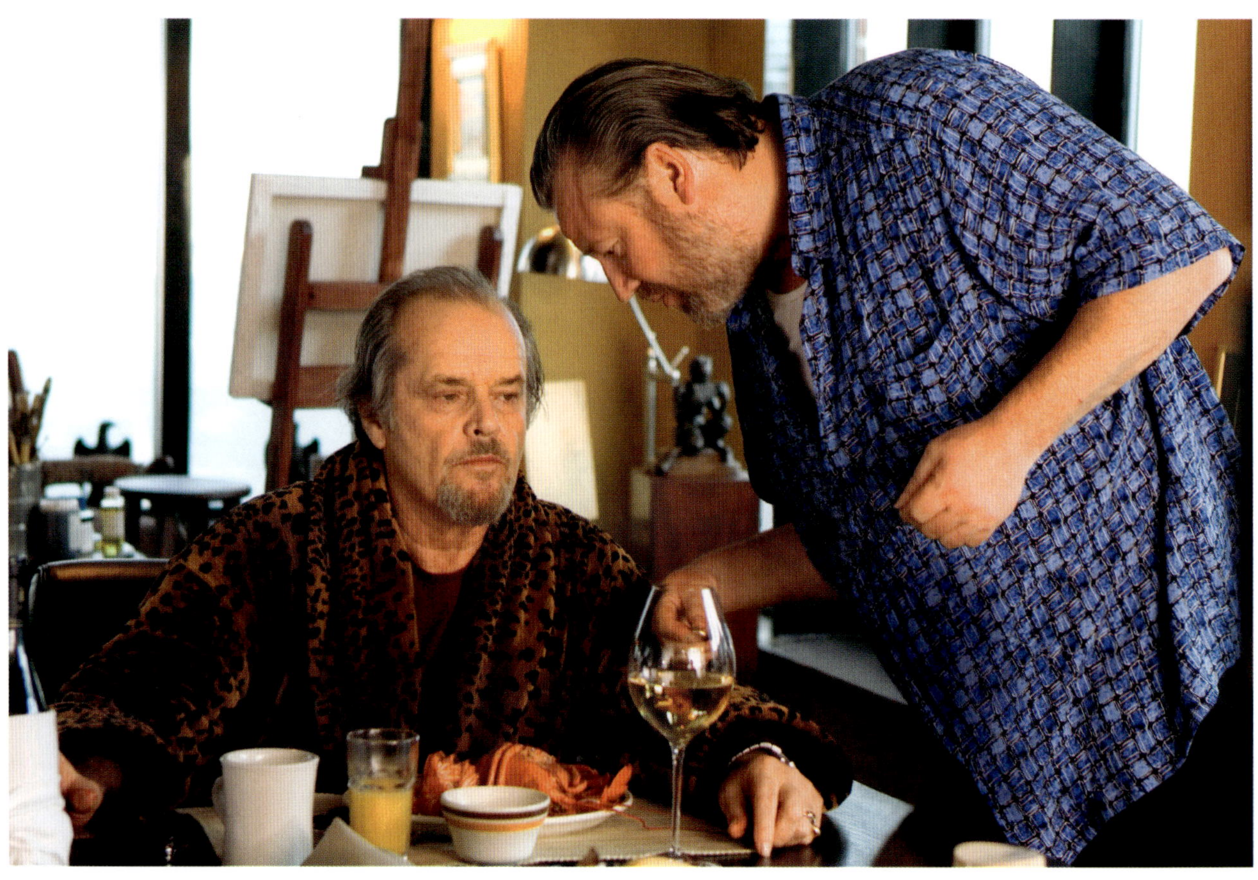

Below: *Frank Costello (Jack Nicholson) gets the lowdown from chief lieutenant Arnold 'Frenchie' French (Ray Winstone). Nicholson imagined the villain as a man of appetites: for food, drink, women, and power.*

2007
THE KEY TO RESERVA (Short) Director

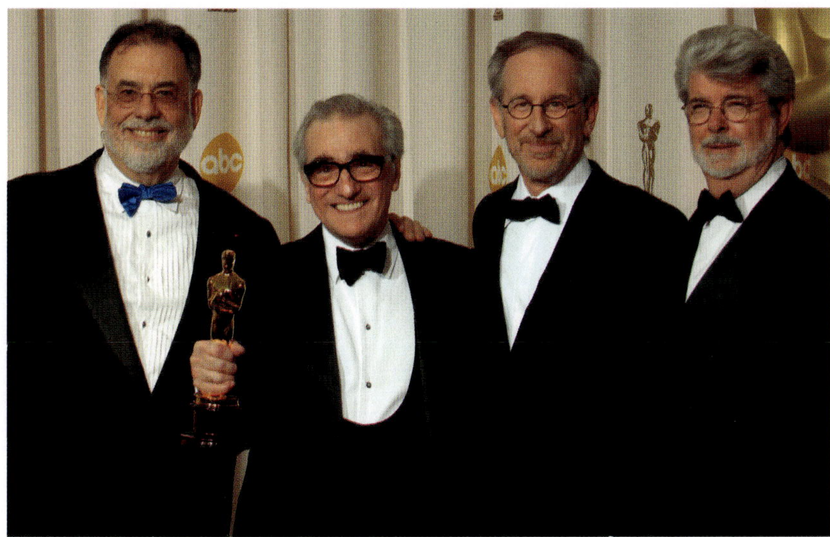

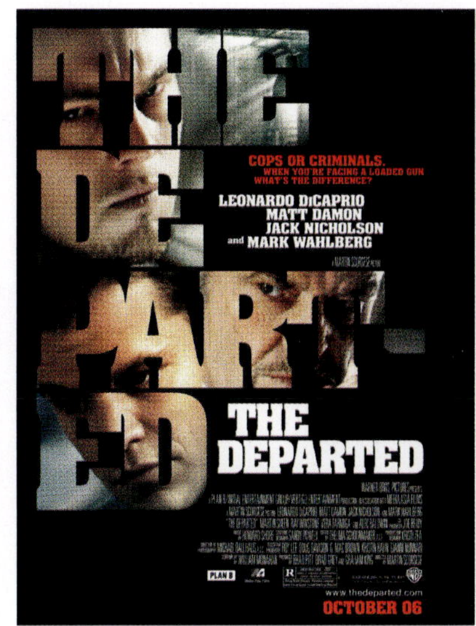

both lost souls. Scorsese admitted that it wasn't until the fifth week of production that he found his stride. They shot on location in Boston through the spring of 2006 (though there are some New York locations disguised as Boston).

It is wrong to think of *The Departed* as unambitious or compromised. Schoonmaker's Oscar for Editing was undoubtedly deserved. The wiring of story is intricate, with months devoted to how the drama moves back and forth between its twinned moles. Indeed, early in the editing, Scorsese sat down to watch their assembly and paled. At the end, he turned to Schoonmaker and instructed her to throw out the entire cut and to begin again.

This is a new rhythm for Scorsese, so devoted to the biographical mode – those flights of recollection. 'It has to do with the nature of betrayal,' he recalled. 'The nature of morality which, after 2001, became suspect to me.'[35] This is what had finally convinced him to make the film. In the shadow of 9/11, he found himself questioning the values of America. That old Catholic guilt courses through its veins (and it is set in America's most Catholic city), even Costello turns out to be an FBI informant. It is also about the riddle of identity. If *Goodfellas* explored a man who discovers where he belongs (before turning rat), *The Departed* exposes how identity can fragment for those who find themselves where they don't belong. The very thing that may have been troubling Scorsese. He did hardly any press for *The Departed*, admitting he was 'tired of it.'[36]

He was never lost in the maze of his frenetic film. There is the Irish-stamped punk on the soundtrack, and references to *Scarface* (in the repeated use of the X-symbol) and that masterpiece of betrayal *The Third Man* as Farmiga walks away from Damon at the funeral, not even meeting his eyes. And he got his sheepish Oscar. But as Scorsese left the stage, he began to wonder if it was worth making studio pictures anymore.

Above left: *The unexpected Oscar? Martin Scorsese finally receives his Best Director trophy from a trio of old comrades: Francis Ford Coppola, Steven Spielberg, and George Lucas.*

Above right: The Departed *was the great success it needed to be, another experiment with popular entertainment on his own terms.*

2008
SHINE A LIGHT (Documentary) Director

As Martin Scorsese's twenty-first feature begins, the hero – for now that description fits – stares at his stricken face in a mirror. 'Come on Teddy, pull yourself together,'[1] Leonardo DiCaprio's fragmenting US Marshal Teddy Daniels implores his twitchy reflection. Mirror shots are, of course, essential to the great Scorsesean fusion of substance and style. So often his films bring their characters into confrontation with themselves, and a director into contemplation of his own reflection: *Mean Streets* opens with Charlie face to face with Charlie; *The Aviator* ends with DiCaprio's Howard Hughes bleakly repeating 'way of the future'[2] to himself; in *Raging Bull*, Jake La Motta recites Brando from *On the Waterfront* to his corpulent double. Scorsese claimed it began in his childhood, when he re-enacted films in front of the mirror. How many have done the same thing in response to his films, even his mirror shots, De Niro pulling a gun on De Niro in the swelling psychosis of *Taxi Driver*?

'You talkin' to me?'[3]

Shutter Island draws deeply from the distorted perspective of Travis Bickle. For all its horror-movie devices, the dark-and-stormy night whipped up by author Dennis Lehane's 1954-set novel, this is squarely Scorsese's turf – American insanity. Genre reflected in a funhouse mirror.

Yet at face value, the film appears to be Scorsese-lite: another vacation in a studio thriller with Paramount footing the bill. Just as he had apparently done with *Cape Fear* and, despite its Oscars, fellow Boston-set suspense story *The Departed*, to be scolded for straying from the chosen path – the pursuit of the personal document. Lehane readily admitted the novel was 'a homage to B-movies and pulp.'[4] On an island asylum, a mist-swallowed fortress in Boston Harbour, repository for the criminally insane, a dangerous female patient (Emily Mortimer) has vanished into thin air. Enter Daniels and his new partner Chuck (a soft-tempered Mark Ruffalo, cast after writing a fan letter to Scorsese), who, like the audience, are to be bamboozled at every turn.

Opposite: *US Marshals Mark Ruffalo and Leonardo DiCaprio find themselves as confounded as the viewer in Martin Scorsese's Gothic mystery* Shutter Island *(2010).*

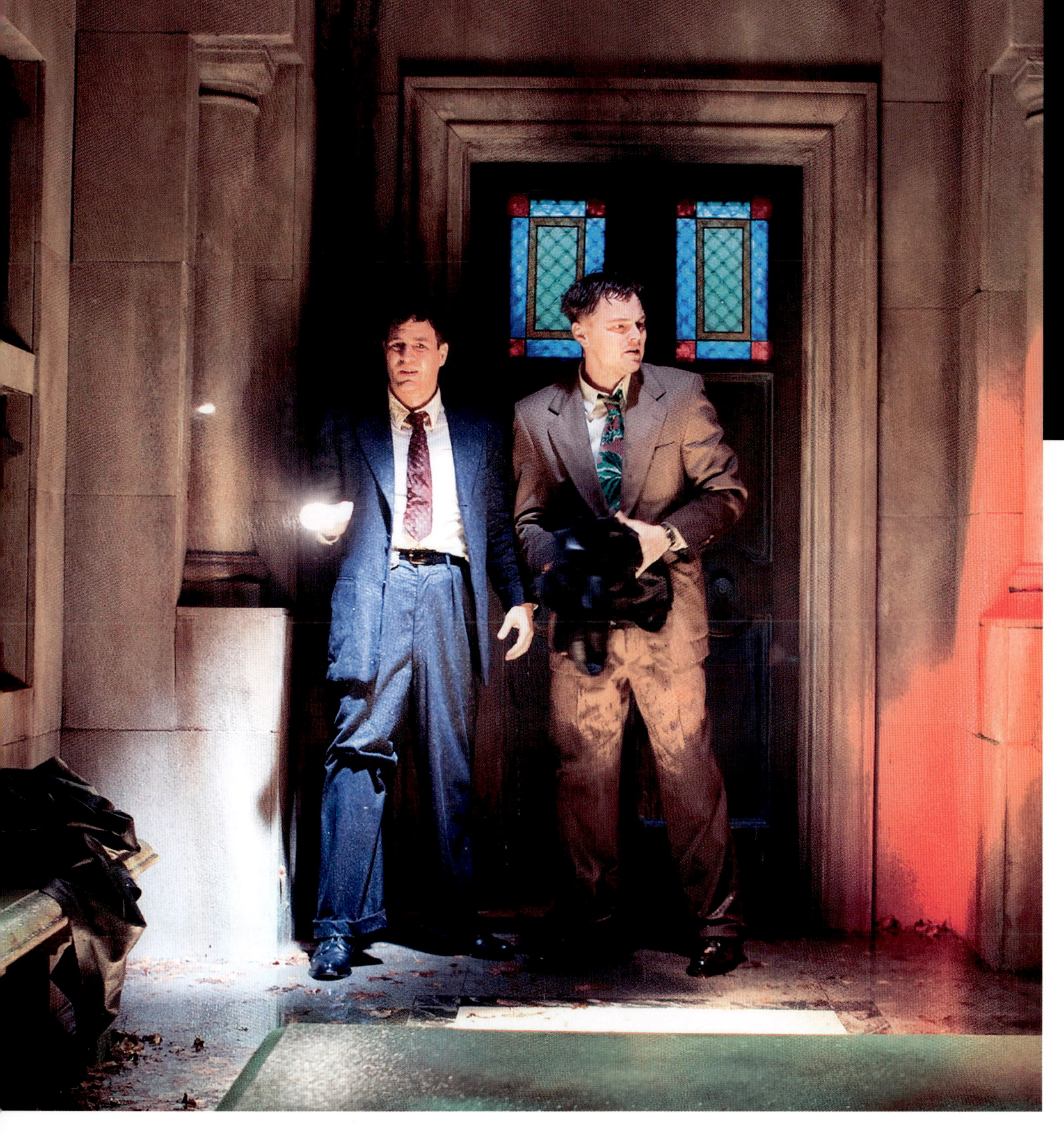

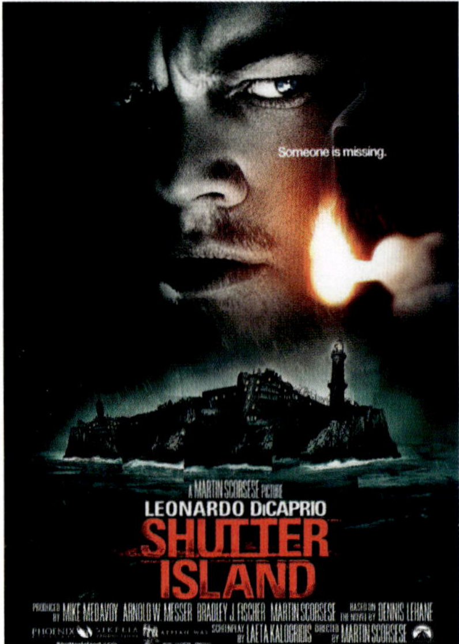

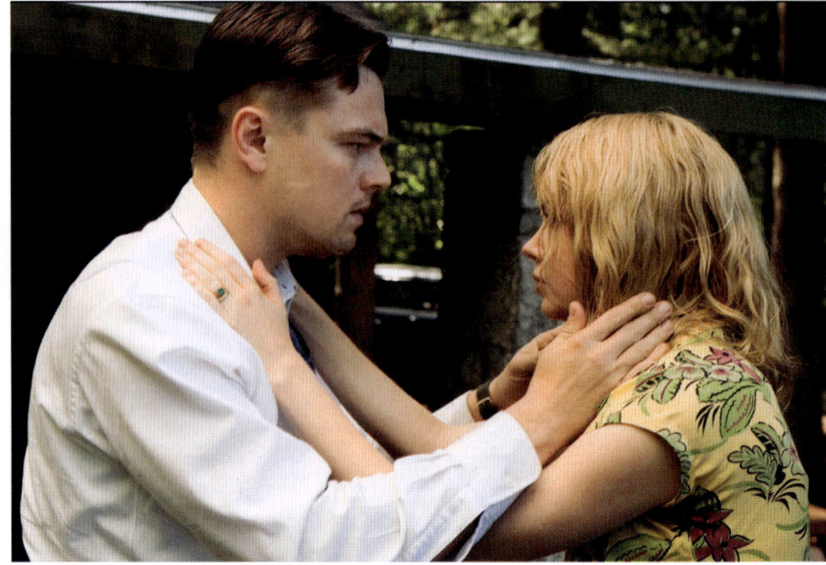

Above left: *Based on Dennis Lehane's novel,* Shutter Island *recalled* Cape Fear*-era Martin Scorsese – it was another chance to test himself against the demands of genre.*

Above right: *Past imperfect – Teddy Daniels (Leonardo DiCaprio) is tormented by the belief that the sudden memories of his wife (Michelle Williams) are trying to tell him something.*

Opposite: *DiCaprio was drawn to peeling open a character, layer by psychological layer. Teddy is another Scorsesean protagonist in search of himself.*

Echoing the author's sentiments, Scorsese maintained that the film 'started out as an entertainment.' But something gets into the filmmaking, something he can't avoid: 'It always seems to become something else.'[5]

He had dismissed the offer of Laeta Kalogridis' script, until he read it. Then immediately read it again. It wasn't the film he thought it was. He was intrigued by how it danced with perception. And Teddy played to DiCaprio's desire to unpeel the layers of character; how far the actor was willing to travel psychologically and emotionally. Sometimes you chose a film because it is right there in front of you.

Teddy is in no shape to unravel the knotted clues, which lead in every direction from evil experiments to personal tragedy. Why is it that everyone seems touched by lunacy in this bedevilled establishment, the predatory doctors as much as the freaks of Block C? Teddy is all migraines and trembling fingers, his brainwaves disrupted by flashes from a nightmare past. Scorsese shoots the present as a gravestone-grim tableau of gothic standards: clinking chains, dripping water, cliff edges, inmates as gnarly as tree bark. The dreamlike past has a sickly, oversaturated psychedelia even more extreme than *Taxi Driver*, and the ghostly Michelle Williams, Teddy's wife, imparts Cassandra-like warnings from beyond the grave.

Superstition was not unknown to Scorsese on a personal level. There was a time, in the seventies, when he became fearful of the number eleven, refusing to travel on the 11th, avoiding flights whose numbers added up to eleven, avoiding the eleventh floor of a hotel.

'It was a way of trying to grab at the chaos of the world and say, "Well, maybe this makes sense..."' he reflected, aware of how it looked. 'Strange things kept happening with that number during that period. I found that when I'd had a bad experience, or maybe I'd been fired from a project, the numbers in the address of a building added up to eleven, or it was the eleventh day...'[6]

Interiors were shot in Medfield State Hospital, an abandoned Massachusetts mental institute, where the walls told their own stories. Scorsese loves his locations to weave their way into the spell of the film. The island's wind-bent landscape, as jagged underfoot as the Moon (there is no firm footing to be found, physically or psychically), was an amalgam of Peddocks Island in Boston Harbour and Acadia National Park in Maine, a fairy-tale exaggeration finessed by CGI (then the vertiginous cliff-sides could be the figment of Teddy's mind).

We are hypnotized by an almost arrogantly accomplished display of filmmaking as illusion. That Ben Kingsley's dapper shrink speaks only through zephyrs of pipe smoke. That cinematographer Robert Richardson's camera whips and pans as if itself beset by terror. That Thelma Schoonmaker's editing can cut as swift as thought between delusion and fact. *Shutter Island* is a film trapped in a narrative labyrinth made up of precise interlocking pieces. 'If you take one piece out,' the director insisted, 'the story falls apart.'[7] We are a world away from the improvisational sparks of *Mean Streets* and the character-driven urges of *Raging Bull* and *Goodfellas*. That famous looseness. But still we are resident in a psyche every bit as fractured as those of Travis Bickle or Jake La Motta.

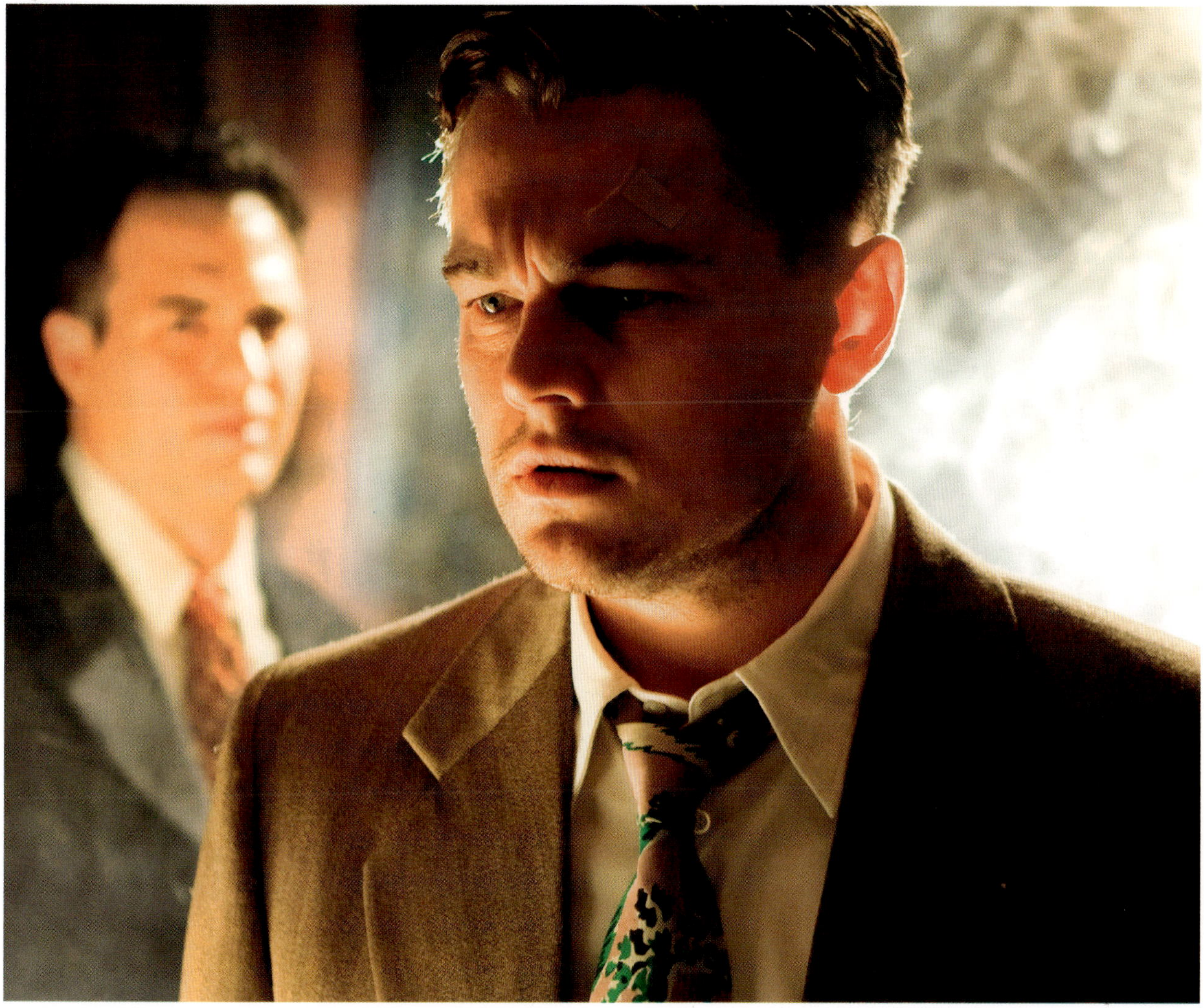

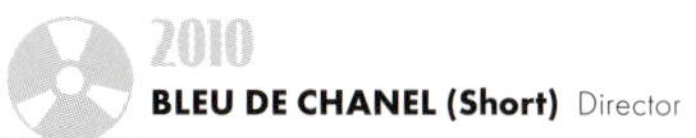

2010
BLEU DE CHANEL (Short) Director

We are awed once more by the ease at which Scorsese plucks inspiration from the branches of film history. Nonchalant references to Hitchcock, Hammer Horror, and Val Lewton's conformity-busting exploitation flicks *Bedlam* and *Isle of the Dead*. *Shutter Island* could almost be a remake of Sam Fuller's *Shock Corridor*, set in an insane asylum – a taut metaphor for America itself.

'We shouldn't be afraid to make a homage,' Scorsese told his team, 'but it has to be serious, not ironic.'[8] This was the legacy of films he had discovered in the fifties at the age of ten or eleven. 'There was a small theatre on Second Avenue that would show third, fourth or fifth-run movies.'[9] We can glimpse it in *Mean Streets*.

There were era-specific noirs about obsessive detectives – *Laura*, *Out of the Past*, and *Vertigo* – that he screened for his cast to fix their bearings (or lack of them). The august presence of Max von Sydow as another doctor recalls the psychological traumas both of Ingmar Bergman and *The Exorcist*.

'It's like he is accessing his dreams or something, the dreams being all these movies,' observed DiCaprio. 'They're like memories coming back to him.'[10]

There's a decent, logical twist: Teddy is revealed to be a murderous inmate

Below: *On the set of* Shutter Island, *Martin Scorsese confers with Ben Kingsley, Leonardo DiCaprio, and Mark Ruffalo. What is so fascinating is that the roles required the actors to maintain layers of reality within the film. They were often acting acting.*

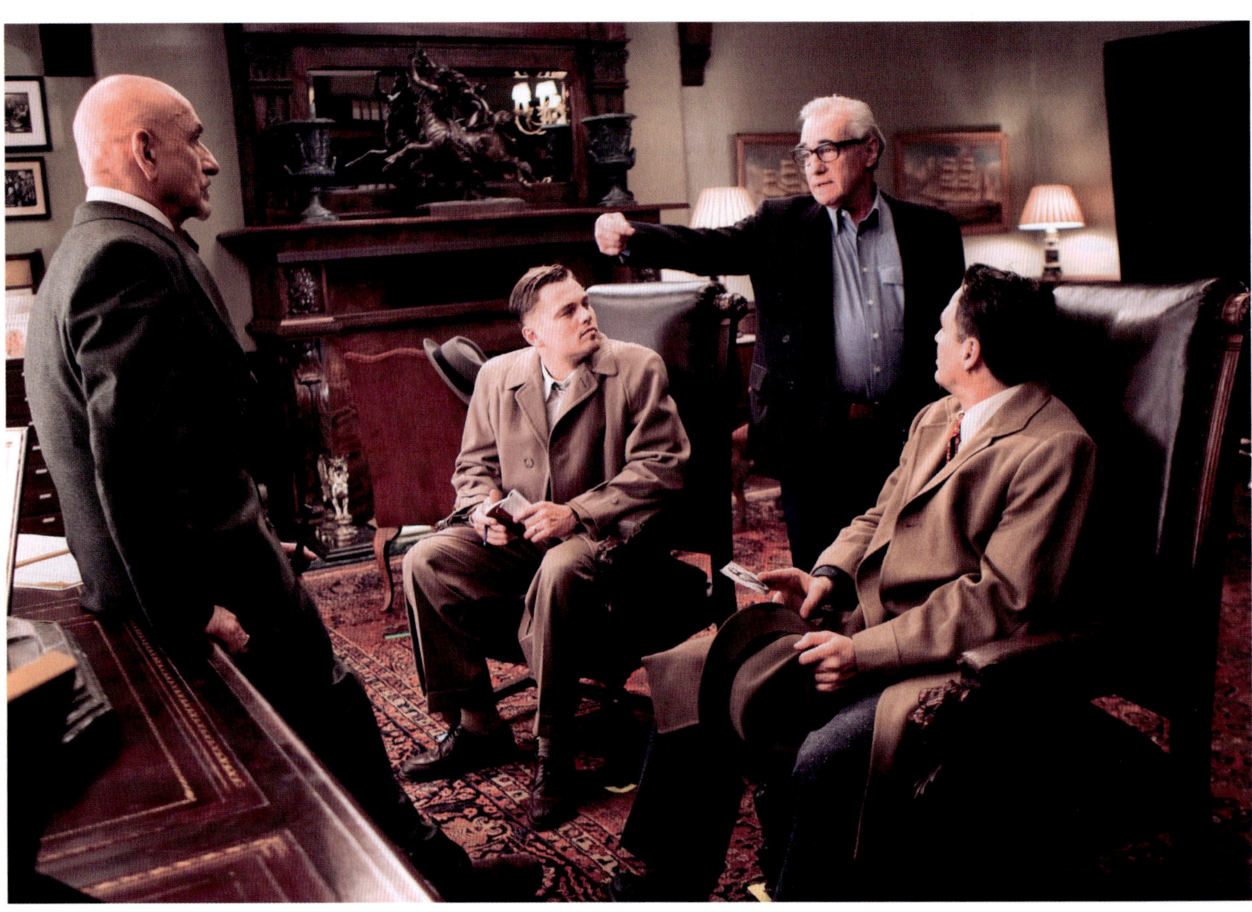

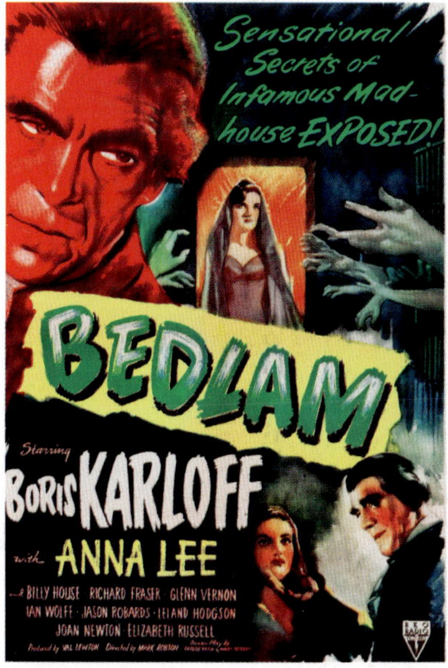

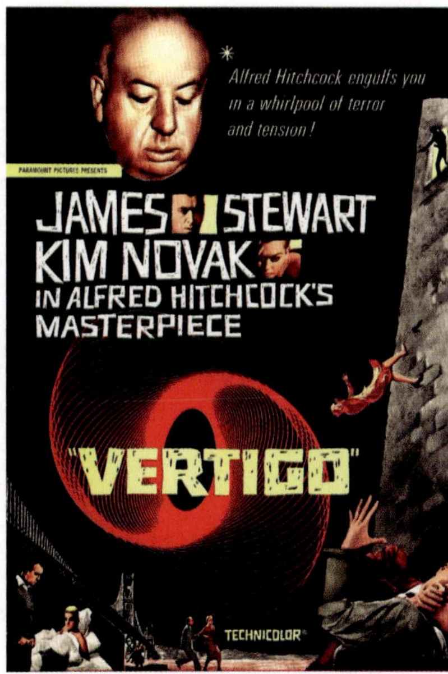

Left: Shutter Island *is arguably Scorsese's most consciously derivative film, drawing on numerous classic thrillers, among them Mark Robson's* Bedlam *(1946) and Hitchcock's* Vertigo *(1958).*

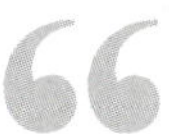

It's like he is accessing his dreams or something, the dreams being all these movies. They're like memories coming back to him.

LEONARDO DiCAPRIO

and the 'plot' an absurdly elaborate method of treatment. The entire film has been pulling the wool over Teddy's eyes and our own. Scorsese was only pretending to make a B-movie.

Return to *Shutter Island*, our senses alerted, and we see a film riddled with deliberate continuity errors, allowing scenes that can be read in entirely different ways. Directors, Scorsese is fond of saying, are 'illusionists' or 'magicians.'[11] He is turning a mirror to the very nature of film. 'It's something not tangible because it's projected electricity, images on a wall. And it's that we somehow make up the film in our minds, in a sense.'[12]

The world beyond the asylum-island is gripped by its own insanity: Teddy is an ex-trooper who walked, aghast, into Dachau. Piles of frozen bodies lurk in his treacherous memory. Inmates mutter fretfully of bombs that can shatter cities. This was the Age of Anxiety.

The final line allows for alternative takes, deeper paranoias. 'Which would be worse: to live as a monster, or to die as a good man?'[13] Is Teddy being brainwashed into thinking he's an inmate? Has he chosen to be lobotomized? It's a line that could apply to any number of Scorsese's films.

Shutter Island opened to a career-best $40 million, going on to make $293 million around the world, and yet Scorsese has spoken of his regrets at making his 'last studio film.'[14] In its wake, he decreed that studios would merely act as distributors, with the budgets raised independently. Beneath the visceral mechanics of *Shutter Island* lies a fascinating dialogue with Scorsese's own anxieties, the uncertainty of his relationship with Hollywood (inmate or visitor?), and with the art of film itself. He confessed that after winning the Oscar with *The Departed*, he had been talked into the film by his own reflection. He should have leapt straight into his passion project *Silence*, based on the novel by Shūsaku Endō about Jesuit missionaries in 17th-century Japan.

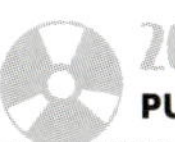
2010
PUBLIC SPEAKING (Documentary) Director / Producer / Writer

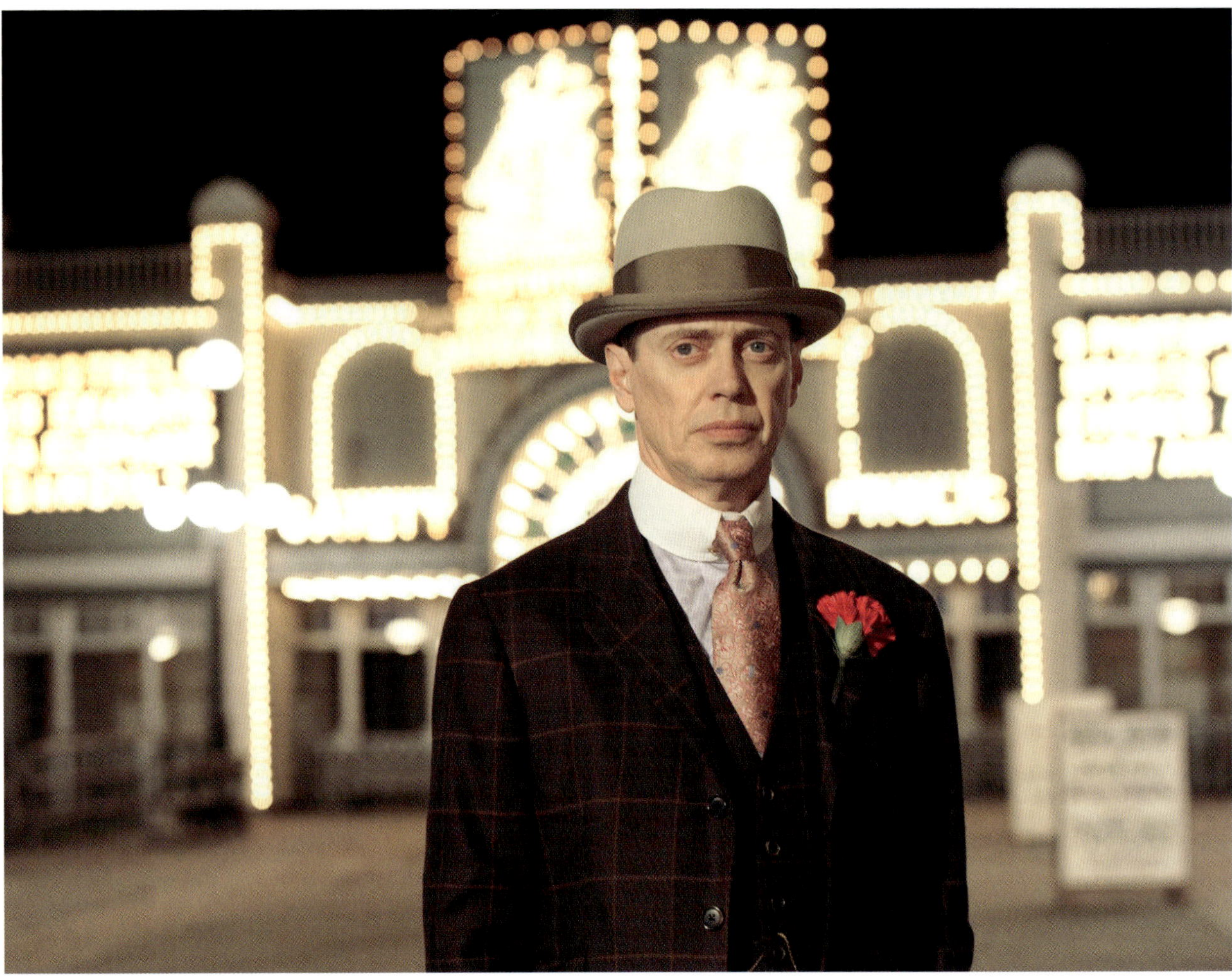

Yet *Silence* would be delayed again when two more temptations crossed his path. The first one was traditional, though it was an unusual venture into television. Scorsese served as executive producer and director of the pilot for gangster series *Boardwalk Empire*, set in a lavishly recreated Prohibition Atlantic City and borne along by the schemes of Machiavellian treasurer Nucky Thompson (Steve Buscemi), with Al Capone (Stephen Graham) still a skid-row hustler. It was a safe harbour. Scorsese finding succour in his own myths. Genre had come full circle: writer-creator Terence Winter had worked on *The Sopranos*, sired by *Goodfellas*. Scorsese was more figurehead, godfather if you will, departing soon enough to leave television to its long, classy five-season haul. Cinema still his unshakeable calling. 'The show more properly belongs to Winter than to Scorsese,' detected the *Los Angeles Times*, 'but the director's symphonic style is unmistakably evident in the pilot...'[15] The sense of place, the choreography of crowds, the poetry of the sidewalk, those stabs of intensity...

Above: *Old hat – Martin Scorsese enjoyed a brief return to the mob, directing the pilot for the period gangster series* Boardwalk Empire *(2010), starring Steve Buscemi.*

Opposite: *Young at heart – Scorsese confers with his youthful stars Chloë Grace Moretz and Asa Butterfield on the set of* Hugo *(2011), his tribute to the early days of cinema.*

2010–2014
BOARDWALK EMPIRE (TV Series, 56 episodes) Director / Executive Producer

The second temptation was another twist. A family film – of all things – named *Hugo*, made with all the artifice modern technology afforded the blockbusting age, including filming in 3D. We were left to wonder if Scorsese had taken leave of his senses. But as Richard Brody intuited in the *New Yorker*, there was another way of looking at the change of pace: 'Like *Shutter Island*, *Hugo*... is, among other things, something of a cinematic confession, even a wild auto-analysis.'[16] Only Scorsese would use state-of-the-art technology to spin a fairy-tale about the silent era's first auteur. In that sense, it also serves as a spiritual prequel to *The Aviator*.

The source material was a graphic novel by Brian Selznick, which laid a fictional veneer of Dickensian whimsy and clockwork fantasy over genuine history. The orphaned Hugo Cabret (Asa Butterfield, with huge, questioning, glacially blue eyes) lives within the walls of a French railway station, where he dutifully keeps the clocks wound.

Gare Montparnasse was built at Shepperton Studios with the dream-like theatricality of Scorsese's beloved Powell and Pressburger. The pervading aesthetic is a steampunk mix of pipes and wheels, cogs and gears, born out of Jules Verne. Scorsese doing science fiction!

From his eyrie inside the station clock, like James Stewart in *Rear Window*, Hugo watches the stories of the Montparnasse regulars take shape. Among the characters is a sullen old man who runs a kiosk selling wind-up trinkets, who turns out to be the real-life figure of Georges Méliès (a gruff, quizzical Ben Kingsley), the great film pioneer, who indeed fell upon hard times after the First World War. With the assistance of Méliès's fictional goddaughter, the excitable Isabelle (Chloë Grace Moretz), whose head is full of books, Hugo will set about repairing Méliès. One of the numerous reasons Scorsese chose this quaint tale was that his wife, Helen Morris, turned to him one day and asked, 'Why don't you make a film our daughter can see for once?'[17] His 12-year-old Francesca had come late in life, when he was in his late fifties. The experience was life-changing.

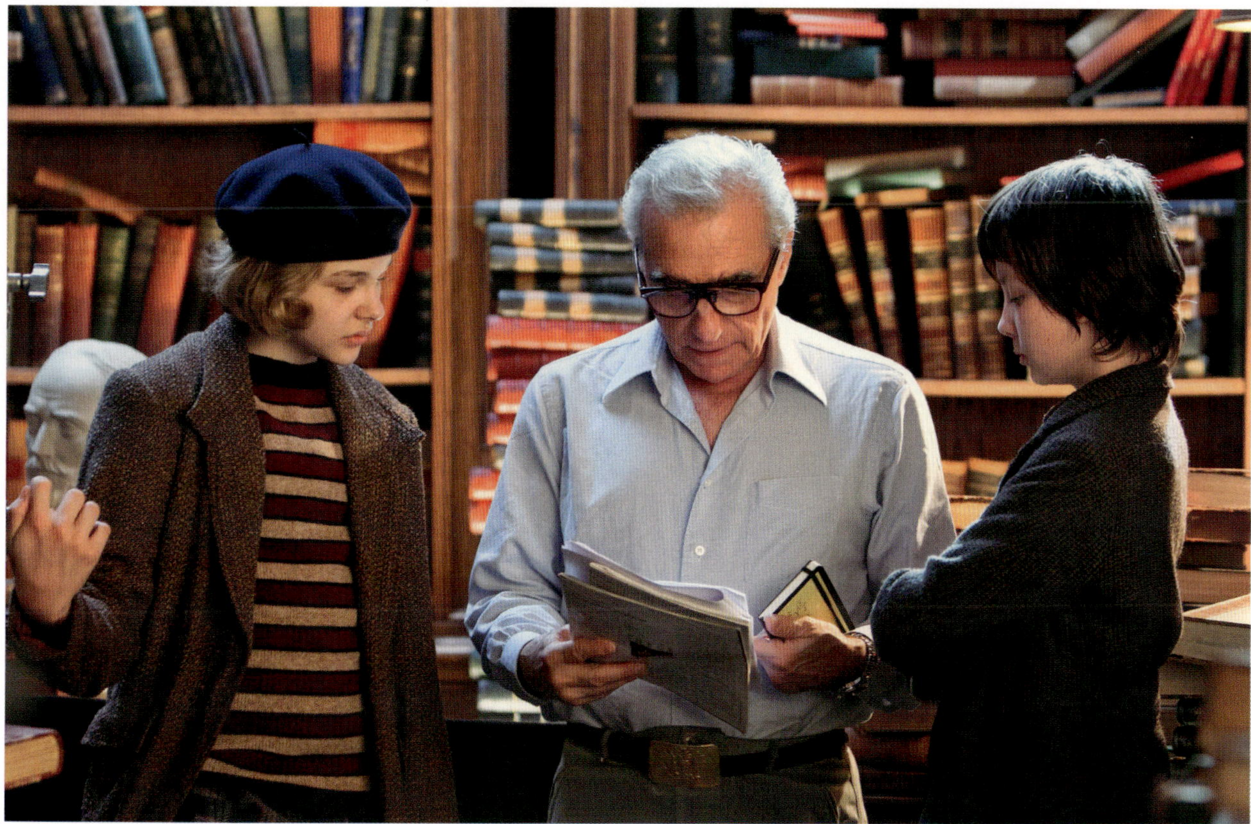

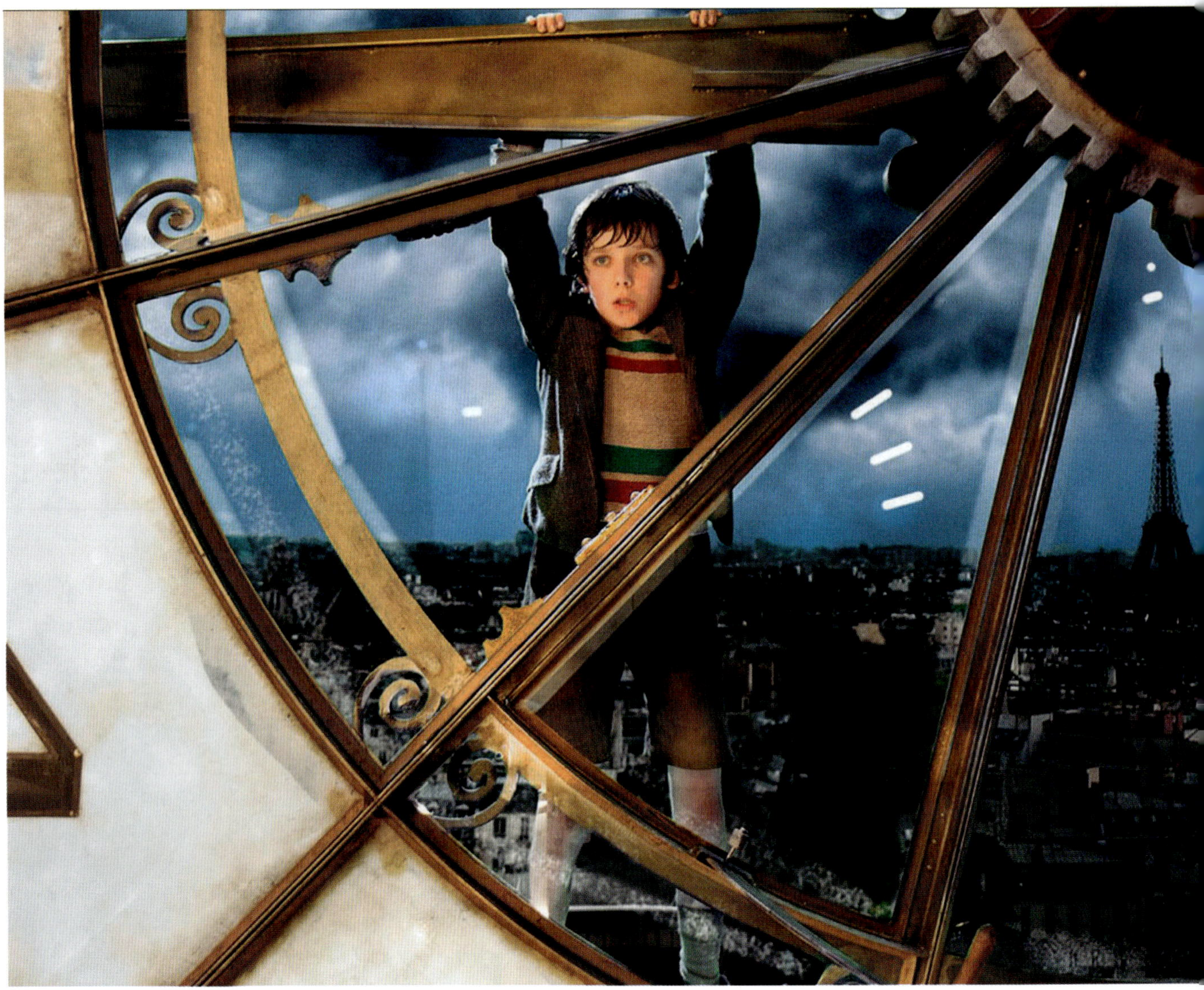

Above: *Time as theme – Asa Butterfield's titular character dangles from the hands of a Paris clock tower in* Hugo, *a reference to Harold Lloyd's* Safety Last! *(1923)*

The world of *Hugo* resolves into a vast network of storytelling inheritance and metaphor as intricate as the steam-cloaked warrens of the station. The language of silent cinema holds sway over the action, with Sacha Baron Cohen as the station police officer drawn into antic chases with orphan brats, a leg clamped from an unhealing war wound. References abound, from Hitchcock's *The Lodger* to Renoir's *La Bête Humaine*. We gain a scene of Hugo sneaking Isabelle into a cinema to see Harold Lloyd's *Safety Last*, which naturally translates into a scene of Hugo dangling from the station's clock tower. Fictional film historian René Tabard (Michael Stuhlbarg), arrives to spell out the part Méliès played in it all. Wielding a massive

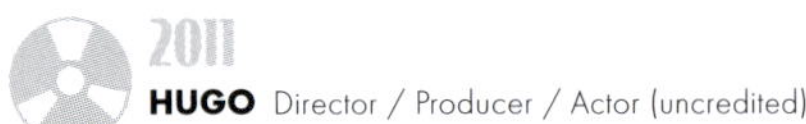

budget of $150 million, Scorsese made a children's film about cinema's childhood.

If he saw himself in Hugo, the timid boy gazing on the tumult of the world, he doubly saw himself in Méliès, the great innovator, raging, wounded, yearning. He could instantly recall the day the Parisian first came into his life. It was 1956, he was thirteen. *A Trip to the Moon* played as part of a gala screening of *Around the World in Eighty Days*, a compendium of Verne on the big screen. The audience still laughed as the rocket pierced the eye of the Moon. 'Méliès actually was a magician,' he reflected. 'And so he understood the possibilities of the motion picture camera.'[18] Méliès pioneered genre, films as vessels of fantasy; then cinema itself was a marvel grasped from the future. For six days of the six-month shoot in 2010, Scorsese revelled in the opportunity to reinvent the world of Méliès' rambunctious glass studio, conjuring dreams out of the air.

Not all the parts of *Hugo* fit together. It tends to the contrived, the Christmassy, even the twee; Scorsese's hand lies heavy on the tiller. Joe Morgenstern in the *Wall Street Journal* saw a glittering wind-up jewellery case of a film, 'but dramatically it is a clockwork lemon.'[19] There were eleven Oscar nominations, awards for Art Direction, Cinematography, and Visual Effects, but commercially the film was a calamity ($186 million worldwide). Kids wanted superheroes, the modern tilt of genre, not odes to the silent era; fans wondered what Scorsese was doing making a film in a chocolate box.

Where *Shutter Island* was disturbed by the idea of film as a deception, *Hugo* pays honour to the strange magic of the medium: this mechanical process that can create its own reality. From Méliès to Marty, the miracle remains the same.

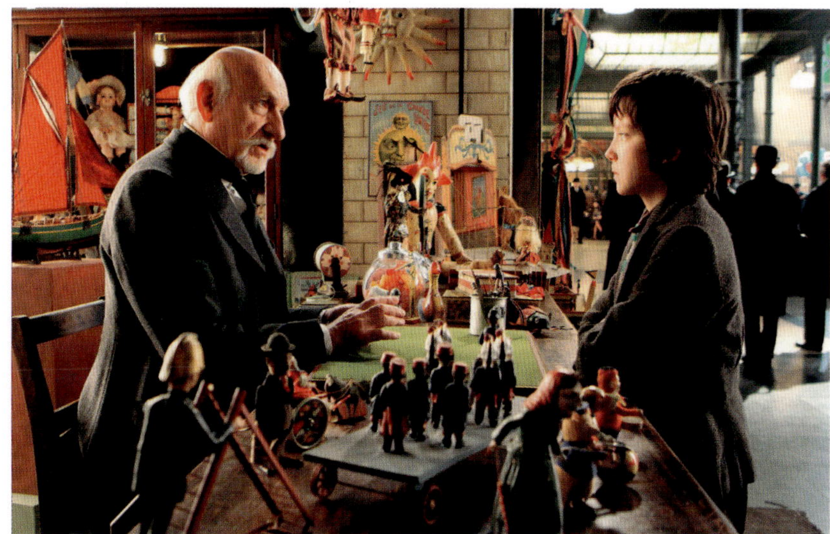

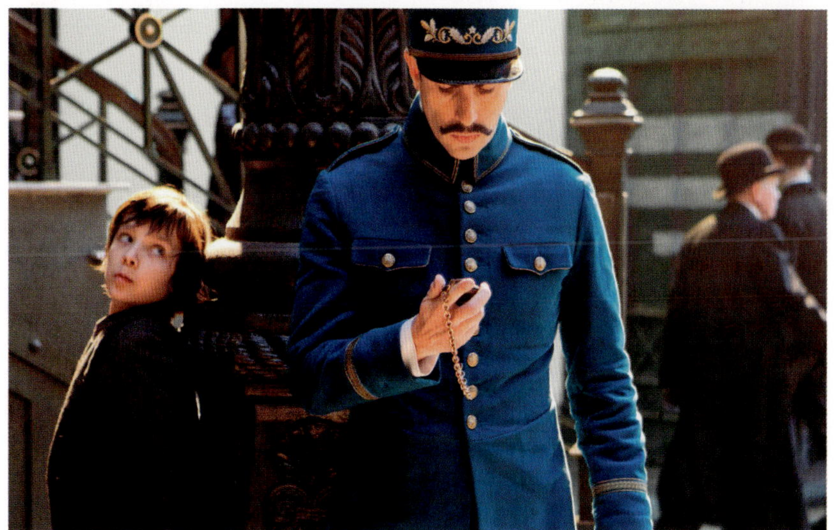

Top: *Life crossing paths with fiction – Ben Kingsley plays the great silent director Georges Méliès, who has fallen on hard times.*

Above: *Hugo (Asa Butterfield) tries to evade being captured by station Inspector Gustave Dasté (Sacha Baron Cohen), another of* Hugo's *clock watchers.*

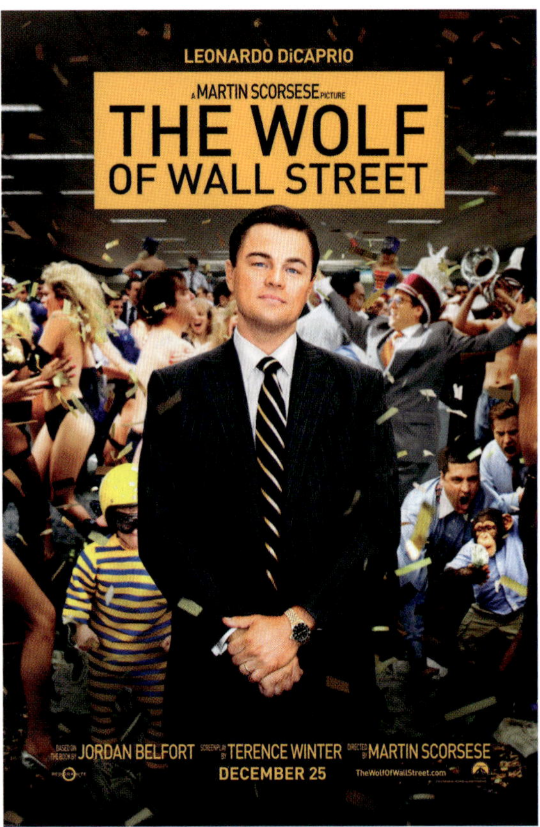

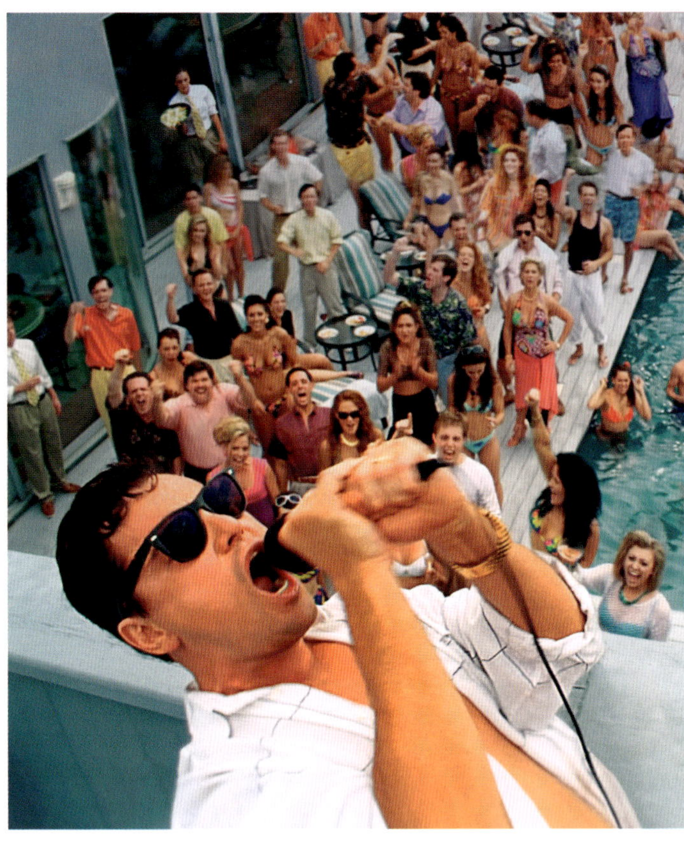

Above left: The Wolf of Wall Street *(2013) marked Martin Scorsese's return to comedy – yet there was a scathing report on modern America hidden beneath the surface.*

Above right: *The age of insolence – Leonardo DiCaprio as hard-partying Wall Street conman Jordan Belfort.*

And still *Silence* was postponed. This time for Scorsese to make another gangster movie in New York. With a topical twist. The characters are not wiseguys, though they are crooks, and the hit film (his highest grossing at a global $407 million) is a kindred spirit to *Goodfellas*, where a true story is jazzed into a morally aloof study in lifestyle. When you think about it, *The Wolf of Wall Street*, starring DiCaprio again, is another essay in American insanity, set on another island-asylum, that of Manhattan. Rather than a thriller, it is Scorsese's first comedy since *After Hours*, the tale of stockbrokers run amok. DiCaprio mentioned Caligula as an inspiration.

They had been on the verge of production in 2007 (before the crash of 2008 made it even more piquant a ride), when DiCaprio brought the biography of Wall Street rapscallion Jordan Belfort to Scorsese's attention. But Warner Brothers grew nervous at the decadence and drug abuse depicted on page and in Terence Winter's screenplay. It was a black comedy, excess was the point, insisted Scorsese, galled that six months of development had come to nothing. This was the Hollywood that exhausted him: the narrowness of focus, the endless second-guessing. Could it be an element of studio satire crept into the film's depiction of the FBI as humourless stiffs?

Five years and two films later, independent production company Red Granite offered Scorsese the opportunity

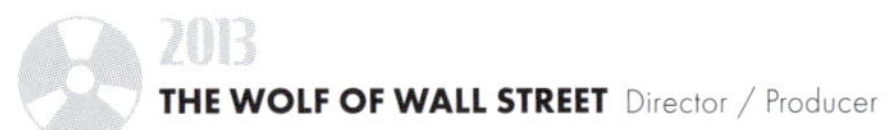

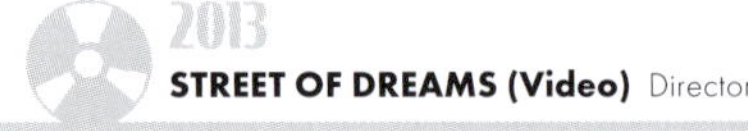

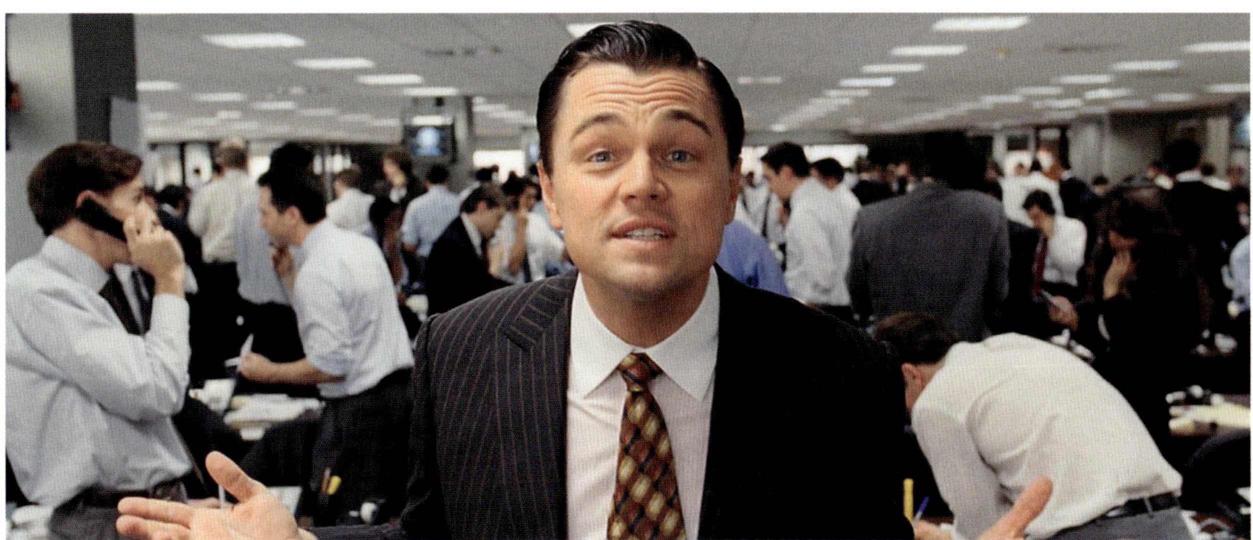

Above: *Shattering the fourth wall – to capture the reality behind the chaos, Scorsese went one step further than simply a voice-over by having DiCaprio turn to camera and address the viewer directly, as if this was an instructional video.*

to make the film as he saw fit, with Paramount distributing in America and Universal abroad. With heavy irony, Red Granite would subsequently be embroiled in a financial scandal, one of the charges being that the film was financed with embezzled money.

'I don't think we'll be able to do a movie like this too many times in the future,'[20] DiCaprio urged Scorsese, knowing there was no one better to catch the right tone – caustic, compelling, unnerving – with which to depict these robber barons. For Scorsese, the attraction of the book lay in Belfort's 'brutal honesty.'[21] Belfort did awful things, defrauded innocent people, but how he enjoyed the fruits of his sin: cocaine, hookers, quaaludes, yachts, nitrous oxide, Lamborghinis, wrestling strippers, apes on roller-skates, marching bands on the office floor. It was Sodom and Gomorrah in Downtown Manhattan, with Belfort and his geek sharks egging each other on. In their research, the filmmakers found that these dealers had fetishized *Goodfellas*.

Crucial to Scorsese was the question of whether the system, and in a bigger sense America, actually celebrated Belfort's swindles. 'Aren't people *expected* to go too far?'[22] he wondered. Like Travis Bickle or Henry Hill or Bill the Butcher, on some level we should relate to their wickedness. Only Belfort is even more persuasive. That's the rub. Lap it up, Scorsese says, this could easily be you.

Blessed with a carny-barker's magnetism, Belfort is the master of pump-and-dump, a financial illusionist, selling worthless, pink-paper stock (known as penny stocks) to none-the-wiser backers, pumping up the price, then dumping his own shares before the market gets wise. 'Was all this illegal?' shrugs Belfort straight to camera, infomercial slick. 'Absolutely fucking not.'[23] Through the illusion of propriety at Stratton Oakmont (named because it simply sounded official), untold money flowed.

As far back as he could remember, Belfort had wanted to be rich. Then richer. To the point where money itself becomes meaningless. Yet DiCaprio makes him a superstar of the superficial, a fusion of cult-leader, stand-up comic (working

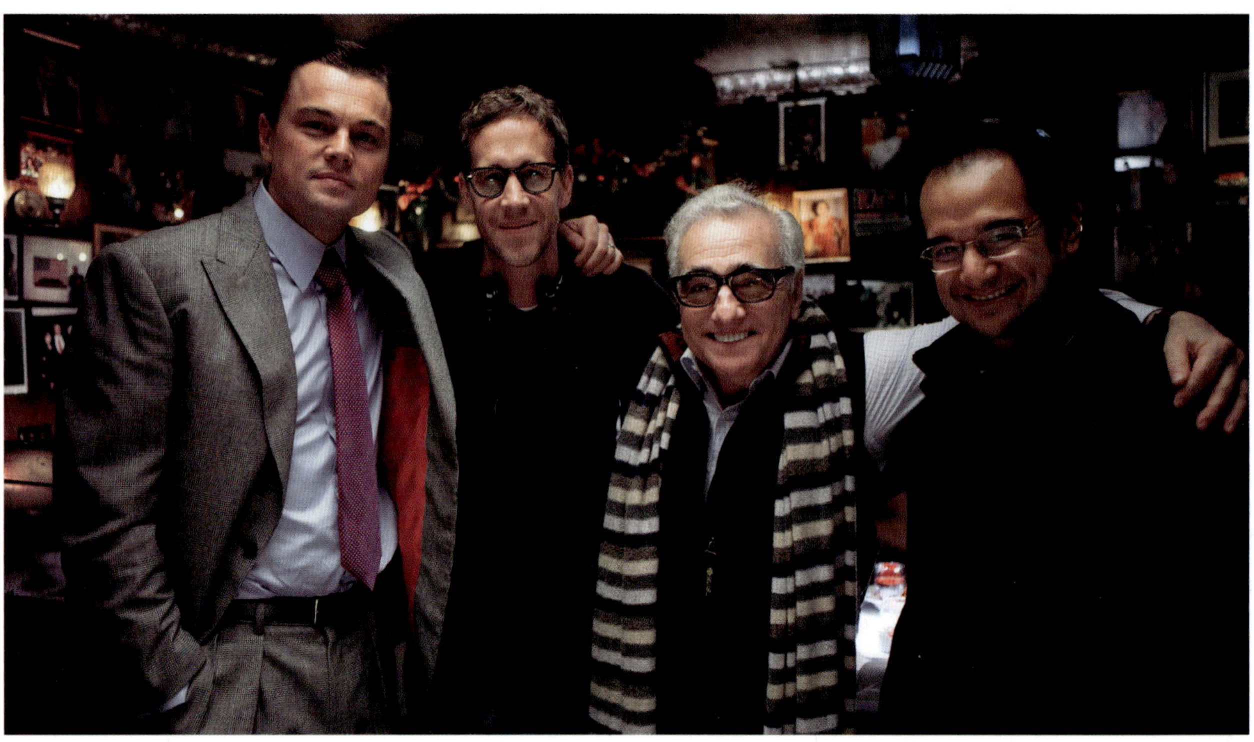

Above: *Striking a pose on the set of* The Wolf of Wall Street *– Leonardo DiCaprio, producer Joey McFarland, Martin Scorsese, and producer Riza Aziz.*

the room, mic in hand), and motivational speaker spinning ironic homilies over another voice-over. It might just be the performance of his career. This is a study in charisma. The lustre of the conman.

Shooting through late 2012, Scorsese genuflects to Chaplin and Keaton, Laurel & Hardy, Hope & Crosby, and Martin & Lewis. Jonah Hill provides DiCaprio with a double-act as debauched, beloved, giggling sidekick Donnie Azoff, and they gurn and scheme through Scorsese's buzzing montages and anecdotal grooves – masterfully controlled pandemonium – a rise and fall that consumes three hours. 'There is a riffing ease here, a swell air of deserved chaos...'[24] savoured David Thomson in the *New Republic*. Cinematographer Rodrigo Prieto changed lens depending on Belfort's state of intoxication. Belfort is another of Scorsese's addicts, but of more than drugs, or even money. He was obsessed with *making* money.

With a camera strapped to the leading man, as Scorsese had done with Harvey Keitel as an inebriated Charlie swaying through the nightlife of *Mean Streets*, Belfort collapses at a payphone and we collapse with him. The film's turning point is a tour de force of slapstick hysteria. Felled by a suspect lude, Belfort tries to drive his Lamborghini home without motor neurone control. This is the last frenetic act of *Goodfellas* concentrated into a single sequence, reducing DiCaprio to a babbling toddler and the comic register to the absurdist school of Andy Kaufman and John Belushi. Entering a weaker final act, we are exhausted, which may be the point. Fate, the FBI (in the shape of Kyle Chandler), and their

2014
THE 50 YEAR ARGUMENT (Documentary) Director / Producer

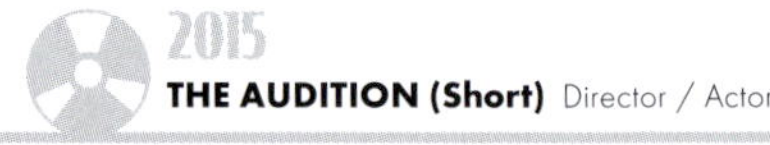

2015
THE AUDITION (Short) Director / Actor

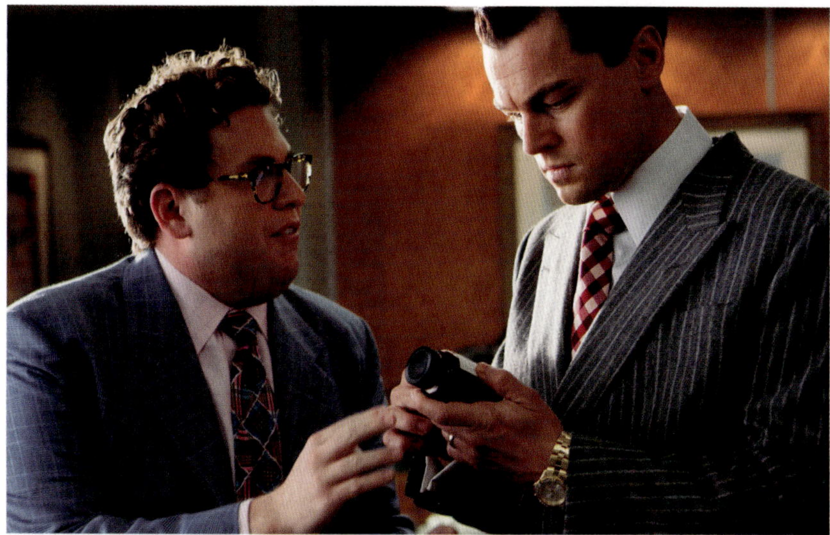

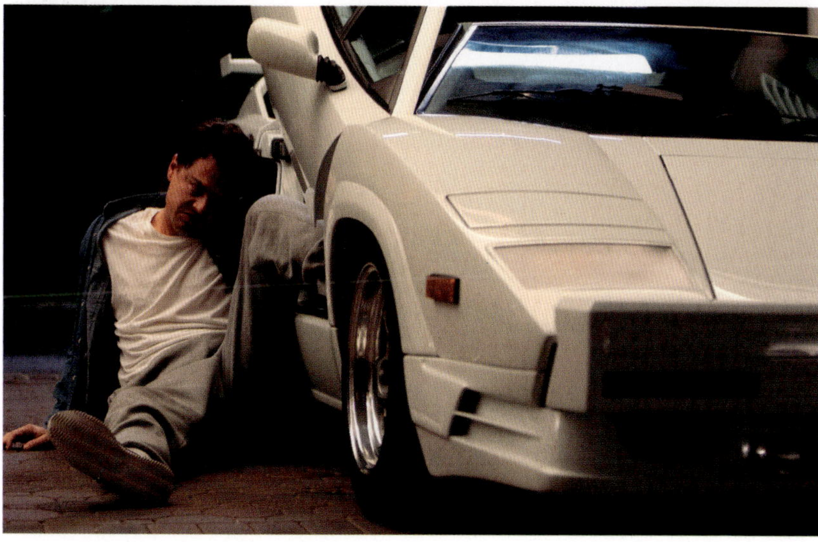

Top: *Recipe for disaster – partner Donnie Azoff (Jonah Hill) tempts Jordan Belfort (DiCaprio) with a batch of Quaaludes of suspect origin…*

Above: *…the result of which is a tour de force of slapstick mania as DiCaprio's Belfort attempts to drive home without motor neurone control.*

surge of unchecked id will catch up with Stratton Oakmont.

Who would have thought that critics could affect shock at anything the director of *Taxi Driver, Raging Bull,* or *Goodfellas* might choose to do? Yet there was a backlash to *The Wolf of Wall Street*. Critics mithered about Scorsese depicting Belfort's dizzying crimes in an entertaining light. 'Movies shouldn't provide moral instruction but the best incorporate competing philosophies,'[25] chided Ryan Gilbey in the *New Statesman*.

'It's an old story, really: people can take their identification with movies and novels to some alarming places,'[26] accepted Scorsese. But how much more daring it is to leave it to the audience to pass their own sentence. To take a look at themselves in the mirror.

Even in its deafening absence, guilt remains Scorsese's signature theme. Watch the film again, and you'll notice moments that cut into the hedonism like the shards of champagne flutes: the woman dared into shaving her head forlornly clutching her severed locks, Belfort's infant daughter staring at her bawling father, the excellent Margot Robbie's gradual transformation from trophy wife to cold voice of reason.

What lies beneath the veneer of civilization, the film wonders? What kind of animals are we if social constraint is stripped away by wealth and drugs? By the end, the staff of Stratton Oakmont have been rendered infantile, a pack of misogynist Benjamin Buttons. The only god worshipped here is Mammon. Scorsese devised a swinging camera move to repeatedly pierce the hot commotion of the trading floor, parting the partying brokers like a wrecking ball. He's back among the brawling thugs of *Gangs of New York*.

After so much hedonism, the great director at last turned to serious matters. '*Silence* needed 20 years just to even think about,'[27] laughed Scorsese, having been entranced by the novel while taking a cameo in Kurosawa's *Dreams* in 1989. He and Jay Cocks had struggled with the screenplay for fifteen years. 'At first, I didn't really immediately know, while I was reading the book, how to realize it, make it real, stage it, because I didn't know the heart of it,'[28] he confessed.

Intriguing permutations never came to pass, involving Daniel Day-Lewis, Benicio del Toro, and Gael García Bernal. Scorsese had got as far as scouting Japanese locations in 2009. And still this flinty epic seemed to evade him, or he evaded *Silence*. But in the early months of 2015, buoyed by recent success, the time had finally come, shooting in Taiwan where the windswept beaches and lush, rolling hills offered a fair facsimile of 17th-century Japan. The glowering, elemental look was based on the Baroque painters, a mix of deep blues and cyans for the coastal regions, then an arid yellow once the protagonist is in captivity in Nagasaki. Taiwan made for a cost-effective alternative, but the budget still rose to $50 million.

It is strange that a project that meant so much to Scorsese occupies such a muted place in his filmography. This could be down to the fact that it is a gruelling watch, and hardly an easy sell after the fizz of his Wall Street rogues. The film remained a boutique item, arty and sombre, making under $24 million worldwide. Reviews were as polarized as Scorsese has ever got. Either forbidding masterpiece: 'A sincere, austere, intellectually rigorous attempt to grapple with God's silence in the face of human suffering,'[29] clamoured *The Scotsman*. Or cinematic endurance test: 'It is an exhausting film to watch, but it's

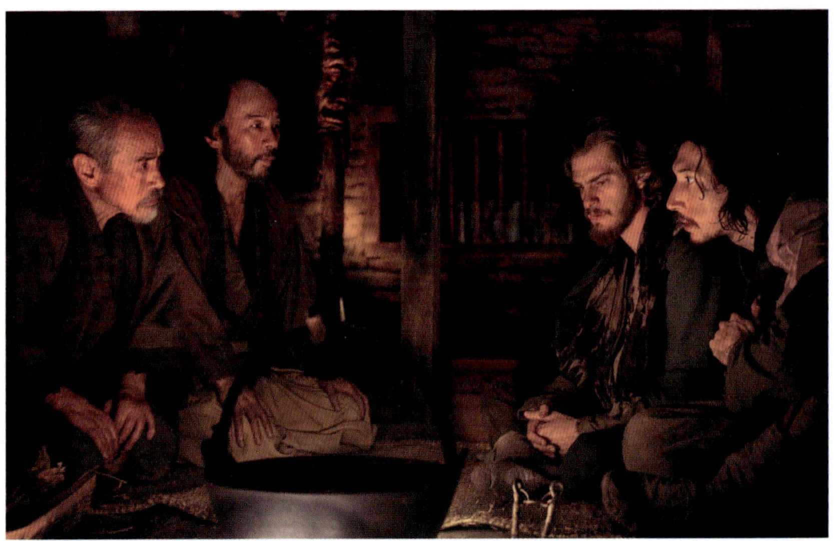

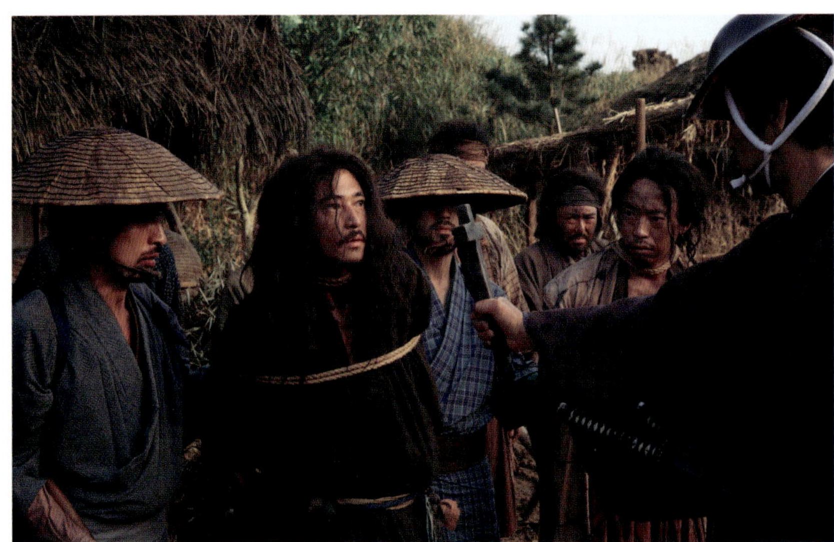

Top: *Andrew Garfield (second from right) and Adam Driver (right) feature as missionary priests in* Silence *(2016), the third of Martin Scorsese's trilogy of faith pictures.*

Above: *Yōsuke Kubozuka as the untrustworthy Kichijirō, who finds himself accused of Christianity.*

Opposite: *The cruelty of history – one of the many punishments for taking up the Catholic faith in Shogunate Japan was to be crucified within an incoming tide.*

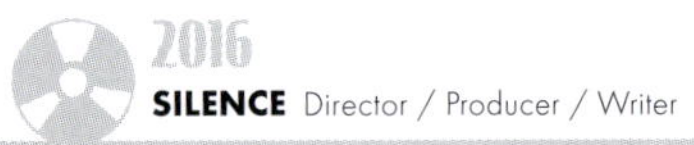

not exhausting emotionally, because it barely engages the emotions,'[30] moaned the *San Francisco Chronicle*.

In truth, the film is both a trial (quite consciously) and a compelling, philosophical story involving two Jesuit priests, Rodrigues (Andrew Garfield) and Garupe (Adam Driver), Portuguese men smuggled into Shogunate Japan, where Catholicism is outlawed upon pain of death (with great emphasis on pain) to discover what has become of their mentor Father Ferreira (another ghostly cameo from Liam Neeson), rumoured to have done the unthinkable and committed apostasy – recanted his faith. Captured, Rodrigues will find his own faith put to an agonizing test under the imperious eye of the inquisitor Inoue (Issey Ogata, whose needling voice is its own torture instrument), confined to a slatted prison, giving him and us only half-glimpses of the world outside.

What was it about *Silence* that held Scorsese in its grip? There was a precedent, a category of troubled-priest movies in which to enlist: Bresson's *Diary of a Country Priest* (which had helped fuel *Taxi Driver's* rages), the colonial brutality of *The Mission* (which featured Robert De Niro), and Bergman's *Winter Light*. Patterns repeat in Scorsese's career. After another cycle of relatively commercial ventures, he was drawn again to a 'faith' picture. *Silence* completed a meditative trilogy with *The Last Temptation of Christ* and *Kundun*. Films that recalled the other side of his character, the boy nurtured by the Catholic Church, who came so close to the priesthood. A contemplation of the young man who had committed apostasy by choosing movies over the haven of faith.

His memories often stole back to Father Francis Principe – his first mentor, when he was a teenager. Principe was the first to suggest there might be more to life than the cycle of marriage and family. That there was a way through literature, music, and movies. 'He loved Westerns, but he didn't like *Johnny Guitar*,'[31] laughed Scorsese.

Endō's novel is about a crisis of faith. '*Silence* is the story of a man who learns

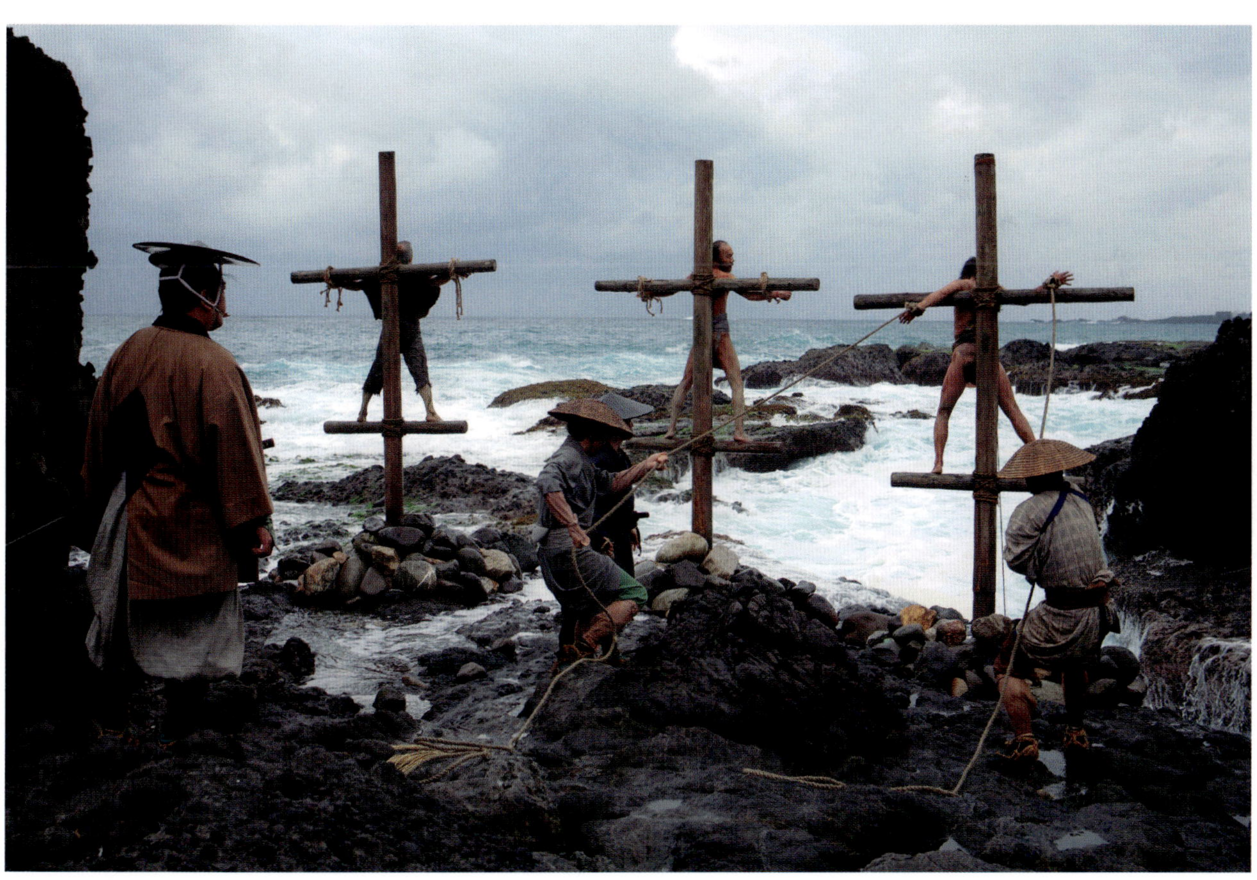

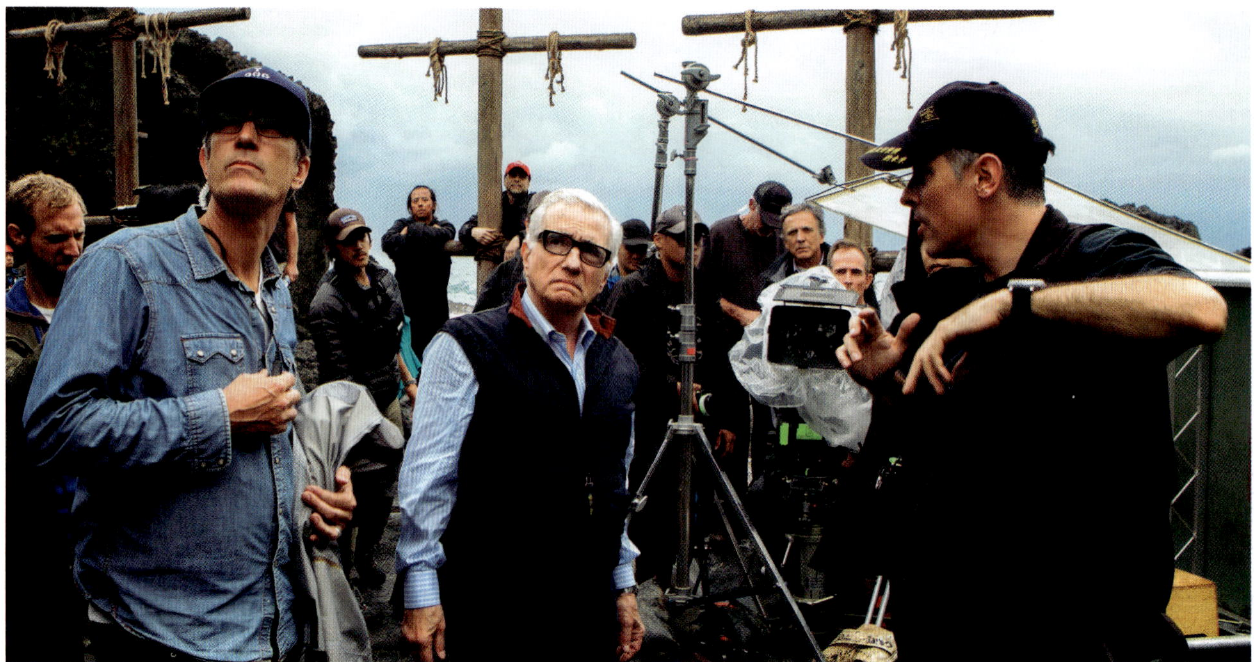

Above: *Braving the elements – Martin Scorsese (centre) and cinematographer Rodrigo Prieto (right) found the perfect mix of moody climate and rugged terrain for* Silence *in Taiwan.*

– so painfully – that God's love is more mysterious than he knows, that He leaves more to the ways of men than we realize...'[32] Scorsese wrote in his introduction to the novel. Rodrigues comes to understand the necessity of Judas to salvation. That betrayal – another key Scorsesean theme – is a complex beast. The film's most fascinating character is Kichijirō (the wonderful Yōsuke Kubozuka), the vagabond who serially betrays Rodrigues, only to return begging for absolution like an addict. The lead actors immersed themselves in the teachings of the Jesuit faith for over a year, physically losing weight, until they were raw and ready, but it is the Japanese cast who stand out.

In its absorbing, textured, disturbing way, *Silence* is another study in psychosis. Rodrigues gazes at his bearded face mirrored in a pool of water, seeing a mockery of Christ gaze back. He is as obsessed as Travis Bickle, trapped in the fever of his faith, even as others – villager converts, a ready supply of victims for the authorities – suffer exquisite tortures for his arrogance. As Rodrigues finally gives way to his captors' demands (the release is almost a physical relief for the viewer), God breaks His silence, assuring him that Christ is still with him, a voice-over direct from Heaven.

Silence epitomizes Scorsese's recurring personal crisis. What constituted art in the realm of the filmic senses? Should cinema attempt to wrestle with higher things? With the existence of God even? Should he, the great Martin Scorsese, be pursuing a nobler cause? The film continued his search for 'something more,'[33] he said; something more than family, more than cinema. What is it, finally, you devoted your life to?

KEEPING IT REAL

Martin Scorsese the documentarian

As a director, Scorsese doesn't make a distinction between his approach to fact and fiction – his fictional films aspire to realism as his numerous documentaries are feats of storytelling. Each parallels the other.

1. *Italianamerican* (1974)
With great affection, Scorsese illuminates the immigrant experience through the prism of his parents, Charles and Catherine, sat on the sofa in their New York apartment. A style is established, with the director a conscious presence (see Little Italy, page 10).

2. *American Boy: A Profile of Steven Prince* (1978)
The extraordinary account of the life of Steven Prince – friend, army brat, road manager for Neil Diamond, actor (see God's Lonely Man, page 40), hustler, and junkie, as regaled in the subject's living room and hot tub. Trusting the power of a storyteller, Scorsese's camera rests on Prince as his tales spiral from comedy into American tragedy.

3. *The Last Waltz* (1978)
The final concert of seventies troubadours The Band was filmed in 1976, and included guest appearances from Eric Clapton and Bob Dylan. But Scorsese conceived it as a musical, storyboarding the gig, lighting it for 35mm, designing the sets, and taking two years to edit. This was about the end of the seventies, *his* seventies (see The Dark Arts, page 58).

4. *Lady By The Sea: The Statue of Liberty* (2004)
Made for the History Channel with Kent Jones, this is a tribute to New York's great statue – and her continued symbolism post-9/11.

5. *No Direction Home: Bob Dylan* (2005)
Scorsese's work with major musical artists is an extension of his passion for music, such an inspiration for his feature films. Here is the New York phase of Bob Dylan's life from 1961 to 1966, including the aftermath of the 1965 Newport Folk Festival, when he walked on stage with an electric guitar. 'It's betrayal again,'[1] recalled Scorsese. Someone yelled 'Judas!'[2] from the audience.

6. *Shine a Light* (2008)
A history of his beloved Rolling Stones, pivoting around their performances at New York's Beacon Theatre in 2006. Something in the 'tone and mood of their music,'[3] he said, inspired his style of filmmaking.

7. *Public Speaking* (2010)
Following the performative structure of *American Boy*, this is an enchanting profile of New York writer and iconoclast Fran Lebowitz. Again it is the personality that rings true. 'When I was a child it was called talking back,' she laughs. 'Now it's called public speaking.'[4]

8. *George Harrison: Living in the Material World* (2011)
The life of the quiet Beatle, focusing on his search for spiritual serenity (mirroring Scorsese's faith pictures), including five years of archival research.

9. *The 50 Year Argument* (2014)
An exhilarating celebration of the *New York Review of Books*, captured from a working editorial office. The central theme is the power of the cultural argument.

10. *Personality Crisis: One Night Only* (2023)
A fourth film co-directed with David Tedeschi (editor on Scorsese's earlier documentaries), this is another combination of concert film and anecdotal biography. In this case centering on David Johansen, witty and anarchic former lead singer of the New York Dolls.

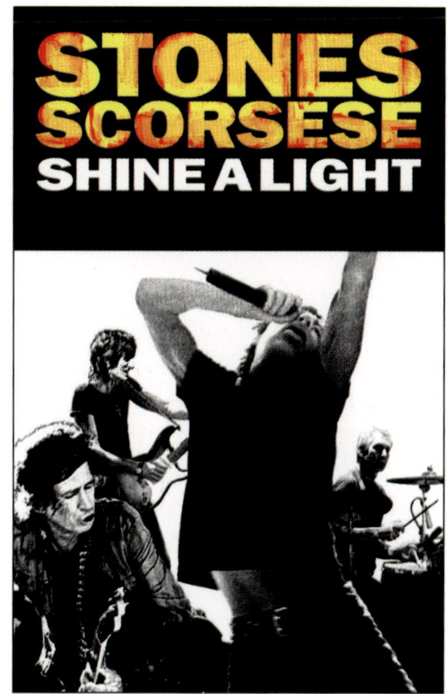

Right: *The release poster for Scorsese's 2008 study of the Rolling Stones.*

The great director had been clear on the matter. The mob scene was all played out. 'What do we explore?'[1] he implored. His trilogy was complete, New York hustlers to Vegas peacocks, three ages of gangster: *Mean Streets, Goodfellas,* and *Casino*. Of course, even as Martin Scorsese declared a moratorium on his beloved wiseguys, he admitted that there was perhaps one area he might still explore. A view of the world, he said, 'from the perspective of somebody who's in their seventies, looking back.'[2] A film that could only be made when he was equally as old and reflective, such as the elegiac saga christened (with no little irony) *The Irishman*, his longest, arguably his deepest cut on the subject, a memoir that doubles back over Scorsese's entire career.

As the cameras rolled on Randall's Island, Manhattan, first of twenty-five locations spread across New York, New Jersey, and as far south as Florida, the year was 2017 and Scorsese seventy-five. He had indeed grown old, America's greatest living director: silver-haired and contemplative, but the whiplash-fast talk, all those roaming thoughts, had not diminished. Nor had his ravenous desire to pursue film as an extension of life. 'Thankfully, the curiosity doesn't end,'[3] he laughed. By now, he had read all of Joyce (bar *Finnegans Wake*), all of Tolstoy, Melville, and Dostoevsky. He had become a literary director, not so much in terms of material (*The Age of Innocence* remains his only classic adaptation), but in the length and texture and mood of his choices, and that dialogue with the nature of cinema itself. He is discussed with the same reverence as a great painter who may have worked in many genres and dabbled in many themes, but whose achievements are summed up in the utterance of a single, all-encompassing name. 'This is the new *Scorsezze...*' Everything is filtered through our perception of the artist, who catches out his own seriousness with gusts of deprecating laughter.

Applauding *The Irishman* in the *New York Times*, A.O. Scott noted how the movie was 'long like a novel by Dostoyevsky or Dreiser, dark like a painting by Rembrandt.'[4]

Opposite: *A movie brat in his dotage – Martin Scorsese dresses up for a gala screening of* The Irishman *at the BFI London Film Festival in 2019.*

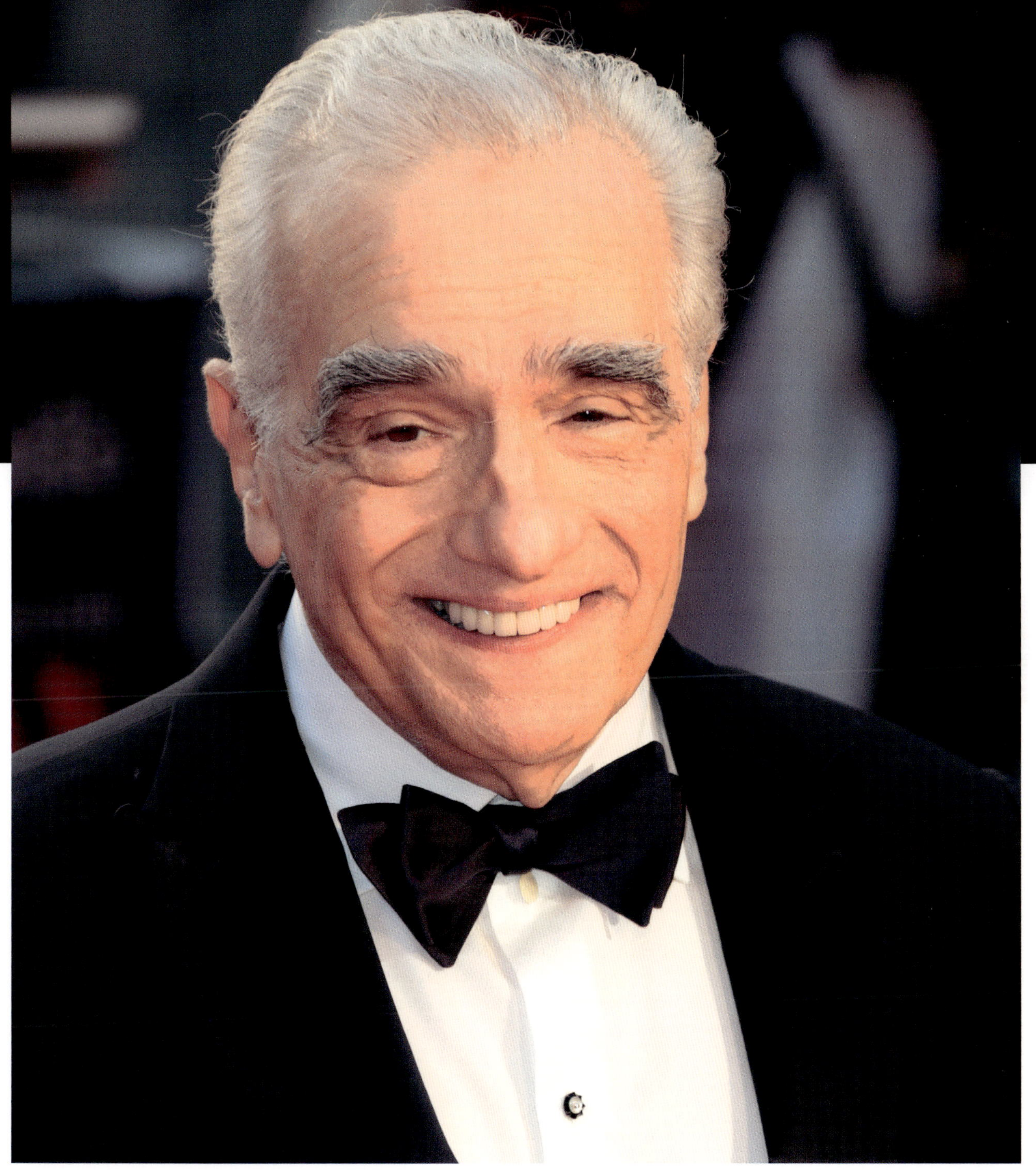

The septuagenarian Scorsese was firmly rooted in New York, his grand Midtown apartment looming high above those Bosch-like streets, happy in the company of his fifth wife (the publisher Helen Schermerhorn Morris, a descendant of Edith Wharton), three daughters, and two grandchildren. Sikelia Productions, his filmmaking facility, was a few blocks away in the Director's Guild Building on 57th Street, where, beneath a view of the Queensboro Bridge, and shelves crowded with books and walls lined with movie posters, he edited and wrote. Like Kubrick and Spielberg, he hates to fly (is there some correlation with directing - this fear of putting control into another's hands?) L.A. is a mystery to him now, populated by a new generation, his friends mostly gone. Unless he's with DiCaprio, or seeing George or Steven or Francis, those left from the old gang, or showing his pensive face to strike a deal, he stays away.

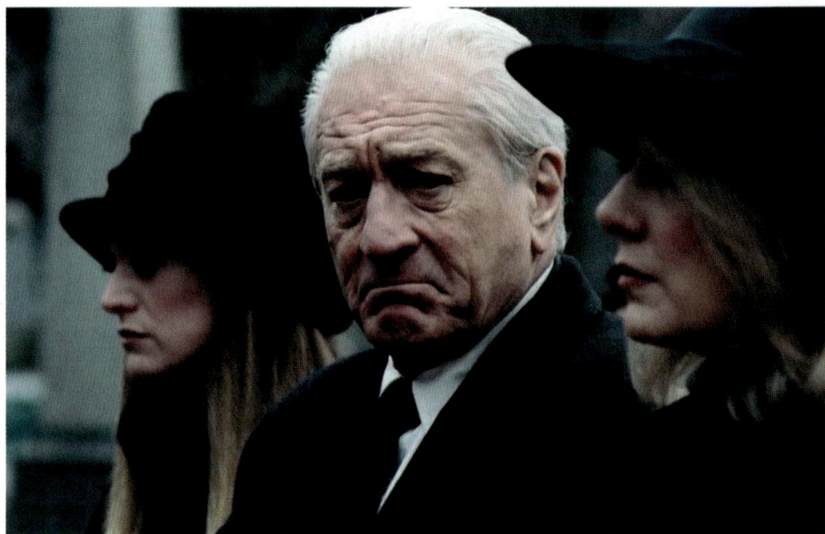

After directing films for over fifty years, it remains only on set that his calling truly makes sense. Once seated beside the camera, he demands quiet in order to contemplate the scene in front of his eyes as if already sitting in the stalls, blessed light falling upon his wrinkled face. His sets are as still as a church in which the ritual of filmmaking is enacted.

In interviews, he still recalled Elizabeth Street. Some part of him remained the young director eager to tell the stories that surrounded him. But this new film was clothed in age and stalked by death - a confession of a life not well spent, tuned to the meditative frequency of *Kundun* or *Silence* rather than the racing heart of *Goodfellas*. *The Irishman* moves like an ocean liner.

Blame Robert De Niro. They were working on an adaptation of Don Winslow's veteran-hitman thriller *The Winter of Frankie Machine*, alongside talk of remaking *The Bad and The Beautiful* (concluding a films-on-film trilogy with *The Aviator* and *Hugo*). It was like this between them: a rolling discussion, certain they would work together again. Often it was through De Niro's perception of a character that Scorsese knew there was 'something here.'[5] And as was also often the case, it was the afterthought that caught fire. De Niro happened to mention this other book that had struck a nerve, *I Heard You Paint Houses*, the life story of mob hitman Frank Sheeran as told to former prosecutor James Brandt. Where Henry Hill had spilled the beans in middle age, exiled from the good life, Sheeran was closing in on the coffin, wheelchair-bound, and ready to confess. Age had withered him.

In Steve Zaillian's script, erstwhile truck driver Sheeran reads as the epitome of the ennobled American working man. Except that this Irish-American Second World War vet had made the FBI list of known Cosa Nostra associates, having risen from small-time fixer and union plant to hitman. Painting houses was wiseguy vernacular for a hired killing, decorating the walls in Pollock-like splashes of blood, and Scorsese will punctuate Sheeran's recollections with trademark rimshots of violence: the pop of a revolver and a body dropping in a final heartbeat. Then, as Sheeran advises in laconic voice-over, toss the gun from a bridge.

Beneath the unhurried governance of Philly mob boss and lifelong associate Russell Bufalino, Sheeran is positioned as bodyguard to James Riddle Hoffa, fulsome head of the Teamsters union. Bigger than Elvis, Hoffa is becoming a liability. In his stoic way, Sheeran comes to love Hoffa - they are almost another Scorsesean marriage - a turbulent man he will ultimately be instructed to dispose of with clinical efficiency. What was so fascinating to De Niro was why loyalty outranked love. Was Sheeran a weak man irrevocably programmed by the mob code? Or, in his tidy way, was he as much a psychopath as Max Cady? 'Has he got a soul?'[6] wondered Scorsese.

There followed ten years of development, with Scorsese and his

Opposite: *Oldfella – Robert De Niro portrays the mob hitman Frank Sheeran who has somehow survived into old age in* The Irishman *(2019).*

Below: *Joe Pesci and De Niro play younger versions of their characters with the assistance of de-ageing CGI. For Scorsese it was essential that his stars portrayed these men throughout.*

leading man (and producer) awaiting age to catch up with them as Clint Eastwood had paused *Unforgiven* until his wrinkles matched. The film passed from a nervy Paramount to the swaggering streamer Netflix, where it was greenlit at an eye-watering $159 million. Twenty-two years had passed since Scorsese had last worked with De Niro (on *Casino*). That Joe Pesci was persuaded out of retirement to play Bufalino (he always needed persuading) and that Harvey Keitel was in the mix, beneath a bouffant of white locks as mob prince Angelo Bruno, added to the meta-aura of a grand reunion – a farewell to all that. De Niro was behind everything, even the casting of an eye-rolling, bellicose Al Pacino as Hoffa. Pacino had never worked with Scorsese (there had been passing talk, long ago, of Scorsese directing *Serpico*), but knew it wasn't a matter of if but when. Cinema demanded it, just as it had with Jack Nicholson, who had symbolically starred in the 1992 biopic *Hoffa*. Big men needed big actors.

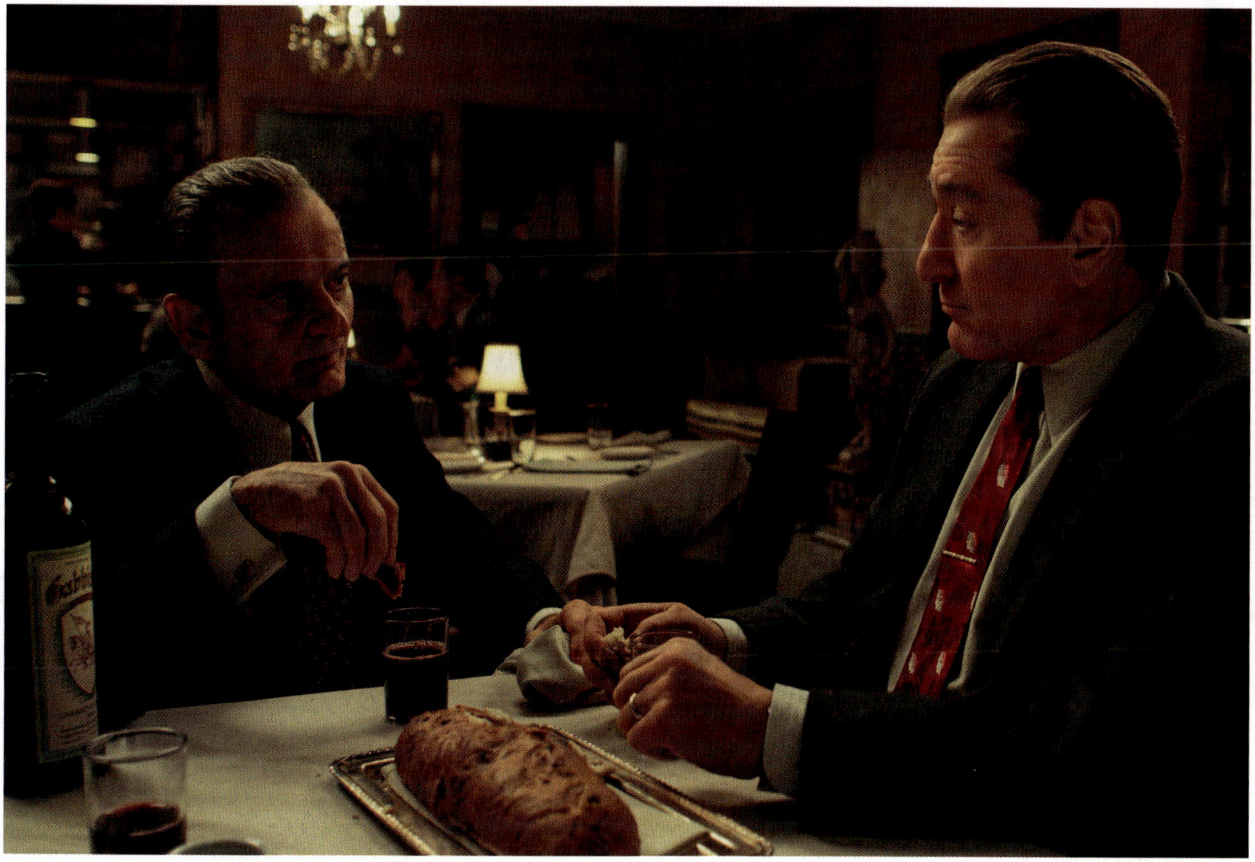

The Irishman opens with an ironic flourish. A slow, twisting tracking shot to The Five Satins' *In the Still of the Night*, not into a nightclub, or through a casino, but down the bleak municipal corridors of a care home to an old man in a wheelchair. This is the decrepit Sheeran (De Niro ancient with make-up), who looks straight into camera

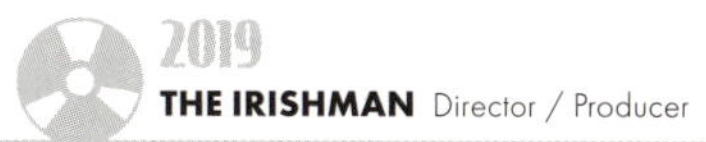

and begins his confession. To whom is unclear. A priest? Brandt? The long-dead Hoffa? To Scorsese as documentarian? Or is it simply we, the innocent viewers, who are being addressed?

Sheeran's narrative expands into a reflection on Scorsese's entire storytelling methodology. This beautifully, novelistically structured Russian doll of a picture: meandering, tangential, idling in backstories, gliding to and fro in time, an old man recalling events at his own ruminative pace. Flashbacks lie within flashbacks, voice-overs within voice-overs, framing devices within framing devices, as Sheeran's story leads us first to 1975 and a car journey that will map out a fresco of mob life.

Backed by those men at Netflix, things had come full circle. Such a studied, digressive approach compares to the great tapestries of modern television that Scorsese had inspired. Would the long game of *The Irishman* have been a better fit for a series? Perhaps, but that is a betrayal Scorsese could never contemplate.

We will discover how Sheeran began painting houses for a living. 'You followed orders...' he explains. 'You got rewarded.'[7] And we find out how he was chosen to sit by the side of Hoffa. Storm-tossed American history is witnessed through ordinary eyes. With gothic understatement, Sheeran's steady progress through the mob rank and file intersects with an underworld of conspiracies of mafia fermentation, real James Ellroy/Oliver Stone 'secret history'[8] terrain: stolen elections, the Bay of Pigs, Bobby Kennedy's crusades, Watergate. 'If they can whack a President,' whispers Russell to an incredulous Sheeran, 'they can whack a president of the union.'[9]

The road trip Russell and Sheeran are taking, with their kvetching wives, from Kingston, Pennsylvania to Detroit aboard an ambling Lincoln Continental (which travels, like every car in *The Irishman*, at the pace of a hearse) is headed not only for a Bufalino wedding, but towards the event to which all this granular history has been adding up – the killing of Hoffa. Sheeran's sharpest memory and confounding regret are depicted with ghostly detachment, Scorsese's control absolute. Then out of the quiet, the crack of Sheeran's gun, two shots, and the plume of red across a wall. In effect, the entire film, almost three and a half hours long, with 300-something scenes, 215 costume changes, is the biography of an assassination.

According to Brandt, this is the solution to Hoffa's fabled disappearance on 30 July 1975, though the book had been derided as more hot air. Scorsese didn't care about speculation, he sought emotional veracity over factual truth, the personal within the

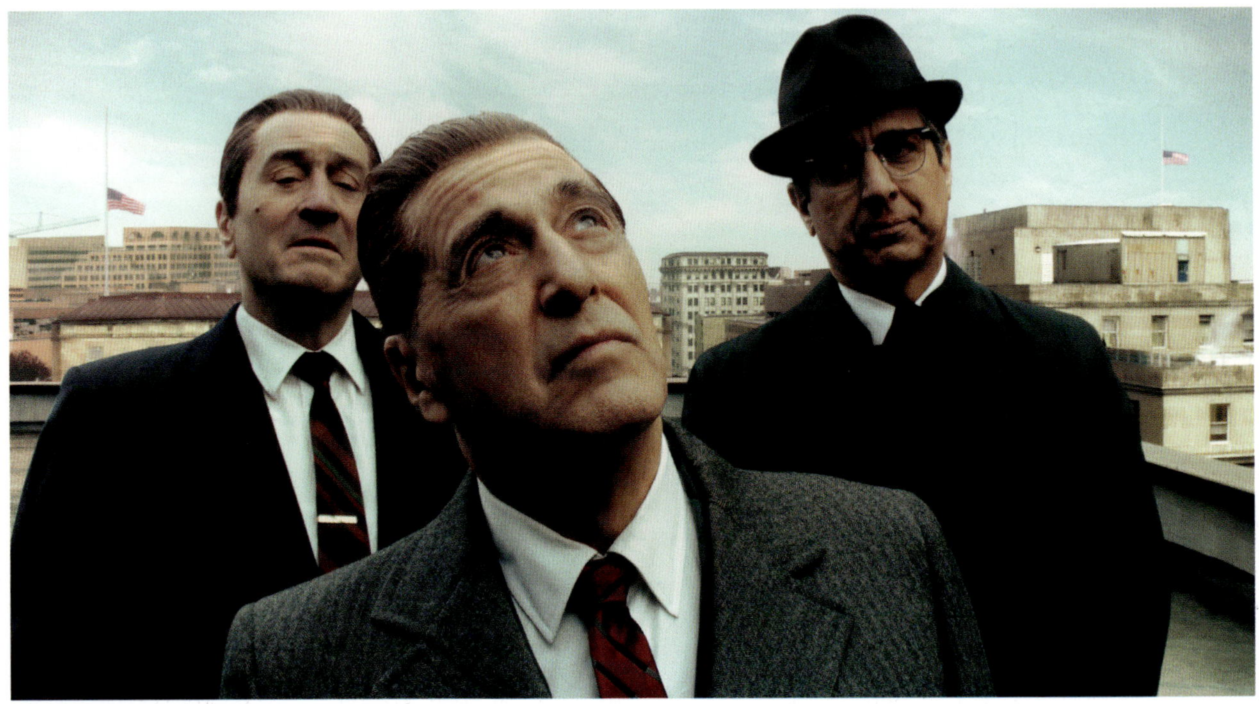

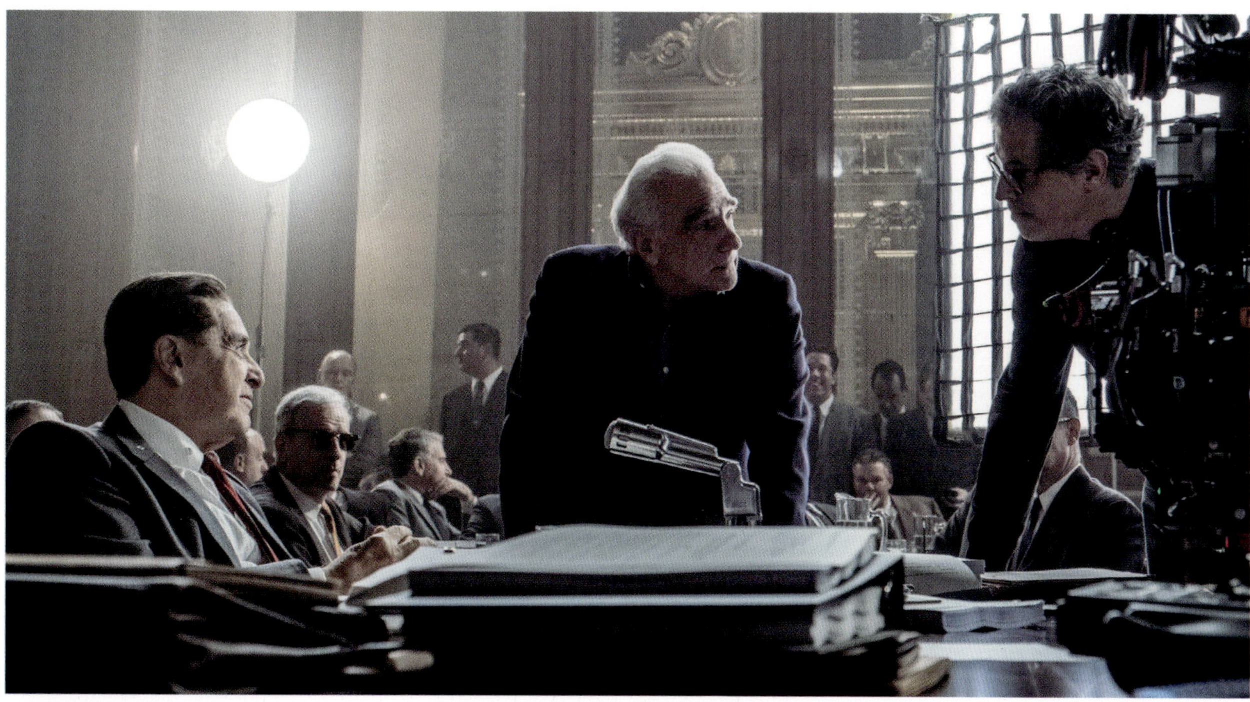

Above: *Making history – Martin Scorsese confers with cinematographer Rodrigo Prieto (right) while shooting* The Irishman *with Al Pacino.*

Opposite: *Friends until the end – Frank Sheeran (Robert De Niro) serves as confidant and bodyguard to Jimmy Hoffa (Pacino), with lawyer Bill Bufalino (Ray Romano).*

mythical. 'What are the essentials? The essentials are the characters,'[10] he declared.

Where once De Niro and Pacino had shared an iconic coffee in Michael Mann's *Heat*, here they are conferring on hotel beds in pinstripe pyjamas. It's as if Scorsese is pastiching their reputations, portraying those twinned American greats as *The Odd Couple*, and the effect is oddly moving. In *Film Comment* Jonathan Romney hailed Pacino's 'self-conscious, almost self-caricaturing vaudeville turn.'[11] Whereas De Niro is a study in perplexed *froideur*, the straight man. It is almost unnerving to see him play subordinate.

No one is as subdued as Pesci. It was what finally seduced him to the part – the chance to go against type. The polar opposite of Tommy DeVito or Nicky Santoro, Russell is the hushed embodiment of assured power. '[He] does everything with his sad, watchful eyes and his lovely, walnut-shell face,' extolled Scott in the *New York Times*. 'When he and De Niro are onscreen together, you believe in the power of art.'[12]

Every day, as soon as the cameras rolled, Scorsese's nervousness melted away. The world of filmmaking became the world of the film. The only element of *The Irishman* that risked marring such authenticity was the most modern. Aghast at the idea of casting younger actors for the younger versions of his leads – 'I would be shooting half the movie without Bob!'[13] – Scorsese was convinced de-ageing CGI would do the trick. A complex process that required each camera to be equipped with three lenses, and months of additional postproduction, for only partial success. We get used to it, but in early scenes the effect is distracting, these younger, AI-like faces on bodies that can't disguise the weight of age. And still flaw can be read as

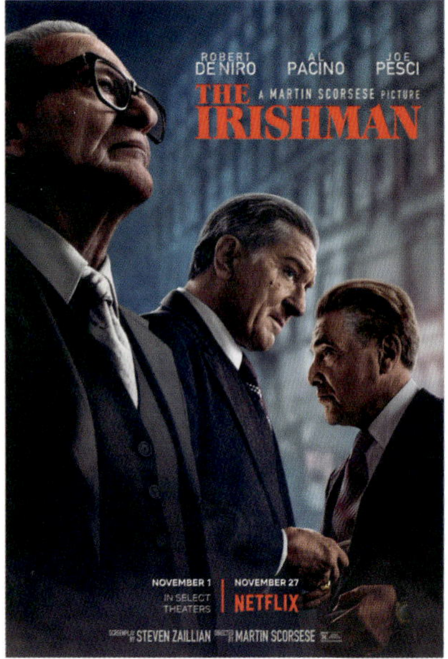

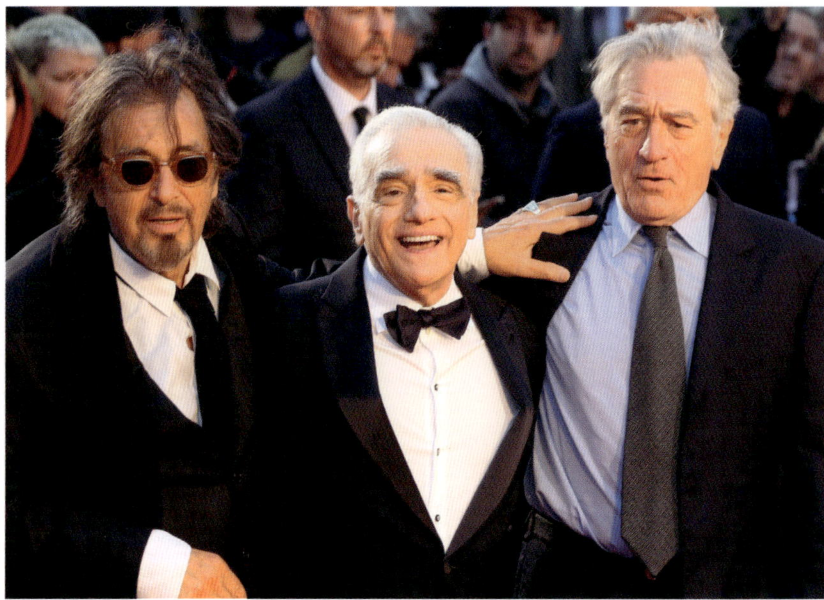

feature – could this be Sheeran's distorted view of himself slowly coming into focus?

Moreover, *The Irishman* cascades with wonderful human faces, another ensemble embracing their Scorsese moment: Ray Romano, Stephen Graham, Anna Paquin (as Sheeran's estranged daughter Peggy, whose silence is damnation), Bobby Cannavale, Jesse Plemons.

This is a story told by an old man, full of silences, a chamber piece, where the Scorsesean blaze is damped down into those woody Rembrandt-like hues, overcast greys, and the creeping shadows of nightfall. Where the sparks of the French New Wave ignited his former gangster films, now the director is calling upon the Ingmar Bergman of *Wild Strawberries*, another road trip into memory. Alongside the statutory jukebox of hits (that other voice-over), there is an inescapable sensation of a self-curated retrospective about *The Irishman*. Not only in its reliquary of mob tales (including revisiting the Copa), but in how it recalls the solemnity of his faith pictures, the social rubric of *The Age of Innocence*, or the passage of life through *Raging Bull*. The shot of Sheeran laying out his guns on the bed is an undeniable reference to Travis Bickle.

Every road in *The Irishman* leads to death, via a muzzle flash or an inglorious decline. In a brilliant Scorsese touch, where once he simply captioned his cast of hoods, now he adds a brief obituary as if they are already ghosts: 'Phil Testa – blown up by a nail bomb under his porch. March 15, 1981.'[14] This sombre, complex, valedictory epic asks: What does a life add up to? What does a career amount to? And surely now serves as Scorsese's last word on the mob – an end to all that. 'To watch this movie, especially in its long, graceful final movement, is to feel a circle closing,'[15] divined Scott in that *New York Times* review.

Wait, not so fast. Scorsese wasn't saying absolutely not. 'What else could you learn?' he wondered. 'As a filmmaker, what else can you learn about yourself and this

Above left: *Backed by Netflix, it is impossible to quantify the financial success of* The Irishman, *but its stature as a film is inarguable.*

Above right: *The new old boy – Al Pacino joins Martin Scorsese and Robert De Niro on the red carpet of the film's premiere at the Venice International Film Festival.*

Opposite: *Table talk – Leonardo DiCaprio, Lily Gladstone, Scorsese, and De Niro get to grips with* Killers of the Flower Moon *(2023).*

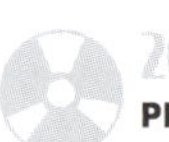
2022
PERSONALITY CRISIS: ONE NIGHT ONLY (Documentary) Director / Executive Producer

subject matter with these characters in this world?... I hope to explore a little more, if I have time.'[16]

Here's the rub. Creative freedom comes at a cost. Swiftly embedded in the small-screen chocolate box of Netflix and Apple, Scorsese's latest two films don't resonate as they should. It is impossible to tell if *The Irishman* was in any way successful. The revenues for its brief run in American cinemas went undeclared (it made less than $1 million internationally), and streaming success is almost impossible to quantify – in effect, *The Irishman* was a loss leader encouraging potential subscribers that Netflix was working in the big leagues. Yet despite eleven Oscar nominations, it won nothing. His next, *Killers of the Flower Moon*, which made $105 million in cinemas before taking its streaming berth, managed ten Oscar nominations, but won nothing.

These two late films are comparable in many ways. Both are three hours plus. Both serve as a fitting capstone on his career, even if retirement remains far from his mind. They feature familiar faces, familiar themes, a tide of regret – each centres on a weak man unwilling to look too closely at his own image. Yet each is an American epic.

Scorsese had been handed David Grann's *Killers of the Flower Moon* while finishing *Silence*, and was immediately intrigued by how the title poeticized a tragedy. 'It was an impression, like a haiku, almost,'[17] he said. He was soon transfixed by a story that refused to be pinned down to a genre. It could be any one of a Western, police procedural, film noir, big sky epic, costume drama, and twisted romance. Or all at once. Some critics wondered if it was a horror movie. Scorsese foresaw the sensual possibilities of a *Kundun*, a study in organized evil as deep-rooted as *Casino* (in a different hat, this is a return to his mob milieu), and ultimately a character piece as intense as *Taxi Driver*. At the heart of the story lay guilt as thick and black as oil.

Grann's non-fiction best seller unearthed the shocking story of how members of the Osage Nation were systematically swindled and murdered after the oil discovered on their Oklahoma reservation had made them rich in the 1920s. Local law enforcement did nothing. It would take the arrival of the Bureau

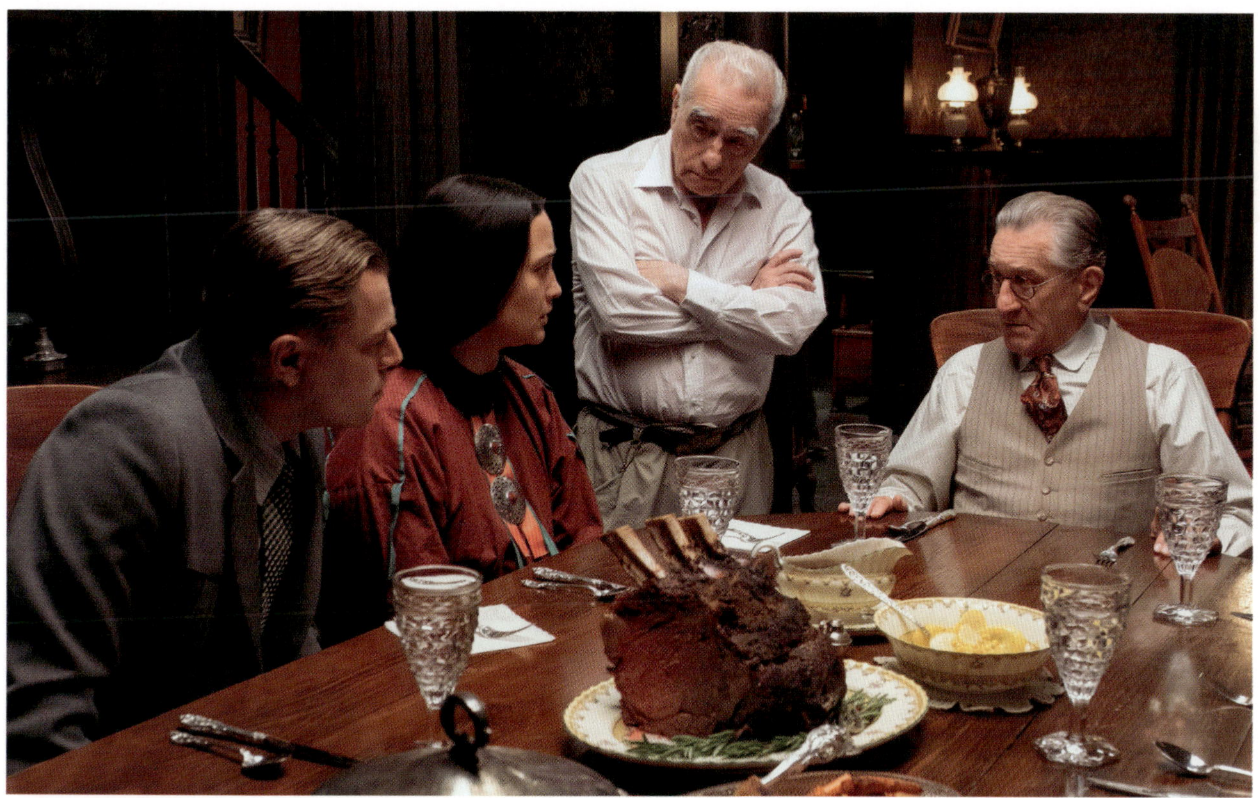

of Investigation (the incipient FBI), in stoic detective Tom White, to unravel a conspiracy that involved the entire white community of Osage County. The finger was finally pointed at cattle rancher William King Hale when his dim-witted nephew and co-conspirator Ernest Burkhart turned state's evidence. What was so insidious about Hale's scheme was that he directed his subordinates – thugs and thieves as mindlessly committed to the cause as Frank Sheeran – to ensnare Osage women in sham marriages, plotting to murder their brides in order to inherit the headrights.

Screenwriter Eric Roth's initial forays into the book produced a script that ostensibly followed White's investigation. The cast was taking fine shape with Leonardo DiCaprio playing the honourable White and De Niro as his Mephistophelean foe Hale (in a perverse way, a tribal man himself: Klan, Mason, politician). Then, deep in discussion one night, DiCaprio asked his friend and director a pertinent question.

'Where's the heart of the film?'[18]

Scorsese realized the answer lay not in the crimes but in the marriage of Ernest to Mollie Kyle, one of five Osage sisters rich in oil. Despite Ernest's hardly well-concealed embroilment in the serial murder of her siblings, they did actually love each other. Scorsese had the right book, but was making the wrong film. He loved the tangents, not the main story. Why not turn it inside out? What if DiCaprio played dull, deceitful, tormented Ernest instead?

As with *Cape Fear*, Scorsese had found his way into the story. Reworking the script, the heavy lifting of plot that had made *The Departed* so painful was confined to the third act (with an excellent Jesse Plemons as White), and, like *Cape Fear* or *Casino* or *Raging Bull*, the marriage became the story. How Ernest, like Sheeran, could have devotion and betrayal inhabiting the same soul.

'There was some decency there,' said Scorsese. 'But for whatever reasons, the weakness of character is interesting to me. And so he's weak, and he's dangerous, but there's still love there. And that's kind of disturbing but, at the same time, it's human. It's what we are.'[19]

This is what makes *Killers of the Flower Moon* so extraordinary and so Scorsesean. The personal burns at the heart of the mythical, as Richard Brody wrote in the *New Yorker*, 'transforming a tale of collective and individual crime into a vision of love that is mysterious, almost religious, and ultimately terrifying.'[20]

The new script also gave the Osage people their voice, something else that had been troubling Scorsese. 'After a certain

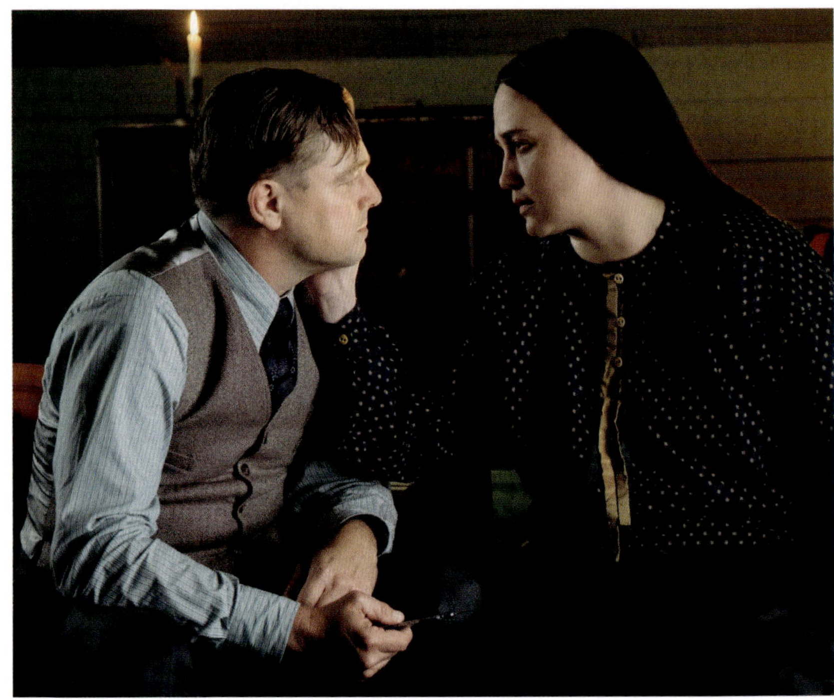

Right: *Ernest Burkhart (Leonardo DiCaprio) shares an intimate moment with his wife Mollie (Lily Gladstone). Among its many themes and potential genres,* Killers of the Flower Moon *is another of Martin Scorsese's portraits of marriage under stress.*

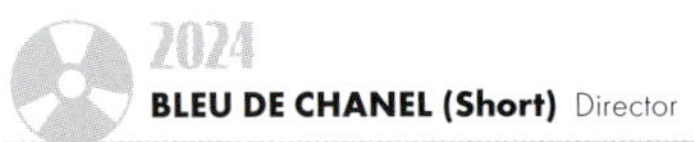

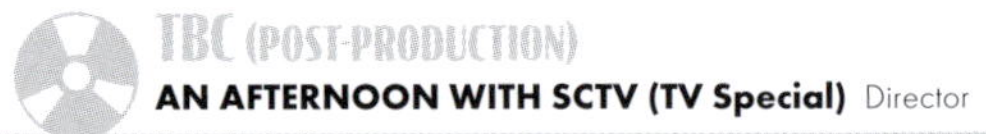

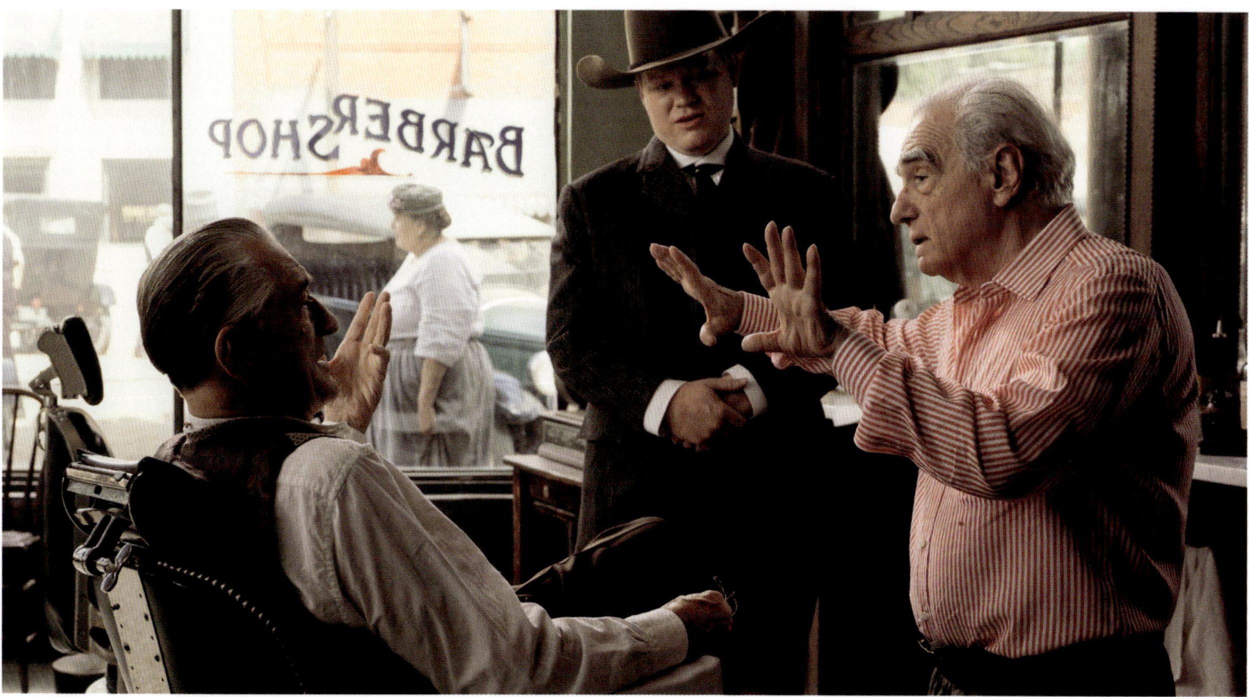

Above: *Justice in focus – Scorsese frames a shot of De Niro as corrupt rancher William Hale, being interrogated by Agent Thomas Bruce White Sr. (Jesse Plemons).*

point, I realized I was making a movie about all the white guys.'[21]

In 1974, he had spent two days with the Oglala Lakota (Sioux) tribe at the Pine Ridge Reservation in South Dakota, with the idea of a feature involving Dee Brown's 1970 classic *Bury My Heart at Wounded Knee*. The film hadn't worked out, but the experience stuck with him. This was America's original sin – the side effect of his own immigrant story. The poison of colonialism and assimilation.

The Osage world was vital to the film's authenticity. In terms of design, portrayal, language, and blessing, Scorsese sought the counsel of the principal of the Osage, Chief Geoffrey Standing Bear, with most of the Osage cast from within the local community. The director pushed for ritual scenes to be improvised as they saw fit. On the first day of shooting on 13 April 2021, elder Archie Mason began proceedings with a prayer.

Above all, Mollie was key. Lily Gladstone was recommended by casting director Ellen Lewis, after her stand-out performance in Kelly Reichardt's *Certain Women*. She was of Blackfeet and NiMíiPuu heritage rather than Osage, but following a Zoom call in which they discussed Catholic indoctrination of tribal youth, Scorsese was left in no doubt. Working her way toward an Oscar nomination, and overcoming her nerves, Gladstone took absolute ownership of Mollie, knowing what she represented. 'You're humanizing these characters more, and in doing that, the history hits you harder.'[22]

Scorsese is not concerned with echoing modern-day headlines of toxic masculinity (though that takes on a literal meaning when Ernest starts poisoning her insulin injections; the Osage were prone to diabetes), so much as the riddle of human relationships.

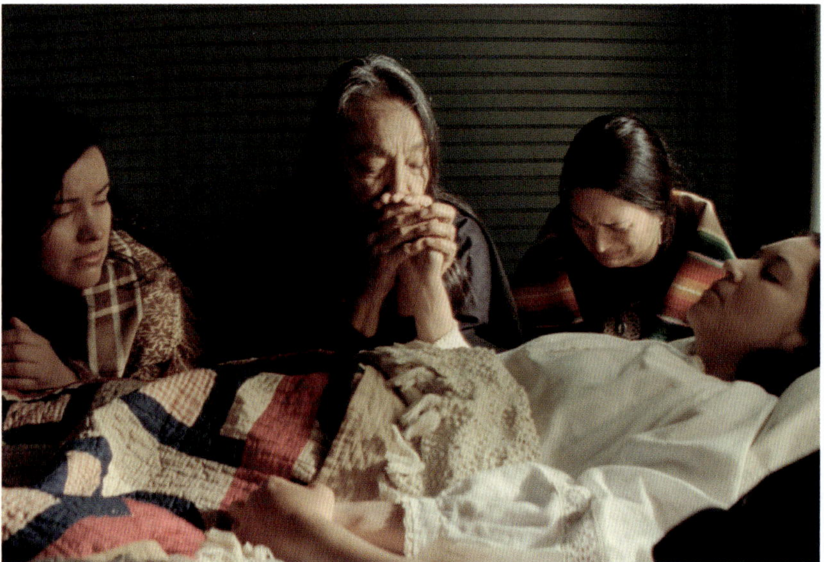

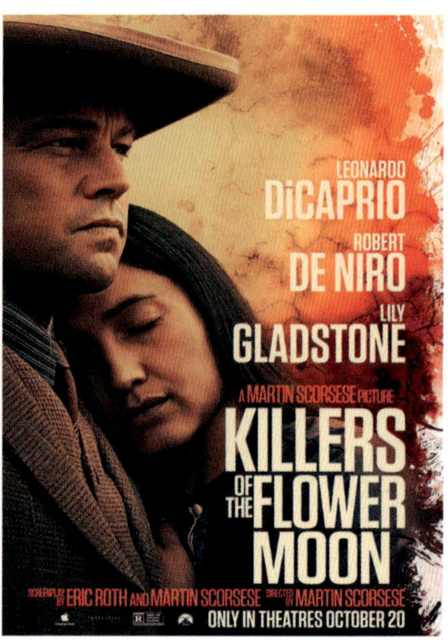

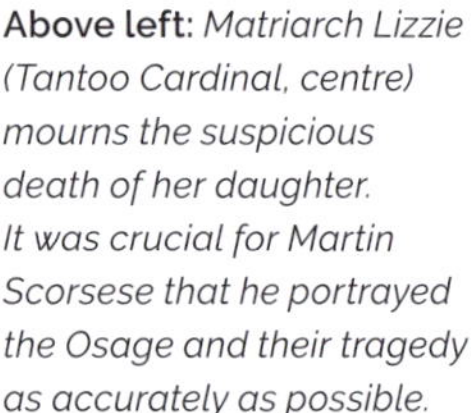

Above left: *Matriarch Lizzie (Tantoo Cardinal, centre) mourns the suspicious death of her daughter. It was crucial for Martin Scorsese that he portrayed the Osage and their tragedy as accurately as possible.*

Above right: Killers of the Flower Moon *benefitted from a significant run in American cinemas before streaming on Apple. In 2023, the cash-rich streamers are more likely to back a Scorsese project than a studio.*

'Don't forget this, that Ernest and Mollie were in love,' he reiterated. 'Why the hell did she stay? Not *why* did she stay with him? *How* did she stay with him? Why one person stays with another, we don't know.'[23]

DiCaprio embraces an unflattering physical transformation that no CGI could augment. Beneath greasy, centre-parted hair, he juts out his chin and knits his brow, a dullard wrestling with a guilt he cannot rationalize.

Scorsese is driven to tell the truth about people who lie to themselves: Travis Bickle, Jake La Motta, Rupert Pupkin, Henry Hill, Teddy Daniels, Frank Sheeran, and now Ernest Burkhart. And here were his two great leading men who have played many of those parts, De Niro and DiCaprio, symbolically united for the first time in one of his feature films (they had previously shared the screen in Scorsese's 2015 short *The Audition*).

There were those who remained unsure of the wisdom of putting such a shockingly average intellect centre stage. Paul Schrader for one thought the film would have benefitted from DiCaprio playing White as originally planned. Of course, it was a good movie, he said, but the investigation was what mattered, this parable about the birth of modern justice. 'Spending three-and-a-half hours in the company of an idiot is a long time.'[24]

The inversion also lost them a studio. Once the thriller dynamic retreated into the background, Paramount again got cold feet and it was cash-rich streamer Apple who agreed to the staggering $214 million it would still take to fulfil Scorsese's vision.

It was so freeing, to be 1400 miles from New York within a self-contained world, a flat, green expanse rolling to the horizon. All they needed to do was build their sets and place their cameras (though CGI was used for the forest of derricks), moving between fifty locations over six months of production. They had the town of Pawhuska virtually to themselves like their own studio. 'We had the control,' he said. 'And that, in a funny way, made it feel like we were making a smaller picture.'[25]

TBC (PRE-PRODUCTION)
THE WAGER: A TALE OF SHIPWRECK, MUTINY, AND MURDER Director / Producer

What makes this such a mesmerizing film, shifting through its moods, daring longer and longer scenes, is a refusal to conform to what is expected of it. A thriller about marriage, it is also a Western in denial. As far as Scorsese was concerned the genre concluded with Sam Peckinpah's blood-strewn elegy *The Wild Bunch*. We are in the 1920s, automobiles bump along patchy roads, oil spews from the ground, and Ernest has returned from a World War on another continent (a veteran like Travis Bickle). Nonetheless, Oklahoma resists the overtures of the future. This is a land still governed by Frontier codes where guns mete out justice. The idea of Manifest Destiny is what pollutes Hale's mind – that God had given the white man this land.

Killers of the Flower Moon is almost a linear piece of storytelling, moving along Time's arrow with only grace notes of voice-over, such as Ernest reading aloud a children's history of the Osage. Stylistically the film verges on the classical – the big sky treatment of *East of Eden* and *Giant* that filled Scorsese's head with America as a child. Naturally, there were specific quotations: Gary Cooper silent *The Winning of Barbara Worth* for the goggles De Niro wears at the wheel of his Model T; Robert Mitchum thriller *Blood on the Moon* for the brooding way the men walk; a ceiling-high view of De Niro getting a shave as his Capone did in *The Untouchables*. The late Robbie Robertson's spellbinding score, mixing tribal drums with electric guitars, is a satisfyingly Scorsesean anachronism.

He was coming full circle once more, as he found himself copying his own protégés, responding to the feedback loop of cinema. He had adored Ari Aster's approach to horror in *Midsommar*: 'Just going a little slower. A little quieter… One has to take these chances. At this age, what else can I do?'[26]

Below: *Burning ambition – part epic, part Western, part crime story,* Killers of the Flower Moon *was the largest production of Scorsese's career.*

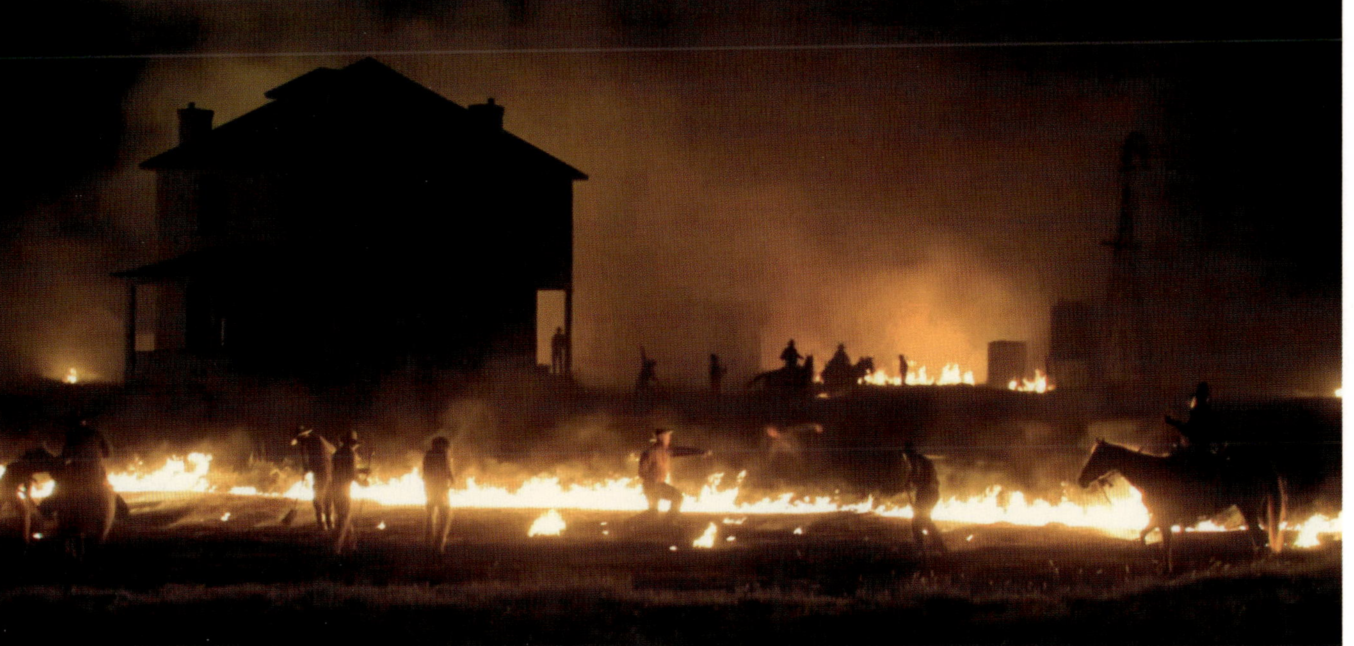

TBC (PRE-PRODUCTION)
UNTITLED MARTIN SCORSESE HAWAIIAN EVENT Director / Producer

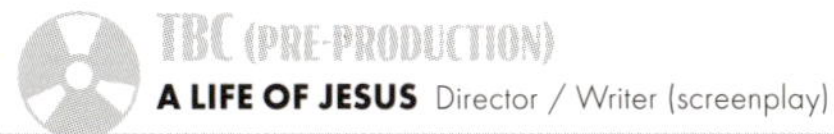

TBC (PRE-PRODUCTION)
A LIFE OF JESUS Director / Writer (screenplay)

The great director's legacy reaches through generations. We see it in the cultural touchstones of Spike Lee; the narrative impulses of Quentin Tarantino; the double helix of life and artifice in Wes Anderson. He is revered as a patron saint of cinema by Paul Thomas Anderson, Damien Chazelle, Aster, the Safdie brothers. Scorsese's shifts of tone, tracking shots, the crackle of montages, voice-overs, and unrepentant close-ups: these are now part of the cinematic language.

Killers of the Flower Moon, his journey into this heart of American darkness, ends on two, contrasting visions. Both are versions of a cultural ritual. First, we get a quirky re-enactment of events being broadcast as a mid-century radio play, sponsored by the FBI and Lucky Strike cigarettes. Was this the hidden storyteller all along, or just Scorsese's sly joke about the proliferation of true-crime podcasts? We learn that both Ernest and Hale were freed before concluding their sentences. Then Scorsese himself steps up to the antique mic and solemnly reveals, to camera, what became of Mollie, who remarried but died of diabetes in 1937. Any greater justice for the Osage was swept away by the force of white man's history.

'There's an iconography to it, and it's Marty recognizing that we're telling a story, and this is our burden of the story,' recalled Eric Roth. 'I almost started crying because I was just so moved by it. I thought Marty was wonderful.'[27]

The final shot is a stunning aerial image of the formations of a contemporary Osage powwow, taking shape as an eye or a flower. Like the essence of Buddhism preserved by the Dalai Lama of *Kundun*; like the power of art amid the commodification of Hollywood, something endures.

And Scorsese endures.

> I thought a few years ago I could stop, but I don't think so anymore.
>
> MARTIN SCORSESE

Below: *Honouring the dead – Lily Gladstone and Martin Scorsese share a reflective moment on the set of* Killers of the Flower Moon.

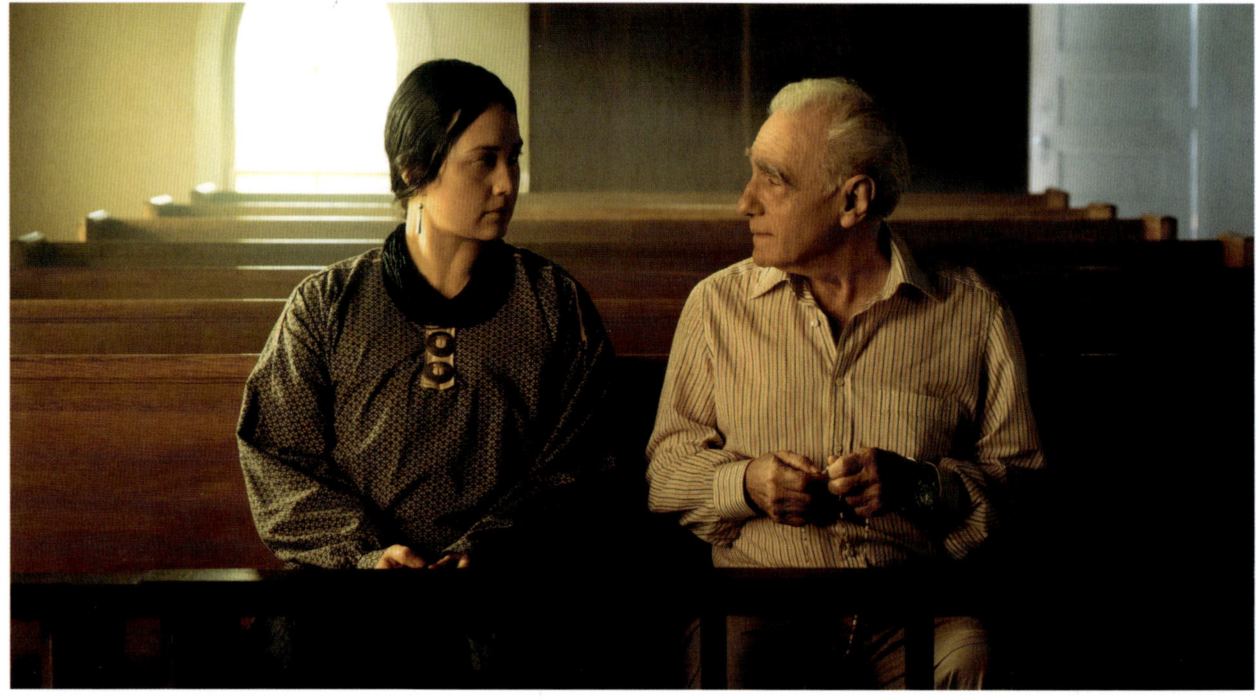

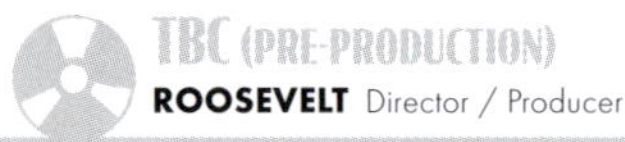

TBC (PRE-PRODUCTION)
ROOSEVELT Director / Producer

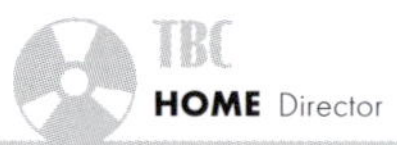

TBC
HOME Director

Aged 82, as this book is finished, there is fast talk of new projects; that itch to be back behind the camera remains as irresistible as any drug. He is toying with a film about Sinatra with DiCaprio, a Roosevelt picture, a new biography of Christ in *The Life of Jesus* (in which he might act), or an adaptation of Marilynne Robinson's homily on Midwestern life *Home*.

'I thought a few years ago I could stop, but I don't think so anymore,' he reflected, before that laugh broke free. 'Look, what do you want me to do – be 100 years old and making Roosevelt? You're going to have me coming in, giving me oxygen while I shoot!'[28]

Then film is oxygen for little Marty, our greatest living director. His has been a quest to get life onto celluloid, all of it, from the spiritual to the venal, the comforting and the violent. The world refracted through the lens of a camera. Something that might speak to the soul.

Life *is* film. Film *is* life.

From his lofty perch in New York, the unlikely doyen, this patron saint, venerable but uncompromising, looks warily about him at an industry and art-form that has lost its way. All these franchises and superheroes, not bad in themselves, but that's not film, not in the way he understands it. That isn't the cinema of human beings trying to convey emotional experiences for other human beings sat alone in the dark (even in company, as Scorsese was with his father, you are always alone with those images).

If there is an abiding image in his films, it is a figure (hero or villain, or the multitudes between) sat in the stalls watching a picture. He can't resist it – that tease. From *Mean Streets* and *Taxi Driver* to *The Aviator* and *Hugo* (of course), to *Kundun*, *The Departed*, and *Killers of the Flower Moon*, their eyes are absorbed by the screen, the light from the projector dancing above their head.

Scorsese has become one of those mysterious figures his younger self would venerate. The great artists. But he remains humble. 'You may have affected certain people's lives – maybe. You may have made people think differently. And that's what you were meant to do.'[29]

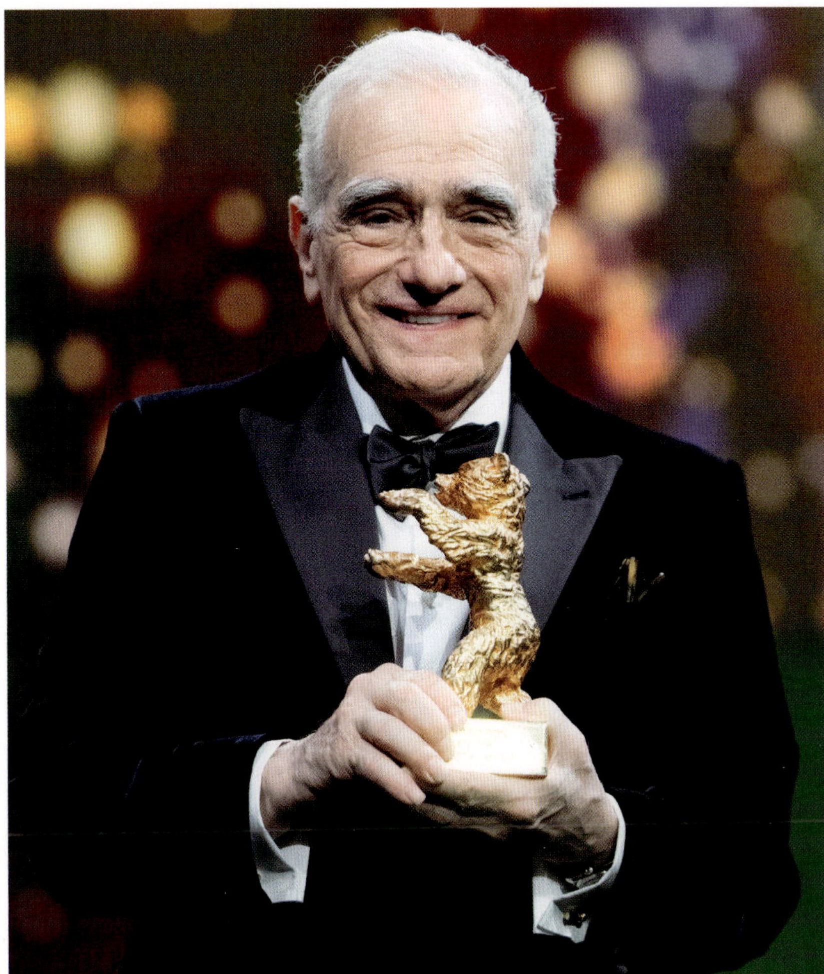

Above: *Scorsese proudly holds an Honorary Golden Bear, presented at the Berlin International Film Festival in February 2024. But he's not done yet.*

SOURCES

BIBLIOGRAPHY

Bach, Steven, *Final Cut: Dreams and Disaster in the Making of Heaven's Gate*, Faber & Faber, 1986

Biskind, Peter, *Easy Riders, Raging Bulls*, Simon & Schuster, 1998

Brunette, Peter (editor), *Martin Scorsese Interviews*, University Press of Mississippi, 1999

Christie, Ian and Thompson, David (editors), *Scorsese On Scorsese*, Faber & Faber, 1990

Ebert, Roger, *Scorsese by Ebert*, The University of Chicago Press, 2008

Jackson, Kevin (editor), *Schrader On Schrader* (Revised Edition), Faber & Faber, 2004

Kael, Pauline, *Taking it All In*, Henry Holt & Co., 1984

Kelly, Mary Pat, *Martin Scorsese – A Journey*, Martin Secker & Warburg, 1992

Kenny, Glenn, *Made Men: The Story of Goodfellas*, Hanover Square Press, 2020

Romney, Jonathan, *Short Orders: Film Writing*, Serpent's Tail, 1997

Sangster, Jim, *Scorsese*, Virgin Books Ltd, 2002

Schickel, Richard, *Conversations with Scorsese*, Alfred A. Knopf, 2011

Schrader, Paul, *Taxi Driver (Screenplay)*, Faber & Faber, 1990

Schwartz, Sanford, *The Age of Movies: Selected Writings of Pauline Kael*, Library of America, 2011

Shone, Tom, *Martin Scorsese: A Retrospective*, Thames & Hudson, 2022

Taubin, Amy, *Taxi Driver – BFI Modern Classics (2nd Edition)*, British Film Institute/Palgrave Macmillan, 2012

Thomson, David, *Have You Seen...? a Personal Introduction to 1000 Films*, Penguin, 2008

Thomson, David, *The New Biographical Dictionary of Film*, Little Brown, 2002

Woods, Paul A. (editor), Scorsese – *A Journey Through the American Psyche*, Plexus, 2005

DOCUMENTARIES

30 Years of The Film Foundation: Martin Scorsese and Ari Aster in Conversation, Criterion, 2020

The Aviator – Q&A interview with Cate Blanchett, Charlie Rose via YouTube, December 2004

After Hours – Documentary about the making of the film, featuring Dunne, Robinson, Schoonmaker, and Scorsese, Criterion, 2023

From the Classroom to the Streets: The Making of Who's That Knocking At My Door, Warner Bros. Home Video, 2003

The Hollywood Masters: Willem Dafoe on The Last Temptation of Christ, LMU School of Film and Television via YouTube, 27 February 2018

Leonardo DiCaprio interview, Charlie Rose via YouTube, December 2004

A Life Without Limits: The Making of The Aviator, Miramax, 2005

Making Taxi Driver, Sony Pictures Home Entertainment, 1999

Making The Irishman, Criterion, 2020

Martin Scorsese interview on Casino, Charlie Rose via YouTube, 1995

Gangs of New York, interview with Martin Scorsese and Daniel Day-Lewis, Charlie Rose via YouTube, December 2002

Martin Scorsese on The Last Temptation of Christ, Cinematographos via YouTube, uploaded 2014

No Direction Home: Bob Dylan, Paramount Home Entertainment, 2005

A new conversation between director Martin Scorsese and film critic Farran Smith Nehme, Scorsese Shorts, Criterion, 2020

The New York, New York Stories, Twentieth Century Fox Home Entertainment, 2008

A Personal Journey With Martin Scorsese Through American Movies, BFI, 1995

Public Speaking, HBO Documentary Films, 2010

The Irishman: roundtable conversation featuring Scorsese and actors Robert De Niro, Al Pacino and Joe Pesci (originally recorded 2019), Criterion, 2020

A Shot at the Top: The Making of The King of Comedy, Twentieth Century Fox Home Entertainment, 2014

Tribeca Film Festival: A Conversation with Martin Scorsese, Robert De Niro and Jerry Lewis, Twentieth Century Fox Home Entertainment, 2014

INTRODUCTION

1. Scorsese, Martin, *The Persisting Vision: Reading the Language of Cinema, New York Review*, 15 August 2013
2. Schickel, Richard, *Conversations with Scorsese*, Alfred A. Knopf, 2011
3. Christie, Ian and Thompson, David (editors), *Scorsese On Scorsese*, Faber & Faber, 1990

LITTLE ITALY

1. Behar, Henri, *Bringing It All Back Home..., Empire*, November 1990
2. Ibid
3. *Italianamerican*, Scorsese Shorts, Criterion, 2020
4. *A new conversation between director Martin Scorsese and film critic Farran Smith Nehme, Scorsese Shorts*, Criterion, 2020
5. Schickel, Richard, *Conversations with Scorsese*, Alfred A. Knopf, 2011
6. Ibid
7. *A new conversation between director Martin Scorsese and film critic Farran Smith Nehme, Scorsese Shorts*, Criterion, 2020
8. Baron, Zach, *Martin Scorsese: 'I have to find out who the hell I am', GQ*, 25 September 2023
9. Christie, Ian and Thompson, David (editors), *Scorsese On Scorsese*, Faber & Faber, 1990
10. Ibid
11. *A new conversation between director Martin Scorsese and film critic Farran Smith Nehme, Scorsese Shorts*, Criterion, 2020
12. Christie, Ian and Thompson (editors), David, *Scorsese On Scorsese*, Faber & Faber, 1990
13. Ibid
14. *A new conversation between director Martin Scorsese and film critic Farran Smith Nehme, Scorsese Shorts*, Criterion, 2020
15. Baron, Zach, *Martin Scorsese: 'I have to find out who the hell I am', GQ*, 25 September 2023
16. Ibid
17. Christie, Ian and Thompson, David (editors), *Scorsese On Scorsese*, Faber & Faber, 1990
18. *A new conversation between director Martin Scorsese and film critic Farran Smith Nehme, Scorsese Shorts*, Criterion, 2020
19. Christie, Ian and Thompson, David (editors), *Scorsese On Scorsese*, Faber & Faber, 1990
20. Ebiri, Bilge, *A Singular Voice, in Short, Scorsese Shorts* (booklet), Criterion, 2020
21. Ibid
22. Schickel, Richard, *Conversations with Scorsese*, Alfred A. Knopf, 201
23. Ibid

REEL LIFE

1. Schickel, Richard, *Conversations with Scorsese*, Alfred A. Knopf, 2011
2. Ibid
3. Ibid
4. Ebert, Roger, *Scorsese by Ebert*, The University of Chicago Press, 2008
5. Sragow, Michael, *Who's That Knocking At My Door Review, New Yorker*, 12 January 2017
6. *From the Classroom to the Streets: The Making of Who's That Knocking At My Door*, Warner Bros. Home Video, 2003
7. Kelly, Mary Pat, *Martin Scorsese – A Journey*, Martin Secker & Warburg, 1992
8. Marlow, Jonathan, *Thelma Schoonmaker: A Personal Journey With Scorsese and Powell, Green Cine*, 6 October 2006
9. Ibid
10. *Who's That Knocking At My Door*, BFI, 2017
11. Kelly, Mary Pat, *Martin Scorsese – A Journey*, Martin Secker & Warburg, 1992
12. Schickel, Richard, *Conversations with Scorsese*, Alfred A. Knopf, 2011
13. Ibid
14. Ibid
15. Ibid
16. Biskind, Peter, *Easy Riders, Raging Bulls*, Simon & Schuster, 1998

17. Nashawaty, Chris, *Crab Monsters, Teenage Cavemen, and Candy Stripe Nurses – Roger Corman: King of the B Movie,* Abrams, 2013
18. Ibid
19. Schickel, Richard, *Conversations with Scorsese,* Alfred A. Knopf, 2011
20. Phipps, Keith, *Martin Scorsese's Forgotten Gangster Movie, The Ringer,* 30 October 2019
21. Lochte, Dick, *Boxcar Bertha Review, Los Angeles Free Press,* 7 January 2020
22. Christie, Ian and Thompson, David (editors), *Scorsese On Scorsese,* Faber & Faber, 1990
23. Ibid
24. Ibid
25. Ibid
26. Bramesco, Charles, *'To me, Manhattan is the universe': Scorsese and De Niro reunite on stage, Guardian,* 18 June 2024
27. Bradshaw, Peter, *Mean Streets Review, Guardian,* 12 October 2023
28. Ibid
29. Chandler, Raymond, *The Simple Art of Murder,* Vintage Books, 1988
30. Christie, Ian and Thompson, David (editors), *Scorsese On Scorsese,* Faber & Faber, 1990
31. Ibid
32. Scorsese, Martin, *Extract from Martin Scorsese Seminar,* The American Film Institute's Center for Advanced Film Studies, 12 February 1975
33. Christie, Ian and Thompson, David (editors), *Scorsese On Scorsese,* Faber & Faber, 1990
34. Ibid
35. Lanier, Hunter, *Mean Streets Review, Film Threat,* 6 May 2021
36. Kael, Pauline, *Everyday Inferno, New Yorker,* 8 October 1973
37. Biskind, Peter, *Easy Riders, Raging Bulls,* Simon & Schuster, 1998
38. Ibid
39. Ibid
40. Schickel, Richard, *Conversations with Scorsese,* Alfred A. Knopf, 2011
41. Kelly, Mary Pat, *Martin Scorsese – A Journey,* Martin Secker & Warburg, 1992
42. Ibid
43. Ibid

GOD'S LONELY MAN

1. Trimarchi, Ivan, *Working Life as a Metaphor in Director-Screenwriter Paul Schrader's Controversial Cinema, Living Life Fearless,* 2023
2. *Making Taxi Driver,* Sony Pictures Home Entertainment, 1999
3. Schrader, Paul, *Taxi Driver,* Faber & Faber, 1990
4. Taubin, Amy, *Taxi Driver – BFI Modern Classics (2nd Edition),* British Film Institute/Palgrave Macmillan, 2012
5. Schrader, Paul, *Taxi Driver,* Faber & Faber, 1990
6. Ebert, Roger, *Scorsese by Ebert,* The University of Chicago Press, 2008
7. Thomson, David, *Have You Seen...? a Personal Introduction to 1000 Films,* Penguin, 2008
8. *Making Taxi Driver,* Sony Pictures Home Entertainment, 1999
9. Ibid
10. Taubin, Amy, *Taxi Driver – BFI Modern Classics (2nd Edition),* British Film Institute/Palgrave Macmillan, 2012
11. Zuckerman, Esther, *Living With the Men of Paul Schrader's 'Man in a Room' Trilogy, New York Times,* 21 May 2023
12. Lopate, Phillip (editor), *American Movie Critics: An Anthology From the Silents Until Now,* Library of America, 2006
13. Biskind, Peter, *Easy Riders, Raging Bulls,* Simon & Schuster, 1998
14. Bose, Swapnil Dhruv, *How Paul Schrader inspired himself to write Taxi Driver, Far Out,* 24 August 2021
15. Ibid
16. Wolfe, Thomas, *Thomas Wolfe: Complete Works: Look Homeward, Angel, Of Time and the River, The Web and the Rock, You Can't Go Home Again...,* Bauer Books, 2024
17. Taubin, Amy, *Taxi Driver – BFI Modern Classics (2nd Edition),* British Film Institute/Palgrave Macmillan, 2012
18. Christie, Ian and Thompson, David (editors), *Scorsese On Scorsese,* Faber & Faber, 1990
19. Schrader, Paul, *Taxi Driver,* Faber & Faber, 1990
20. Schwartz, Sanford, *The Age of Movies: Selected Writings of Pauline Kael,* Library of America, 2011
21. Taubin, Amy, *Taxi Driver – BFI Modern Classics (2nd Edition),* British Film Institute/Palgrave Macmillan, 2012
22. de Semlyen, Nick, *Martin Scorsese Interview, Empire,* 7 October 2019
23. Schrader, Paul, *Taxi Driver,* Faber & Faber, 1990
24. Christie, Ian and Thompson, David (editors), *Scorsese On Scorsese,* Faber & Faber, 1990
25. Ibid
26. *Making Taxi Driver,* Sony Pictures Home Entertainment, 1999
27. Taubin, Amy, *Taxi Driver – BFI Modern Classics (2nd Edition),* British Film Institute/Palgrave Macmillan, 2012
28. Ebert, Roger, *Scorsese by Ebert,* The University of Chicago Press, 2008
29. Ibid
30. Christie, Ian and Thompson, David (editors), *Scorsese On Scorsese,* Faber & Faber, 1990
31. Ebert, Roger, *Scorsese by Ebert,* The University of Chicago Press, 2008
32. Biskind, Peter, *Easy Riders, Raging Bulls,* Simon & Schuster, 1998
33. Ibid
34. *Making Taxi Driver,* Sony Pictures Home Entertainment, 1999
35. Taubin, Amy, *Taxi Driver – BFI Modern Classics (2nd Edition),* British Film Institute/Palgrave Macmillan, 2012
36. Schrader, Paul, *Taxi Driver,* Faber & Faber, 1990
37. Ebert, Roger, *Scorsese by Ebert,* The University of Chicago Press, 2008
38. Taubin, Amy, *Taxi Driver – BFI Modern Classics (2nd Edition),* British Film Institute/Palgrave Macmillan, 2012
39. Ibid
40. Ibid

SAVED BY CINEMA

1. *A new conversation between director Martin Scorsese and film critic Farran Smith Nehme, Scorsese Shorts,* Criterion, 2020
2. Schickel, Richard, *Conversations with Scorsese,* Alfred A. Knopf, 2011
3. Laskin, Nicholas, *Watch: Study Cinema History With Full Doc 'A Personal Journey With Martin Scorsese Through American Movies', IndieWire,* 17 December 2014
4. *A Personal Journey With Martin Scorsese Through American Movies,* BFI, 1995
5. Ibid
6. Ibid
7. *30 Years of The Film Foundation: Martin Scorsese and Ari Aster in Conversation,* Criterion, 2020

THE DARK ARTS

1. Kaplan, Jonathan, *Taxi Dancer: Martin Scorsese Interviewed, Film Comment,* July/August 1977
2. *The New York, New York Stories,* Twentieth Century Fox Home Entertainment, 2008
3. Schickel, Richard, *Conversations with Scorsese,* Alfred A. Knopf, 2011
4. Kelly, Mary Pat, *Martin Scorsese – A Journey,* Martin Secker & Warburg, 1992
5. Bowen, Chuck, *Review: New York, New York Movingly Wrestles with the Musical's Legacy, Slant,* 28 January 2020
6. Canby, Vincent, *Film: New York In a Tuneful Era, New York Times,* 23 June 1977
7. Kelly, Mary Pat, *Martin Scorsese – A Journey,* Martin Secker & Warburg, 1992
8. Ibid
9. Biskind, Peter, *Easy Riders, Raging Bulls,* Simon & Schuster, 1998
10. Kelly, Mary Pat, *Martin Scorsese – A Journey,* Martin Secker & Warburg, 1992
11. Biskind, Peter, *Easy Riders, Raging Bulls,* Simon & Schuster, 1998
12. Ibid
13. Boorman, John (editor), *Director's Cut: Best of Projections,* Faber & Faber, 2006
14. Christie, Ian and Thompson, David (editors), *Scorsese On Scorsese,* Faber & Faber, 1990
15. Ibid
16. Bach, Steven, *Final Cut: Dreams and Disaster in the Making of Heaven's Gate,* Faber & Faber, 1986
17. Ibid
18. *Raging Bull,* Criterion Edition, 2022
19. Henry, Michael, *Raging Bull, Positif,* 11–12 February 1981
20. Christie, Ian and Thompson, David (editors), *Scorsese On Scorsese,* Faber & Faber, 1990
21. Ibid
22. Ibid
23. Kelly, Mary Pat, *Martin Scorsese – A Journey,* Martin Secker & Warburg, 1992
24. Ibid
25. Ibid
26. Bach, Steven, *Final Cut: Dreams and Disaster in the Making of Heaven's Gate,* Faber & Faber, 1986

27. Kael, Pauline, *Religious Pulp, or the Incredible Hulk, New Yorker,* December 1980
28. Biskind, Peter, *Slouching Toward Hollywood, Premiere,* November 1991
29. Kelly, Mary Pat, *Martin Scorsese – A Journey,* Martin Secker & Warburg, 1992
30. *A Shot at the Top: The Making of The King of Comedy,* Twentieth Century Fox Home Entertainment, 2014
31. *Tribeca Film Festival: A Conversation with Martin Scorsese, Robert De Niro and Jerry Lewis,* Twentieth Century Fox Home Entertainment, 2014
32. *A Shot at the Top: The Making of The King of Comedy,* Twentieth Century Fox Home Entertainment, 2014
33. Ibid
34. *The King of Comedy,* Twentieth Century Fox Home Entertainment, 2014
35. Kael, Pauline, *Taking it All In,* Henry Holt & Co., 1984
36. Butt, Thomas, *Rupert Pupkin of The King of Comedy is Scorsese's Most Deranged Protagonist, Collider,* 18 February 2023

TEMPTATIONS

1. *New Conversation Between Director Martin Scorsese and Fran Lebowitz, After Hours,* Criterion, 2023
2. Lattanzio, Ryan, *Martin Scorsese's After Hours Paved the Anxious, Paranoid Road for the Safdies and Beau Is Afraid, IndieWire,* 15 August 2023
3. Ibid
4. Morris, Brogan, *'Everything was ass-backwards': Griffin Dunne on shooting After Hours with Martin Scorsese, BFI,* 20 March 2024
5. Christie, Ian and Thompson, David (editors), *Scorsese On Scorsese,* Faber & Faber, 1990
6. Ibid
7. Woods, Paul A. (editor), *Scorsese – A Journey Through the American Psyche,* Plexus, 2005
8. Ibid
9. Peachment, Chris, *Night of the Living Dead, Time Out,* 28 May–3 June 1986
10. O'Malley, Sheila, *No Exit, After Hours* (booklet), Criterion, 2023
11. *New Conversation Between Director Martin Scorsese and Fran Lebowitz, After Hours,* Criterion, 2023
12. *After Hours – Documentary about the making of the film, featuring Dunne, Robinson, Schoonmaker, and Scorsese,* Criterion, 2023
13. Ebert, Roger, *Scorsese by Ebert,* The University of Chicago Press, 2008
14. *After Hours,* Criterion, 2023
15. Schickel, Richard, *Conversations with Scorsese,* Alfred A. Knopf, 2011
16. Dunne, Griffin, *The Friday Afternoon Club: A Family Memoir,* Grove Press UK, 2024
17. *New Conversation Between Director Martin Scorsese and Fran Lebowitz, After Hours,* Criterion, 2023
18. Biskind, Peter and Linfield, Susan, *Chalk Talk,* American Film, November 1986
19. Christie, Ian and Thompson, David (editors), *Scorsese On Scorsese,* Faber & Faber, 1990
20. Ibid
21. Ebert, Roger, *Scorsese by Ebert,* The University of Chicago Press, 2008
22. Floyd, Nigel, *Altar Egos, Time Out,* 14–21 September 1988
23. Ibid
24. *Martin Scorsese on The Last Temptation of Christ, Cinematographos* via YouTube, uploaded 2014
25. *The Last Temptation of Christ,* Criterion, 2019
26. Shone, Tom, *Martin Scorsese: A Retrospective,* Thames & Hudson, 2022
27. Corliss, Richard, *... And Blood, Film Comment,* September/October 1988
28. Ibid
29. Schickel, Richard, *Conversations with Scorsese,* Alfred A. Knopf, 2011
30. *The Hollywood Masters: Willem Dafoe on The Last Temptation of Christ,* LMU School of Film and Television via YouTube, 27 February 2018
31. Ibid
32. Mantel, Hilary, *The Last Temptation of Christ Review, The Spectator,* 24 September 1988
33. Schickel, Richard, *Conversations with Scorsese,* Alfred A. Knopf, 2011
34. Benson, Shelia, *Intense, Utterly Sincere, Frequently Fascinating Work, Los Angeles Times,* 12 August 1988
35. Sragow, Michael, *The Last Temptation of Christ Review, San Francisco Examiner,* 12 August 1988
36. Shone, Tom, *Martin Scorsese: A Retrospective,* Thames & Hudson, 2022
37. Christie, Ian and Thompson, David (editors), *Scorsese On Scorsese,* Faber & Faber, 1990

WISEGUYS

1. Denby, David, *Meaner Streets, New York Magazine,* 24 September 1990
2. Flint, Hanna, *Goodfellas at 30: The making of one of film's greatest shots, BBC,* 21 September 2020
3. Ibid
4. Ibid
5. Ebert, Roger, *Scorsese by Ebert,* The University of Chicago Press, 2008
6. *Goodfellas: Screenplay,* Faber & Faber, 2000
7. Christie, Ian and Thompson, David (editors), *Scorsese On Scorsese,* Faber & Faber, 1990
8. Ibid
9. Denby, David, *Meaner Streets, New York Magazine,* 24 September 1990
10. Ebert, Roger, *Scorsese by Ebert,* The University of Chicago Press, 2008
11. Schickel, Richard, *Conversations with Scorsese,* Alfred A. Knopf, 2011
12. Willens, Michele, *Pileggi, the Fella Behind 'Goodfellas', Los Angeles Times,* 22 March 1991
13. Ibid
14. Christie, Ian and Thompson, David (editors), *Scorsese On Scorsese,* Faber & Faber, 1990
15. Smith, Gavin, *Martin Scorsese Interviewed, Film Comment,* September 1990
16. *Goodfellas: Screenplay,* Faber & Faber, 2000
17. Christie, Ian and Thompson, David (editors), *Scorsese On Scorsese,* Faber & Faber, 1990
18. Smith, Gavin, *Martin Scorsese Interviewed, Film Comment,* September 1990
19. Kenny, Glenn, *Made Men: The Story of Goodfellas,* Hanover Square Press, 2020
20. Ebert, Roger, *Scorsese by Ebert,* The University of Chicago Press, 2008
21. Unattributed, *Martin Scorsese's Goodfellas: A Complete Oral History,* GQ, 20 September 2010
22. Ibid
23. Ibid
24. 63rd Academy Awards Ceremony 1991, Oscars.org
25. *Goodfellas: Screenplay,* Faber & Faber, 2000
26. Ibid
27. Unattributed, *Martin Scorsese's Goodfellas: A Complete Oral History, GQ,* 20 September 2010
28. *Goodfellas: Screenplay,* Faber & Faber, 2000
29. Unattributed, *Martin Scorsese's Goodfellas: A Complete Oral History, GQ,* 20 September 2010
30. Smith, Gavin, *Martin Scorsese Interviewed, Film Comment,* September 1990
31. Christie, Ian and Thompson, David (editors), *Scorsese On Scorsese,* Faber & Faber, 1990
32. DeCurtis, Anthony, *What the Streets Mean, South Atlantic Quarterly,* Spring 1992
33. Unattributed, *Martin Scorsese's Goodfellas: A Complete Oral History, GQ,* 20 September 2010
34. *Goodfellas: Screenplay,* Faber & Faber, 2000
35. Smith, Gavin, *Martin Scorsese Interviewed, Film Comment,* September 1990
36. Ibid
37. Walker, Alexander, *Reared by the Mob, Evening Standard,* 25 October 1990
38. de Semlyen, Nick, *Martin Scorsese Interview, Empire,* 7 October 2019
39. Unattributed, *Martin Scorsese's Goodfellas: A Complete Oral History, GQ,* 20 September 2010
40. Ibid
41. Murphy, Kathleen, *Goodfellas Review, Film Comment,* October 1990
42. Biskind, Peter, *Slouching Toward Hollywood, Premiere,* November 1991

ACTING UP

1. Schickel, Richard, *Conversations with Scorsese,* Alfred A. Knopf, 2011
2. Christie, Ian and Thompson, David (editors), *Scorsese On Scorsese,* Faber & Faber, 1990
3. Vivarelli, Nick, *Martin Scorsese to Play Dante Alighieri's Mentor in Julian Schnabel's Upcoming In the Hand of Dante, Hollywood Reporter,* 20 February 2024

THE PARADOX

1. Christie, Ian, *Martin Scorsese's Testament, Sight and Sound,* January 1996
2. Biskind, Peter, *Slouching Toward Hollywood, Premiere,* November 1991
3. Ibid
4. Fitzgerald, F. Scott, *The Stories of F. Scott Fitzgerald, Vol. 2: The Crack-up, with Other Pieces And Stories,* Penguin Modern Classics, 1986
5. Biskind, Peter, *Slouching Toward Hollywood, Premiere,* November 1991
6. Ibid
7. Ansen, David, *The Horror, The Horror, Newsweek,* 24 November, 1991
8. Ebert, Roger, *Scorsese by Ebert,* The University of Chicago Press, 2008
9. Biskind, Peter, *Slouching Toward Hollywood, Premiere,* November 1991
10. Schickel, Richard, *Conversations with Scorsese,* Alfred A. Knopf, 2011
11. Ibid

12. Freer, Ian, *Doctor Martin, Empire,* May 1998
13. Christie, Ian and Thompson, David (editors), *Scorsese On Scorsese,* Faber & Faber, 1990
14. Cocks, Jay and Scorsese, Martin, *The Age of Innocence: The Shooting Script,* Newmarket Press, 1996
15. Canby, Vincent, *The Age of Innocence; Grand Passions and Good Manners, New York Times,* 17 September 1993
16. Cocks, Jay and Scorsese, Martin, *The Age of Innocence: The Shooting Script,* Newmarket Press, 1996
17. Lane, Anthony, *The Age of Innocence, New Yorker,* 31 July 1993
18. *Martin Scorsese interview on Casino, Charlie Rose* via YouTube, 1995
19. Smith, Gavin, *Martin Scorsese Interviewed, Film Comment,* November/December 1993
20. Pileggi, Nicholas and Scorsese, Martin, *Casino,* Faber & Faber, 9 September 1996
21. Ibid
22. Schickel, Richard, *Conversations with Scorsese,* Alfred A. Knopf, 2011
23. Ibid
24. Christie, Ian, *Martin Scorsese's Testament, Sight and Sound,* January 1996
25. *Martin Scorsese interview on Casino, Charlie Rose* via YouTube, 1995
26. Pileggi, Nicholas and Scorsese, Martin, *Casino,* Faber & Faber, 9 September 1996
27. Rafferty, Terrence, *Casino: Review, New Yorker,* 22 November 1995
28. Pileggi, Nicholas and Scorsese, Martin, *Casino,* Faber & Faber, 9 September 1996
29. Lyne, Susan, *The Filmmaker Series: Scorsese, Premiere,* December 1995
30. Schickel, Richard, *Conversations with Scorsese,* Alfred A. Knopf, 2011
31. Ibid
32. Smith, Gavin, *The Art of Vision: Martin Scorsese's Kundun, Film Comment,* January/February 1998
33. Corliss, Richard, *Kundun review, Time,* 3 April 1998
34. Denby, David, *Kundun review, New York Magazine,* 1 January 2000
35. Schickel, Richard, *Conversations with Scorsese,* Alfred A. Knopf, 2011
36. Ibid

AMERICAN DREAMS

1. Schickel, Richard, *Conversations with Scorsese,* Alfred A. Knopf, 2011
2. Schrader, Paul, *Bringing Out the Dead: Screenplay,* Faber & Faber, 6 March 2000
3. Ibid
4. Sangster, Jim, *Scorsese,* Virgin Books Ltd, 2002
5. Ibid
6. Rudolph, Eric, *Urban Gothic, American Cinematographer,* November 1999
7. *Martin Scorsese: Bringing Out the Dead, Bobbie Wygant Archive,* 19 September 1999
8. Schickel, Richard, *Conversations with Scorsese,* Alfred A. Knopf, 2011
9. Lane, Anthony, *White Nights, New Yorker,* 1 November 1999
10. Schrader, Paul, *Bringing Out the Dead: Screenplay,* Faber & Faber, 6 March 2000
11. Sante, Lucy, *Martin Scorsese's Gangs of New York: Making the Movie (including The Complete Screenplay),* Headline, 2003
12. Mantel, Hilary, *A Memoir of My Former Self,* John Murray, 2023
13. Ebert, Roger, *Scorsese by Ebert,* The University of Chicago Press, 2008
14. *Gangs of New York, interview with Martin Scorsese and Daniel Day-Lewis, Charlie Rose* via YouTube, December 2002
15. Schickel, Richard, *Conversations with Scorsese,* Alfred A. Knopf, 2011
16. Ibid
17. Ebert, Roger, *Scorsese by Ebert,* The University of Chicago Press, 2008
18. Scott, A.O., *To Feel A City Seethe, New York Times,* 20 December 2002
19. *Gangs of New York, interview with Martin Scorsese and Daniel Day-Lewis, Charlie Rose* via YouTube, December 2002
20. *Gangs of New York,* Entertainment in Video, 2007
21. Ebert, Roger, *Scorsese by Ebert,* The University of Chicago Press, 2008
22. Denby, David, *High Rollers, New Yorker,* 12 December 2004
23. LaSalle, Mick, *Scorsese's Aviator is a sumptuous, entertaining look at the life of Howard Hughes – even if it doesn't have a point, San Francisco Chronicle,* 17 December 2004
24. *The Aviator: Leonardo DiCaprio Exclusive Interview, ScreenSlam* via YouTube, uploaded 15 April 2015
25. *Leonardo DiCaprio interview, Charlie Rose* via YouTube, December 2004
26. *A Life Without Limits: The Making of The Aviator,* Miramax, 2005
27. *Cate Blanchett interview on The Aviator, Charlie Rose* via YouTube, December 2004
28. Winter, Jessica, *The Aviator review, Guardian,* 10 June 2005
29. Thomson, David, *The New Biographical Dictionary of Film,* Little Brown, 2002
30. LaSalle, Mick, *Review – Scorsese scores with cop drama that's spy caper, too, San Francisco Chronicle,* 6 October 2006
31. Ibid
32. Brown, Mick, *Martin Scorsese interview for Shutter Island, The Telegraph,* 7 March 2010
33. Schickel, Richard, *Conversations with Scorsese,* Alfred A. Knopf, 2011
34. *The Departed,* Warner Brothers Home Video, 2007
35. Schickel, Richard, *Conversations with Scorsese,* Alfred A. Knopf, 2011
36. Harrod, Horatia, *Martin Scorsese interview: sex, drugs, and the suffering that came before Silence, Telegraph,* 17 December 2016

ILLUSIONISTS

1. *Shutter Island,* Paramount Home Entertainment, 2019
2. Logan, John, *The Aviator: A Screenplay,* Hyperion, 2004
3. Schrader, Paul, *Taxi Driver,* Faber & Faber, 1990
4. Weich, Dave, *Dennis Lehane Meets the Bronte Sisters,* Powell's Books author interviews, 10 October 2006
5. Rafferty, Terrence, *Cue the Director's Adrenaline, New York Times,* 5 February 2010
6. Brown, Mick, *Martin Scorsese interview for Shutter Island, The Telegraph,* 7 March 2010
7. Rafferty, Terrence, *Cue the Director's Adrenaline, New York Times,* 5 February 2010
8. Brown, Mick, *Martin Scorsese interview for Shutter Island, The Telegraph,* 7 March 2010
9. Ibid
10. Rafferty, Terrence, *Cue the Director's Adrenaline, New York Times,* 5 February 2010
11. *A Personal Journey With Martin Scorsese Through American Movies,* BFI, 1995
12. Schickel, Richard, *Conversations with Scorsese,* Alfred A. Knopf, 2011
13. *Shutter Island,* Paramount Home Entertainment, 2019
14. Baron, Zach, *Martin Scorsese: 'I Have To Find Out Who The Hell I Am', GQ,* 25 September 2023
15. Lloyd, Robert, *Television review: Boardwalk Empire, Los Angeles Times,* 17 September 2010
16. Brody, Richard, *Martin Scorsese on "Hugo", New Yorker,* 15 December 2011
17. Unattributed, *Martin Scorsese on Hugo: A very personal film, CBS News,* 23 April 2012
18. Ibid
19. Morgenstern, Joe, *Hugo: A Dazzler, but No Victor, Wall Street Journal,* 25 November 2011
20. Schilling, Mary Kaye, *DiCaprio and Scorsese on The Wolf of Wall Street, Vulture,* 25 August 2013
21. Ibid
22. Ibid
23. *The Wolf of Wall Street,* Universal Home Entertainment, 2016
24. Thomson, David, *The Wolf of Wall Street: No Moralizing, Great Filmmaking, New Republic,* 9 January 2014
25. Gilbey, Ryan, *The Wolf of Wall Street: Beyond the boiler room, New Statesman,* January 2014
26. *DiCaprio and Scorsese on The Wolf of Wall Street, Vulture,* 25 August 2013
27. Feinberg, Scott, *Martin Scorsese Defends The Wolf of Wall Street: 'The Devil Comes With a Smile' (Q&A), Hollywood Reporter,* 31 December 2013
28. Martin, James (Society of Jesus), *Exclusive: Martin Scorsese discusses his faith, his struggles, his films and Silence, America – The Jesuit Review,* 6 December 2016
29. The Newsroom, *Film reviews: Silence, A Monster Calls, Assassin's Creed, Monster Trucks, The Scotsman,* 4 January 2017
30. LaSalle, Mick, *'Silence' is Scorsese at his worst, San Francisco Chronicle,* 5 January 2017
31. Martin, James (Society of Jesus), *Exclusive: Martin Scorsese discusses his faith, his struggles, his films and Silence, America – The Jesuit Review,* 6 December 2016
32. Endō, Shūsaku, *Silence* (Introduction), Picador Classics, 2015
33. *A new conversation between director Martin Scorsese and film critic Farran Smith Nehme, Scorsese Shorts,* Criterion, 2020

KEEPING IT REAL

1. Schickel, Richard, *Conversations with Scorsese,* Alfred A. Knopf, 2011
2. *No Direction Home: Bob Dylan,* Paramount Home Entertainment, 2005
3. Shone, Tom, *Martin Scorsese: A Retrospective,* Thames & Hudson, 2022
4. *Public Speaking,* HBO Documentary Films, 2010

THE LONG GAME

1. Shone, Tom, *Martin Scorsese: A Retrospective,* Thames & Hudson, 2022
2. Schickel, Richard, *Conversations with Scorsese,* Alfred A. Knopf, 2011
3. Itzkoff, David, *Martin Scorsese is Letting Go, New York Times,* 19 October 2023
4. Scott, A.O., *'The Irishman' Review: The Mob's Greatest Hits, in a Somber Key, The New York Times,* 27 September 2019
5. Shone, Tom, *Martin Scorsese: A Retrospective,* Thames & Hudson, 2022
6. *Making The Irishman,* Criterion, 2020
7. *The Irishman,* Criterion, 2020
8. Woods, Sean, *James Ellroy's American Apocalypse, Rolling Stone,* 15 October 2009
9. *The Irishman,* Criterion, 2020
10. *Roundtable Conversation featuring Scorsese and actors Robert De Niro, Al Pacino and Joe Pesci* (originally recorded 2019), *The Irishman,* Criterion, 2020
11. Romney, Jonathan, *Film of the Week: The Irishman, Film Comment,* 1 November 2019
12. Scott, A.O., *The Irishman Review: The Mob's Greatest Hits, in a Somber Key, New York Times,* 27 September 2019
13. *Making The Irishman, The Irishman,* Criterion, 2020
14. *The Irishman,* Criterion, 2020
15. Scott, A.O., *The Irishman Review: The Mob's Greatest Hits, in a Somber Key, New York Times,* 27 September 2019
16. Hibberd, James, *Martin Scorsese: The Irishman Interview, Entertainment Weekly,* 24 October 2019
17. Zacharek, Stephanie, *Martin Scorsese Still Has Stories To Tell, Time,* 12 September 2023
18. Brody, Richard, *Martin Scorsese on Making Killers of the Flower Moon, New Yorker,* 17 October 2023
19. Horne, Philip, *'We are the killers, and we have to understand that': Martin Scorsese on 'Killers of the Flower Moon', Sight and Sound,* 17 October 2023
20. Brody, Richard, *The Silent Thunder of Killers of the Flower Moon, New Yorker,* 20 October 2023
21. Zacharek, Stephanie, *Martin Scorsese Still Has Stories To Tell, Time,* 12 September 2023
22. Keegan, Rebecca, *'I Felt an Atonement': The Making of Killers of the Flower Moon, Hollywood Reporter,* 11 December 2023
23. Brody, Richard, *Martin Scorsese on Making Killers of the Flower Moon, New Yorker,* 17 October 2023
24. Tonet, Aureliano, *Filmmaker Paul Schrader: 'If I am gonna make a film about dying, I better hurry up', Le Monde,* 2 January 2024
25. Brody, Richard, *Martin Scorsese on Making Killers of the Flower Moon, New Yorker,* 17 October 2023
26. Brady, Tara, *Martin Scorsese: 'One has to take chances. At this age, what else can I do?', Irish Times,* 14 October 2023
27. Coggan, Devan, *Martin Scorsese explains his Killers of the Flower Moon cameo, Entertainment Weekly,* 16 November 2023
28. de Semlyen, Nick, *Martin Scorsese Interview, Empire,* 7 October 2019
29. The THR Staff, *Martin Scorsese Talks Hugo, Recurring Nightmares and How His 12-Year-Old Rules the Roost, Hollywood Reporter,* 16 November 2011

ACKNOWLEDGEMENTS

Coming to the end of writing a book about Martin Scorsese, there's a real sense that you have only just begun. Like the conclusion to one of his extraordinary films, you feel wrung out, more uncertain of the world, but more alive nonetheless. Early on in the writing of this book, I attended a talk given by the great Thelma Schoonmaker, Scorsese's primo editor for decades. She explained something very profound about working with Scorsese, something I took as a guiding light. Great films, she said, do not answer questions, they only ask more questions. I can't help but feel that going on this journey with the maestro has made me a better writer, as his films have made me a better viewer. I only hope that I have managed to ask more questions on the subject of the Little Italian who has stood tall over the medium, and above all, my thanks go to the great Martin *Scorsezze* for challenging me and every one of us to expect more from movies, and from life.

Thanks, of course, are due elsewhere. To my editor Jessica Axe, who will never let me rest on my laurels. To my endlessly patient and hugely talented designer Sue Pressley at Stonecastle Graphics, who genuinely appreciates the subjects of our books together. To my copy editor Nick Freeth, fearlessly contesting my grammar, my dates, and my occasionally erratic spelling. He has saved my bacon on so many occasions. And to the friends and colleagues, with whom I have spent many years discussing Scorsese: Ian Freer, Simon Braund, Steve Hornby, Nick de Semlyen, Phil Thomas, Mark Dinning, Julian Alcantara, Ron Fogelman, Lyndy Saville, Stephen Armstrong, and Neil Norman.

Above all, this book is dedicated to Wai, who I love and dream of walking through a swish New York club to a front-row seat. Only without having to join the mob.

PICTURE CREDITS

Abaca Press / Alamy Stock Photo 171; Album / Alamy Stock Photo 13, 25, 63b, 81r, 89r, 92, 94l, 97, 105b, 110, 113, 114b, 134b, 150l; Allstar Picture Library Ltd / Alamy Stock Photo 17r, 41, 55l, 145r; ARCHIVIO GBB / Alamy Stock Photo 12r; BFA / Alamy Stock Photo 79r, 164l, 168r; Bill Waterson / Alamy Stock Photo 117l; Cinematic / Alamy Stock Photo 17l, 53, 106, 117c; Collection Christophel / Alamy Stock Photo 4, 20, 21a, 21b, 22, 23, 26, 27, 28a, 28b, 54, 57r, 59, 60, 63a, 72r, 75, 77b, 87, 88l, 116b, 126, 133, 147; Entertainment Pictures / Alamy Stock Photo 112r, 161; Everett Collection Inc / Alamy Stock Photo 16l, 16r, 29, 30l, 30r, 31, 32r, 36, 39l, 55c, 55r, 57l, 64l, 64r, 72l, 89l, 95a, 122r, 157; FlixPix / Alamy Stock Photo 44b; Glasshouse Images / Alamy Stock Photo 81l; GRANGER – Historical Picture Archive / Alamy Stock Photo 14; JJs / Alamy Stock Photo 145l; LANDMARK MEDIA / Alamy Stock Photo 151, 166, 168l, 169, 170; Maximum Film / Alamy Stock Photo 69; Moviestore Collection Ltd / Alamy Stock Photo 52a, 104, 107, 135; PA Images / Alamy Stock Photo 8; Photo 12 / Alamy Stock Photo 6-7, 116a, 122l, 146; Pictorial Press Ltd / Alamy Stock Photo 35, 79l; PictureLux / The Hollywood Archive / Alamy Stock Photo 98l; RGR Collection / Alamy Stock Photo 71l, 84a; ScreenProd / Photononstop / Alamy Stock Photo 84b, 86l, 86r, 88r, 91, 115; Sipa US / Alamy Stock Photo 164r; Stan Pritchard / Alamy Stock Photo 117r; Steve Schapiro / Getty Images 9, 56; Stills Press / Alamy Stock Photo 159; STUDIOCANAL FILMS LTD / Alamy Stock Photo 18; TCD/Prod.DB / Alamy Stock Photo 12l, 19a, 19b, 33a, 33b, 34l, 34r, 37, 38a, 38b, 39r, 42, 43, 44a, 45, 46, 47a, 47b, 48-49l, 49r, 50, 51a, 51b, 52b, 61l, 61r, 62, 65, 66, 67a, 67b, 68l, 68r, 70, 71r, 73, 76, 77a, 78, 80, 82a, 82b, 83, 85, 93, 95b, 96, 98r, 99, 100, 101a, 101b, 102l, 102r, 103, 105a, 109, 111l, 111r, 112l, 118l, 118r, 119, 120, 121, 123r, 125, 127, 128-129l, 130, 131l, 131r, 132, 134a, 136, 137a, 137b, 138, 139r, 141, 142l, 142r, 143, 144, 148, 149a, 149b, 150r, 152, 153a, 153b, 154a, 154b, 155, 156, 160, 162, 163, 165, 167; Underwood Archives, Inc / Alamy Stock Photo 15; United Archives GmbH / Alamy Stock Photo 32l, 114a, 129r; UPI / Alamy Stock Photo 139l; WWD / Getty Images 11, 94r; ZUMA Press, Inc. / Alamy Stock Photo 123l.